SOCIAL PROBLEMS: CONTEMPORARY READINGS

SOCIAL PROBLEMS:

CONTEMPORARY READINGS
SECOND EDITION

John Stimson — *William Paterson College*

Ardyth Stimson — *Kean College*

Vincent N. Parrillo — *William Paterson College*

F. E. PEACOCK PUBLISHERS, INC.
ITASCA, ILLINOIS

Copyright © 1991
F. E. Peacock Publishers, Inc.
All rights reserved.
Library of Congress Catalog Card No. 90-162257
ISBN 0-87581-351-8
Printed in the United States of America.
10 9 8 7 6 5 4 3 2 1
1995 1994 1993 1992 1991

SUBJECT CONTENTS

I. Introduction: Defining Social Problems   1

II. Alcohol and Drug Abuse   21

III. Sexual Expressions   63

IV. Crime and Violence   103

V. Ethnic and Class Discrimination   139

VI. Sexism and Problems of the Aging   185

VII. The Disrupted Family   239

VIII. Educational Problems   281

IX. Concentrations of Economic and Political Power   297

X. Health Care Deficiencies   327

XI. Cities   349

XII. Population and Ecological Problems   375

XIII. Work and Technology   397

XIV. Conflict and War   411

Index   441

DETAILED CONTENTS

PREFACE — xv

CHAPTER I

INTRODUCTION: DEFINING SOCIAL PROBLEMS — 1

1. "Assessing the Seriousness of Social Problems" by Jerome G. Manis, from *Social Problems* — 3

Television news shows us at least one new problem every evening. How are we to judge which are important enough to receive societal attention?

2. "Quasi-Theories and Research Origination: Quasi-Theories as Substitute Cures" by John Stimson and Ardyth Stimson, from *Sociological Practice* — 13

Scientific research is often thought to be unnecessary and therefore is never carried out on some of our most important problems. Everyday culture makes us feel we already know their causes and cures.

CHAPTER II

ALCOHOL AND DRUG ABUSE — 21

3. "Tinydopers: A Case Study of Deviant Socialization" by Patricia A. Adler and Peter Adler, from *Symbolic Interaction* — 23

This case study describes a lifestyle in which infants and children are taught to use drugs by their parents.

4. "Forgotten Victims: Children of Alcoholics" by Elizabeth Stark, from *Psychology Today* — 37

Alcoholics' children are often guilt-ridden and socially isolated and are therefore unaware that they have suffered emotional damage because of their parents' problems.

Detailed Contents

    5. "Drugs-Crime Connections: Elaborations from the Life Histories of Hard-Core Heroin Addicts" by Charles E. Faupel and Carl B. Klockars, from *Social Problems*   44

The myth that drug use inevitably leads to a criminal involvement is shown to be an oversimplification of a number of complex addict lifestyles.

CHAPTER III

SEXUAL EXPRESSIONS   63

    6. "Walking the Line: The Personal and Professional Risks of Sex Education and Research" by Richard R. Troiden, from *Teaching Sociology*   65

The process of sexual labeling is examined by showing how being publicly associated with sexual behavior, even engaging in its scientific study, places an individual in jeopardy of social stigmatization as ''sexually suspect.''

    7. "Exposure to Pornography and Aggression Toward Women: The Case of the Angry Male" by Susan H. Gray, from *Social Problems*   78

Pornography makes men who are already angry with women much angrier, and this will continue until the male role is understood and modified.

    8. "An Overview of Sexual Abuse" by Renitta L. Goldman and Virginia R. Wheeler, from *Silent Shame: The Sexual Abuse of Children*   91

Many myths have arisen around the recently publicly recognized problem of child abuse, and they can only be dispelled by a clear statement of the types of abuse that actually exist.

CHAPTER IV

CRIME AND VIOLENCE   103

    9. "Warehousing Criminals" by Donald R. Cressey, from *Society*   105

Prisons have become crime factories because we lock away offenders and define them as wild aliens.

    10. "How Moral Men Make Immoral Decisions" by J. Patrick Wright, from *On a Clear Day You Can See Gen-*

Detailed Contents

eral Motors: John Z. DeLorean's Look Inside the Automotive Giant   112

The decision to sell the Corvair automobile, even though it was known to be dangerous, was made by businessmen who considered themselves moral.

11. "Tomorrow's Thieves" by Jay S. Albanese, from *The Futurist*   117

Computer fraud and larceny will become the most prevalent forms of crime in the near future, and so far we know little about how to spot them or control them.

12. "Political Terrorism" by Ovid Demaris, from *Brothers in Blood*   123

In the past, terrorists attacked only people who represented their enemies. Now, no one is safe.

13. "The Education of a Torturer" by Janice T. Gibson and Mika Haritos-Fatouros, from *Psychology Today*   132

A study of Greek military police shows the disturbing result that almost anyone can be taught to obey orders and inflict torture on people defined as enemies.

CHAPTER V

ETHNIC AND CLASS DISCRIMINATION   139

14. "How to Keep the Poor Always with Us" by William Ryan, from *Equality*   141

The history of the development of our welfare programs reveals a two-tiered policy in which the well-to-do receive the bulk of government assistance.

15. "The Feminization of Ghetto Poverty" by Diana M. Pearce, from *Society*   149

Three-quarters of the poor are women and children. Many are in households headed by females who must overcome both racial discrimination and sexism in order to earn any income.

16. "Race-specific Policies and the Truly Disadvantaged" by William Julius Wilson, from *The Truly Disadvantaged: The Inner City, The Underclass and Public Policy*   158

It was incorrect to assume that race-specific programs would help all Blacks. The policies developed during the civil rights movement

Detailed Contents

benefited mostly middle-class Blacks, and the truly disadvantaged were not assisted.

17. "Shattering Myths about the Homeless" by David Whitman, from *U. S. News and World Report*   171

The visibility of the homeless on city streets makes them seem too numerous to be helped by government programs, but this is only one myth among many about the homeless.

18. "Additive Multiculturalism: A Specific Proposal" by Harry C. Triandis, from "The Future of Pluralism," *Journal of Social Issues*   175

Instead of attempting an homogenizing integration of all groups into one American lifestyle, we need to preserve the distinctive characteristics of all who make up America.

CHAPTER VI

SEXISM AND PROBLEMS OF THE AGING   185

19. "Sexual Harassment on a University Campus: The Confluence of Authority Relations, Sexual Interest and Gender Stratification" by Donna J. Benson and Gregg E. Thomson, from *Social Problems*   187

Berkeley undergraduate women sense a disruptive sexual atmosphere when dealing with male instructors, and almost one third of them report receiving unwanted sexual attention.

20. "The Invisible Hands: Sex Roles and the Division of Labor in Two Local Political Parties" by Diane R. Margolis, from *Social Problems*   204

Women are much more politically active than it appears; it is just that men take on the visible roles, while women are confined to making arrangements and stuffing envelopes.

21. "Sexual Terrorism," by Carol Sheffield   215

Sexual terrorism maintains patriarchy in the same ways that political terrorism maintains totalitarian regimes.

22. "Elders under Siege" by Peggy Eastman, from *Psychology Today*   235

Elder abuse, or "gram-slamming," is a newly recognized problem with characteristics similar to child abuse and other forms of the abuse of the subordinate and dependent.

Detailed Contents

CHAPTER VII

THE DISRUPTED FAMILY 239

23. "The Love Lost in Cliches" by Robert C. Solomon, from *Love: Emotion, Myth & Metaphor* 241

An analysis of the figures of speech used to express romantic love helps us understand why it is so difficult to achieve lasting relationships.

24. "The Social Construction of Deviance: Experts on Battered Women" by Donileen R. Loseke and Spencer E. Cahill, from *Social Problems* 250

The process of the creation of social services for a newly recognized problem is illustrated by seeing how "battered women" were socially defined and a new type of expert came forward to treat them.

25. "Divorce and Stigma" by Naomi Gerstel, from *Social Problems* 269

Interviews with the recently divorced and separated show that, even though many new family forms are now acceptable, the divorced still feel devalued and stigmatized.

CHAPTER VIII

EDUCATIONAL PROBLEMS 281

26. "Expect and Ye Shall Receive" by William Ryan, from *Equality* 283

Teachers' expectations for students' achievements become self-fulfilling prophecies that tend to encourage only children from middle-class backgrounds.

27. "Class of 2000: The Good News and the Bad News" by Marvin J. Cetron, from *The Futurist* 289

By the year 2000 almost all occupations will require advanced preparation, and this will demand costly revisions of the educational system.

CHAPTER IX

CONCENTRATIONS OF ECONOMIC AND POLITICAL POWER 297

28. "The Bureaucratic Ethos" by Arthur Vidich and Joseph Bensman, from *The New American Society* 299

Detailed Contents

The social interaction in bureaucracies seems to be informal and friendly, but you must be able to translate the hidden meanings to understand the real and rigid rules.

29. "The Limits to Complexity: Are Bureaucracies Becoming Unmanageable?" by Duane S. Elgin and Robert A. Bushnell, from *The Futurist* 304

Bureaucratic organizations were supposed to improve efficiency, but now we are wondering if they have become too large and complex to even survive.

30. "Citizenship" by Robert N. Bellah, Richard Madsen, William M. Sullivan, Ann Swidler, and Steven M. Tipton, from *Habits of the Heart* 320

Even though most Americans distrust government, they remain patriotic and believe that there is a national value consensus that should be supported.

CHAPTER X

HEALTH CARE DEFICIENCIES 327

31. "AIDS 2000: Where the Fight Will Be Fought" by Richard Merritt and Mona J. Rowe, from *The Futurist* 329

The prediction of a large number of AIDS patients raises questions about the adequacy of our combined private/public health care delivery system.

32. "The All-Frills Yuppie Health Care Boutique" by Emily Friedman, from *Society* 341

A consumer-oriented health care system is developing that could lead to a number of trendy retail doctor-patient arrangements and will probably rule out adequate care for the poor.

CHAPTER XI

CITIES 349

33. "Woodlawn: The Zone of Destruction" by Winston Moore, Charles P. Livermore, and George F. Galland, Jr., from *The Public Interest* 351

A case study of one Chicago neighborhood illustrates the urban cycle of decay, violence, abandonment, and devastation.

Detailed Contents

34. "The Aging Central City: Some Modest Proposals" by Norman Krumholz, from *New Directions for the Mature Metropolis* — 365

There is hope for the rejuvenation of central cities if we settle for constructive shrinkage and realize that most of the growth will occur in the surrounding residential suburbs.

CHAPTER XII

POPULATION AND ECOLOGICAL PROBLEMS — 375

35. "Hidden Effects of Overpopulation" by Paul R. Ehrlich and John P. Holdren, from *Saturday Review* — 377

The ecosystem is fragile because it contains a number of intricate balances that we do not yet understand and that could, if upset, cause massive chain reactions.

36. "A Guide to Some of the Scariest Things on Earth," from *The New York Times* — 380

A sampling from around the world lists the problems that environmentalists consider to be most threatening.

37. "Ill Winds: Air Pollution's Toll on Trees and Crops" by James J. Mackenzie and Mohamed T. El-Ashry, from *Technology Review* — 383

Evidence is now available for us to understand how air pollution kills forests and damages crops, costing billions of dollars each year.

38. "Whither Water? The Fragile Future of the World's Most Important Resource" by Bruce K. Ferguson, from *The Futurist* — 391

Water appears to be in endless supply, but our enormous consumption rate may force the recycling of sewage and the conversion of sea water.

CHAPTER XIII

WORK AND TECHNOLOGY — 397

39. "Living Dangerously" by Abigail Trafford and Andrea Gabor, from *U.S. News and World Report* — 399

The agencies that were supposed to assess the risks of new technologies have not been successful. In order to predict future risks we must reduce our arrogant technological overconfidence.

xiii

Detailed Contents

40. "Management by Stress: Behind the Scenes at Nummi Motors" by Mike Parker and Jane Slaughter, from *The New York Times*   406

Before American businessmen rush to improve efficiency by adopting Japanese management techniques, they should look at the adjustments necessary to survive a typical day on the oppressive Japanese production line.

CHAPTER XIV

CONFLICT AND WAR   411

41. "The Shattered Crystal Ball: How Might a Nuclear War Begin?" by The Harvard Nuclear Study Group, from *Living with Nuclear Weapons*   413

A group of realistic future scenarios describe various ways nuclear war could begin and make us realize that safety is fragile as long as any international conflict exists.

42. "The Moral Equivalent of War" by William James, from *McClure's Magazine*   429

This is a classic statement of how societal values channel our emotions to make war attractive and how this process can be redirected toward constructive social actions.

INDEX   441

PREFACE

We feel it is essential that an introductory social problems course, taught mostly to first- and second-year college students, include many examples of the impact of social problems on individuals' everyday lives. The proper study of social problems is based on theoretical analyses of social structural dislocations and the historical development of social inequalities. All too often, however, these discussions become abstract or lost in the comparisons of rival theoretical positions. Students react to these discussions with dissatisfaction and the questions, "So what? What does this mean for my life? What can I do about it?" We did not, however, want to go too far in the direction of popularization and collect topical articles representing current headlines. Our selections therefore had to be sociological but emphasize the involvement of society's individual members in social problems.

We saw two other needs that should be met when adding readings to a social problems course. Students are not too interested in things that have already happened. They care about what will happen to them. The articles should emphasize future possibilities: both future damage estimates and future policy solutions. We become interested in where we have been, only when it can help us understand where we are going.

The final emphasis is perhaps the most important. Students often come to social problems courses feeling that they already know the causes, and therefore the solutions, of problems. Common culture experience provides abundant class, ethnic, and gender stereotypes and other value-based faulty ways to assign blame for problems. Students need not be bigoted to adopt these quasi-explanations—they are the common stuff of daily life. We have found that is not sufficient to provide the "scientific" explanation and hope that its truth will automatically displace the common cultural solution. You will therefore find a number of articles that attempt to dispel myths that supposedly explain problems such as sexual abuse, divorce, the drugs-crime connection, and the homeless. Such articles are given a general introduction by the article on defining quasi-theories in Chapter I.

Preface

Half of the selections in the second edition are new. Articles are arranged in fourteen chapters that follow what has come to be the standard social problems text order of presentation. Two new chapters have been added. One covers the problems of work and technology, and the other conflict and war. New emphasis has been placed on health care with articles on AIDS ("AIDS 2000") and the problems of health care delivery ("The All-Frills Yuppie Health Care Boutique"). The poverty and sexism chapters have been expanded by adding articles that recognize the feminization of poverty and the role of sexual terrorism in supporting patriarchal social systems.

J. Stimson
A. Stimson
V. N. Parrillo

CHAPTER I

INTRODUCTION: DEFINING SOCIAL PROBLEMS

Reading 1
ASSESSING THE SERIOUSNESS OF SOCIAL PROBLEMS

Jerome G. Manis, *Western Michigan University*

> *If we were to rely on the media's reflection of public opinion, our list of major social problems would change almost every day. Manis shows us how to avoid this confusion through a scientific definition of social problems using standards of magnitude, severity, and primacy.*

The definition of a concept inevitably influences the nature of the related hypotheses or theory. A well-conceived concept is heuristic and realistic—that is, it generates hypotheses that improve our understanding of phenomena. Such a concept will direct researchers toward significant data. As Max Planck (1962:841) has contended, however, there are many "phantom problems—in my opinion, far more than one would ordinarily suspect—even in the realm of science." It is the recognition of anomalies in "normal science" that results in the collapse of accepted paradigms (Kuhn, 1962)....

Exponents of leading sociological perspectives—symbolic interactionism and functionalism—have essentially similar conceptions of social problems. To Blumer (1971:298, 301–302), "social problems are fundamentally products of collective definition...A social problem does not exist for a society unless it is recognized by that society to exist." Merton (1971:799) is somewhat more inclusive: "The first and basic ingredient of a social problem consists of a substantial discrepancy between widely shared standards and actual conditions of social life." Although he distinguishes between manifest or recognized and latent or unrecognized discrepancies, his definition centers upon "widely shared standards," i.e., society's norms and values.

One of the shortcomings of the public definition of social problems is the inclusion of possibly spurious or "phantom" conditions....Indeed, the "subjective" definition must include witchhunting, long hair, and

---

Reprinted with permission from *Social Problems* 22 (1974): 1–15 by The Society for the Study of Social Problems and the author.

Chapter I
Defining Social Problems

possession of marihuana as social problems as long as the public is in opposition to them. So defined, the concern of the sociology of social problems is with social issues or controversies rather than the objective conditions detrimental to human or societal well-being.

A related deficiency of the "public opinion" approach to social problems is its inability to assess the seriousness of social problems. Some advocates of this viewpoint are aware of the limitation.

> ...it is the values held by people occupying different social positions that provide the rough basis for the relative importance assigned to social problems...this sometimes leads to badly distorted impressions of various problems, even when these are judged in the light of reigning values (Merton, 1971:801).

> Nor are public definitions sound guides to the magnitude of social problems....Influential publics, moreover, have little if any basis on which to *compare* the relative seriousness—extent and effects—of problems....This definition of social problems explores certain absurdities. Public recognition is in nearly all respects a bad basis for collective judgment....In spite of these difficulties, the definition stands: A social problem is a condition that has been defined by significant groups as a deviation from some social standard, or breakdown of social organization (Dentler, 1971:14-15).

Despite these admissions of "distortions" and "absurdities," sociologists have continued to use popular values as the only criteria of social problems....

THE IDENTIFICATION OF SOCIAL PROBLEMS

For present purposes, social problems are defined as "those social conditions, identified by scientific inquiry and values as detrimental to the well-being of human societies" (Manis, 1974). Four perspectives or viewpoints appear useful in determining and specifying such conditions. These are: (1) public conceptions; (2) the views of appropriate professionals; (3) sociological knowledge; (4) the norms and values of science. The order in which the categories are presented is based upon their increasing importance as criteria for identifying social problems. Consistent application of these criteria can help to reduce or eliminate the anomalies arising from current definitions of social problems.

PUBLIC CONCEPTIONS

A basic source of information concerning social problems are the opinions and attitudes of the members of a group or society. This information

Reading 1
Assessing the Seriousness of Social Problems

is necessary for understanding social behavior. As Blumer (1971:301) points out, "the process of collective definition determines the career and fate of social problems, from the initial point of their appearance to whatever may be the terminal point in their course." Though most textbooks accept "collective definition" as the essence of social problems, they do not disclose any evidence for the choice of their topics.

The content of the sociological literature—crime, divorce, alcoholism, etc.—*appears* to be congruent with the views of the populace. However, the justification for their inclusion or for the assessment of their assumed seriousness is not revealed to the reader. The absence of such data is a major deficiency in our knowledge....

Public conceptions of deviance, and of social problems generally, are necessary but insufficient knowledge. Certainly, we need to know what a society abhors and why it does so. We also need to know the consequences of these conceptions. Accepting social values as criteria of "harmful people" or "undesirable conditions" lends an aura of scientific respectability to beliefs which may be based on ignorance or prejudice. Accepting these values as the ultimate criteria of social problems is a specious justification for claims of value-neutrality.

PROFESSIONAL EXPERTISE

At times, public opinion differs substantially from the views of experts. A current example is the widespread antagonism to users of marihuana. The public position seems to be based upon many erroneous beliefs: that it is addictive; that it is debilitating; that it invariably leads to other addictions; that users are sexually depraved. The differing views of physicians, psychiatrists, and sociologists apparently have not greatly altered its popular image.

According to current definitions, marihuana is a social problem since it is contrary to social values. Presumably it is a serious problem if many people are strongly opposed to its usage. The views of trained experts are considered relevant because of their disagreement with the public, not for their technical knowledge. Sociologists may agree with the professional definition—but the public definition is the usual standard for identifying social problems.

There are, of course, many experts; and they are not always in agreement. But in agreement or not, their professional training and intimate contact with conditions viewed by the public as undesirable can provide needed correctives. Sociologists do question the medical perspective of psychiatry. Should they not also raise questions about the category of "crazy people"? The latter conception helps to explain the responses of society to those so identified and the effects of these labels. It is less helpful in the search for social causation and consequences.

Chapter I
Defining Social Problems

Sociologists draw upon the data of other experts and disciplines in their analyses of mental disorder, drop-outs, divorce, and riots. This expertise receives special weight in the analyses but not in the definition of social problems. To be consistent with current definitions, the seriousness of social problems should be based not on the weight of technical data but the extent of popular concern.

To propose that the expert's interpretation be included in defining and assessing social problems is not a claim for their absolute correctness. It is only a means for incorporating more technical knowledge into our inquiries. Such knowledge can help to recognize trivial or spurious social problems as well as to identify serious ones.

SOCIOLOGICAL KNOWLEDGE

Although social problems are defined in terms of public conceptions, values, and controversies, sociologists do not ignore the causes and the consequences of the "undesirable conditions." Indeed, Blumer (1971:300) has contended that sociologists have concentrated on the latter and have "conspicuously failed...to study the process by which a society comes to recognize its social problems." What sociologists actually do is different from what they say about social problems.

The discrepancy stems, I believe, from the unwillingness of researchers to accept the implications of the accepted definition. If the public views busing, atheism, subversives, women's liberation, and radical professors as major social problems, will the textbook writers allocate substantial sections to these topics? If not, why not?...Understanding of everyday knowledge is needed by sociology; understanding does not require its endorsement....

THE VALUES OF SCIENCE

A major justification for the accepted definitions of social problems is the presumed value-neutrality of science. A scientific sociology must avoid any appearance of bias derived from personal values. The aim is laudable. The accepted solution—adopting popular values as standards for identifying social problems—is a substitution of values, not their elimination. The outcome is an illusory value-neutrality....

That science is a social institution with distinctive norms and values can hardly be questioned. Among the accepted values are the search for knowledge, the empirical testing of belief, the provisional standing of accepted viewpoints, the freedom of critics to dissent and propose new interpretations, and the dissemination of knowledge (Merton, 1967). The socialization of would-be scientists includes the inculcation of these values.

Reading 1
Assessing the Seriousness of Social Problems

Scientists seldom discuss, since they take for granted, certain underlying values. In totalitarian states, protection of life, safety, subsistence, and freedom of inquiry for the scientist may be uncertain. The institution of science depends upon societal tolerance and support. Obviously, science cannot exist without society and functioning scientists. Is it less obvious to contend that science must value an open, supportive society?

A current value-controversy among scientists concerns the social responsibility of science. To take an extreme illustration, does the nuclear scientist have the obligation to test a fission hypothesis which will set off a continuous, endless, chain reaction (Z-bomb?)? Traditionally, scientists have contended that science can only describe "what is, not should be." Contemporary science is *not* limited to this role of passive observation. The rapid tempo of discovery and, particularly, the creation of new phenomena—synthetic atoms, plastics, nylon, etc.—reflect the intentional innovations which have helped to transform the world around us. These creations have blurred the lines between basic and applied science as well as between science and technology.

The thesis here is that the knowledge and the values of science can provide sociology with needed guidelines for appraising social phenomena. Certainly, scientists neither possess all of the needed knowledge nor agree upon scientific values. Nevertheless, existing knowledge and values are more uniform, more rational, and more fruitful criteria than the divergent beliefs and values of any given society....

Proposing the use of scientific criteria to assess the existence or the severity of social problems need not imply absolutism. Specifying their criteria does not require the crowning of scientists. The concepts, hypotheses, theories, and values of science are open to continuing criticism, revision, or rejection on the basis of rational judgments and knowledge. No implication that science be empowered to coerce society to accept its conclusions is intended. All that is suggested here is to permit the knowledge and values of science to identify and to assess conditions deemed harmful to science and to society.

To summarize, scientific knowledge and values are proposed as criteria for identifying socially harmful conditions. These criteria can help to distinguish spurious from genuine social problems. We also need to consider ways of differentiating minor or trivial social problems from major or serious ones. By seriousness is meant the primacy, the magnitude, and the severity of social problems.

THE PRIMACY OF SOCIAL PROBLEMS

An examination of the interrelationships among social problems provides one way of assessing their importance. To illustrate, let us consider the hypothesis that poverty is associated with higher rates of malnutri-

Chapter I
Defining Social Problems

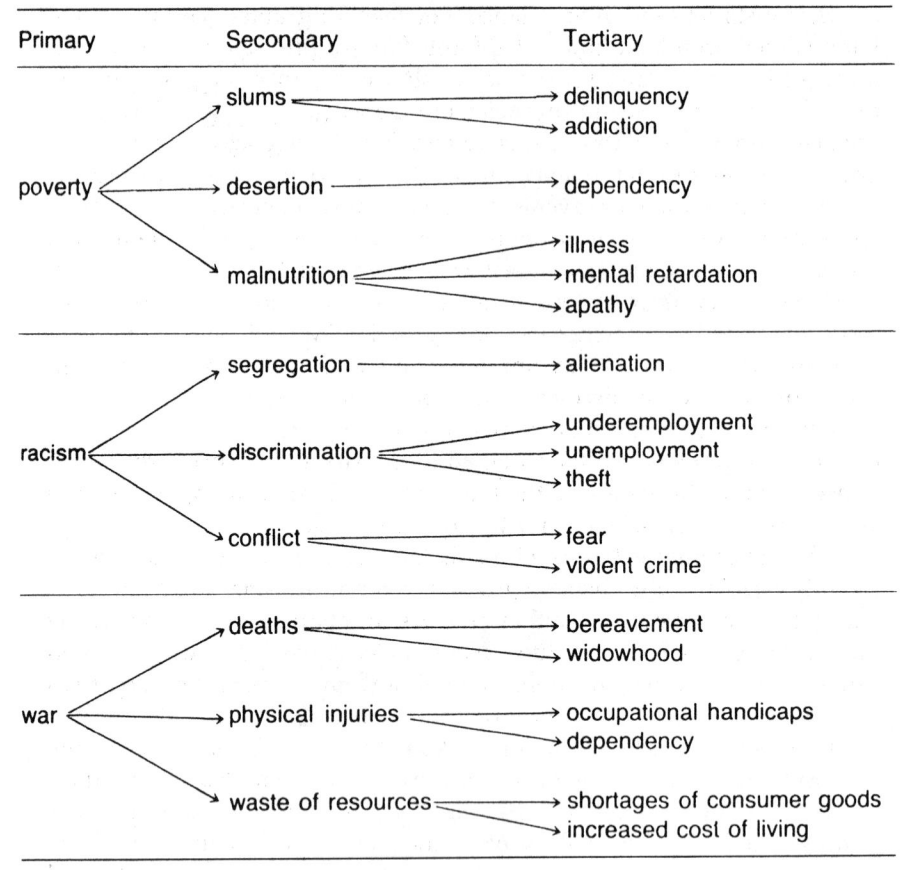

Primary	Secondary	Tertiary
poverty	slums	delinquency, addiction
	desertion	dependency
	malnutrition	illness, mental retardation, apathy
racism	segregation	alienation
	discrimination	underemployment, unemployment, theft
	conflict	fear, violent crime
war	deaths	bereavement, widowhood
	physical injuries	occupational handicaps, dependency
	waste of resources	shortages of consumer goods, increased cost of living

Figure 1. A paradigm for classifying social problems on the basis of hypothesized influences.

tion, mortality, desertion, delinquency, drop-outs, addiction, and mental disorder.... Viewing poverty as an antecedent to many other social problems is a basis for appraising its importance or primacy.

Social problems which produce or exacerbate other social problems are more serious or critical to society than those which have less effects. On such grounds, Perrucci and Pilisuk (1971:xix) refer to "central" or "underlying" social problems as distinguished from the "peripheral" ones produced by the former. Despite the brevity of their discussion, it is evident that they consider cause-effect relationships as their basic criterion....

Primary social problems are influential social conditions which have multiple detrimental consequences for society. For example, we may predict that a conventional war will result in higher death rates, waste of human and other resources, increases in family disorganization, disruption of careers, and neglected solutions to other undesirable conditions. Racism seems conducive to separatism, conflict, individual alienation, etc. On the basis of their multiplicative influences, war and racism can be viewed as primary social problems; their socially harmful effects may be defined as secondary or tertiary problems....

In the absence of detailed, accurate, and precise knowledge, the proposed distinctions between specific primary and secondary or tertiary social problems remain as hypotheses rather than established conclusions. Even so, they are preferable to such criteria as numbers of concerned citizens or level of their emotional outrage. Not only is the distinction more objective, but it requires empirical data concerning the relationships between problem variables. The formulation of more and improved social indicators would facilitate study of such relationships.

Secondary social problems are less critical for a society than primary ones in that the former are products of the latter. Likewise, tertiary social problems are least important in that they are the products of primary and secondary problems. Secondary social problems may be viewed as intervening variables or as the immediate influences upon tertiary social problems....

THE MAGNITUDE OF SOCIAL PROBLEMS

...prevalence and incidence are accepted indicators of the seriousness of social problems. Difficulties arise when attempts are made to compare the magnitude of different phenomena. Some of the suggested difficulties may be exaggerated, particularly when the differences in the units are emphasized. For example, Merton (1971:801) asks, "Shall we conclude that the approximately 9000 murders in 1969 represent about one-fifth as great a social problem as the approximately 56,700 deaths from vehicular accidents in that year?" Although his response is negative, one may respond, why not? Certainly, the causes differ and the public concern about homicide differs from the public apathy toward traffic fatalities. The consequences *are* similar, as they are also for suicide and for war-related deaths. Vital statistics provide useful sources for appraising the magnitude of social problems.

Another useful comparison can be made of the prevalence of forms of addiction. While the public is more greatly aroused by heroin addiction than by addiction to alcohol or barbituates, it is the resulting legal penalties for the former which compound its seriousness. That there are about ten million alcoholics as compared to several hundred thousand heroin addicts is considered by medical professionals to be the more serious health problem. Should not sociologists adopt similar criteria?

Chapter I
Defining Social Problems

Comparing more divergent conditions, of course, is much more difficult. Assessing the magnitude of poverty requires different standards from those used in appraising the rates of juvenile delinquency. Are equal numbers of the poor and of juvenile delinquents equivalent in seriousness as social problems? Though their differences appear to defy attempts to compare their magnitude, the effort to do so is important. One method of comparing their seriousness would be a consideration of their effects—as noted in the previous section. If poverty is indeed a major source of other problems, we can give its prevalence a greater emphasis or weighting in our deliberations. Furthermore, we can appraise the differential severity of its consequences.

THE SEVERITY OF SOCIAL PROBLEMS

By severity is meant the varying impact, the degree of damage, harshness, or impairment, of social conditions upon the well-being of individuals and society. The harmfulness of some social problems can be assessed more readily than others. Loss of life is clearly a more critical outcome of war than minor injuries. A ten-year prison term is a harsher penalty than a one-year term; these differences of sentence are imposed on the basis of some judgment of differential social injury. In these comments, no implication is intended that assessing severity is a simple or easy task. Here, as elsewhere in this analysis, the aim is to further discussion of the topic.

In the absence of clearcut criteria for defining social problems, evaluation of their severity may be begun with conditions harmful to the physical well-being of individuals. Severity can be ranked from the finality of death, through total, major, and minor incapacity. These are crude but useful categories for assessing impairment. The distinctions are no more arbitrary than those used to distinguish social classes, small groups, or subcultures.

Similar procedures have been applied to the severity of mental disorders. The *American Psychiatric Association* (1952) has considered "psychiatric impairment" in terms of mild to severe categories. Their ratings are based on judgments of the individual's ability to function socially and occupationally. Such evaluations are appropriate ways of assessing social problems.

Also similar are the methods used in comparing the severity of crimes. Homicide and aggravated assault are characterized as major crimes while disorderly conduct is not. The alleged criterion is differential harmfulness. On this basis, some sociologists have favored the decriminalization of gambling, homosexual behavior, and other acts which are not clearly detrimental to individuals or to the society. The concept of "crimes without victims" helps to identify trivial or spurious problems.

Closely related to the degree of severity of a social problem is its duration or recurrence. Ignoring their other effects, addictive drugs are considered to be more harmful than non-addictive drugs. Other parallels to this temporal aspect of severity are the medical concern with "chronic" conditions and the penologist's concern with recidivism. Transitory conditions may be considered less severe than continuing or permanent ones....

CONCLUSION

An aim of this discussion has been to emphasize the importance of demonstrable knowledge and reasoned evaluation in identifying and appraising social problems. The knowledge and values of science are less ethnocentric, less erratic, and less influenced by vested interests than those of a majority or significant numbers of a society. Using the views of the latter as the criterion of social problems is a more knowledge-free than value-free definition of social problems.

Adopting scientific knowledge and values as criteria does not imply disregard for public perceptions. Certainly, research is needed to clarify the ways by which individuals come to believe that certain social conditions are undesirable. We need to know more of the processes of collective action, of the influences of mass media and pressure groups, and of the consequences of group reactions. Knowledge of public concerns can reduce the risk of an ivory-towered isolation of sociology.

The effort to determine the seriousness of social problems requires procedures for distinguishing between trivial or spurious and important or genuine ones. That public judgments are made, at times, on the basis of erroneous information or emotionality can harldy be doubted. Such judgments need not be given equality in assessing social problems with those based on facts and reasoned judgments....

To espouse scientific knowledge and values for the appraisal of social phenomena implies no claims of omniscience and certainly not of omnipotence. Similar limitations are applicable to public opinion. The latter is influenced by advertising, political ideologies, religious beliefs, etc. Accepting public opinion as the standard for defining and assessing social problems is incongruent with the rational basis of scientific inquiry.

The place of values remains the central dilemma of the sociological enterprise. Values are involved in the choice of concepts, research topics, and methods of inquiry. They are clearly relevant to the definition of social problems and to assessments of their seriousness. The knowledge

Chapter I
Defining Social Problems

values of science provide a more appropriate perspective for sociology than those of "significant numbers" of a given society.

REFERENCES

American Psychiatric Association. 1952. *Diagnostic and Statistical Manual, Mental Disorders.* Washington, D.C.

Blumer, Herbert. 1971. "Social problems as collective behavior." *Social Problems* 18(Winter): 298–306.

Dentler, Robert A. 1971. *Basic Social Problems.* Chicago: Rand McNally.

Kuhn, Thomas S. 1970. *The Structure of Scientific Revolutions.* Chicago: University of Chicago Press.

_____. 1974. "The concept of social problems: Vox populi and sociological analysis." *Social Problems* 21:305–315.

Merton, Robert K. 1967. *On Theoretical Sociology.* New York: Free Press.

_____. 1971. "Social problems and sociological theory," pp. 793–845 in Robert K. Merton and Robert Nisbet (eds.), *Contemporary Social Problems.* New York: Harcourt Brace Jovanovich.

Perrucci, Robert, and Marc Pilisuk (eds.). 1971. *The Triple Revolution Emerging: Social Problems in Depth.* Boston: Little, Brown.

Planck, Max. 1962. "Phantom problems in science," pp. 840–852 in Dagobert D. Runes (ed.), *Treasury of World Science.* New York: Philosophical Library.

Reading 2
QUASI-THEORIES AND RESEARCH ORIGINATION: QUASI-THEORIES AS SUBSTITUTE CURES

John Stimson, *William Paterson College*
Ardyth Stimson, *Kean College*

> Many social problems never receive attention or even get researched. Our society just explains them away using culturally accepted quasi-theories. Stimson and Stimson provide a list of rationalizations and pseudo explanations that keep us from finding out the truth.

NEGOTIATED REALITY

Sociologists continue to uncover and debate the ramifications of W. I. Thomas's statement (1951) that typically we do not make our decisions statistically or scientifically, that we lead our lives by inference. Recent extensions and explorations of the nonscientific nature of social life can be summarized as Negotiated Reality theory—a view that sees the process of daily interaction interrupted by discussion of motivation, causation, or planning only when a problem arises that directly disrupts the normal flow. The immediate goal is to reinstate nondisturbing normality. If the disturbance, or disturber, cannot be labeled and put aside, then reality must be examined and redefined to include it as normal. It is not necessary that any "real" disturbance, or solution, exist: The explanation process, itself, will solve the situation in any case (Mills, 1940; Rains, 1975:5).

Merton (1971) and Blumer (1971) developed "constructionist" descriptions of the collective process of social-problem definition that demonstrated that group values define what is or is not a problem. Hewitt and Hall (1973) have extended the relevance of this perspective by examining the collective definition of the supposed causes and solutions of so-

Reprinted with permission from *Sociological Practice* (Spring 1977): 38–48. Copyright © 1977 by Human Sciences Press, 72 Fifth Avenue, New York, NY, 10011.

Chapter I
Defining Social Problems

cial problems. They show that quasi-theories exist in all our minds and can be called up to quiet the effects of disturbing events.

There is a strong similarity between the social negotiation of reality process that Hewitt and Hall (1973) describe and the formulation of many applied research programs. We have often found it a battle to propose that an applied research be allowed to try to find answers that others around the table thought they already knew. Hewitt and Hall's description of quasi-theory structure places these conflicts in a meaningful social-psychological context. It can help explain why each person thinks he is an adequate sociologist and how he is supported in this belief by the typical social process of problem solving.

GOALS

Three main suggestions will be made. First, researchers, especially when hoping to affect policy, must recognize that a powerful competitor really does exist—that there are traditional alternatives to science that more easily alleviate the tension that leads to problem solving. Second, each of these alternatives is a quasi-theory with a specific time-ordered structure of social construction that can be interrupted so that meaningful research can be originated. Finally, research results can find an interested audience among policy makers only if researchers return to a normal conversational style of presentation that argues for "scientific" cures in the same manner in which competing cures are justified.

We will extend Hewitt and Hall's concept by showing that social science research is but a special case within this normal process—a special case that has, perhaps, lost touch with the normal structure of problem discussion and definition. Quasi-theorizing is the normal procedure. Science, for all its organization and supposed protections against introspection, rearranges the usual chronological pattern of problem solution. Science, thereby, places itself at a severe disadvantage during the argumentation that must take place when applied research is either formulated or presented.

QUASI-THEORY STRUCTURE

Hewitt and Hall describe a series of steps with a recognizable structure that directly contradicts scientific procedure. "What is essential to a quasi-theory is its logic, which is one of cause and effect, though quite disarranged temporally if viewed from a scientific viewpoint. The use of quasi-theories involves postulation of a cure, followed by an analysis of cause and effect, that supports the cure" (1973:370). Analysis is post hoc. What represents causal research in this normal talk-structure of problem solution is a "build-around" of justifying definitions. The stages of this process are: (a) choice of a cure (a way to stop the disturbance); (b) definition of what can be cured (i.e., the "real" problem is distinguished from its false aspects, "false" usually meaning those that can't be affected by the chosen cure); (c) selection of examples from cultural and biographical experience that support the efficacy of the cure and the problem definition....

Hall and Hewitt (1970) used the quasi-theory of communication to demonstrate how 1960s political disturbances were explained away before they were properly analyzed. The process moved directly from public notice of conflict to a cure that stated: "We all share the same values and goals, we are just having trouble communicating our common humanity, Americanism or interest in progress, etc." The apparent value conflicts were seldom examined. A solution was selected, ready-made, from the cultural context in order to calm the disturbance.

Two other familiar examples from the political process are quoted by Hall and Hewitt. Real analysis or action has often been avoided by assigning causal power to either "outside agitators" or a "conspiracy by a controlling elite." Quasi-theories are also used to alleviate tension and confusion that can be handled in no other way. When human problems seem to have no solution, a quasi-theory will be submitted, for example, "Time will heal it," or the behavior is ascribed to some invisible unconscious instinct that is "natural."...

SOME QUASI-THEORIES THAT REPLACE RESEARCH

The goal of this section is to stimulate an exchange of experiences among sociologists by providing a preliminary list of quasi-theories that we have heard explain away problems that needed research.

1. Some version of the notion that *man is rational*, materialistic, and able quickly to recognize the route to the greatest reward is a concept often used to oversimplify potential research situations. It is used especially in commercial research to explain away labor-management or consumer-intention studies. Its central notion is that "dollar-profit" overrides mere social values or definitions of the situation because it is somehow more basic or natural. This view does not recognize profit as just one value among many. It sees profit as a normal outcome of man's basic utility-seeking efficiency in avoiding unrewarded effort. Advertising research has often shown that, on the contrary, "profit" can be a function of created, manipulated desire. This "thing-rational" notion of man occasionally closes out social problem research, for example, the notion that low pay is the central problem of ghetto life—better salaries would be more motivating and thereby cure everything else....

Chapter I
Defining Social Problems

2. "We can't wait; *immediate action* is needed" has signaled the end of many research proposals (Blalock, 1970:5). It is based on the assumption that the obvious problems are the real problems. It has been an effective call to action *instead of study,* especially when phrased in terms of "a war on..." or "a crusade against..." by a charismatic political or business leader. There are real time pressures. Problems are urgent, but this does not reduce the need for knowledge before action or excuse the belief that an area is over-simple.

Banfield (who has proposed some research-aborting quasi-theories of his own) does make a telling point when he describes "Incessant Politics and Perpetual Service" as our twin national afflictions (cited in Nisbet, 1974). Nisbet ends his review of *The Unheavenly City* with the hope that the next wave of politicians and administrators will be devoted to the apothegm: "Don't just do something. Sit there!" (1974:152).

The entire Banfield controversy is a good example of a battle of quasi-theories. We remember only the "cures" he has criticized, and what his critics said. Banfield's contribution is his attack on the popular notions that cities are rapildy deteriorating and are "cauldrons of repressed revolt" (in Nisbet, 1974:143–144). Banfield thereby helped to place urbanology back in historical perspective, back into the arena where research might be allowed.

The alternative that Banfield presents, however, supports another series of popular quasi-theories that also preclude research.

3. *Panglossian* quasi-theories are based on the notion that time will cure all. They state that life is difficult and that we are in the grip of major long-term processes (Demographic Transition or Racial Assimilation) that cannot be substantially affected. We are in the best of all possible worlds, considering the changes we are living through. Banfield's urbanology is a current example: "The mere act of *doing for* others, especially when armed with the might and wealth of the democratic state, cannot help but destroy, or set back grievously, processes of an adaptive nature in the [local] areas" (in Nisbet, 1974:150). That is, immigrants must assimilate or poverty cultures must adapt, and artificial assistance can only slow the natural process.

This is the most extreme research killer, and we should remember that it is partly an attempt to destroy the quasi-theory of Perpetual Service. Even Killian, the proponent of sociological pessimism, leaves a place for research: "If the pessimistic sociologist is impelled to be an activist, he can still address himself to the question, 'What sorts of adjustments do individuals and groups make to living in a world that is not and never will be a utopia?' " (Killian, 1971:284).

4. A related quasi-theory develops from the attempt to rank interventions by *measuring the human suffering* that each would alleviate. Crisis

Reading 2
Quasi-Theories and Research Origination

intervention is the normal operation of most social-problem practitioners. They are concerned with research and method, in the abstract, but have come to believe that they must alleviate the immediately presented severe symptom before more-lasting change can take place.

The notion of directing immediate action at areas of maximum individual pain is not invalid. It becomes a research-stifling quasi-theory only when extended so that possible *causes* or problems are chosen using an estimate of their destructive impact. We have often seen this orientation in juvenile problems research, for example, a working mother *must* cause such deprivation that the child will be disorganized, or broken homes are so traumatic that they *must* produce delinquency.

The supposed traumatic effects of inadequate housing have probably received more governmental attention than any other form of suffering, but recent study shows that little evidence can be found to support new housing as an effective cure, or even a major correlate, of other problems (Mitchell, 1974). Housing construction has probably been chosen so often because of economic (it stimulates finance and employment) and political (it provides tangible achievements) considerations.

Its appeal to the public, its plausibility, is probably based on a quasi-theory that equates, somehow, a man's castle with his worth. Mitchell comments that "decent housing and a suitable living environment are rapidly being elevated to the status of fundamental human rights" (1974:276). The quasi-theory that accompanies this value states that a man or family cannot function properly, rationally and morally, when this fundamental right or need is violated (i.e., when too much suffering is caused, it is not a motivation toward change, but a degradation).

5. The *"sweet mystery of life"* quasi-theory is used, almost seasonally, during congressional investigations of basic research grants. It states that research on such things as love, marriage, birth, death, etc., is useless because these subjects are so basic that the answers are automatically known by all. An extreme form of this view states that it is better not to study sex or marriage, for example, because it is better to suffer the high divorce rates of today than to risk the disenchanting coldness that might result from scientific analysis. We refer you to Lazarsfeld's work (1969) combating the notion of the obvious and offer only one additional comment. The culture is generous. It offers contradictory advice: He who hesitates is lost! Look before you leap! . . .

6. The *"ask the contact-person"* quasi-theory is mentioned by Blalock (1970) and by Foote (1974). It avoids research by assuming that the person who deals with the situation (salesperson, community organizer, local politician) can easily report the most important variables and the causal structure.

Blalock blames sociologists because "we have not seriously challenged the nonsensical idea that there is little point in analyzing "cold" statistics when real insights are to be obtained by seeing life as it actually is and by getting out and doing things, rather than living in the "ivory tower" (1970:7).

Foote's example explains how marketing research is often cut short by asking the salesperson to act as the expert on the consumer. The answer is always that price is the most powerful variable. Foote points out, however, that the real consumption process is complete by the time the salesperson becomes involved. Price can be the last, and the least important, variable.

Other examples that ignore the fallacy of assuming that participants have a clear view of their surroundings include asking police about crime or social workers about poverty. Contact-people serve symptoms and have developed a set of quasi-theories that is peculiar to their occupational positions.

One result of this acceptance of the contact-person as expert is that most statistics that are regularly collected are designed by, and for, the contact-operators. They are assumed to know the important items that will predict the future and assist understanding of the situation.

7. The *"jusk ask those living in the situation"* quasi-theory is quite similar, but it is in error for a different reason. People living in even a very difficult situation have usually adjusted or adapted to it. Selltiz and her co-workers base their discussion of exploratory research on this assumption. They suggest that the quickest way to discover the potent variable is to ask strangers, deviants, outcasts, or marginal men. These respondents' views are not as likely to have been neutralized, repressed, or subculturally socialized (Selltiz et al., 1959:65). Again, there is nothing wrong with client or consumer surveys—as long as they are not proposed as causal analyses. . . .

8. Finally, researchers must be careful to avoid activating the quasi-theory of *hopeless overdetermination*. In some areas, especially urban problems and juvenile delinquency, sociologists have been too convincing in their destruction of simplistic theories. The authors have often lost a committee's attention when trying to lay out a complicated causal structure. This experience demonstrated that quasi-theory structures are important. One cure, or cause, is all that can be handled and justified in one discussion. . . .

The feeling of helplessness that develops in an administrator or lay committee during too complicated a discussion is the surest killer of research proposals. The listener feels justified in retreating to popular quasi-theories when science violates his structure of thought. The analysis has become more threatening than the problem itself, and traditional simplifications are sought, quickly.

Reading 2
Quasi-Theories and Research Origination

The implicit value orientation of this paper is that research can be valid, and that whatever sociology's problems are, more exploratory and descriptive studies will be helpful. This orientation does *not* include the belief that sociologists' theories are the "real" theories and the public's are merely "quasi." The goal is for sociologists to be allowed to research to learn and inform.

REFERENCES

Blalock, Hubert M., Jr. 1970. *An Introduction to Social Research.* Englewood Cliffs, N.J.: Prentice-Hall

Blumer, Herbert. 1971. "Social problems as collective behavior." *Social Problems* 18:298–306.

Foote, Nelson. 1974. "Putting sociologists to work." *American Sociologist* 9:125–134.

Hall, Peter M., and John P. Hewitt. 1970. "The quasi-theory of communication and the management of dissent." *Social Problems* 18:17–27.

Hewitt, John P., and Peter M. Hall. 1973. "Social problems, problematic situations, and quasi-theories." *American Sociological Review* 38:367–374.

Killian, Lewis M. 1971. "Optimism and pessimism in sociological analysis." *American Sociologist* 6:281–286.

Lazarsfeld, Paul F. 1969. "What do attitude surveys tell us?" *Public Opinion Quarterly* 13:378–390.

Merton, Robert K. 1971. "Social problems and sociological theory," pp. 793–845 in Robert K. Merton and Robert Nisbet (eds.), *Contemporary Social Problems.* New York: Harcourt Brace Jovanovich.

Mills, C. Wright. 1940. "Situated actions and vocabularies of motive." *American Sociological Review* 5:904–913.

Mitchell, Robert E. 1974. "Sociological research on the economic myths of housing." *Social Problems* 22:259–280.

Nisbet, Robert. 1974. "The urban crisis revisited," pp. 142–151 in George Riter (ed.), *Social Realities.* Boston: Allyn and Bacon.

Rains, Prudence 1975. "Imputations of deviance." *Social Problems* 23:1–11.

Selltiz, Claire, et al. 1959. *Research Methods in Social Relations.* New York: Holt, Rinehart and Winston.

Thomas, W. I. 1951. *Social Behavior and Personality,* E. H. Volkart, ed. New York: Social Science Research Council.

CHAPTER II

ALCOHOL AND DRUG ABUSE

Reading 3

TINYDOPERS: A CASE STUDY OF DEVIANT SOCIALIZATION

Patricia A. Adler, Peter Adler, *University of California, San Diego*

> Not all marijuana use is hidden from parents. Increasingly, very young children are beginning to smoke with their parents. These "tinydopers," ranging in age from 0 to 8, are picking up drug use as part of their "normal" socialization experience. This phenomenon raises interesting questions about changes in social mores and patterns of socialization.

Marijuana smoking is now filtering down to our youngest generation; a number of children from 0–8 years old are participating in this practice under the influence and supervision of their parents. This phenomenon, *tinydoping*, raises interesting questions about changes in societal mores and patterns of socialization. We are not concerned here with the desirability or morality of the activity. Instead, we will discuss the phenomenon, elucidating the diverse range of attitudes, strategems and procedures held and exercised by parents and children.

An examination of the history and cultural evolution of marijuana over the last several decades illuminates the atmosphere in which tinydoping arose. Marijuana use, first located chiefly among jazz musicians and ghetto communities, eventually expanded to "the highly alienated young in flight from families, schools and conventional communities" (Simon and Gagnon, 1968:60; see also Goode, 1970; Carey, 1968; Kaplan, 1971; and Grinspoon, 1971). Blossoming in the mid-1960s, this youth scene formed an estranged and deviant subculture offsetting the dominant culture's work ethic and instrumental success orientation. Society reacted as an angry parent, enforcing legal, social and moral penalties against its rebellious children. Today, however, the pothead subculture has eroded and the population of smokers has broadened to include large numbers of middle class and establishment-oriented people.

Reprinted with permission from *Symbolic Interaction* 1 (2) (Spring 1978): 90–105.

Chapter II
Alcohol and Drug Abuse

Marijuana, then, may soon take its place with alcohol, its "prohibition" a thing of the past. These two changes can be considered movements of moral passage:

> Movements to redefine behavior may eventuate in a moral passage, a transition of the behavior from one moral status to another.... What is attacked as criminal today may be seen as sick next year and fought over as possibly legitimate by the next generation. (Gusfield, 1967:187. For further discussions of the social creation of deviance, see also Matza, 1969; Kituse, 1962; Douglas, 1970; and Becker, 1963.)

Profound metamorphoses testify to this redefinition: frequency and severity of arrest is proportionately down from a decade ago; the stigma of marijuana-related arrest is no longer as personally and occupationally ostracizing; and the fear that using grass will press the individual into close contact with hardened criminals and cause him to adopt a deviant self-identity or take up criminal ways has also largely passed.

The transformation in marijuana's social and legal status is not intrinsic to its own characteristics or those of mood-altering drugs in general. Rather, it illustrates a process of becoming socially accepted many deviant activities or substances may go through. This research suggests a more generic model of social change, a sequential development characteristic of the diffusion and legitimation of a formerly unconventional practice. Five stages identify the spread of such activities from small isolated outgroups, through increasing levels of mainstream society, and finally to such sacred groups as children.[1] Often, however, as with the case of pornography, the appearance of this quasi-sanctioned conduct among juveniles elicits moral outrage and a social backlash designed to prevent such behavior in the sacred population, while leaving it more open to the remainder of society.

Most treatments of pot smoking in the sociological literature have been historically and sub-culturally specific (see Carey, 1968; Goode, 1970; Grupp, 1971; Hochman, 1972; Kaplan, 1971; and Simon and Gagnon, 1968), swiftly dated by our rapidly changing society. Only Becker's (1953) work is comparable to our research since it offers a generic sequential model of the process for becoming a marijuana user.

The data in this paper show an alternate route to marijuana smoking. Two developments necessitate a modification of Becker's conceptualization. First, there have been many changes in norms, traditions

---

[1] The period of childhood has traditionally been a special time in which developing adults were given special treatment to ensure their growing up to be capable and responsible members of society. Throughout history and in most cultures children have been kept apart from adults and sheltered in protective isolation from certain knowledge and practices (see Aries, 1965).

and patterns of use since the time he wrote. Second, the age of this new category of smokers is cause for reformulation. Theories of child development proposed by Mead (1934), Erikson, (1968) and Piaget (1948) agree that prior to a certain age children are unable to comprehend subtle transformations and perceptions. As we will see the full effects and symbolic meanings of marijuana are partially lost to them due to their inability to differentiate between altered states of consciousness and to connect this with the smoking experience. Yet this does not preclude their becoming avid pot users and joining in the smoking group as accepted members.

Socialization practices are the final concern of this research. The existence of tinydoping both illustrates and contradicts several established norms of traditional childrearing. Imitative behavior (Piaget, 1962), for instance, is integral to tinydoping since the children's desire to copy the actions of parents and other adults is a primary motivation. Boundary maintenance also arises as a consideration: as soon as their offspring can communicate, parents must instruct them in the perception of social borders and the need for guarding group activities as secret. In contrast, refutations of convention include the introduction of mood-altering drugs into the sacred childhood period and, even more unusual, parents and children get high together. This bridges, often to the point of eradication, the inter-generational gap firmly entrenched in most societies. Thus, although parents view their actions as normal, tinydoping must presently be considered as deviant socialization.

METHODS

Collected over the course of 18 months, our data include observations of two dozen youngsters between the ages of birth and eight, and a similar number of parents, aged 21 to 32, all in middle-class households. To obtain a complete image of this practice we talked with parents, kids and other involved observers (the "multi-perspectival" approach, Douglas, 1976). Many of our conversations with adults were taped but our discussions with the children took the form of informal, extemporaneous dialogue, since the tape recorder distracts and diverts their attention. Finally, our study is exploratory and suggestive; we make no claim to all-inclusiveness in the cases or categories below.

THE KIDS

The following four individuals, each uniquely interesting, represent many common characteristics of other children and adults we observed.

Chapter II
Alcohol and Drug Abuse

"Big Ed": The Diaperdoper. Big Ed derives his name from his miniature size. Born three months prematurely, now three years old, he resembles a toy human being. Beneath his near-white wispy hair and toddling diapered bottom, he packs a punch of childish energy. Big Ed's mother and older siblings take care of him although he often sees his father who lives in a neighboring California town. Laxity and permissiveness characterize his upbringing, as he freely roams the neighborhood under his own and other children's supervision. Exposure to marijuana has prevailed since birth and in the last year he advanced from passive inhalation (smoke blown in his direction) to active puffing on joints. Still in the learning stage, most of his power is expended blowing air into the reefer instead of inhaling. He prefers to suck on a "bong" (a specially designed waterpipe), delighting on the gurgling sound the water makes. A breast fed baby, he will go to the bong for oral satisfaction, whether it is filled or not. He does not actively seek joints, but Big Ed never refuses one when offered. After a few puffs, however, he usually winds up with smoke in his eyes and tearfully retreats to a glass of water. Actual marijuana inhalation is minimal; his size renders it potent. Big Ed has not absorbed any social restrictions related to pot use or any awareness of its illegality, but is still too young to make a blooper as his speech is limited.

Stephanie: The Social Smoker. Stephanie is a dreamy four-year-old with quite good manners, calm assurance, sweet disposition and a ladylike personality and appearance. Although her brothers are rough and tumble, Stephanie can play with the boys or amuse herself sedately alone or in the company of adults. Attendance at a progressive school for the last two years has developed her natural curiosity and intelligence. Stephanie's mother and father both work, but still find enough recreational time to raise their children with love and care and to engage in frequent marijuana smoking. Accordingly, Stephanie has seen grass since infancy and accepted it as a natural part of life. Unlike the diaperdoper, she has mastered the art of inhalation and can breathe the smoke out through her nose. Never grasping or grubbing for pot, she has advanced from a preference for bongs or pipes and now enjoys joints when offered. She revels in being part of a crowd of smokers and passes the reefer immediately after each puff, never holding it for an unsociable amount of time. Her treasure box contains a handful of roaches (marijuana butts) and seeds (she delights in munching them as snacks) that she keeps as mementos of social occasions with (adult) "friends." After smoking, Stephanie becomes more bubbly and outgoing. Dancing to records, she turns in circles as she jogs from one foot to the other, releasing her body to the rhythm. She then eats everything in sight and falls asleep—roughly the same cycle as adults, but faster.

Reading 3
Tinydopers

When interviewed, Stephanie clearly recognized the difference between a cigarette and a joint (both parents use tobacco), defining the effects of the latter as good but still being unsure of what the former did and how the contents of each varied. She also responded with some confusion about social boundaries separating pot users from non-users, speculating that perhaps her grandmother did smoke it but her grandfather certainly did not (neither do). In the words of her father: "She knows not to tell people about it but she just proably wouldn't anyway."

Josh: The Self-gratifier. Everyone in the neighborhood knows Josh. Vociferous and outgoing, at age five he has a decidedly Dennis-the-Menace quality in both looks and personality. Neither timid nor reserved, he boasts to total strangers of his fantastic exploits and talents. Yet behind his bravado swagger lies a seeming insecurity and need for acceptance, coupled with a difficulty in accepting authority, which has led him into squabbles with peers, teachers, siblings and parents.

Josh's home shows the traditional division of labor. His mother stays home to cook and care for the children while his father works long hours. The mother is always calm and tolerant about her youngster's smart-alec ways, but his escapades may provoke an explosive tirade from the father. Yet this male parent is clearly the dominating force in Josh's life. Singling Josh out from his younger sister and brother, the father has chosen him as his successor in the male tradition. The parent had himself begun drinking and smoking cigarettes in his early formative years, commencing pot use as a teenager, and now has a favorable attitude toward the early use of stimulants which he is actively passing on to Josh.

According to his parents, his smoking has had several beneficial effects. Considering Josh a "hyper" child, they claim that it calms him down to a more normal speed, often permitting him to engage in activities which would otherwise be too difficult for his powers of concentration. He also appears to become more sedate and less prone to temper tantrums, sleeping longer and more deeply. But Josh's smoking patterns differ significantly from our last two subjects. He does not enjoy social smoking, preferring for his father to roll him "pinners" (thin joints) to smoke by himself. Unlike many other tinydopers, Josh frequently refuses the offer of a joint saying, "Oh that! I gave up smoking that stuff." At age five he claims to have already quit and gone back several times. His mother backs this assertion as valid; his father brushes it off as merely a ploy to shock and gain attention. Here, the especially close male parent recognizes the behavior as imitative and accepts it as normal. To others, however, it appears strange and suggests a surprising sophistication.

Josh's perception of social boundaries is also mature. Only a year older than Stephanie, Josh has made some mistakes but his awareness of

Chapter II
Alcohol and Drug Abuse

the necessity for secrecy is complete; he differentiates those people with whom he may and may not discuss the subject by the experience of actually smoking with them. He knows individuals but cannot yet socially categorize the boundaries. Josh also realizes the contrast between joints and cigarettes down to the marijuana and tobacco they contain. Interestingly, he is aggressively opposed to tobacco while favoring pot use (this may be the result of anti-tobacco cancer propaganda from kindergarten).

Kyra: The Bohemian. A worldly but curiously childlike girl is seven-year-old Kyra. Her wavy brown hair falls to her shoulders and her suntanned body testifies to many hours at the beach in winter and summer. Of average height for her age, she dresses with a maturity beyond her years. Friendly and sociable, she has few reservations about what she says to people. Kyra lives with her youthful mother and whatever boyfriend her mother fancies at the moment. Their basic family unit consists of two (mother and daughter), and they have travelled together living a free life all along the West Coast and Hawaii. While Josh's family was male dominated, this is clearly female centered, all of Kyra's close relatives being women. They are a bohemian group, generation after generation following a hip, up-to-the-moment, unshackled lifestyle. The house is often filled with people, but when the visitors clear out, a youthful, thrillseeking mother remains, who raises this daughter by treating her like a sister or friend. This demand on Kyra to behave as an adult may produce some internal strain, but she seems to have grown accustomed to it. Placed in situations others might find awkward, she handles them with precocity. Like her mother, she is being reared for a life of independence and freedom.

Pot smoking is an integral part of this picture. To Kyra it is another symbol of her adulthood; she enjoys it and wants to do it a lot. At seven she is an accomplished smoker; her challenge right now lies in the mastery of rolling joints. Of our four examples, social boundaries are clearest to Kyra. Not only is she aware of the necessary secrecy surrounding pot use, but she is able socially to categorize types of people into marijuana smokers and straights. She may err in her judgment occasionally, but not more so than any adult.

STAGES OF DEVELOPMENT

These four and other cases suggest a continuum of reactions to marijuana that is loosely followed by tinydopers.

From birth to around 18 months a child's involvement is passive. Most parents keep their infants nearby at all times and if pot is smoked the room becomes filled with potent clouds. At this age just a little marijuana smoke can be very powerful and these infants, the youngest

Reading 3
Tinydopers

diaperdopers, manifest noticeable effects. The drug usually has a calming influence, putting the infant into a less cranky mood and extending the depth and duration of sleep.

After the first one and a half years, the children are more attuned to what is going on around them: they begin to desire participation in a "monkey see, monkey do" fashion. During the second year, a fascination with paraphernalia generally develops, as they play with it and try to figure it out. Eager to smoke with adults and older children, they are soon discouraged after a toke (puff) or two. They find smoking difficult and painful (particularly to the eyes and throat)—after all, it is not easy to inhale burning hot air and hold it in your lungs.

But continual practice eventually produces results, and inhalation seems to be achieved somewhere during the third or fourth year. This brings considerable pride and makes the kids feel they have attained semi-adult status. Now they can put the paraphernalia to work. Most tinydopers of this age are wild about "roachclips," itching to put their joints into them as soon as possible after lighting.

Ages four and five bring the first social sense of the nature of pot and who should know about it. This begins as a vague idea, becoming further refined with age and sophistication. Finally, by age seven or eight kids have a clear concept of where the lines can be drawn between those who are and aren't "cool," and can make these distinctions on their own. No child we interviewed, however, could verbalize about any specific effects felt after smoking marijuana. Ironically, although they participate in smoking and actually manifest clear physical symptoms of the effects, tinydopers are rationally and intellectually unaware of how the drug is acting upon them. They are too young to notice a change in their behavior or to make the symbolic leap and associate this transformation with having smoked pot previously. The effects of marijuana must be socially and consensually delineated from non-high sensations for the user to fully appreciate the often subtle perceptual and physiological changes that have occurred. To the youngster the benefits of pot smoking are not at all subtle: he is permitted to imitate his elders by engaging in a social ritual they view as pleasurable and important; the status of adulthood is partially conferred on him by allowing this act, and his desire for acceptance is fulfilled through inclusion in his parents' peer group. This constitutes the major difference in appreciation between the child and adult smoker.

PARENTS' STRATEGIES

The youth of the sixties made some forceful statements through their actions about how they evaluated the Establishment and the conven-

Chapter II
Alcohol and Drug Abuse

tional American lifestyle. While their political activism has faded, many former members of this group still feel a strong commitment to smoking pot and attach a measure of symbolic significance to it. When they had children the question then arose of how to handle the drug vis-à-vis their offspring. The continuum of responses they developed ranges from total openness and permissiveness to various measures of secrecy.

SMOKING REGULARLY PERMITTED

Some parents give their children marijuana whenever it is requested. They may wait until the child reaches a certain age, but most parents in this category started their kids on pot from infancy. These parents may be "worried" or "unconcerned."

Worried. Ken and Deedy are moderate pot smokers, getting high a few times a week. Both had been regular users for several years prior to having children. When Deedy was pregnant she absolutely refused to continue her smoking pattern.

> I didn't know what effect it could have on the unborn child. I tried to read and find out, but there's very little written on that. But in the "Playboy Advisor" there was an article: they said we advise you to stay away from all drugs when you're pregnant. That was sort of my proof. I figured they don't bullshit about these types of things. I sort of said now at least somebody stands behind me because people were saying, "You can get high, it's not going to hurt the baby."

This abstinence satisfied them and once the child was born they resumed getting high as before. Frequently smoking in the same room as the baby, they began to worry about the possible harmful effects this exposure might have on his physical, psychological, and mental development. After some discussion, they consulted the family pediatrician, a prominent doctor in the city.

> I was really embarrassed, but I said, "Doctor, we get high, we smoke pot, and sometimes the kid's in the room. If he's in the room can this hurt him? I don't want him to be mentally retarded." He said, "Don't worry about it, they're going to be legalizing it any day now—this was three years ago—it's harmless and a great sedative."

This reassured them on two counts: they no longer were fearful in their own minds, and they had a legitimate answer when questioned by their friends.[2]

---

[2]Particularly relevant to these "justifications" is Scott and Lyman's (1968) analysis of accounts, as statements made to relieve one of culpability. Specifically, they can be seen as "denial of injury" (Sykes and Matza, 1957) as they assert the innocuousness of giving marijuana to their child. An "excuse" is further employed, "scapegoating" the doctor as the one really responsible for this aberration. Also, the appeal to science has been made.

Reading 3
Tinydopers

Ken and Deedy were particularly sensitive about peer reactions:

> Some people say, "You let your child get high?!" They really react with disgust. Or they'll say, "Oh you let your kids get high," and then they kind of look at you like, "That's neat, I think." And it's just nice to be able to back it up.

Ken and Deedy were further nonplussed about the problem of teaching their children boundary maintenance. Recognizing the need to prevent their offspring from saying things to the wrong people, they were unsure how to approach this subject properly.

> How can you tell a kid, how can you go up to him and say, "Well you want to get high, but don't tell anybody you're doing it"? You can't. We didn't really know how to tell them. You don't want to bring the attention, you don't want to tell your children not to say anything about it because that's a sure way to get them to do it. We just never said anything about it.

They hope this philosophy of openness and permissiveness will forestall the need to limit their children's marijuana consumption. Limits, for them, resemble prohibitions and interdictions against discussing grass: they make transgressions attractive. Both parents believe strongly in presenting marijuana as an everyday occurrence, definitely not as an undercover affair. When asked how they thought this upbringing might affect their kids, Deedy offered a fearful but doubtful speculation that their children might one day reject the drug.

> I don't imagine they'd try to abuse it. Maybe they won't even smoke pot when they get older. That's a big possibility. I doubt it, but hopefully they won't be that way. They've got potheads for parents.

Unconcerned. Alan and Anna make use of a variety of stimulants—pot, alcohol, cocaine—to enrich their lives. Considered heavy users, they consume marijuana and alcohol daily. Alan became acquainted with drugs, particularly alcohol, at a very early age and Anna first tried them in her teens. When they decided to have children the question of whether they would permit the youngsters to partake in their mood-altering experiences never arose. Anna didn't curtail her drug intake during pregnancy; her offspring were conceived, formed and weaned on this steady diet. When queried about their motivations, Alan volunteered:

> What the hell! It grows in the ground, it's a weed. I can't see anything wrong with doing anything, inducing any part of it into your body any way that you possibly could eat it, smoke it, intravenously, or whatever, that it would ever harm you because it grows in the ground. It's a natural thing. It's one of God's treats.

Chapter II
Alcohol and Drug Abuse

All of their children have been surrounded by marijuana's aromatic vapor since the day they returned from the hospital. Alan and Anna were pleased with the effect pot had on their infants; the relaxed, sleepy and happy qualities achieved after inhaling pot smoke made child-rearing an easier task. As the little ones grew older they naturally wanted to share in their parents' activities. Alan viewed this as the children's desire to imitate rather than true enjoyment of any effects:

> Emily used to drink Jack Daniels straight and like it. I don't think it was taste, I think it was more of an acceptance thing because that's what I was drinking. She was also puffing on joints at six months.

This mimicking, coupled with a craving for acceptance, although recognized by Alan in his kids, was not repeated in his own feelings toward friends or relatives. At no time during the course of our interview or acquaintance did he show any concern with what others thought of his behavior; rather, his convictions dominated, and his wife passively followed his lead.

In contrast to the last couple, Alan was not reluctant to address the problem of boundary maintenance. A situation arose when Emily was three, where she was forced to learn rapidly:

> One time we were stopped by the police while driving drunk. I said to Emily—we haven't been smoking marijuana. We all acted quiet and Emily realized there was something going on and she delved into it. I explained that some people are stupid and they'll harm you very badly if you smoke marijuana. To this day I haven't heard her mention it to anyone she hasn't smoked with.

As each new child came along, Alan saw to it that they learned the essential facts of life.

Neither Alan nor Anna saw any moral distinction between marijuana smoking and other, more accepted pastimes. They heartily endorsed marijuana as something to indulge in like "tobacco, alcohol, sex, breathing or anything else that brings pleasure to the senses." Alan and Anna hope their children will continue to smoke grass in their later lives. It has had beneficial effects for them and they believe it can do the same for their kids:

> I smoked marijuana for a long time, stopped and developed two ulcers; and smoked again and the two ulcers went away. It has great medicinal value.

SMOKING OCCASIONALLY PERMITTED

In contrast to uninterrupted permissiveness, other parents restrict marijuana use among their children to specific occasions. A plethora of rea-

*Reading 3
Tinydopers*

sons and rationalizations lie behind this behavior, some openly avowed by parents and others not. Several people believe it is okay to let the kids get high as long as it isn't done too often. Many other people do not have any carefully thought-out notion of what they want, tending to make spur-of-the moment decisions. As a result, they allow occasional but largely undefined smoking in a sporadic and irregular manner. Particular reasons for this inconsistency can be illustrated by three examples from our research:

1. *Conflicts between parents* can confuse the situation. While Stella had always planned to bring her children up with pot, Burt did not like the idea. Consequently, the household rule on this matter varied according to the unpredictable moods of the adults and which parent was in the house.
2. Mike and Gwen had trouble *making up their minds.* At one time they thought it probably couldn't harm the child, only to decide the next day they shouldn't take chances and rescind that decision.
3. Lois and David didn't waver hourly but had *changing ideas over time.* At first they were against it, but then met a group of friends who liked to party and approved of tinydoping. After a few years they moved to a new neighborhood and changed their lifestyle, again prohibiting pot smoking for the kids.

These are just a few of the many situations in which parents allow children an occasional opportunity to smoke grass. They use various criteria to decide when those permissible instances ought to be, most families subscribing to several of the following patterns:

Reward. The child receives pot as a bonus for good behavior in the past, present or future. This may serve as an incentive: "If you're a good boy today, Johnny, I may let you smoke with us tonight," or to celebrate an achievement already completed like "going potty" or reciting the alphabet.

Guilt. Marijuana can be another way of compensating children for what they aren't getting. Historically, parents have tried to buy their kids off or make themselves loved through gifts of money or toys but pot can also be suitable here. This is utilized both by couples with busy schedules who don't have time for the children ("We're going out again tonight so we'll give you this special treat to make it up to you") and by separated parents who are trying to compete with the former spouse for the child's love ("I know Mommy doesn't let you do this but you can do special things when you're with me").

Chapter II
Alcohol and Drug Abuse

Cuteness. To please themselves parents may occasionally let the child smoke pot because it's cute. Younger children look especially funny because they cannot inhale, yet in their eagerness to be like Mommy and Daddy they make a hilarious effort and still have a good time themselves. Often this will originate as amusement for the parents and then spread to include cuteness in front of friends. Carrying this trend further, friends may roll joints for the little ones or turn them on when the parents are away. This still precludes regular use.

Purposive. Giving marijuana to kids often carries a specific anticipated goal for the parents. The known effects of pot are occasionally desired and actively sought. They may want to calm the child down because of the necessities of a special setting or company. Sleep is another pursued end, as in "Thank you for taking Billy for the night; if he gives you any trouble just let him smoke this and he'll go right to bed." They may also give it to the children medicinally. Users believe marijuana soothes the upset stomach and alleviates the symptoms of the common cold better than any other drug. As a mood elevator, many parents have given pot to alleviate the crankiness young children develop from a general illness, specific pain or injury. One couple used it experimentally as a treatment for hyperactivity (see Josh).

Abstention. Our last category of marijuana smoking parents contains those who do not permit their children any direct involvement with illegal drugs. This leaves several possible ways to treat the topic of the adults' own involvement with drugs and how open they are about it. Do they let the kids know they smoke pot? Moreover, do they do it in the children's presence?

Overt. The great majority of our subjects openly smoked marijuana in front of their children, defining marijuana as an accepted and natural pastime. Even parents who withhold it from their young children hope that the kids will someday grow up to be like themselves. Thus, they smoke pot overtly. These marijuana smokers are divided on the issue of other drugs, such as pills and cocaine.

1. *Permissive.* One group considers it acceptable to use any drug in front of the children. Either they believe in what they are doing and consider it right for the kids to observe their actions, or they don't worry about it and just do it.
2. *Pragmatic.* A larger, practically oriented group differentiated between "smokable" drugs (pot and hashish) and the others (cocaine and pills), finding it acceptable to let children view consumption of the former group, but not the latter. Rationales varied for this, ranging from safety to morality:

Reading 3
Tinydopers

> Well, we have smoked hashish around them but we absolutely *never ever* do coke in front of them because it's a white powder and if they saw us snorting a white powder there goes the drain cleaner, there goes the baby powder. Anything white, they'll try it; and that goes for pills too. The only thing they have free rein of is popping vitamins.

Fred expressed his concern over problems this might engender in the preservation of his children's moral fibre:

> If he sees me snorting coke, how is he going to differentiate that from heroin? He gets all this anti-drug education from school and they tell him that heroin is bad. How can I explain to him that doing coke is okay and it's fun and doesn't hurt you but heroin is something else, so different and bad? How could I teach him right from wrong?

3. *Capricious.* A third group is irregular in its handling of multiple drug viewing and their offspring. Jon and Linda, for instance, claim that they don't mind smoking before their child but absolutely won't permit other drugs to be used in his presence. Yet in fact they often use almost any intoxicant in front of him, depending on their mood and how high they have already become.

In our observations we have never seen any parent give a child in the tinydoper range any kind of illegal drug other than marijuana and, extremely rarely, hashish. Moreover, the treatment of pot has been above all direct and open: even those parents who don't permit their children to join have rejected the clandestine secrecy of the behind-closed-doors approach. Ironically, however, they must often adopt this strategy toward the outside world; those parents who let it be known that they permit tinydoping frequently take on an extra social and legal stigma. Their motivation for doing so stems from a desire to avoid having the children view pot and their smoking it as evil or unnatural. Thus, to de-stigmatize marijuana they stigmatize themselves in the face of society.

REFERENCES

Adler, Peter, and Patricia A. Adler. 1979. "Symbolic interactionism," in Patricia A. Adler, Peter Adler, Jack D. Douglas, Andrea Fontana, C. Robert Freeman and Joseph Kotarba, *An Introduction to the Sociologies of Everyday Life*. Boston: Allyn and Bacon.

Adler, Patricia A., Peter Adler, and Jack D. Douglas. Forthcoming. "Organized crime: Drug dealing for pleasure and profit," in Jack D. Douglas (ed.), *Deviant Scenes*.

Aries, Phillipe. 1965. *Centuries of Childhood: A Social History of Family Life*. New York: Vintage.

Chapter II
Alcohol and Drug Abuse

Becker, Howard S. 1953. "Becoming a Marijuana user." *American Journal of Sociology* 59 (November).
_____. 1963. *Outsiders,* New York: Free Press.
Carey, James T. 1968. *The College Drug Scene.* Englewood Cliffs, N.J.: Prentice-Hall.
Douglas, Jack D. 1970. "Deviance and respectability: The social construction of moral meanings," in Jack D. Douglas (ed.), *Deviance and Respectability.* New York: Basic Books.
_____. 1976. *Investigative Social Research.* Beverly Hills, Calif.: Sage Publications.
Erikson, Erik. 1968. *Identity, Youth and Crisis.* New York: W. W. Norton.
Goode, Erich. 1969. *Marijuana,* New York: Atherton.
_____. 1970. *The Marijuana Smokers.* New York: Basic Books.
Grinspoon, Lester. 1971. *Marihuana Reconsidered.* Cambridge, Mass.: Harvard University Press.
Grupp, Stanley E. (ed.). 1971. *Marihuana.* Columbus, Ohio: Charles E. Merrill.
_____. 1973. *The Marihuana Muddle.* Lexington, Mass.: Lexington Books.
Gusfield, Joseph R. 1967. "Moral passage: The symbolic process in public designations of deviance." *Social Problems* 15:2 (Fall).
Hochman, Joel S. 1972. *Marijuana and Social Evolution.* Englewood Cliffs, N.J.: Prentice-Hall.
Kaplan, John. 1971. *Marihuana: The New Prohibition.* New York: Pocket Books.
Kituse, John I. 1962. "Societal reactions to deviant behavior." *Social Problems.* 9:3 (Winter).
Lyman, Stanford, and Marvin B. Scott. 1968. "Accounts." *American Sociological Review* 33:1.
_____. 1970. *A Sociology of the Absurd.* New York: Appleton-Century-Crofts.
Matza, David. 1969. *Becoming Deviant.* Englewood Cliffs, N.J.: Prentice-Hall.
Mead, George H. 1934. *Mind, Self and Society.* Chicago: University of Chicago Press.
Piaget, Jean. 1948. *The Moral Judgment of the Child.* New York: Free Press.
_____. 1962. *Play, Dreams and Imitation in Childhood.* New York: W. W. Norton.
_____, and B. Inhelder. 1969. *The Psychology of the Child.* New York: Basic Books.
Simon, William, and John H. Gagnon. 1968. "Children of the drug age." *Saturday Review,* September 21.
Sykes, Gresham, and David Matza. 1957. "Techniques of Neutralization." *American Sociological Review* 22 (December).

Reading 4

FORGOTTEN VICTIMS: CHILDREN OF ALCOHOLICS

Elizabeth Stark

> *Children of alcoholics often have feelings of guilt and self-blame. The family isolates itself trying to hide its turmoil from the outside world. Because of this isolation, alcoholics' children develop problems without being aware of them. They appear to be just super-responsible or oversensitive. Children of alcoholics must be told of their susceptibility to certain problems in order to be more able to deal with them, and society must be made aware of their special problems so they will not be stigmatized.*

When one member of a family is an alcoholic the entire family suffers. But the problems of the alcoholic often overshadow those of the rest of the family, especially the children. An 11-year-old girl comes home from school each day, leads her drunken mother to bed and prepares dinner for her younger brothers and sisters. A withdrawn teenager is reluctant to make friends because he is too embarrassed to have them over to his house. An unruly third-grader is told his misbehavior is the reason his father drinks. These are just some of the situations children face.

There are approximately seven million children in this country under the age of 18 living with an alcoholic parent, according to the Children of Alcoholics Foundation. These children live in an atmosphere of anxiety, tension, confusion and denial, often having no idea of what a normal family life is like, according to psychologist Joseph Kern, director of Alcoholism Treatment Services in Nassau County, New York.

Counselors and therapists see a great deal of guilt and self-blame among alcoholics' children, who often believe that there is something they could be doing to change things. "They are given subtle messages or told directly that if they were better, mom or dad wouldn't drink so much," Kern says.

Reprinted with permission from *Psychology Today* magazIne, copyright © 1987 (PT Partners, L.P.).

Chapter II
Alcohol and Drug Abuse

These children are never sure how to deal with their parents; a certain action is praised one day, then punished or ignored the next, depending on the parent's sobriety. Ellen Morehouse, a social worker and director of the Student Assistance Program in White Plains, New York, has found that children are confused by the difference between "dry" behavior and "drunk" behavior. A father who, while drunk, promises to take his son to a hockey game may have no recollection of the promise by the night of the game.

Numerous studies have shown that children of alcoholics have low self-confidence and are insecure about their parents' love. They say to themselves, "If he really loved me he wouldn't drink," according to Morehouse. They are very fearful of accidents. Will a parent pass out while smoking a cigarette and set the house on fire? Will she injure herself during a fall? Will he lose control of the car? Children are also terrified of the arguments that usually go on between their parents. The atmosphere of argument and tension in an alcoholic household is frequently more upsetting to children than the parents' actual drinking. And children often have reason to fear for their own safety. Victims of incest and child abuse often come from alcoholic families.

The anxiety and tension are magnified by the family isolation. The goings-on in an alcoholic household are kept from the outside at almost any cost. Children are often afraid to bring friends home and avoid activities that would involve their parents. They become coconspirators in a pact of silence. According to Morehouse, parents tell their children that they are not to discuss the drinking with anyone, stating or implying "what goes on in this family is OUR business."

This environment can cause serious problems for children. Psychosomatic ailments such as headaches, upset stomachs and insomnia are common, and many children suffer from depression. These children are more likely to develop learning disabilities, as well as deviant and antisocial behavior, according to numerous studies.

In addition, sons of alcoholics have an increased risk of alcoholism when they grow up, as research on families, twins and adopted children has shown. For example, studies by psychiatrist Donald Goodwin of the University of Kansas in the 1970s in Denmark showed that adopted sons of alcoholics were four times more likely than sons of nonalcoholics to become alcoholics, despite being raised by nonalcoholic parents.

Although daughters of alcoholics are less likely to grow up as alcoholics, they are more prone than women without an alcoholic parent to marry alcoholic men and to become severely depressed. Children of alcoholics are also more likely to develop other problems, such as drug abuse and eating disorders.

Children from alcoholic families often use a variety of coping meth-

Reading 4
Children of Alcoholics

ods to survive. Denial is one of the most common mechanisms. Some children split their parents into two people, a good half and a bad half. Others simply downplay the importance of their emotions to alleviate the pain, becoming numb to the world. They convince themselves that they don't really want the things that they can't obtain or brag and lie to their peers to cover up the things they lack.

These children often take certain roles to try to survive their chaotic childhood. Family therapist Sharon Wegscheider has described four such roles. The "hero," or caretaker, usually the oldest child, becomes a surrogate parent, supervising the other children and running the household. The caretaker is often a superachiever, doing extremely well in school and athletics. The "scapegoat," or problem child, on the other hand, gets into trouble and misbehaves to draw attention away from the alcoholism. The "mascot" puts on a facade of being carefree and tries to minimize the problems by joking and clowning. Last is the "lost child" who fades into the background, withdrawn and isolated from the turmoil.

Whether these roles are helpful or harmful in the long run is unclear. Psychologist Claudia Black, a founder of the National Association for Children of Alcoholics, has come up with similar categories to define these roles. She believes that they are often only superficial cures for later problems.

But not all children from alcoholic homes have trouble. "There is a whole group of children who don't have problems," says Jeannette Johnson, a psychologist with the National Institute on Alcohol Abuse and Alcoholism, who is studying resilient children. "The question is 'What makes them invulnerable?'"

There is no simple answer to that question. The reason that some children do better than others depends on many complicated and interwoven factors. The severity of the parent's drinking, the amount of marital conflict in the home, the presence of siblings, the sex of the alcoholic parent and the child's relationship with the nonalcoholic parent can all make a difference.

Emmy Werner, a psychologist at the University of California, Davis, has been studying a group of children of Kauai, Hawaii, who were born in 1955. Of the almost 700 children she has been following, 49 were children of alcoholics, and some of them revealed classic learning and behavior problems. But 29 of the 49 children did not display any of those problems when they were interviewed at age 18 by Werner.

There were a number of factors that affected how well a child made out in an alcoholic family. Girls were more resilient than were boys; almost three-quarters of the 29 resilient children were female. Werner also found that having an alcoholic mother was more damaging than having an alcoholic father. Only one resilient child had an alcoholic mother. In contrast, most children of alcoholic mothers that Werner saw had serious psychosocial problems by the age of 18.

One reason children of alcoholic mothers are vulnerable, Werner says, is because of the risk of fetal alcohol syndrome; if the mother abuses alcohol during her pregnancy the child may have various birth defects.

In addition, since it is usually the mother who is the primary caretaker, her inaccessibility due to alcoholism can be especially detrimental, Werner explains. She found that most of the resilient children had received a great deal of attention from their primary caretakers during their first year, while the less resilient children often had not. Children from alcoholic families were also better off if a younger sibling was not born until they were at least 2 years old, assuring them some time alone in the limelight.

If children in an alcoholic home do not get the time and attention they need from their family, caring outsiders can make a difference. The positive influences of outside social supports has been shown in the work of psychologist Janette Beals and her colleagues at the Program for Prevention Research at Arizona State University. They found that teachers, coaches, counselors and adult friends who play, talk with and advise children from alcoholic homes can make a real difference to a child.

The amount of alcohol the parents consume affects the family's equilibrium, and based on the cases she sees, Morehouse says that the more disrupted the household, the worse off the child. A child from a home in which parents only drink some on weekends has an advantage over the one whose parents are out of it all week. And, "If the parents present the image of a harmonious marriage," she says, "the child is better off."

An important way to preserve the sense of a normal home despite family alcoholism is by observing family holidays and rituals. Studies by psychiatrist Steven Wolin and his colleagues at George Washington University's Center for Family Research have shown that when these rituals are altered by heavy drinking, the families are more likely to pass on alcohol problems to their children.

"People tend to evaluate their families on holidays," says Morehouse. "If your mom ignores your birthday, even if she's been great to you all year, you won't forget that."

Aside from outside factors, some children just seem to have better inner resources than others to deal with growing up in an alcoholic home. Werner found that children whom parents considered "cuddly" and "affectionate" as children did better than other children. "Easy to love" children may garner more attention and care from adults because of their appealing personalities.

Reading 4
Children of Alcoholics

Psychologist Johnson is just beginning to study these resilient children from alcoholic homes. She suspects that some children's resilience comes from the caretaking responsibility they acquire early in life. In her view, helping to run the household and looking after brothers and sisters "may not necessarily be a bad thing. In fact it might serve as a protective measure. When you are skillful you are intrinsically rewarded."

But others, such as Kern, who sees many adult children of alcoholics (ACoA's) in the addiction programs he runs, believe that these "super-copers," as they're called, "pay the price somewhere down the line."

"On the surface things may be OK, but when you scratch the surface things are not OK. The strategies they used in their childhoods will not work in adulthood," he says.

There are 21 million adult children of alcoholics according to the Children of Alcoholics Foundation, and many carry the emotional scars of their childhood into their adult lives. ACoA's often look for external solutions to feel good about themselves and to fill "a gaping hole inside," says Kern. They may become superachievers in their quest to tackle the world outside instead of working on the problems inside. As adults, children of alcoholics often reveal some type of addictive behavior, whether it's an addiction to alcohol, drugs, food, gambling or even work.

Many ACoA's have a great need for control and tend to see issues in black and white, according to Rudolph Edens, a social worker who directs the Addictions Program at George Washington University Health Plan in Washington, D.C. "There is no middle ground for many of them," he says. "They tend to criticize themselves unmercifully. A lot of them are walking around with a coat of armor—they think there is no one else like them." Edens says that as adults, children of alcoholics often create trouble for themselves because they feel more comfortable when there is a crisis. They are so used to things going badly, they don't know what to do with success.

ACoA's frequently have problems with relationships and are unable to get close to someone, Kern says. They often marry unstable mates or alcoholics in an attempt to "fix" them, to succeed with their spouses where they failed with their parents.

Kern feels that the recent publicity being given to children of alcoholics is a good thing. "I think the label is wonderful news. Finally a lot of these people can say, 'Ah! That's what's the matter with me.' " Kern says that whenever he goes out and speaks about ACoA's, people always come to him afterward, relieved to discover at last that there are others who have the same problems that they do.

Of course, if children of alcoholics can be helped while they are still children, many of these adult problems can be avoided. One of the biggest obstacles is identifying these children early enough. Guilt and the family code of silence often prevent children from seeking help on their own, so most of those who receive help are children whose parents are being treated for alcoholism. And only 15 percent of alcoholics ever receive treatment.

But even children whose parents are being treated are often ignored. "There's a mistaken belief that once the alcoholic gets better, the family problems will get better," says Morehouse. She points out that a parent's abstinence may occasionally make problems worse. Children often have impossible expectations for what life will be like when the alcoholic stops drinking, Morehouse says, and can't understand, for example, why their parents are still arguing. On top of that, children often lose the freedom they had when their parents were drinking. All of a sudden the parent is back in control and there are restrictions on what the child is allowed to do. The roles that children formerly assumed may no longer work within the family.

Al-Anon and Alateen, organizations affiliated with Alcoholics Anonymous that serve family members, can help children of alcoholics. But without the support and encouragement of a parent, a child or teenager is very unlikely to attend meetings. Most professionals agree that the schools are the best place to reach children of alcoholics. There are various signs that teachers, nurses and guidance counselors should look for, Morehouse says. Children are often dressed inappropriately, don't bring in permission slips, absence slips or homework, are fearful of their parents meeting the teacher and are consistently late for school and stranded without a ride after school.

A possible problem for the schools in singling out children of alcoholics is stigmatization. Does labeling children as "potential alcoholics," or "at risk" for other serious problems, create a self-fulfilling prophecy? Will teachers, parents and even the children themselves have a different set of expectations?

Morehouse believes that children of alcoholics should know what risks they face, but they should also know that it isn't a foregone conclusion that they'll become alcoholics or drug abusers. By knowing their susceptibilities they can take the proper precautions. The risks associated with being the child of an alcoholic can be buffered by the inner resources of the child and the care and attention of supportive adults.

To avoid stigmatization in school, Morehouse suggests that information about alcoholism be presented to all students, encouraging those with family problems to seek out a teacher on their own. Teachers can assign the class to read a book on alcoholism, or pass out pamphlets that present children with questions such as "Do you worry about your parent's drinking?" or "Do you think your parents shouldn't drink so much or shouldn't drink at all?" The odds are good that a classroom teacher

Reading 4
Children of Alcoholics

will have at least 1 child from a family with an alcoholic parent; estimates are that in a class of 25 children, 5 students will come from a home with either alcohol or drug problems.

In addition to educating schoolchildren, teaching the public at large can help. As Migs Woodside, president of the Children of Alcoholics Foundation, says, "Anybody can help. Be a good listener. Invite one of these youngsters over for dinner, or to do homework. Give them your phone number and tell them to call you if they need help. What these children need is a sympathetic friend."

Reading 5

DRUGS-CRIME CONNECTIONS: ELABORATIONS FROM THE LIFE HISTORIES OF HARD-CORE HEROIN ADDICTS

Charles E. Faupel, *Auburn University*
Carl B. Klockars, *University of Delaware*

> *It is usually assumed that being a hard-core heroin addict necessarily leads to engaging in criminal activity. Two specific hypotheses are often proposed: (1) that the pressure to obtain money for the drugs forces the addict into crime; and, (2) the addict subculture encourages criminal solutions. Analysis of the life histories of 32 addicts suggests that neither hypothesis is wholly true. There are a great many addict career patterns. Different routes of access to drugs and the different life structures selected by addicts interact to form the specific pattern adopted by a given individual.*

The debate over the nature and extent of the relationship between heroin use and criminal activity is a long-standing one which has generated a voluminous literature. A 1980 survey (Gandossey et al., 1980) lists over 450 citations to books, articles, and research reports which directly or indirectly bear upon the heroin-crime relationship. Since 1980 the study of this relationship has continued, and several large-scale quantitative studies (Anglin and Speckart, 1984; Ball et al., 1981, 1983; Collins et al., 1984, 1985; Johnson et al., 1985) generally support the thesis that an increase in criminality commonly occurs in conjunction with increased heroin use in the United States. These studies, together with a host of others preceding them (e.g., Ball and Snarr, 1969; Chein et al., 1964; Inciardi, 1979; McGlothlin et al., 1978; Nash, 1973; Weissman et al., 1974) have moved the focus of the debate from the empirical question of whether or not

---

Reprinted with permission from *Social Problems* 34(1987): 54–63m, 66m–68 by the Society for the Study of Social Problems and the authors.

there is a heroin-crime connection to empirical and theoretical questions about the dynamics of that connection.

In particular, two hypotheses, neither of which is new, currently occupy center stage in the drugs-crime controversy. The first, stated by Tappan a quarter of a century ago, maintains that the "addict of lower socio-economic class is a criminal primarily because illicit narcotics are costly and because he can secure his daily requirements only by committing crimes that will pay for them" (1960:65–66). This hypothesis maintains that heroin addict criminality is a consequence of addiction, albeit an indirect one. As physical dependence upon and tolerance for heroin increase, and the cost of progressively larger dosages of heroin increase proportionally, the addict is driven to criminal means to satisfy his or her habit. Empirically, this hypothesis predicts a linear increase in heroin consumption and a corresponding increase in criminal activity necessary to support it. In contrast, a second hypothesis maintains that the "principal explanation for the association between drug abuse and crime...is likely to be found in the subcultural attachment" (Goldman, 1981:162) comprised of the criminal associations, identifications, and activities of those persons who eventually become addicted. The basis for this hypothesis can only be understood in the context of the contemporary socio-legal milieu in which narcotics use takes place. Since the criminalization of heroin in 1914, the social world of narcotics has become increasingly intertwined with the broader criminal subculture (Musto, 1973). Consequently, would-be narcotics users inevitably associate with other criminals in the highly criminal copping areas of inner cities, and, indeed, are often recruited from delinquent and criminal networks. Through these criminal associations, therefore, the individual is introduced to heroin, and both crime and heroin use are facilitated and maintained. Empirically, this second hypothesis predicts increases in heroin use following or coinciding with periods of criminal association and activity.

A shorthand title for the first hypothesis is "Drugs cause crimes"; for the second "Crimes cause drugs." Each, as we shall see below, is subject to a number of qualifications and reservations; but each, as we shall also see below, continues to mark a rather different approach to understanding the drugs-crime connection. Furthermore, each hypothesis has quite different policy implications associated with it.

METHODOLOGY

Our contribution to understanding the dynamics of the drugs-crime connection is based upon life-history interviews with 32 hard core heroin addicts in the Wilmington, Delaware area. We purposely selected the respondents on the basis of their extensive involvement in the heroin subculture. All of the respondents had extensive contact with the criminal justice system. At the time of interview, 24 of the 32 respondents were incarcerated or under some form of correctional authority supervision (e.g., supervised custody, work release, parole, or probation). While this places certain limits on the generalizations that can be made from these data, the focus of this study is the dynamics of addiction among heavily-involved street addicts. For example, controlled users or "chippers" will not have experienced many of the dynamics reported here. Similarly, physicians, nurses, and middle class "prescription abusers" are not typically subject to many of the constraints experienced by lower-class street users. Hence, it is important to emphasize that the findings we report here are intended to describe "hard core" urban heroin addicts.

Women are slightly overrepresented, constituting 14 of the 32 respondents. Ethnically, the sample consists of 23 blacks and nine whites; Hispanics are not represented because there is not a sizable Hispanic drug-using population in the Wilmington area.

Respondents were paid five dollars per hour for their interview time, which undoubtedly contributed to the 100 percent response rate. The interviews ranged from 10 to 25 hours in length, with each interview session averaging between three and four hours. With a single exception, all of the interviews were tape recorded and transcribed. Respondents were promised confidentiality and, without exception, they spoke openly of their drug, crime, and life-history experience.

The incarcerated respondents and most of the street respondents were selected with the aid of treatment personnel who were carefully instructed regarding the goals of the research and selection criteria. This strategy proved invaluable for two reasons. First, by utilizing treatment personnel in the screening process, we were able to avoid the time-consuming task of establishing the "appropriateness" of respondents for the purposes of this research; the treatment personnel were already intimately familiar with the drug-using and criminal histories of the respondents. Second, the treatment personnel had an unusually positive relationship with Wilmington-area drug users. The treatment counselor in the prison system was regarded as an ally in the quest for better living conditions, appeals for early release, etc., and was regarded as highly trustworthy in the prison subculture. His frequent confrontations with prison authorities over prisoner rights and privileges enhanced his reputation among the inmates. Similarly, the treatment counselor who aided in the selection of street respondents was carefully selected on the basis of his positive involvement with street addicts. His relationship with area addicts is a long-standing and multifaceted one. His reputation among street addicts was firmly established when he successfully negotiated much needed reforms in one of the local treatment agencies. Because of the long-standing positive relationship they had with area addicts, this initial contact by treatment personnel greatly facilitated our establishing necessary rapport.

After a few initial interviews were completed, several broad focal areas emerged which formed the basis for future questioning. Respondents were interviewed regarding: (1) childhood and early adolescent experiences which may have served as *predisposing factors* for eventual drugs/criminal involvement; (2) *initial encounters* with various types of drugs and criminality; (3) the *evolution* of their drug and criminal careers; (4) their patterns of activity during *peak periods* of drug use and criminality, including descriptions of *typical days* during these periods; (5) their *preferences* for types of crimes and drugs; (6) the *structure of understanding* guiding drug use and criminal activity; and (7) their perceptions of the nature and effectiveness of *drug treatment.* Structuring the life-history interviews in this way insured that most relevant career phases were covered while at the same time it permitted the respondents a great deal of flexibility in interpreting their experiences.

DRUGS CAUSE CRIMES VERSUS CRIMES CAUSE DRUGS

One of the earliest strategies for testing the Drugs-cause-crimes versus Crimes-cause-drugs hypotheses involved trying to establish a temporal sequence to drug use and criminal behavior. If it can be established that a pattern of regular or extensive criminal behavior typically precedes heroin addiction, that finding would tend to support the Crimes-cause-drugs hypothesis. Conversely, if a pattern of regular or extensive criminality tends to develop after the onset of heroin addiction, that finding would tend to support the Drugs-cause-crimes hypothesis. Previous research on this question is mixed, but mixed in a systematic way. Most of the early studies found little criminality before the onset of opiate addiction (Pescor, 1943; Terry and Pellens, 1928). Later studies, by contrast, have shown a high probability of criminality preceding heroin addiction (Ball and Chambers, 1970; Chambers, 1974; Jacoby et al., 1973; Inciardi, 1979; O'Donnell, 1966; Robins and Murphy 1967).

Our life-history interviews are consistent with the findings of the recent studies. All of our respondents reported some criminal activity prior to their first use of heroin. However, for nearly all of our respondents, both their criminal careers and their heroin-using careers began slowly. For the respondents in our study, a median of 3.5 years elapsed between their first serious criminal offense and subsequent involvement in criminal activity on a regular basis. Likewise, all of our respondents reported

Chapter II
Alcohol and Drug Abuse

at least occasional use of other illicit drugs prior to their first experience with heroin. Moreover, many of our respondents indicated that they spent substantial periods of time—months and even years—using heroin on an occasional basis ("chipping" or "chippying"), either inhaling the powder ("sniffing" or "snorting"), injecting the prepared ("cooked") mixture subcutaneously ("skinpopping"), or receiving occasional intravenous injections from other users before becoming regular users themselves. Perhaps most importantly, virtually all of our respondents reported that they believed that their criminal and drug careers began independently of one another, although both careers became intimately interconnected as each evolved. In the earliest phases of their drug and crime careers, the decision to commit crimes and the decision to use drugs were choices which our respondents believe they freely chose to make and which they believe they could have discontinued before either choice became a way of life (also see Fields and Walters, 1985; Morris, 1985).

DRUG AND CRIME CAREER PATTERNS

From our interviews it appears that two very general factors shape and influence the drug and crime careers of our respondents, not only during the early stages of each career but as each career evolves through different stages. The first of these factors is the *availability* of heroin rather than the level of physical tolerance the user has developed. "The more you had the more you did," explains "Mona" a thirty-year-old female. "And if all you had was $10 then that's all you did.... But if you had $200 then you did that much." Addicts are able to adjust to periods of sharply decreased availability (e.g., "panic" periods when supplies of street heroin disappear) by reducing consumption or by using alternative drugs (e.g., methadone). They are also able to manipulate availability, increasing or decreasing it in ways and for reasons we discuss below.

As we use the term, availability also means something more than access to sellers of heroin who have quantities of the drug to sell. By availability we also mean the resources and opportunities to buy heroin or obtain it in other ways as well as the skills necessary to use it. In short, availability is understood to include considerations of all of those opportunities and obstacles which may influence a heroin user's success in introducing a quantity of the drug into his or her bloodstream.

The second general factor shaping the drugs and crime careers of our life-history interviewees is *life structure*. By "life structure" we mean regularly occurring patterns of daily domestic, occupational, recreational, or criminal activity. Recent ethnographic accounts of heroin-using careers in several major cities reveal that, like their "straight" counterparts, most addicts maintain reasonably predictable daily routines (Beschner and Brower, 1985; Walters, 1985). Throughout their lives our respondents fulfilled, to one degree or another, conventional as well as criminal and other subcultural roles. In fact, during most periods of their crime and drug careers, our interviewees spent far more time engaged in conventional role activities than in criminal or deviant ones. Many worked conventional jobs. Women with children performed routine housekeeping and child-rearing duties. Many leisure-time activities did not differ from those of non-addicts. These hard core addicts spent time grocery shopping, tinkering with cars, visiting relatives, talking with friends, listening to records, and watching television in totally unremarkable fashion.

Life structure in the hard core criminal addict's life can be also provided by some rather stable forms of criminal activity. Burglars spend time staking out business establishments. Shoplifters typically establish "runs," more or less stable sequences of targeted stores from which to "boost" during late morning, noon, and early afternoon hours, saving the later afternoon for fencing what they have stolen. Prostitutes typically keep a regular evening and night-time schedule, which runs from 7 P.M. to 3 A.M. Mornings are usually spent sleeping and afternoons are usually occupied with conventional duties.

It is within this structure of conventional and criminal roles that buying ("copping"), selling ("dealing"), and using ("shooting") heroin take place. For example, shoplifters typically structure their runs to allow times and places for all three activities. Likewise, prostitutes seek to manage their drug use so that neither withdrawal symptoms ("joneses") nor periods of heroin-induced drowsiness will interfere with their work. In order to meet the demands of criminal or conventional roles, addicts in our sample often used other drugs (e.g., marijuana, barbituates, alcohol, amphetamines, methadone) to alter their moods and motivations, saving heroin as a reward for successfully completing a job or meeting other obligations.

A Typology of Career Patterns

These two dimensions—*availability* and *life structure*—are critical to understanding the dynamics of addict careers. According to our respondents, differences in the ways addicts manage these functions and variations in these two dimensions that are beyond the control of addicts combine to produce fairly distinct patterns, periods, or stages in their careers. The interaction of availability and life structure may be understood to describe addict career phases that are familiar to participants or observers of the heroin scene.

In Figure 1, we identify four such familiar career phases, each of

Chapter II
Alcohol and Drug Abuse

Figure 1
A TYPOLOGY OF HEROIN USE CAREER PHASES

Availability	Life Structure	
	High	Low
High	The Stabilized Junkie	The Free-Wheeling Junkie
Low	The Occasional User	The Street Junkie

which is marked by a different interaction of heroin availability and life structure. It is important to note that while each denotes an addict type, none of the "types" imply a single career pattern. That is, throughout their drug-crime careers, addicts typically move through periods in which they may at one time be described as one type and later as another. In our discussion of each type, we describe some of the ways in which transitions seem to occur.

The Occasional User—Low Availability/High Life Structure. Initiates into the heroin-using subculture typically begin as occasional users. For the beginning heroin user, a variety of factors typically serve to limit the availability of heroin. The initiate has usually not spent enough time in the heroin subculture to develop extensive drug connections. In addition, the beginner must be taught how and where to buy heroin, and also must learn how to use it. Moreover, the typical beginning heroin user is unlikely to have sufficient income to maintain any substantial level of heroin consumption, and is most unlikely to have either the connections or the knowledge necessary to increase availability through low-level dealing or through shrewd buying and reselling as experienced addicts sometimes do.

In addition to these factors which tend to limit the availability of heroin to the beginning user and hold him or her to an occasional user role, a variety of factors related to life structure also tend to oblige the beginning heroin user to play an occasional user role, or at least to do so until that life structure can be modified to accommodate a higher level of heroin use. In many cases beginning heroin users are young, dependent, involved in school, and bear family roles and obligations which are not easily changed. Likewise, adult role obligations, such as full-time employment, housekeeping, and child rearing, can be altered so as to be compatible with occasional patterns of heroin use, but not without considerable difficulty if those patterns include high or even moderately high levels of addiction.

One of our respondents, "Belle," explained how she and her husband, "Taps" maintained a very long period of occasional use, due largely to Taps' determination to keep his full-time job:

> I know of people that does half a bag generally. Do you understand what I'm saying? That they automatically live off of half a bag and got a jones. Like I said, Taps worked—and he would shoot no more than half a bag of dope at any time he took off and wouldn't do no wrong. He would not do no wrong. He worked each and every day. And this is what I told you before—I said I don't know how he had a jones and worked, but he worked every day.

Moreover, Belle went on to explain that when the life structure Taps provided for her lapsed—and availability increased—she did not remain an occasional user:

> Taps had me limited a long, long time. I mean a long time limited to nothing but a half a bag of drugs, until he completely stopped hisself. Then when he stopped, I went "Phwee!"—because I didn't have anybody to guide me. I didn't have to take half a bag and divide it in half for him. And I went from one bag to more.

"Ron," another addict in our sample, played the role of "occasional user" without interruption for nearly eight years. During this period he consumed an average of $10–15 in street heroin per day, while holding down a full-time job and living with his mother, who refused to allow him to use drugs in her home. Toward the end of the eight-year period he became a "tester" for a local drug dealer, a role which increased the availability of heroin. At about the same time, he also lost his job and moved out of his mother's home. Having lost the support of the stable routine imposed by his job and living arrangements at the same time heroin became more readily available to him in his role of "tester," his drug use escalated dramatically within a very short time.

Interestingly, the low availability/high life structure pattern of occasional use, which typically marks the beginning addict's entrance into the drug-using world, is characteristic of many addicts' attempts to leave it. Many formal drug rehabilitation programs impose conditions of low (or no) heroin availability combined with high life structure upon addicts enrolled in their programs (Faupel, 1985). Likewise, as Biernacki (1986) and Waldorf (1983) have extensively demonstrated, addicts who attempt to quit on their own often seek to do so by limiting or eliminating altogether their contacts with addict friends, self-medicating with "street" methodone, and devoting themselves intensively to some highly de-

Chapter II
Alcohol and Drug Abuse

manding routine activity such as a full-time job or caring for young children.

The Stabilized Junkie—High Availability/High Life Structure. For the occasional user to become a stabilized junkie, heroin must become increasingly available in large and regular quantities, and his or her daily structure must be modified to accommodate regular heroin use. Making heroin regularly available in sufficiently large quantities is not only a matter of gaining access to reliable sources of supply of the drug; it also involves learning new and more sophisticated techniques for using and obtaining it as well as getting enough money to be able to buy it regularly.

During the time beginning addicts play occasional user roles, they typically learn the fundamentals of copping, cooking, cutting, and spiking. These are all drug-using skills that take time to learn. It was not uncommon for the addicts in our sample to report that a sharp increase in their level of heroin use followed their learning to shoot themselves. When an occasional user learns to self-inject and no longer requires the more knowledgeable drug-using friends to "get off," this new level of skill and independence, in effect, increases the availability of heroin.

Likewise, copping skills and contacts which might have been sufficient to support occasional use require upgrading to support the needs of the stabilized junkie. The would-be stabilized junkie who must rely solely on low-quality, "street" heroin, who gets "ripped" by paying high prices for "bad dope," or who is totally dependent on what quality or quantity of heroin a single supplier happens to have available must seek to stabilize both the quantity and quality of regularly available heroin. Doing so seems to require extending and developing contacts in the drug subculture. In the words of one of our respondents:

> ...you got to start associating with different people. You got to be in touch with different people for the simple reason that not just one person has it all the time. You got to go from one person to the other, find out who's got the best bag and who hasn't.... You want to go where the best bag is for your money, and especially for the money *you're* spending. You got to mingle with so many different people.

Making, developing, and maintaining the contacts that are helpful if not absolutely necessary to stable heroin use seem to invite natural opportunities for the most common modification in the stabilized junkie's life structure: dealing. From the point of view of the would-be stabilized junkie, dealing has two major advantages over most other forms of routine daily activity. First, it can be carried on in the course of the stabilized junkie's search for his or her own supply of drugs and, second, it can be a source of money for the purchase of drugs or a source of drugs itself.

Dealing can be rather easily accommodated to the needs of both availability and life structure.

All of our respondents reported that at some time in their drug-using careers they had played the role of dealer, if only occasionally. Becoming an occasional dealer is almost an inevitable consequence of becoming a competent, regular user. A stabilized junkie will not only be approached to "cop" for occasional users and addicts whose suppliers are temporarily out of stock, but the stabilized junkie will come to recognize occasions on which especially "good dope" can be purchased and resold at a profit to drug-using friends.

Because the work of dealing drugs on a small scale does not require much more time or effort than that which goes into buying drugs regularly for one's own use, dealing also has another advantage which makes it an attractive activity for the stabilized junkie. Namely, it can be carried on as a source of drugs or income without undue interference with whatever other "hustle," if any, constitutes the stabilized junkie's additional source of support. This is particularly true if, in the course of carrying on the hustle—be it theft, shoplifting, pimping, prostitution, bookmaking, or dealing in stolen property—the stabilized addict is likely to come into regular contact with other drug users.

The extent to which dealing can be carried on along with other hustles depends, of course, both on the nature of that hustle and on the extent of the dealing. The stabilized junkie will tend to divide his or her hustling efforts between dealing and other hustles with an eye toward which one delivers the highest profit. However, dividing those efforts will also involve other considerations such as the stabilized junkie's personal preference for one type of work, life style and community reputation considerations, opportunities to practice one type of hustle or another, and the physical demands each type of hustle tends to require. Among female heroin users, a rather common accommodation to the profits and opportunities of dealing and those of other hustles is a live-together arrangement with a male user. In this division of labor each tries to conduct their outside hustle during hours when the other can be at home to handle dealing transactions. An important feature of this arrangement is that, if necessary, it can be structured so as to permit the stabilized female junkie to be at home for housekeeping and child-rearing duties as well as dealing.

The Free-Wheeling Junkie—High Availability/Low Life Structure. Although most heroin users spend some portion of their drug-using careers as stabilized junkies and many manage to live for years with high heroin availability and highly-structured daily routines, at least two properties of the stabilized junkie's situation tend to work against the maintenance of stability. One is the pharmacological property of heroin.

Chapter II
Alcohol and Drug Abuse

It is a drug to which users tend to develop a tolerance rather rapidly, although as Zinberg (1984) has demonstrated, such tolerance is neither necessary nor universal. Moreover, as we have pointed out earlier, numerous factors in the social setting of heroin use mitigate the destabilizing effect of the drug. Work routines, household duties, and even subcultural roles all serve to structure drug consumption. However, in the absence of external structures of constraint, or when such routines are temporarily disrupted, the pharmacalogical properties of heroin tend to destabilize the lifestyle of the addict further. In sum, contrary to popular belief, heroin use does not inevitably lead to a deterioration of lifestyle. Rather, the physiological dynamics of narcotics use tend to be most destabilizing under conditions where life structure is already weak and incapable of accommodating the physiological demands imposed by increased tolerance.

The other property of the stabilized junkie's life which tends to undermine stability is the hustle the junkie uses to finance his or her habit. According to our respondents, it is not hard times or difficulties in raising money through hustles which tend to destabilize the stabilized junkie's life. "You can adjust yourself to a certain amount of drugs a day," explained Belle, "that you don't have to have but just that much." In addition to reducing their drug consumption, stabilized junkies accommodate themselves to such lean periods by substituting other drugs for heroin, working longer and harder at their hustling, or changing the type of hustle they work.

On the contrary, it is the unusual success, the "big sting" or "big hit," that tends to destabilize the stabilized junkie's high degree of life structure. The "big sting" or "big hit" can come in many forms. One of our respondents—an armed robber who usually limited his robbing to street mugging, gas stations, and convenience stores—"hit" a bank, which to our respondent's surprise, produced a "take" of over $60,000. He increased his heroin consumption dramatically and, while doing so, abandoned virtually all the stabilizing routines which marked his life prior to his windfall take. In another instance, a relatively stable junkie dealer was "fronted" several thousand dollars of heroin on consignment. Instead of selling it as he had agreed to do, he absconded with it to another state, shot up most of it himself, and gave the rest away. In still another case, a relatively low-level burglar/thief came across $10,000 in cash in the course of one of his burglaries. He took the money to New York where he intended to cop a "big piece" that he could bring back to the city in which he lived and sell for a nice profit. However, instead of selling it, he kept it for his own use and his habit rapidly increased from a stable three bags per day to nearly a "bundle"—25 bags per day.

Although the "big hit" or "big sting" appears to be the most common precipitator of the transition from the status of stabilized or occasional heroin user to the status of free-wheeling junkie, many other variants of similar destabilizing patterns are common. The stabilized junkie may not be the one who makes the big sting. It may be his or her spouse, roommate, paramour, addict friend, or regular trick who receives a windfall of drugs or money and invites the stabilized junkie to share in the benefits of good fortune. "Goody," a part-time street prostitute, moved in with a big-time drug dealer who provided her with all the heroin she wanted in exchange for domestic services, sexual favors, and some modest help in cutting and packaging drugs. Although her supply of drugs was virtually limitless, she took her childraising obligations and responsibilities very seriously and they kept her to a modest level of use. However, after a year of domestic living she began to miss the "street" life and the friends she had there and to resent her total ("bag bitch") dependence on her dealer boyfriend. She returned to the street and used the money she earned from " 'hoing," and "ripping" her tricks to purchase drugs in addition to what she got at home for free. This behavior not only destabilized her drug use, but it also disrupted her home life to such an extent that she parted with her dealer and returned to the street full-time. Interestingly, this return to prostitution, theft, and robbery as her sole means of support forced her to develop a new life structure and abandon the free-wheeling pattern into which she had drifted when she had a dual source of supply.

Unless heroin addicts are disciplined by a life structure to which they are so committed and obligated that it effectively prevents them from doing so, they will expand their consumption of heroin to whatever level of use the availability of drugs or funds to buy them makes possible. What marks the career stage of the free-wheeling junkie is the almost total absence of structures of restraint. In the words of "Little Italy," who described a "free-wheeling" stage of his addict career:

> I can remember, I wouldn't be sick. I wouldn't need a shot. . . . And some of the guys might come around and get a few bags [and say] "Hey man, like I don't have enough money. Why don't you come down with me?" . . . I'm saying [to myself], "Oh-oh, here I go!" and I would shoot drugs I didn't even need to shoot. So I let it get out of control.

The problem for the first free-wheeling junkie is that the binge cannot last forever and is typically fairly short-lived. After a month or two of free-wheeling heroin use—during which time the free-wheeling junkie may have no idea of how much heroin he or she is consuming daily—not only is a modest usage level unsatisfying but the life structure within which he or she might support it is likely to have been completely abandoned or at least be in severe disrepair.

Chapter II
Alcohol and Drug Abuse

The Street Junkie—Low Availability/Low Life Structure. At this point in a free-wheeling junkie's career when heroin availability drops precipitiously and life structure does not provide the support necessary to stabilize heroin use, the free-wheeling junkie may manage to rebuild that life structure and accommodate to a new and lower level of availability. To the extent that this rebuilding and accommodation can be managed, the free-wheeling junkie may be able to return to the life of a stabilized junkie. However, if the rebuilding of life structure cannot be managed, the free-wheeling junkie may become a street junkie.

Street junkies most closely approximate the public stereotype of heroin addicts, if only because their way of life—both where and how they live—make them the most visible variety of heroin addict. Cut off from a stable source of quality heroin, not knowing from where his or her next "fix" or the money to pay for it will come, looking for any opportunity to make a buck, getting "sick" or "jonesing," being pathetically unkempt and unable to maintain even the most primitive routines of health or hygiene, the street junkie lives a very difficult, hand-to-mouth (or more precisely arm-to-arm) existence.

In terms of our typology, the street junkie's life may be understood as a continuous but typically unsuccessful effort to stabilize life structure and increase heroin availability. The two problems are intimately related in such a way that, unless the street junkie can solve both problems at once, neither problem will be solved at all. That is, unless the street junkie can establish a stable life structure, he or she will be unlikely to increase the availability of heroin. Likewise, unless the street junkie is able to increase the availability of heroin, he or she will be unlikely to establish a stable life structure.

To illustrate how this relationship works in less abstract terms, it is helpful to begin with a description of what low life structure means in the life of the street. Goldstein (1981:69) captures the tenor of the street junkie's situation nicely when he observes that

> [if] any single word can describe the essence of how street opiate users "get over," that word is *opportunism*. Subjects were always alert to the smallest opportunity to earn a few dollars. The notion of opportunism is equally relevant to predatory criminality, nonpredatory criminality, employment, and miscellaneous hustling activities.

The cause of the street junkie's opportunism is his or her failure to establish a stable life structure which regularly produces enough income to support an addiction. Consequently, the street junkie's life is a series of short-term crimes, jobs, and hustles. Street junkies steal or rob when opportunites arise to do so. For a price or in exchange for heroin, they will "cop" for an out-of-towner, "taste" for a dealer, "tip" for a burglar, rent their "works" to another junkie, sell their "clinic meth" and food stamps, or share their "crib" (accommodations) with a junkie who needs a place to "get off" or a " 'hoe" who needs a room to take her "tricks." They will do odd jobs, wash cars, paint apartments, deliver circulars, move furniture, carry baggage, or snitch to the police. The problem is not only that this opportunistic crime, hustling, or legitimate work pays very little, but that none of it is stable. While one or more of these activities may produce enough income today, none of them may be counted on to do so tomorrow. Moreover, because typical street addict crimes pay so little, because such crimes must be repeated frequently to produce any sizable income, and because they are so unpredictably opportunistic, the chance that the street addict will be arrested sooner or later is very, very high. This was the unfortunate experience of Little Italy who, after falling out with his supplier, was forced to discontinue drug sales as a major means of income and turned to armed robbery to support his use.

> I know today, I can say that if you don't have a plan you're gonna fuck up man.... Now those robberies weren't no plan. They didn't fit in nowhere ...just by the spur of the moment, you know what I mean? I had to find something to take that place so that income would stand off properly, 'cause I didn't have a plan or didn't know anything about robbery...

As Little Italy's experience demonstrates, street junkies' lives are further complicated by the fact that "big dealers"—vendors of quantities of good quality heroin—often refuse to sell to them. The reasons they refuse are directly related to the instability of street junkies' lives. Because street junkies can never be certain when and for how much they will "get over," they are frequently unable to afford to buy enough drugs to satisfy their "jones." In the face of such a shortage they will commonly beg drugs from anyone they know who might have them or have access to them, try to "cop short" (buy at less than the going rate), attempt to strike a deal to get drugs loaned or "fronted" (given on consignment) to them on a short-term basis, or, if necessary, engage in opportunistic hustling. Also, because street junkies are the type of addict most vulnerable to arrest they are also the most likely category of addict to be "flipped" by police into the role of an informant. Usually street junkies will be promised immunity from prosecution on the charge for which they were arrested if they "give up" somebody "big." Given the frequency with which street addicts "come up short," the relatively small amount of profit to be made in each individual transaction with them, and the higher than normal risk of police involvement, few "big dealers" are willing to put up with all of the attendant hassles and hustles that dealing with street junkies typically involves.

While there are exceptions—the most common being big dealers who are relatives of street junkies or their friends of long standing—street addicts are mainly limited to "street dope," heroin that has been repeatedly "stepped on" (diluted) as it is passed from the highest level of dealer to the lowest. In fact, some studies (Leveson and Weiss, 1976:119) have shown that as much as 7 percent of street dope may have no heroin in it at all, while other studies (Smith, 1973) show a heroin concentration of from 3 to 10 percent in street dope as compared with an average concentration of nearly 30 percent to bags seized from "big dealers." The irony in this situation is that, as a consumer of "street dope," the street addict pays a higher per/unit price for heroin than any other person in the distribution chain. Furthermore, this very low and often unpredictable quality of heroin available to the street junkie serves to destabilize his or her life structure further. . . .

REFERENCES

Anglin, M. Douglas, and George Speckart. 1984. "Narcotics Use and Crime: A Confirmatory Analysis." Unpublished report, University of California Los Angeles.

Ball, John C., and Carl D. Chambers. 1970. *The Epidemiology of Heroin Use in the United States.* Springfield, Ill.: Charles C Thomas.

Ball, John C., Lawrence Rosen, John A. Flueck, and David Nurco. 1981. "The criminality of heroin addicts when addicted and when off opiates," pp. 39-65 in James A. Inciardi (ed.), *The Drugs-Crime Connection.* Beverly Hills, Calif.: Sage Publications.

Ball, John C., John W. Shaffer, and David Nurco. 1983. "The day to day criminality of heroin addicts in Baltimore: A study of the continuity of offense rates." *Drug and Alcohol Dependence* 12:119-142.

Ball, John C., and Richard W. Snarr. 1969. "A test of the maturation hypothesis with respect to opiate addiction." *Bulletin of Narcotics* 21:9-13.

Beschner, George M., and William Brower. 1985. "The scene," pp. 19-29 in Bill Hanson, George Beschner, James M. Walters, and Elliot Bovelle (eds.), *Life with Heroin: Voices from the Inner City.* Lexington, Mass.: Lexington Books.

Biernacki, Patrick. 1986. *Pathways from Heroin Addiction: Recovery without Treatment.* Philadelphia: Temple University Press.

Chambers, Carl D. 1974. "Narcotic addiction and crime: An empirical overview," pp. 125-142 in James A. Inciardi and Carl D. Chambers (eds.), *Drugs and the Criminal Justice System.* Beverly Hills, Calif.: Sage Publications.

Chein, Isidor, Donald L. Gerard, Robert S. Lee, and Eva Rosenfeld. 1964. *The Road to H: Narcotics, Juvenile Delinquency, and Social Policy.* New York: Basic Books.

Collins, James J., Robert L. Hubbard, and J. Valley Rachal. 1984. *Heroin and Cocaine Use and Illegal Income.* Center for Social Research and Policy Analysis. Research Triangle Park, N.C.: Research Triangle Institute.

Reading 5
Drugs-Crime Connections

———. 1985. "Expensive drug use and illegal income: A test of explanatory hypotheses." *Criminology* 23:743-764.
Dembo, Richard, James A. Ciarlo, and Robert W. Taylor. 1983. "A model for assessing and improving drug abuse treatment resource use in inner city areas." *The International Journal of Addictions* 18:921-936.
Dole, Vincent P., Marie E. Nyswander, and Alan Warner. 1968. "Successful treatment of 750 criminal addicts." *Journal of the American Medical Association* 206:2708-2711.
Dole, Vincent P., J. Waymond Robinson, John Orraca, Edward Towns, Paul Searcy, and Eric Caine. 1969. "Methadone treatment of randomly selected criminal addicts." *New England Journal of Medicine* 280:1372-1375.
Faupel, Charles E. 1981. "Drug treatment and criminality: methodological and theoretical considerations," pp. 183-206 in James A. Inciardi (ed.), *The Drugs-Crime Connection.* Beverly Hills, Calif.: Sage Publications.
———. 1985. "A theoretical model for a socially oriented drug treatment policy." *Journal of Drug Education* 15:189-203.
Fields, Allen, and James M. Walters. 1985. "Hustling: supporting a heroin habit," pp. 49-73 in Bill Hanson, George Beschner, James M. Walters, and Elliot Bovelle (eds.), *Life with Heroin: Voices from the Inner City.* Lexington, Mass.: Lexington Books.
Gandossy, Robert P., Jay R. Williams, Jo Cohen, and Hendrick J. Harwood. 1980. *Drugs and Crime: A Survey and Analysis of the Literature.* National Institute of Justice. Washington, D.C.: U.S. Government Printing Office.
Gearing, Frances R. 1974. "Methadone maintenance treatment five years later— where are they now?" *American Journal of Public Health* 64:44-50.
Goldbart, Stephen. 1982. "Systematic barriers to addict aftercare program implementation." *Journal of Drug Issues* 12:415-430.
Goldman, Fred. 1976. "Drug markets and addict consumption behavior," pp. 273-296 in *Drug Use and Crime: Report of the Panel on Drug Use and Criminal Behavior.* National Technical Information Service publication number PB-259 167. Springfield, Va.: U.S. Department of Commerce.
———. 1981. "Drug abuse, crime and economics: The dismal limits of social choice," pp. 155-181 in James A. Inciardi (ed.), *The Drugs-Crime Connection.* Beverly Hills, Calif.: Sage Publications.
Goldstein, Paul. 1981. "Getting over: Economic alternatives to predatory crime among street drug users," pp. 67-84 in James A. Inciardi (ed.), *The Drugs-Crime Connection.* Beverly Hills, Calif.: Sage Publications.
Hanson, Bill, George Beschner, James M. Walters, and Elliot Bovelle. 1985. *Life with Heroin: Voices from the Inner City.* Lexington, Mass.: Lexington Books.
Hawkins, J. David. 1979. "Reintegrating street drug abusers: Community roles in continuing care," pp. 25-79 in Barry S. Brown (ed.), *Addicts and Aftercare.* Beverly Hills, Calif.: Sage Publications.
Inciardi, James A. 1974. "The villification of euphoria: Some perspectives on an elusive issue." *Addictive Diseases* 1:241-67.
———. 1979. "Heroin use and street crime." *Crime and Delinquency* 25:335-46.
Jacoby, Joseph E., Neil A. Weiner, Terence P. Thornberry, and Marvin E. Wolfgang. 1973. "Drug use in a birth cohort," pp. 300-43 in *National Commis-*

Chapter II
Alcohol and Drug Abuse

    sion on Marijuana and Drug Abuse, *Drug Use in America: Problem in Perspective,* Appendix I. Washington, D.C.: U.S. Government Printing Office.

Johnson, Bruce D., Paul J. Goldstein, Edward Preble, James Schmeidler, Douglas S. Lipton, Barry Spunt, and Thomas Miller. 1985. *Taking Care of Business: The Economics of Crime by Heroin Abusers.* Lexington, Mass.: Lexington Books.

Judson, Barbara, Serapio Ortiz, Linda Crouse, Thomas Carney, and Avram Goldstein. 1980. "A follow-up study of heroin addicts five years after admission to a methadone treatment program." *Drug and Alcohol Dependence* 6:295-313.

Leveson, Irving, and Jeffrey H. Weiss. 1976. *Analysis of Urban Health Problems.* New York: Spectrum.

Lukoff, Irving, and Debra Quatrone. 1973. "Heroin use and crime in a methadone maintenance program: A two year follow-up of the Addiction and Research Corporation Program: A preliminary report," pp. 63-112 in Gil J. Hayim, Irving Lukoff, and Debra Quatrone (eds.), *Heroin Use in a Methadone Maintenance Program.* Washington, D.C.: U.S. Department of Justice, National Institute of Law Enforcement and Criminal Justice.

McGlothlin, William H., M. Douglas Anglin, and Bruce D. Wilson. 1978. "Narcotic addiction and crime." *Criminology* 16:293-315.

Morris, Richard W. 1985. "Not the cause, nor the cure: Self-image and control among inner city black male heroin users," pp. 135-153 in Bill Hanson, George Beschner, James M. Walters, and Elliot Bovelle (eds.), *Life with Heroin: Voices from the Inner City.* Lexington, Mass.: Lexington Books.

Musto, David. 1973. *The American Disease: Origins of Narcotic Control.* New Haven, Conn.: Yale University Press.

Nash, George. 1973. "The impact of drug abuse treatment upon criminality: A look at 19 programs." Upper Montclair, N.J.: Montclair State College.

Newman, Robert G., Sylvia Bashkow, and Margot Gates. 1973. "Arrest histories before and after admission to a methadone maintenance treatment program." *Contemporary Drug Problems* 2:417-424.

O'Donnell, John A. 1966. "Narcotic addiction and crime." *Social Problems* 13:374-385.

Pescor, Michael J. 1943. "A statistical analysis of the clinical records of hospitalized drug addicts." *Public Health Reports Supplement,* 143.

Robins, Lee N., and George E. Murphy. 1967. "Drug use in a normal population of young Negro men." *American Journal of Public Health* 570:1580-1596.

Smith, Jean Paul. 1973. "Substances in illicit drugs," pp. 13-30 in Richard H. Blum and associates (eds.), *Drug Dealers—Taking Action.* San Francisco: Jossey Bass.

Tappan, Paul. 1960. *Crime, Justice and Correction.* New York: McGraw-Hill.

Terry, Charles E., and Mildred Pellens, 1928. *The Opium Problem.* New York: The Haddon Craftsman.

Waldorf, Dan. 1983. "Natural recovery from opiate addiction: Some social-psychological processes of untreated recovery." *Journal of Drug Issues* 13:237-280.

Walters, James M. 1985. " 'Taking care of business' updated: A fresh look at the daily routine of the heroin user," pp. 31-48 in Bill Hanson, George Beschner,

James M. Walters, and Elliot Bovelle (eds.), *Life with Heroin: Voices from the Inner City*. Lexington, Mass.: Lexington Books.

Weissman, James C., Paul L. Katsampes, and Thomas A. Giacienti. 1974. "Opiate use and criminality among a jail population." *Addictive Diseases* 1:269–281.

Zinberg, Norman E. 1984. Drug Set and Setting: The Basis for Controlled Intoxicant Use. New Haven, Conn.: Yale University Press.

CHAPTER III

SEXUAL EXPRESSIONS

Reading 6
WALKING THE LINE: THE PERSONAL AND PROFESSIONAL RISKS OF SEX EDUCATION AND RESEARCH

Richard R. Troiden, *Miami University*

> *It is not just the people who actively engage in nontypical sexual behaviors who are stigmatized by society. There are many risks attached to being a sexologist, one who teaches and does research in sexuality. Personal and professional risks stem from audience-held expectations and misconceptions about what those people who study sex are really like, and why they really do it. Sexologists are often stigmatized because they question the unquestionable. Goffman's stigma theory is used to explain this example of how even the professionals who are only scientifically associated with deviance can become marked as "sexually suspect."*

As Gagnon and Simon (1973) have noted, American cultural messages about sexuality are mixed. Sexuality is presented variously as a sacred act, a form of recreation, a private behavior, something "dirty," a reproductive necessity, a means of intimate expression, a biological drive, or a primitive, mysterious force. Sexuality is both fascinating and frightening, and existing sociocultural arrangements and clandestine learning structures have fostered ambivalent attitudes toward sexuality among Americans.

In the popular mind, the scientific study of sexuality is faintly immoral, even unnatural. By extension, students of sexuality are looked upon as unnaturally interested in sex, and thus sexuality suspect:

> Sex research has an irregular history. Much of this is due to the fact that sex has been a stigmatized subject. Proper people simply did not talk or

---

Reprinted with permission from *Teaching Sociology* 15 (1987): 241–249 by the American Sociological Association and the author.

Chapter III
Sexual Expressions

write about it, and, especially, they did not do research about it during the 19th and first part of the 20th centuries (Bullough 1985, p. 375).

A preliminary analysis of questionnaires administered to approximately 1,000 members of the Society for the Scientific Study of Sex (SSSS) revealed that 32 percent of its members had experienced occupationally related discrimination. The degree of discrimination ranged from

being the object of snickers and brunt of jokes to being subjected to public demonstrations, ostracism (including ostracism of their families), as well as losing jobs and referrals, and being denied raises and promotions ("Sexuality Professionals" 1985, p. 1).

The ambivalent responses to some sexuality experts from other professionals and the lay public support the assertion that human sexuality is a stigmatizing line of work.

STIGMA THEORY

Erving Goffman (1963) uses the term *stigma* to describe a socially disvalued behavior, attribute, or condition that disqualifies the possessor from full social acceptance. A stigma "marks" or "brands" the individual as different, setting him or her apart from "normals"—people who do not vary significantly from the particular expectations under consideration. Jones et al. (1984) use the more neutral term *mark* to describe socially discrediting attributes.

Types of Stigma

Goffman identifies three types of stigma: *abominations of the body, blemishes of individual character,* and *tribal stigmas.* Abominations of the body are disfiguring physical conditions that serve as barriers to full social acceptance, such as being blind, crippled, deaf, or mute. Blemishes of individual character refer to undesirable conditions that are not immediately apparent, but are grounds for discrimination only if discovered. Potentially stigmatized people can hide their stigmas, and may pose as "normal" among conventionals. Homosexuals, prostitutes, strippers, liars, and drug addicts are examples. Tribal stigmas are acquired by virtue of lineage or group ties. In the United States, national origin, race, or religion traditionally have served as bases for unequal social treatment.

This paper describes a form of occupational stigma, a type only indirectly touched upon by Jones et al. and Goffman. Occupational stigmatization renders sexuality educators and researchers socially marked or

*Reading 6
Risks of Sex Education and Research*

markable, depending on the context. Professionally, the status of the sexuality educator or researcher is readily apparent, broadcast by topics of research and instruction. Personally, the sexuality expert has greater latitude for disclosing or disguising his or her occupational status. As I shall demonstrate, some people hold sexuality specialists accountable for their own stigmatization because it stems from or may influence their choice of occupation. Others perceive sex experts as threats to the traditional sexual order or as security risks (Bullough 1985).

PERSONAL RISKS

The general public's personal and professional responses to sexuality professionals reflect ambivalent attitudes toward sexuality and uncertainty about what these professionals do. The stigmatizing aspects of careers in sex research and education are probably most visible in the personal realm; personal stigmatization may occur in casual encounters and in close (intimate) relations. Personal risks stem from the stereotyped expectations held by members of the wider culture regarding the characteristics of sexuality experts. Jones et al. (1984, p. 154) define stereotypes as "overgeneralized, largely false beliefs about members of social categories that are frequently, *but not always,* negative" (emphasis mine).

In casual encounters, nonspecialists typically learn that individuals are sexuality educators or researchers when they are first introduced. Stereotyped expectations cast sexuality professionals into several possible molds: as questioning the unquestionable, multiply flawed, sexually unusual, unworthy of belief, undermining traditional values, or advocating the practices investigated.

QUESTIONING THE UNQUESTIONABLE

Some social audiences view sex education and research as attempts at questioning the unquestionable, making a concerted effort to challenge a sexual order that they believe is based either in nature or in that which is sacred. The theme of sexuality professionals as questioners of the unquestionable is revealed in responses such as "How can you do something so gross for a living?" or "Isn't anything sacred to you?" or "You know, there's more to life than just sex." Sexuality specialists are seen as violating a norm that almost everyone else follows: unquestioning acceptance of the existing sexual order. In these cases, the "sexually suspect" stigma is viewed as voluntarily acquired, a consequence of occupational choice.

Chapter III
Sexual Expressions

MULTIPLY FLAWED

Sometimes audiences react to the knowledge that individuals are sexuality educators and researchers by adding a wide variety of flaws to the original occupational stigma. This process is reflected in such responses as "Isn't it true that many people who do sex research are themselves psychologically disturbed?"; "I've heard that sexual dysfunction is more common among sex therapists and counselors than in the population at large"; "I know of a couple who researched sex, but their marriage was highly unstable"; "People who study sex are the ultimate spectators, afraid to experience their own sexuality"; or (at a sexuality workshop) "I wonder how many people here are taking this workshop to resolve their own sexual problems." In these cases the "sexually suspect" stigma is attributed to developmental flaws such as an obsessive interest in or fear of sex.

OCCUPYING SEXUAL EXTREMES

A third stereotyped response to sexuality specialists is to characterize them as occupying sexual extremes, possessing a number of positive or negative attributes, depending on perspective. Extreme level of sexual desire is one expectation—"I'll bet you can't get it often enough." Extreme sexual prowess is another, as expressed by the statement, "I bet you're something else in bed." Other people assume that the sexuality specialist possesses vast sexual experience. The comment "I'll bet you've tried it all" reflects this expectation. Sexual specialization is yet another presumption: "What kink are you into?" A few people see sex experts as exhibiting all of these extremes. In such cases, sexuality specialists are seen as promiscuous savages, ever on the prowl for sex and driven by the need for sexual variety, improved technique, novelty, and orgasmic release.

At other times, audience expectations regarding sexuality specialists are more positive. Sexuality professionals are sometimes assumed to possess high levels of sexual health. The comments "You seem so together about sex" or "You've done a remarkable job of integrating your sexuality into your personality" reflect these expectations. Finally, sexuality professionals are sometimes looked upon as sexual gurus, possessed of limitless sexual lore, capable of diagnosing and resolving sexual concerns with a few well-chosen words and specific suggestions.

UNWORTHY OF BELIEF

Disbelief is another audience response to the sexuality educator or researcher. Individuals sometimes refuse to honor professionals' claims to being sex researchers or educators, and treat such claims as jokes or attempts at humor. At other times, disbelief stems from the assumption that sexual knowledge is acquired naturally: "Who'd ever think there'd come a time when people would have to be taught about sex or take classes to learn how to have a baby?" In these instances, sexologists' activities are trivialized; they and their work become the objects of snickers and the brunt of jokes.

SOURCES OF PERIL

In another audience response to sexuality professionals, a theory or ideology is constructed to explain their disvalued status and to account for the danger it represents. In these instances, the perils and the historical precedent dimensions of stigma come heavily into play. Members of highly conservative religious groups frequently cast sexuality professionals into the role of "godless secular humanists" set on altering or destroying America's most cherished family values. A female student, for example, recently accused me of "not loving our Lord" because I stated that according to research, homosexuality poses few, if any, threats to traditional family life (AIDS notwithstanding).

Sexuality educators are especially vulnerable to the charge of subverting traditional family values. They are often perceived as influencing their students powerfully by exposing them to potentially harmful (i.e., liberal) attitudes toward sexuality. Jones et al. made a similar point when they discussed public perceptions of ex-mental patients:

> Since the more power someone has, the more harm that person can do, it seems likely that society will be very reluctant to assign mentally questionable people to positions of power and that candidates for important jobs will be carefully screened to be certain that they are balanced and reliable (1984, p. 69).

ADVOCATES AND PRACTITIONERS

Another audience reaction is the presumption that sexuality experts both advocate and practice the sexual pattern they investigate. Thus, homosexuality researchers are presumed to be homosexual, students of nudism are presumed to be nudists, extramarital sex investigators are thought to "swing in wedlock," students of sadomasochism are believed to be devotees, and so forth. As researchers' topics change, so may the expectations surrounding their alleged sexual interests and practices. One expert, who initially researched homosexuality, has recently investigated heterosexual patterns. This change in emphasis apparently altered a colleague's presumptions about the expert's sexual preferences. While lecturing on homosexuality, the colleague used the expert to illustrate how a person's sexual preference may be fluid enough to permit alternation between heterosexual and homosexual patterns. This was a remarkable statement, since the expert had never discussed his sexuality or private life with this colleague.

The stigma attaching to sex research may continue to plague a researcher even after his or her research interests have evolved in directions considered more conventional. One woman, who conducted a landmark study of extramarital sex, recently developed an interest in examining the relatively uncontroversial topic of adult sibling relationships. Her past record as a sex researcher, however, led some of her colleagues to presume that brother/sister incest was the topic of her latest investigations.

Sexuality experts' intimate partners may also harbor ambivalent expectations. They may expect specialists to be "super lovers"—totally attentive, uninhibited, mistresses or masters of erotic technique. They may assume that the professionals expect them to be "wanton" and "wild," which may promote "performance anxiety." At other times, partners may fear that sexuality professionals view sex as an analytical exercise or an applied experiment, and may say, "Are you sure you don't analyze and evaluate everything we do sexually?" Alternatively, intimate partners may fear that specialists prefer the sexual patterns they are investigating to those in which the couple indulge together ("Are you sure prostitutes aren't more exciting to you?").

PROFESSIONAL RISKS IN ACADEMIC SETTINGS

The public image of sexologists as sexually suspect provides a backdrop against which nonsexuality specialists assess and judge the professional contributions of sex experts in academic settings. The presumption that sexuality specialists are sexually unconventional may affect the way in which administrators evaluate research and writing on sexual issues, and their willingness to support such endeavors. Professionals who lack training in relativizing disciplines, such as sociology, psychology, and anthropology, may see deviance and conformity as invariant, internal properties rather than outcomes of culturally and situationally created labeling; thus they lack the training necessary for objective assessment of controversial research and theorizing.

The professional risks encountered by sexuality specialists in academic settings may be traced to several sources: the multidisciplinary approach to sex, the highly specialized nature of sex research, the type of topics investigated, the intrinsic interest of the subject, the controversial course content, the use of instructional audiovisuals, and the expectations of student audiences.

A Multidisciplinary Field

The multidisciplinary nature of sex research and education usually necessitates publishing in multidisciplinary journals. Publishing in journals outside the major discipline may place academic sexuality experts at professional risk within their major disciplines if their department, division, or college places a higher value on works published in mainstream journals within the major discipline than on those appearing in multidisciplinary publications. The multidisciplinary nature of sexuality research may also make it more difficult to locate people within the major discipline to serve as outside reviewers of research papers on sexuality.

Extreme Specialization

Sexuality research is also highly specialized, which may generate the charge of overspecialization. A dean, for example, recently informed a sexuality professional that although his sexuality research was important, he had carved out such a specialized niche that it limited his chances of developing a national reputation in the major discipline—an institutional requirement for promotion.

Anticipated Peril

From an administrative perspective, the anticipated peril of including sexuality professionals on the staff may outweigh the perceived benefits. For this reason, the sexual topics that individuals investigate may affect their initial chances of obtaining a position or the ease of moving from one position to another. When one sexuality expert first applied for a job, for example, his vita informed prospective employers of his research on homosexuality. This individual had applied only to universities that expressed an interest in hiring a "deviance" specialist, but most of these institutions did not acknowledge receipt of the application or inform the applicant that he was being considered for the job. At one university the candidate's name was withdrawn from the candidate pool after a formal interview because—according to a member of the search committee—the administration felt uncomfortable about affiliating a homosexuality researcher with their institution.

Chapter III
Sexual Expressions

INTRINSIC INTEREST

The intrinsic interest that sexuality and sex research hold for professionals and the lay public may also provide grounds for discounting excellent teaching evaluations in sexuality and sex-related courses. During the Spring, 1985 semester, for example, I received an award for outstanding teaching. This award had not been offered in 11 years. 700 people were eligible, 80 were nominated, and 4 received the award. Upon hearing the news of the award, a colleague from another discipline remarked casually, "Well, what do you expect? You teach sex," as if the topic alone guaranteed excellent evaluations.

CONTROVERSIAL TOPICS

Many topics covered routinely in human sexuality classes are controversial, creating yet another source of risk. The potential for conflict is always present when classroom lectures and discussions routinely address abortion, homosexuality, sadomasochism, masturbation, pornography, extramarital sex, and contraception (McKinney 1985). Instructors are often accused of advocacy when they present information challenging the alleged pathology of controversial activities, and in this sense they may be perceived as sources of peril.

One sexuality specialist who discussed nonsexist childrearing practices with her class acknowledged that she did not discourage her son from playing with dolls. She was shocked to learn that a group of students approached her chair to determine if the courts could gain custody of her son for "his own good." Her chair requested that in the future she refrain from discussing her childrearing practices in class. Instructors who find themselves embroiled in controversies stemming from course topics run the risk of being defined institutionally as "troublemakers," sources of peril, or poor risks for tenure and promotion, especially when the controversy spills out of the classroom and into the wider community.

CONTROVERSIAL ADVISING

Sexuality specialists may also incur professional risk because of their willingness to serve as faculty advisors to controversial student groups. A gay campus organization, for example, recently approached a female sexuality specialist and asked her to advise them. When the instructor discussed this request with her chair, the chair was appalled, and claimed that her chances of obtaining tenure might be jeopardized if she advised the group. Nonetheless, she agreed to act as advisor. (She did not gain tenure because of the "overly political and rhetorical nature of her work.")

Use of Audiovisuals

Classroom use of sexually explicit materials may also generate levels of controversy that the untenured neophyte may wish to avoid, especially when the conflict mobilizes community interest groups. Recently an untenured professor showed a college sexuality class an X-rated movie to demonstrate how pornography distorts expectations about the nature of male and female sexuality. Attendance was voluntary, and relevant administrators were informed in advance about the time, date, and purpose of the film. A local community group heard about the project and staged an antipornography demonstration. In this case, the university administration backed the instructor solidly because it places strong emphasis on academic freedom.

In another instance, a first-year, untenured faculty member showed his sexuality class films about homosexual lovemaking to underscore the similarity between heterosexual and homosexual patterns. One student, offended by the sexually explicit nature of the films, complained to the instructor's chair. The chair met with the instructor and expressed his displeasure over the use of such films in class, and ended the conversation with the statement, "I won't have you advocating homosexuality in the classroom." Another chair regarded a sexuality specialist as promoting premarital sex because she showed her sexuality classes films dealing with heterosexual lovemaking.

A departmental chair who supports an individual's decision to show sexually explicit films in his or her classes provides an important source of faculty morale. One chair considered previewing all films shown in human sexuality classes but decided against such a move: he reasoned that such a policy would be discriminatory because he did not preview the films shown in other courses. This chair also felt that the instructor was in a better position to judge what type of sexuality films would be appropriate for the class.

Student Expectations

Student expectations may also create problems for human sexuality instructors (McKinney 1985). Some students assume that they will excel in class because of the vastness of their sexual experiences. These students may be upset when confronted by demanding examinations on multidisciplinary course content rather than on sexual experience and technique. Other students become distressed when instructors refuse to endorse or condemn certain sexual patterns (e.g., premarital sex or homosexuality), and stress instead the importance of active decision making, choices, consequences, self-responsibility, and acting in accordance with deeply held values. Disenchanted students may occasionally retaliate through complaining to the chair and by giving instructors low ratings in course evaluations.

REACTIONS TO OCCUPATIONAL STIGMATIZATION

After they encounter people with stigmatizing expectations, sexuality professionals may experience increasingly ambivalent attitudes about interacting with nonspecialists. They may become unsure of how others will react to them, or wonder what more conventional people really think of them. This awareness may make specialists feel as if they are "on stage," self-aware and calculating, and careful about the impressions they make both inside and outside work. In other cases, sexuality professionals may feel (and fear) that the accomplishments they see as minor will be regarded by nonspecialists as remarkable or noteworthy. Some colleagues, for example, find it amazing that sex educators and researchers can discuss sensitive sexual topics comfortably in large classes peopled by both sexes. At still other times, sexuality professionals may fear that minor failings may be seen as growing out of the disvalued status. A chair, for example, may perceive a sexuality expert's occasional lack of punctuality as evidence of a "sexually irresponsible" attitude. The ambivalence sexuality experts feel toward nonspecialists may be managed through situational strategies, withdrawal, or redefinition.

SITUATIONAL STRATEGIES

Goffman (1963) and Jones et al. (1984) suggest that stigmatized persons react to stereotypic expectations in a number of ways. In the context of sexuality, one obvious response is to leave the field, to stop conducting sexuality research or teaching sexuality classes. One sexuality educator stopped teaching sex courses because the topics covered contain the potential for conflict and strife. Yet another colleague switched the focus of her research when her dean stated, "We don't like sex at this university." Another response involves selective self-disclosure—a general unwillingness to broadcast topics of one's research or teaching with nonintimates (Weinberg and Williams 1972; Troiden 1981). I sometimes tell strangers that I study identity or teach social studies simply because I am tired of explaining and justifying my research and teaching.

Other sexuality experts respond to the stigma by saying or doing nothing in class that is not supported by the literature. Still other specialists may react by using the stigma of sexuality for the secondary gains it provides, such as excuses (justified or not) for failure or a general lack of success: "I would have been promoted or tenured if I had avoided research and teaching in the area of sex."

WITHDRAWAL

The "sexually suspect" stigma surrounding the status of sexuality educator or researcher may also set sexuality professionals apart from society and sometimes from themselves. They may feel discredited socially, nearly alone occupationally, at the fringes of an unaccepting world. As a result, some sexuality experts may confine their interactions to their "own"—those similarly stigmatized—and to the "wise"—sympathetic outsiders who honor claims to equal treatment—who are perceived as sources of support and reassurance. Withdrawal into a community of like-situated others has important implications for the self-esteem of sexuality professionals:

> Exposure to others with similar problems has at least two important consequences. It allows for comparison with respect to coping with the stigma. Second, comparison with people who are similarly marked or stigmatized should allow individuals to focus on attributes and qualities other than the stigmatized ones, and thereby provide the opportunity for them to view themselves as complex and differentiated individuals with valued attributes and abilities (Jones et al. 1984, p. 144).

REDEFINITION

The stigmatizing features of a career in sexuality may be viewed alternatively as a blessing in disguise, creating greater self-awareness, strength of character, or sexual integration. Most of the sexuality specialists I know fall into this category. The SSSS study cited earlier verifies my observations: 68 percent of the SSSS members reported feeling positive about their choice of profession ("Sexuality Professionals" 1985). In a more defensive spirit, sex experts may respond by cataloging the sexual failings of other professionals; they may point out that on balance, the general population possesses the sexual problem, not the sexuality specialists.

WHY REMAIN? A PERSONAL VIEW

Given the risks outlined above, why does a professional remain in the field of sexuality? First, the subject matter is interesting. Sex is fascinating to the specialist and the lay public alike. Keeping up on the literature is more a joy than a chore, a source of fascination rather than boredom. Second, teaching sexuality provides an opportunity to dispel sexual misinformation, to replace myth with fact. Eliminating ignorance is gratifying. Third, a pluralistic approach to sexuality provides a platform for discussing the dangers posed by conservative attempts to impose a moral hegemony on American society. A spirited defense of value pluralism is not without its pleasures.

The renown and popularity of human sexuality courses may also gratify the ego. After all, an instructor seldom has the opportunity to be a "star," forced to turn away hundreds from an already packed classroom. In addition, sexuality research is still in its adolescence. A scholar can conduct pathfinding research and form fresh theories, especially on variant sexualities. Research at the edge of a "forbidden frontier" is appealing on several levels. Also, I would argue that a researcher should not allow the dictates of conventional morality to determine what should or should not be investigated. Yielding to these pressures limits the scope of research to topics considered politically and socially "correct" by the mainstream and relegates social science research to the study of etiquette.

Studying and teaching human sexuality may also be a liberating occasion for personal growth. Instructors must often overcome their own inhibitions to be comfortable in teaching a course on such delicate topics. Finally, professional involvement provides the opportunity to meet fellow specialists, sources of inspiration and support as well as knowledge. As Goffman (1963) would have predicted, I will conclude by saying that managing the stigma of the sexually suspect has made me a better person.

SUMMARY AND CONCLUSION

This paper identified stigmatizing features of a career in sex education and research using stigma theory as a point of departure. Because of their careers, sexuality experts may be "marked" as "sexually suspect." Personally, the sexuality expert status may or may not be disclosed when individuals are first introduced, which may render sexuality professionals discreditable or markable. Professionally, the sexologist status is announced by topics of research, which may socially discredit sexuality experts. Audience expectations cast sexuality professionals into a number of possible stigmatizing modes: as questioners of the unquestionable, multiply flawed, sexually unusual, unworthy of belief, undermining traditional values, or as advocating the practices investigated.

Sexuality professionals may respond to their stigmatization by withdrawing from the field, deciding to "pass" as nonspecialists, electing to do or say nothing that is unsupported by professional literatures, using the stigma for secondary gains, withdrawing into a community of fellow sexuality specialists, or by cataloging the failures of nonspecialists.

Stereotypical expectations surrounding the characteristics of sexuality experts provide a backdrop against which their achievements are assessed and evaluated in academic settings, providing a potential source of bias. Professional risks in academic settings may be traced to several sources: the multidisciplinary nature of the field; the highly specialized nature of sex research; the type of topics investigated; the interest of the subject; the controversial course content; the use of instructional audiovisuals; and the expectations of student audiences....

The benefits of careers in sex education and research include the intrinsic interest of the subject, gratification obtained from eliminating sexual ignorance and reducing sexual guilt, ego enhancement obtained from teaching an immensely popular course, the opportunity to stress the importance of value pluralism, the chance to conduct pathfinding research, and the opportunities for personal growth and professional fellowship. More research is necessary to determine which audience, actor, and institutional variables promote or discourage personal and professional stigmatization.

REFERENCES

Bullough, Vern L. 1985. "Problems of research on a delicate topic: A personal view." *Journal of Sex Research* 21:375–386.
Francoeur, Robert T. 1982. *Becoming a Sexual Person.* New York: Wiley.
Gagnon, John H., and William Simon. 1973. *Sexual Conduct: The Social Sources of Human Sexuality.* Chicago: Aldine.
Goffman, Erving. 1963. *Stigma.* Englewood Cliffs, N.J.: Prentice-Hall.
Jones, Edward E., Amerigo Farina, Albert H. Hastorf, Hazel Markus, Dale T. Miller, and Robert A. Scott. 1984. *Social Stigma: The Psychology of Marked Relationships.* New York: Freeman.
Lofland, John. 1969. *Deviance and Identity.* Englewood Cliffs, N.J.: Prentice-Hall.
McKinney, Kathleen. 1985. "Ethical issues and dilemmas in the teaching of the sociology of human sexuality." *Quarterly Journal of Ideology* 9:23–27.
"Sexuality professionals report discrimination." 1985. *Sexuality Today* 23(49):1.
Troiden, Richard R. 1981. "Research as process: The human dimension of social scientific research," pp. 108–118 in Theodore C. Wagenaar (ed.), *Readings for Social Research.* Belmont, Calif.: Wadsworth.
Weinberg, Martin S., and Colin J. Williams. 1972. "Fieldwork among deviants: Social relations with subjects and others," pp. 165–186 in Jack D. Douglas (ed.), *Research on Deviance.* New York: Random House.

Reading 7

EXPOSURE TO PORNOGRAPHY AND AGGRESSION TOWARD WOMEN: THE CASE OF THE ANGRY MALE

Susan H. Gray, *New York Institute of Technology*

> Exposure to pornography makes men who are already hostile toward women even more angry. Gray points out that since we cannot eliminate either pornography or the anger underlying violence against women, we must develop cultural mechanisms to encourage socially acceptable forms of resolving this anger. Changes in our rigid role expectations and notions of masculinity could be particularly helpful.

WHAT IS PORNOGRAPHY? AND WHO CONSUMES IT?

Defining pornography is the key problem in the debate over, and study of, its effects. Neither the president's commission nor the U.S. courts have come up with a definition acceptable to all. The president's commission examined all sexually explicit materials, including books, manuscripts, photographs and films. The mildest material it considered was depictions of nudity. Believing that the word "pornography" denoted disapproval, the president's commission preferred the words "obscenity" or "sexually explicit materials." Court definitions of obscenity, the legal term for pornography, have ranged from material which on the whole appeals to prurient interests and has no redeeming social value (*Roth* v. *United States*, 1957) to a reluctance to define obscenity and a delegation of that task to local communities (*Miller* v. *California*, 1973). Women Against Pornography targets any materials depicting violence towards women, and has included under this broad category *Vogue* magazine fashion spreads by photographer Richard Avedon and a Warner Brothers billboard advertisement, later discontinued, which read: "I'm black and

---

Reprinted with permission from *Social Problems* 29 (4) (April 1982): 387–398 by The Society for the Study of Social Problems and by the author.

Reading 7
Pornography and Aggression toward Women

blue from the Rolling Stones and I love it."[1] Most contemporary research on pornography studies both soft-core and hard-core materials. Although the distinction between soft-core and hard-core is sometimes fuzzy, "soft-core" generally refers to depictions of nudity or semi-nudity, or depictions of sexual activity without explicit photographs or descriptions of genitals. "Hard-core" generally refers to depictions of nudes engaged in implied sexual activity with a focus upon the genitals. For the purpose of this paper, I define pornography as both soft-core and hard-core depictions of sexual behavior, be they found in magazines, books, films or audiotapes.

Most consumers of pornography are young, married men. They are college educated, politically liberal, high consumers of the mass media in general, and had an average income of $12,000 in 1970 (Nawy, 1973; Wilson and Abelson, 1973). About a quarter of all men have been exposed to sado-masochistic materials. Men use pornography most often as means of enhancing the responsiveness and enjoyment of sexual intercourse with a stable partner. Younger consumers without a stable partner usually use pornography to masturbate (Nawy, 1973; Wilson and Abelson, 1973).

Malamuth and Spinner (forthcoming) analyzed the content of photographs, drawings and cartoons in *Playboy* and *Penthouse* magazines from 1973 to 1977 to see if there had been changes in the number of portrayals of violence against women. They found that violent portrayals have been increasing in both of these periodicals, although they never exceeded 10 percent of all the cartoons and 5 percent of the photographs and drawings. One of Malamuth and Spinner's criteria of sexual violence was scenes that depicted sado-masochism, a form of sexual expression which can take place between consenting adults and is not necessarily exploitative or violent against women. Changing fashions in sexual expression may account for the increase that Malamuth and Spinner found. On the other hand, Diamond (1980) suggests an increasing violence in pornography represents a patriarchal response to increases in the social power of women.

Smith (1976) studied "adults-only" paperback fiction available in "adult" bookstores in the United States and found violent themes in about one third of the 428 books he reviewed. The violence was not always physical, but included blackmail and mental coercion, usually committed by men against women. Typically, the woman was forced to participate in an initially unwanted sexual act and began by protesting but ended up pleading for more, her sexual passion unleashed....

---

[1]See Bullough and Bullough (1977) for further discussion of the problem of defining pornography.

ANGER, HARD-CORE PORNOGRAPHY, AND AGGRESSION

Several studies show that aggression levels in previously angered males are raised by exposure to hard-core pornography, but that aggression is not raised in nonangered males (Meyer, 1972; Baron, 1974, 1978; Donnerstein et al., 1975). Pornography facilitates the expression of anger if anger toward a particular target already exists. Violence is facilitated either through teaching an angered man to view women poorly (the behaviorist model) or through encouraging a cathartic release of anger.

Portrayals of violence without sexual content can facilitate the expression of anger as well as can portrayals of sexually related violence. In Meyer's (1972) study, undergraduate male students were angered by painful electric shocks, which they thought were the result of negative evaluations by another student (gender unspecified) of their performance on a task. The angered students were then shown a violent film segment (a knife fight scene in *From Here to Eternity*), a segment from a hard-core "stag" movie, an exciting but non-violent and sexually neutral film segment (a cowboy saddling and riding a half-broken horse), or not shown any film. Subjects who viewed the violent film clip gave the most electric shocks to the person that had angered them. Viewers of the "stag" film gave more shocks than did viewers of the cowboy clip or those who saw no film. A difficulty of experiments such as this is that retaliatory behavior toward a specific person is different from displaced retaliation toward a more general target. Hurting a known or an unknown person because a woman aroused your anger in a pornographic novel or film is different from hurting the specific person who hurt you. The relationship between these two expressions of anger is not clear from the data available.

Angered men need not be exposed to explicit sexual materials to interpret them sexually. An early study of male sex offenders shown drawings with ambiguous sexual connotations found that the offenders were capable of producing their own pornographic content (Linder, 1953). A more recent study of undergraduates found that angered men rated cartoons with both exploitative and non-exploitative sexual themes from *Playboy* as higher in sexual content than did non-angered men (Baron, 1978). Angered men can easily attribute their arousal to sexual stimuli, rather than to their anger. Where there is no explicit sexual stimuli in the immediate environment, an angered man will conjure up some, if necessary.

The strength of the pornographic stimulus affects whether an angered man acts aggressively. When angered and then subsequently aroused by hard-core pornography, men have difficulty distinguishing between anger and sexual arousal. Soft-core pornography is less likely to trigger subsequent aggression in angered men. Sexual arousal through soft-core pornography either distracts attention from previous anger or defuses anger through recognition of the incompatibility of sexual arousal with aggression (Baron, 1974; Donnerstein et al., 1975).

Men can be distracted from their anger by hard-core as well as soft-core pornography. Zillman and Sapolsky (1977) angered male college students and then exposed them to either neutral photographs (furniture, scenery and abstract art), soft-core pornography, or hard-core pornography. Both soft-core and hard-core materials defused anger, and subjects exposed to either were no more likely to retaliate against the researcher than were the subjects exposed to neutral photographs.

Baron and Bell (1977) found that aggression by angered men was inhibited after exposure to strongly arousing pornography. They point out that it is not just a question of whether pornography is soft-core or hard-core, but whether the themes are tenderness (aggression-inhibiting) or wildness and impulsivity (aggression-facilitating). The issue is further complicated by studies which examine anger and exposure to pornography in reverse order. Men who are shown hard-core pornography and then angered attribute their arousal to anger, rather than sexuality, thus facilitating their aggression (Donnerstein et al., 1975). Anger can also be increased because men are distracted by their anger from a source of sexual stimulation. As the studies reviewed here show, men who are not previously or subsequently angered usually do not become aggressive when exposed to hard-core or soft-core pornography.

In a society in which responses to anger other than aggression are permitted (e.g., seduction), aggression need not be the main response of angered men. Laboratory research subjects sitting in front of a machine which they believe they can use to administer electric shocks to victims do not have many other behavioral options for discharging arousal. Yet, as the studies discussed above show, even with behavioral options curtailed, men confronted with highly arousing pornography usually remain non-aggressive in front of such machines—provided they have not been angered. For angered men, sexuality and aggression are more compatible, particularly where there is difficulty distinguishing anger from sexual arousal and where the sexual arousal does not distract from or diffuse the anger.

PORNOGRAPHY AND AGGRESSION: THE LONG-TERM EFFECTS

Studies of pornography usually measure its effects immediately or 10 minutes after exposure, though some attention has also been given to long-term effects.

Chapter III
Sexual Expressions

People exposed to hard-core pornography who are not angered do not become aggressive over time. In a study of married couples over a 12-week period, Mann et al. (1973) found that viewing weekly hard-core pornographic films with themes including sado-masochism produced no significant changes in sexual behavior, other than an increase in sexual behavior on film-viewing nights. Pornography can also become boring over time, resulting in lowered interest in and response to it (Howard et al., 1973).

There is evidence that pornography gradually erodes inhibitions against aggression toward both men and women. Male subjects in Baron and Bell's (1973) study initially gave weaker electric shocks to female victims than to male victims. When Donnerstein and Hallam (1978) gave men a second opportunity to shock a woman who had angered them, the men's inhibitions decreased drastically after a 10-minute wait in which they sat quietly, if they had previously been shown hard-core films.[2] There has been too little research on the long-term effects of exposure to pornography in potentially deviant or already deviant men. However, there is some evidence that long-term exposure is not detrimental to men who are chronically angry towards, or incompetent with, adult women.

Goldstein and Kant have studied rapists and pedophiles (child molesters) admitted to a state hospital in California (Goldstein, 1973; Goldstein and Kant, 1974; Kant and Goldstein, 1970).[3] Rapists and pedophiles reported less exposure to pornography during adolescence and adulthood than the general male population. Not only did rapists report that

---

[2]In a contradictory study of Jaffe et al. (1974), men were not initially inhibited in their aggression toward women, but gave more intense electric shocks to women than to men. These were research subjects who had *not* been previously angered, but had been strongly aroused. However, a further study by Donnerstein (1980) revealed that when men are exposed to *both* pornography and violence in the same film, more aggression is exhibited toward men than toward women, both on the first and second opportunity. Even with previously angered men, therefore, aggression toward women may still be inhibited under highly arousing conditions, although not consistently so. Men who are aggressive toward other men, after exposure to pornography and violence, may be acting because of the way they see men treat women in violent pornographic materials. This aggressive behavior would indirectly benefit, rather than harm, women.

[3]Another way to gauge the long-term effects of the widespread availability of pornography on sexually deviant men is to examine statistical information from Denmark. Since the Danish ban on pornographic literature was repealed in 1967, sex offenses have been decreasing in Copenhagen (Kutchinsky, 1973). However, prosecutions have also decreased as a greater tolerance has developed for behavior such as "peeping" or verbal indecency. Rape has remained fairly stable over the last few decades, with only several dozen cases reported in Copenhagen each year. Child molestation has decreased. These statistics reveal no harmful social consequences of the repeal.

Reading 7
Pornography and Aggression toward Women

the pornography they found most exciting was the portrayal of nonviolent heterosexual intercourse, but they had less exposure to these portrayals and to photographs or movies of fully-nude women, oral sex, or sado-masochistic activity than the general male population. Rapists had more exposure than the general male population to photographs of explicit sexual acts while they were six to 10 years old, but these photographs did not necessarily portray violence. Goldstein and Kant (1974) theorized that pornography performs an educational function for men during their formative years; deprived of information about sex, rapists and pedophiles have few stimuli which portray society's definition of the "normal sex act." The rapists and pedophiles studied found it more difficult to talk about sex and had fewer sources of sexual information, such as parental explanations.

Goldstein and Kant found that rapists and pedophiles did not initiate the postures or acts they found most exciting in pornography, but used portrayals of these acts for more general sexual arousal and masturbation. Hard-core pornography was not an incitement to rape or child molestation. But violence and brutality, *whether associated with sex or not*, were often mentioned as disturbing—particularly to rapists. Violence and brutality—not sexuality—were the stimuli for aggression.

> We must consider that sex offenders are highly receptive to suggestions of sexual behavior congruent with their previously formed desires and will interpret the material at hand to fit their needs.... [The question becomes] whether the stimulus most likely to release anti-social behavior is one representing sexuality or one representing aggression. (Goldstein and Kant, 1974:109)[4]

A related study by Kercher and Walker (1973) found that convicted rapists exposed to slides containing non-rape sexual cues were not aroused any more than were men from the general population. Moreover, the rapists rated the slides less appealing than the general popula-

---

[4]Groth and Birnbaum (1979) also conclude that rape is related more to the need to express anger than to consumption of pornography. However, a study of sexual offenders by Davis and Braucht (1973) did find a small relationship between childhood exposure to pornography and later rape, statutory rape or homosexual prostitution ($r = +0.26$). Part of the control population in Davis and Braucht's research consisted of members of religious organizations, men who were probably less likely to consume or to admit to the consumption of pornography, thereby affecting the comparative statistic on the general male population's use of pornography. In addition, in any retrospective study, it is unclear whether or not there is a direct causal relationship between early exposure to pornography and sexual deviance. The amount of early exposure to pornography may be a reflection of a character already likely to become involved in sexual offenses. Finding that sexual offenders are consumers of pornography is like finding that many heroin addicts at one point also smoked marijuana. It does not demonstrate that one is an outgrowth of the other.

tion. Avel, Blanchard, Barlow, and Mavissakian (1975) and Abel, Barlow, Blanchard, and Guild (1977) studied the relationship between exposure to audiotaped narration of rape scenes and arousal patterns in rapists. Although they concluded that arousal patterns are idiosyncratic, the rapists they studied did become more sexually aroused by narrations of rape and aggression than did non-rapists. Both Abel, Barlow, Blanchard, and Guild (1977) and Barbaree et al., (1979) suggest that narrations of violent sex do not arouse rapists any more than do narrations of sex between mutually consenting partners. Rather, narrations of violent sex fail to inhibit arousal to the extent that force inhibits the arousal of normal males, or enables them to suppress their arousal.

TYPES OF ANGER, FANTASY, AND IMAGES OF WOMEN

Research to date suggests that anger is a greater social problem than pornography, especially when anger is directed toward those less powerful. Anger is most dangerous in men who are unable to effectively distinguish between aggression, the control of women, and sexual arousal. The goals of social change might be better served by focusing on the source of anger in men, and by helping men to deal with that anger, than by focusing on pornography. Anger not validated by pornography will be validated elsewhere if supported by cultural values. Recent "horror" films such as *I Spit on Your Grave* depict violence against "liberated," independent women (Ebert, 1981).

It is unrealistic to hope to eliminate all anger in men toward women; it is equally unrealistic to hope to eliminate pornography. A complex relationship exists between sex and anger. Both sex and anger involve one person who has less power than the other or others. Relationships between men and women in western culture are generally power relationships. The struggle between men and women for power is often arousing to both, but most people do not translate that arousal into violence.

Nevertheless, the relationship between sex and anger is an important one. What many researchers have not considered is that anger takes different forms. Studies on pornography and aggression in angered men often view anger superficially as a factor leading to erosion of self-esteem in the laboratory. This superficial anger may be a different kind of anger than the anger manifested by chronically disturbed men. The deep anger in disturbed men is a potentially unresolved component of psychoanalytic development (Stoller, 1975). Deep anger may stimulate more socially destructive behavior than the superficial anger stimulated in experimental laboratories. To view the effects of pornography on this deep anger we have only the indirect evidence from studies of sex offenders. An important question is whether those with unresolved deep

Reading 7
Pornography and Aggression toward Women

anger are those more likely to attack women when their superficial anger is stimulated in the laboratory or in everyday life. To stimulate superficial anger in the laboratory, I feel, could help those with deep anger to quickly get in touch with their feelings. The routine insults of everyday life, including the thwarting of expectations derived from pornography, perhaps provide this stimulus for the rapist. More information is needed on the process, and the extent, to which everyday incidents put people in touch with their deep anger.

It has been argued that the consumption of pornography is a cathartic device to discharge momentary aggressive impulses (English, 1980). But pornography can also be a tool for validating a deeper anger toward women. This may be one reason why soft-core pornography generally distracts men who are angry, but hard-core pornography is less likely to do so. If superficially induced anger puts men in touch with a deeper anger, partially validated by pornography, then pornography becomes more dangerous than we might otherwise believe. The process by which men are put in touch with deep anger must become a central question in the debate over pornography.

I believe that non-angered men perceive both soft-core and hard-core pornography as fantasy. Most people can distinguish between fantasy and reality. For those who cannot, it is the unresolved anger and not the pornography which creates the fundamental problem. Artistic media, such as films, novels or even advertising, often employ fantasy, and its creators expect it to be recognized as such. That a particular portrayal is not realistic, or expresses anger toward a group of people, is usually not an effective argument for the portrayal's danger to society. In situations in which lack of realism is a danger to society (e.g., propaganda or racist literature and films), it is usually because consumers cannot easily separate reality from fiction. Both soft-core and hard-core pornography may often be crude—a form of low culture rather than high culture—but they are nevertheless, I believe, folk art forms. Like comic books or murder mysteries, pornography is a manifestation of popular culture, created by members of a society. Should we ask that pornography be more realistic than other forms of fiction? That some of the literature previously labelled pornographic is now regarded as quality literature, rather than pornography, makes the answer to this question particularly difficult. The dividing line between low-brow and high-brow art can be vague.

I believe that the content of most sexual fantasies is not inherently bad simply because it is silly, or angry, or not representative of the "real" sex life of most people—or even because it may shape reality. In sex, there can be elements of objectification, of dominance and submission, of competition, lovelessness and pain. Some people may prefer to repress these in their sex lives; others may take delight in expressing them.

Chapter III
Sexual Expressions

But pornography reveals the options, both exploitative and non-exploitative—options which are there independent of the existence of pornography. Often revealing to consumers what they like, pornography is equally capable of demonstrating what they do not like.

If pornographic images of women are often derogatory, and validate anger, the images of consumers of pornography are often equally so. Consumers are portrayed as tragic figures involved in the exploitation of male sexual desire by female workers in the pornography industry who seek avenues for economic upward mobility. This exploitation is degrading to both the seller and the buyer, as are many other forms of commercial enterprise when the business ethic takes precedence over all else.

If some people nevertheless find the images of women in pornography repulsive, it is futile to try to change images of women by reducing the amount of pornography available. Suppression rarely changes social images over time; more often it drives them underground, thereby giving them a tantalizing flavor. Suppression could even encourage a more extreme pornographic genre.

THE FUTURE OF PORNOGRAPHY

Future research on pornography should endeavor to: (1) provide a more uniform definition of pornography; (2) investigate systematically the link between sexual arousal, anger and aggression when a great range of behavioral options are presented; (3) decide whether to focus on the general male population or a population with greater pathology when investigating angered men; and (4) create unobtrusive measures of arousal and a mechanism for the male subject to differentiate between specific women and unknown and unseen female targets. Greater coordination of research efforts in these ways would help clarify the extent to which angered men are dangerous when exposed to pornography. At present, the move towards suppression of extreme forms of pornography is not supported by solid empirical evidence of the harmful effects of pornography.

Johnson and Goodchilds (1973) suggest an alternative to suppression: a pornography more clearly in line with both feminist and humanist values. In this genre, neither sex would be manipulated or used as an object, as they are in conventional pornography. English (1980) has speculated on a pornography in which older women pair with younger men, body types become more variable, and sexual expression becomes less phallocentric, thereby making pornography more appealing to female consumers. Some would argue that this would no longer be pornography.

Reading 7
Pornography and Aggression toward Women

Faust (1980) has argued that women have their own distinct pornographic genre in escapist romantic fiction whose heroines are often alternately raped and seduced. Brownmiller (1975), on the other hand, insists that there can be no female equivalent of pornography, a male invention. In Brownmiller's sense of pornography as domination, escapist romantic fiction is an exercise in masochism and contrary to humanist and/or feminist values. The content of pornography might be changed if those with humanist and feminist values became involved in its production, thereby creating a new market among feminist and humanist consumers. There is no reason to expect, however, that traditional pornography would not continue to be in demand as well.

If the relationship between exposure to pornography and the degree of violence against women is the key issue in the debate over pornography, it must be recognized that themes of violence have become an integral part of most of our media. A disturbed mind will find exciting stimuli wherever it looks. The amount of violence depicted in pornography is less than the amount of violence shown on television in the United States (Dienstbier, 1977). Dienstbier has pointed out the irony in U.S. society's massive exposure to violence in the media with lower exposure to violence in real life, coupled with society's lower exposure to pornography in the media and higher exposure to sex in real life.

We are not likely to eliminate the anger underlying male violence against women completely. To the extent which we do not, pornography can always evoke that anger. Psychoanalysts claim that a certain amount of frustration and anger is necessary to create a separate ego identity. Without that frustration and developmental anger, normal forms of loving and normal expressions of sexuality would not occur (Stoller, 1975). If we view these expressions as desirable, but if that same anger, when unresolved, produces violence against women,[5] we need cultural mechanisms to encourage socially acceptable forms of resolving this anger or directing it more appropriately: better communication in interpersonal relations, changes in the rigid role expectations and notions of masculinity which lead to pain and anger when they cannot be lived up to, and improved education for men about the nature of being a woman and about female sexuality. Without these, violence toward women can find its expression with or without pornography. With these mechanisms, pornography may once again be viewed as just another form of fantasy, probably not dangerous and maybe no longer attractive to men who are no longer angry.

---
[5] As Chodorow (1978) points out, contemporary family organization contributes to lack of respect for women as well.

Chapter III
Sexual Expressions

REFERENCES

Abel, Gene G., David H. Barlow, Edward B. Blanchard, and Donald Guild. 1977. "The components or rapists' sexual arousal." *Archives of General Psychiatry* 34:895-903.

———, Edward B. Blanchard, David H. Barlow, and Matig Mavissakian. 1975. "Identifying specific erotic cues in sexual deviations by audiotaped descriptions." *Journal of Applied Behavior Analysis* 8:247-260.

Amoroso, Donald M., and Marvin Brown. 1973. "Problems in studying the effects of erotic material." *Journal of Sex Research* 9:187-195.

Barbaree, H. E., W. L. Marshall, and R. D. Lanthier. 1979. "Deviant sexual arousal in rapists." *Behaviour Research and Therapy* 17:215-222.

Baron, Robert A. 1974. "Aggression-inhibiting influences of heightened sexual arousal." *Journal of Personality and Social Psychology* 30:318-322.

———. 1978. "Aggression-inhibiting influences of sexual humor." *Journal of Personality and Social Psychology* 36:189-197.

———. 1979. "Heightened sexual arousal and physical aggression: An extension to females." *Journal of Research in Personality* 13:91-102.

———, and Paul A. Bell. 1973. "Effects of heightened sexual arousal on physical aggression." Paper presented to the annual convention of the American Psychological Association, Montreal, August.

———, and Paul A. Bell. 1977. "Sexual arousal and aggression by males: Effects of type of erotic stimuli and prior provocation." *Journal of Personality and Social Psychology* 35:79-87.

Brownmiller, Susan. 1975. *Against Our Will: Men, Women and Rape.* New York: Bantam.

Bullough, Vern, and Bonnie Bullough. 1977. *Sin, Sickness and Sanity: A History of Sexual Attitudes.* New York: New American Library.

Chodorow, Nancy. 1978. *The Reproduction of Mothering: Psychoanalysis and the Sociology of Gender.* Berkeley: University of California Press.

Commission on Obscenity and Pornography. 1970. *The Report of the Commission on Obscenity and Pornography.* Washington, D.C.: U.S. Government Printing Office.

Davis, Keith, and G. Nicholas Braucht. 1973. "Exposure to pornography, character and sexual deviance: A retrospective survey." *Journal of Social Issues* 29:183-196.

Diamond, Irene. 1980. Pornography and repression: A reconsideration." *Signs* 5:686-701.

Dienstbier, Richard A. 1977. "Sex and violence: Can research have it both ways?" *Journal of Communication* 27:176-188.

Donnerstein, Edward. 1980. "Pornography and violence against women: Experimental studies." *Annals of the New York Academy of Science* 347:277-288.

Donnerstein, Edward, and John Hallam. 1978. "Facilitating effects of erotica on aggression against women." *Journal of Personality and Social Psychology* 36:1270-1277.

Donnerstein, Edward, Marcia Donnerstein, and Ronald Evans. 1975. "Erotic stimuli and aggression: Facilitation or inhibition?" *Journal of Personality and Social Psychology* 32:237–244.

Dworkin, Andrea. 1981. *Pornography: Men Possessing Women.* New York: Putnam.

Ebert, Roger. 1981. "Why movie audiences aren't safe anymore." *American Film* 6 (March): 54–56.

English, Deidre. 1980. "The Politics of Porn." *Mother Jones* 5(April): 44–45.

Faust, Beatrice. 1980. *Women, Sex and Pornography: A Controversial Study.* New York: Macmillan.

Goldstein, Michael J. 1973. "Exposure to erotic stimuli and sexual deviance." *Journal of Social Issues* 29:197–219.

———, and Harold S. Kant. 1974. *Pornography and Social Deviance.* Berkeley: University of California Press.

Gordon, John. 1980. "On sex and sexism." *Inquiry 3* (May 5): 29–31.

Groth, A. Nicholas, and H. Jean Birnbaum. 1979. *Men Who Rape: The Psychology of the Offender.* New York: Plenum.

Hentoff, Nat. 1979. "The new legions of erotic decency." *Inquiry 3* (December 10): 5–7.

Howard, James L., Myron B. Liptzin, and Clifford B. Reifler. 1973. "Is pornography a problem?" *Journal of Social Issues* 29:133–145.

Jaffe, Yoran, Neil Malamuth, Joan Feingold, and Seymour Feshbach. 1974. "Sexual arousal and behavioral aggression." *Journal of Personality and Social Psychology* 30: 759–764.

Johnson, Paula, and Jacqueline D. Goodchilds. 1973. "Pornography, sexuality and social psychology." *Journal of Social Issues* 29:231–238.

Kaminer, Wendy, n.d. "Women against pornography: Where we stand on the first amendment." Mimeographed. Women against pornography, 358 W. 47 Street, New York, N.Y.

Kant, Harold S., and Michael J. Goldstein. 1970. "Pornography." *Psychology Today* 4 (December): 59–61, 76.

Kercher, Glen A., and C. Eugene Walker. 1973. "Reactions of convicted rapists to sexually explicit stimuli." *Journal of Abnormal Psychology* 81:46–50.

Kutchinsky, Bert. 1973. "The effect of easy availability of pornography on the incidence of sex crimes: The Danish experience." *Journal of Social Issues* 29:163–181.

Lederer, Laura (ed.). 1980. *Take Back the Night: Women on Pornography.* New York: William Morrow.

Lindner, Harold. 1953. "Sexual responsiveness to perceptual tests in a group of sexual offenders." *Journal of Personality* 21:364–374.

Malamuth, Neil M., and James V. P. Check. 1980. "Penile tumescence and perceptual responses to rape as a function of victim's perceived reactions." *Journal of Applied Social Psychology* 10:528–547.

———, and Barry Spinner. Forthcoming. "A longitudinal content of analysis of sexual violence in the bestselling erotica magazines." *Journal of Sex Research.*

———, Scott Haber, and Seymour Feshbach. 1980. "Testing hypotheses regarding rape: Exposure to sexual violence, sex differences and the normality of rapists." *Journal of Research in Personality* 14:121–137.

Chapter III
Sexual Expressions

———, Maggie Heim, and Seymour Feshbach. Forthcoming. "Sexual responsiveness of college students to rape depictions: Inhibitory and disinhibitory effects." *Journal of Personality and Social Psychology.*

———, Ilana Reisin, and Barry Spinner. 1979. "Exposure to pornography and reaction to rape." Paper presented to the annual convention of the American Psychological Association, New York City, August.

Mann, Jay, Jack Sidman, and Sheldon Starr. 1973. "Evaluating social consequences of erotic films: An experimental approach." *Journal of Social Issues* 29:113–131.

Meyer, Timothy. 1972. "The effects of sexually arousing and violent films on aggressive behavior." *Journal of Sex Research* 8:324–331.

Nawy, Harold. 1973. "In the pursuit of happiness? Consumers of erotica in San Francisco." *Journal of Social Issues* 29:147–161.

The New York Times. 1977. "Judge in Wisconsin calls rape by boy 'normal' reaction." May 27, p. A9.

Rosen, Raymond C., and Francis J. Keefe. 1978. "The measurement of human penile tumescence." *Psychophysiology* 15:366–376.

Smith, Don D. 1976. "The social content of pornography." *Journal of Communication* 26:16–24.

Stoller, Robert J. 1975. *Perversion: The Erotic Form of Hatred.* New York: Pantheon.

Wilson, W. Cody, and Herbert I. Abelson. 1973. "Experience with and attitudes toward explicit sexual materials." *Journal of Social Issues* 29:19–39.

Zillman, Dorf, and Barry S. Sapolsky. 1977. "What mediates the effect of mild erotica on annoyance and hostile behavior in males?" *Journal of Personality and Social Psychology* 35:587–596.

Cases cited

Miller v. California, 413 U.S. 15, 1973.

Roth v. United States, 354 U.S. 476, 1957.

Reading 8

AN OVERVIEW OF SEXUAL ABUSE

Renitta L. Goldman, Virginia R. Wheeler

> Sexual abuse of children is an example of a problem that has only recently been publicly recognized as powerful, despite having had a long history of causing suffering. The forms of abuse to which children have been subjected are defined. During the long history of abuse many myths have developed about the victims, their families, and sexual abusers. These myths can be dispelled by systematic comparisons with the recently developed facts. Then the current status of sexual abuse can be accurately described and future needs can be assessed.

PREVALENCE

The abuse and neglect of children by adults charged with their care continues to plague society. However, the aspect of child abuse that is recently coming to the attention of professionals working with children is abuse pertaining to the sexual exploitation of children. Sexual abuse of children not only is widespread today, but also has a lengthy history dating back many centuries and is documented through early writings and drawings of the ancient Egyptians and Greeks. It is an old vice, but public inquiry and outrage have increased in the past decade as awareness has increased. Sexual exploitation of children is finally achieving the publicity such a serious societal problem warrants. This publicity which leads to public awareness is a necessary precedent to preventive action and treatment.

Recently the print media as well as television have featured articles and special programs related to child abuse, with emphasis on the sexual abuse of children. Researchers estimate that between 100,000 and 500,000 American children will be sexually molested this year, and few of

From Renitta L Goldman and Virginia R. Wheeler, *Silent Shame: The Sexual Abuse of Children*, Danville, Ill.: Interstate, 1986, pp. 1–6, 10–17. Reprinted by permission of PRO-ED, Inc.

Chapter III
Sexual Expressions

the offenders will be reported to anyone in authority. Fewer still will go to court, be convicted, or be punished for their crime.

An NBC television news special entitled "Silent Shame" reported that one out of every three girls is sexually abused. Four thousand children are sexually abused and many murdered each year. A television station reported that every two minutes a child is sexually abused in the United States (ABC affiliate, August 23, 1984).

As our society becomes more aware of the sexual exploitation of children, there is a proliferation of articles, books, and television programs pertaining to topics that were once taboo. For example, a special ABC telecast on incest, "Something About Amelia," was aired January 9, 1984.

Incest, a secretive act within the confines of the home, is probably the most underreported of all forms of sexual abuse. The taboo regarding incest has not prevented its occurrence. Rather, the taboo has just prevented the subject from being discussed (Stark, 1984). The American Humane Association cites almost 48,000 reported cases of incest in 1982. But Henry Giarretto, founder of the Child Abuse and Sexual Treatment Program in Santa Clara, California, contends that this figure is far too low. He estimates that over 250,000 children in the United States are sexually molested in their homes each year (Stark, 1984). Incest affects over 10 percent of American families (Rush, 1980).

A sociologist at Mills College in Oakland, California, Diana Russell, completed a study of sexual abuse among 930 randomly chosen San Francisco women. She found that 152 of them had been sexually abused by a family member before they were 18 years old, and 44 were abused by their fathers. Of the 152 cases of sexual abuse, only 4 cases were reported to the authorities.

Estimates suggest that one out of every four women will be sexually abused before age 18. Twenty-five percent of college women surveyed recently reported a sexual experience with an adult before age 13. Of these incidents, only 6 percent were reported (Barry, 1984). The unreported rate of child sexual abuse is at least three or four times that of the reported rate (Vander Mey and Neff, 1982). Kempe and Kempe (1984) stated that *reported* cases of sexual abuse of children have increased 200 percent since 1976.

Millions of today's adults are grown-up victims of sexual abuse in one form or another. Authorities are now finding that the perpetrators of this crime were often victims as children. Finkelhor (1979) estimates that 19 percent of all American women and 9 percent of all American men were sexually victimized as children. He also states that between 2 million and 5 million American women have had incestuous relationships.

The exact data on the prevalence of sexual exploitation of children in

Reading 8
Overview of Sexual Abuse

our society is difficult to find. Some even question whether there is actually more sexual abuse of children today. They contend that we are just talking more about it. We now openly acknowledge some of these concerns that have been with us for generations. Others see the women's movement as a catalyst which has exposed such practices and given women the courage to fight for their rights and those of their children....

IMPORTANT DEFINITIONS

CHILD ABUSE AND NEGLECT DEFINED

Congress enacted the Child Abuse Prevention and Treatment Act (PL 93-247) in 1974 and amended the Act in 1978. This act defines child abuse and neglect as the physical or mental injury, sexual abuse or exploitation, negligent treatment, or maltreatment of a child under the age of 18 by a person who is responsible for the child's welfare under circumstances which indicate that the child's health or welfare is harmed or threatened thereby. Categories of harm may include sexual abuse, physical abuse, nutritional deprivation, drug abuse, medical care neglect, emotional neglect, and educational neglect (Irwin, 1982).

Child abuse may be defined as any act of omission or commission that endangers or impairs a child's physical or emotional health or development. Child abuse includes physical abuse and neglect, emotional abuse, and sexual abuse (California Attorney General, 1980).

Individual states have defined child abuse. For example, in the state of Utah child abuse or neglect means causing harm or threatened harm to a child's health or welfare. In Maryland abuse means (1) physical injury or injuries sustained by a child as a result of cruel or inhumane treatment or as a result of a malicious act or acts by any parent, adoptive parent, or other person who has the permanent or temporary care or custody or responsibility for supervision of a minor child, or (2) any sexual abuse of a child, whether physical injuries are sustained or not. In Nevada child abuse and neglect mean physical or mental injury of a nonaccidental nature, sexual abuse, sexual exploitation, or negligent treatment or maltreatment of a child by a person who is responsible for the child's welfare under circumstances which indicate that the child's health or welfare is harmed or threatened.

SEXUAL ABUSE DEFINED

Sexual abuse may be defined as any act which arouses or uses a child for sexual gratification. The act can fall anywhere along a continuum from

Chapter III
Sexual Expressions

fondling to digital penetration. Some "gray areas" of sexual abuse may include children who sleep with their mothers, or families which bathe together (Swann, 1983).

Another definition of sexual abuse is any sexual activity, assaultive or non-assaultive, between an adult and a child (Houston University, 1977). Schlesinger (1982) defines sexual abuse as any exposure of a child to sexual stimulation inappropriate for the child's age, level of psychosexual development, and role in the family. Miller (1979) defines sexual abuse as sexual exploitation of any victim under age 18 years of age by an adult. The exploitation can range from indecent exposure to genital contact.

The National Center on Child Abuse and Neglect (NCCAN) prefers another definition: "Contacts or interactions between a child and an adult when the child is being used for the sexual stimulation of that adult by another person" (Kempe and Kempe, p. 10, 1984).

Several terms fall under the category of sexual abuse:

Incest. Vander Mey and Neff (1982) define incest as all forms of erotic sexual contact, sexual demands or threats, or pornographic exploitation initiated by an adult who is related to the child by family ties or surrogate family ties. Grando (1983) defines incest as sexual abuse that is committed by a family member in either the nuclear or extended family. The abuser may be related by blood or marriage. In the United States no uniformity exists among states regarding the degree of kinship or the age of consent. The majority of states restrict the degree of kinship to first and second blood relatives. Renshaw (1982) identifies incest as a statutory offense, usually a felony, which consists of either marriage or a sexual act (intercourse or deviate sexual conduct) between persons who are too closely related. He further identifies "aggravated" incest as incest between a father and daughter. The term "incest" is derived from the Latin *incestum*. This word means "unchaste and low."

Pedophilia. Pedophilia is a psychosexual perversion in which the adult is sexually attracted to children. The pedophile can be homosexual, bisexual, or heterosexual in orientation. Most pedophiles are men; women are rarely identified as pedophiles and are rarely recognized in modern research. The term *pedophilia* was coined by Richard von Krafft-Ebing, a German physicist in the 19th century. The term literally means "love of children." A common term for "pedophile" is "child molester."

Pederasty. Pederasty refers to the sexual contact between adult males and "consenting" children for reasons of producing satisfactory relationships for both the adults and the children. Pederasty was practiced in ancient Greece.

Reading 8
Overview of Sexual Abuse

Exibitionism. Exhibitionism indicates the exposure of the genitals of an adult male to women and children. The purpose of exhibitionism is to experience sexual excitement and through this activity register surprise and shock of the onlooker.

Molestation. Sexual molestation is defined as sexual contact short of intercourse. Activities may be exposure, touching, or masturbation.

Sodomy. The legal definition of sodomy is carnally knowing a person by the anus or by or with the mouth.

Sexual Sadism. Sexual sadism denotes inflicting bodily harm to a victim as a means of gaining sexual excitement.

Sexual Intercourse. Sexual intercourse refers to fellatio (oral-genital contact), sodomy (anal-genital contact), or penile-vaginal contact.

Rape. Rape refers to sexual intercourse—real or attempted—without the consent of the victim. Two forms of rape have been identified:

1. *Statutory rape.* Statutory rape refers to non-violent penetration (vaginal or oral) with a person who is under the legal age of consent. The legal age of consent varies among states. In 23 states the age of consent falls between 13 and 16. In 14 states the age of consent is 18. In the other states the age of consent is below 12.

2. *Forcible rape.* Forcible rape refers to the degree of damage to a child, which is dependent on the size of the child, the attacker, the violence, and the amount and kind of other physical violence rendered along with the rape.

Frotteurs. Frotteurs are men who rub against women's bodies in crowds.

Chickenhawks. A "chickenhawk" is a pedophile whose sexual preference is limited to boys. It is a term used by some law enforcement personnel, child pornographers, and offenders themselves.

Diddler. A "diddler" is a slang term used in prisons for sex offenders.

Child Pornography. Child pornography refers to the arranging of photographs (by still, video, or film production), or any material which involves minors in sexual acts regardless of parental consent. Child pornography also includes the distribution of such material.

Child Prostitution. Child prostitution denotes children in sexual acts for profit. Generally different partners are involved.

Chapter III
Sexual Expressions

MYTHS

Myths abound about the sexual victimization of children. Only recently has the literature begun to discredit them. Myths about the victims are as prevalent as those about the perpetrator and the family environment from which they come. Some experts report that even after 50 years of scientific research in a supposedly sexually liberated society, the subject of the sexual abuse of children is still taboo (de Young, 1981; Groth, et al., 1978).

To the general public the term "child molester" conjures up visions of a dangerous, anonymous psychopath who haunts playgrounds looking for unsuspecting children in order to lure them into a sexual relationship. Some still think the perpetrator of sexual offenses against children is a lecherous, dirty old man. As more information about this topic comes to light, it is evident that few in our society have a clear picture of the victim, the perpetrator, or their families.

SOME COMMON MYTHS CONCERNING THE PERPETRATOR

1. Myth. Most sexual abuse of children is perpetrated by someone who is a stranger to the child victim.

1. Fact. In most cases of sexual abuse, the perpetrator is an adult known to the victim and one who has easy access to the child. Surveys show that only one out of every five or six victims is abused by a total stranger.

2. Myth. Perpetrators of sexual abuse of children are as likely to be female as male.

2. Fact. Actually the number of male perpetrators far exceeds the number of female perpetrators. It is estimated that 95 percent of the perpetrators are male.

3. Myth. Perpetrators who sexually abuse children are usually inferior in intelligence.

3. Fact. Few sexual abusers are limited in their intellectual capacity. Most, in fact, are of average or above average intelligence.

4. Myth. In an incestuous father-daughter relationship, the father is usually seduced by a promiscuous daughter.

4. Fact. Although incestuous fathers may rationalize their behavior with this logic, this is very seldom the case. The promiscuous or seductive behavior of the daughter is often the result, but seldom the primary cause of an incestuous relationship.

5. Myth. The sexual abuser is usually psychotic.

5. Fact. The perpetrator is seldom psychotic but probably has experi-

Reading 8
Overview of Sexual Abuse

enced emotional deprivation. It may be only when the abuse is discovered that the neurotic behavior is evident.

6. Myth. Men who sexually abuse children are more likely to come from an ethnic minority group and from a lower socio-economic background than those who do not.

6. Fact. The sexual abuser comes from all walks of life. All socioeconomic levels, all ethnic groups, and most occupational groups are represented in the perpetrator category.

7. Myth. The stigma of sexual abuse falls only on the perpetrator, never on the child victim.

7. Fact. Children who are sexually abused often become further victimized by other family members when the abuse is revealed. In cases of incest, victims may be rejected, accused of lying, and held responsible for the breakup of the family. Sometimes agencies involved in investigating or treating sexually abused children inadvertently add to their victimization as do friends, neighbors, and peers.

8. Myth. Incest occurs because men do not have outlets for their sexual needs.

8. Fact. Although it is true that incestuous fathers often have poor marital relationships, the major reason for incest is not the fulfillment of sexual needs. They may turn to their daughters for emotional fulfillment. Some psychologists believe these men are also looking for power (Stark, 1984).

SOME COMMON MYTHS CONCERNING THE VICTIM

1. Myth. A child's report of sexual abuse is usually fantasy rather than actual fact.

1. Fact. Children seldom lie about a matter as serious as sexual abuse. Young children are not sophisticated enough to be aware of sexual acts unless they have been involved sexually with an older person.

2. Myth. Children who make an accusation of sexual abuse and then retract it are merely displaying attention-seeking behavior.

2. Fact. Children are both reluctant to challenge adult authority and fearful of retaliation. Therefore, they may be ambivalent about reporting the abuse and may later deny it.

3. Myth. A child is partially to blame if he/she does not resist the parent's sexual advances.

3. Fact. The child is never to blame when sexually molested by an adult, especially one he/she has learned to love and respect. Children are taught to obey adults and to accept their judgment as to what is right

Chapter III
Sexual Expressions

or wrong. It is logical that a child would submit to a parent or known authority figure.

4. Myth. There is usually only one child victim of sexual abuse in a family.

4. Fact. The oldest daughter is most often the initial victim. Younger girls in the family may be sexually abused when the oldest daughter becomes a teenager and has more social contacts outside the home.

5. Myth. Usually the incest victim is chosen for sexual interaction because she is the most attractive and provocative.

5. Fact. The incest victim is most often the oldest daughter who has moved into a parental role within the family. She may not be the most attractive nor provocative daughter. In some cases the most vulnerable child is selected for the molestation.

6. Myth. Because violence is seldom used, there are no long-lasting, harmful effects to the child as a result of intrafamilial sexual activity.

6. Fact. Untreated victims may maintain victim behaviors throughout their lives. They may end up unassertive and unable to set limits on their behavior or the behavior of others. Untreated sexual abuse in childhood often leads to problems with sexuality in adulthood. Incest may cause more serious psychological problems if untreated because of the length of the abuse.

7. Myth. Children who have been sexually assaulted recover more rapidly if they are encouraged to forget about the incident as soon as possible.

7. Fact. In most cases, the trauma of being sexually abused can be resolved most rapidly when it can be discussed with a supportive, knowledgeable, and compassionate therapist. The impact of the abuse correlates with the reaction of those around the child when the abuse is disclosed.

8. Myth. The process of going through the justice system to prosecute the offender adversely affects the child and should be avoided if possible.

8. Fact. It is true that the court proceedings may add to the trauma the child has experienced. However, in some states, depositions can be videotaped. Most justice systems have specially trained personnel who can deal with the subject without increasing the strain on the victim. The experience of the court process can have a positive side. It can confirm to the victim that he/she is believed and will be protected by those in authority.

9. Myth. If a child has a sexual experience with a person of the same sex, he/she will become homosexual or bisexual, or develop homosexual tendencies.

Reading 8
Overview of Sexual Abuse

9. Fact. Most experts in the field believe that homosexuality is programmed in a child early. Sexual molestation by a homosexual does not shift a child's sexual orientation.

SOME COMMON MYTHS CONCERNING THE FAMILY

1. Myth. Families from low income and social status groups foster most sexual abuse.

1. Fact. Sexually abusive families come from all social and income levels. In fact, the *FBI Law Enforcement Bulletin* (January 1984) reports incest occurring most commonly in middle-class families.

2. Myth. Incest is indigenous to society's lower classes.

2. Fact. There is proportionally higher incidence of *reported* offenses by lower-class men than middle-class men (Gagnon, 1974). Families in the lower socio-economic groups have more contacts with agencies where sexual abuse could be discovered and reported.

3. Myth. Rarely is a mother aware of an incestuous relationship between her daughter(s) and her spouse.

3. Fact. Mothers usually know that "something is wrong" but may choose not to investigate because of fear of disrupting the family or because of economic depencency, apathy, mental or physical illness, etc. However, Judith Herman, Director of the Women's Mental Health Collective in Somerville, Massachusetts, believes that there is considerable "mother blaming" used to get fathers "off the hook" (Stark, 1984).

4. Myth. In an incestuous family there is usually only one victim.

4. Fact. Intrafamilial sexual abuse has an adverse effect on every member of the family. It is now usually viewed by professionals as a family systems problem. Almost every case of incest is found in a dysfunctional family.

5. Myth. Divorce is the usual and most appropriate action taken by a parent who discovers her spouse has been sexually abusing one of their children.

5. Fact. The divorce of parents is not always the best solution to an incestuous parent-child relationship. By involving the entire family in therapy, the marriage may be left intact and a history of positive relationships developed with all members of the family system.

6. Myth. Unlike other forms of child abuse, sexual abuse is not intergenerational.

6. Fact. Sexual abuse, like other forms of child abuse, is a learned behavior. It is often an inappropriate response to emotional needs and tends to become a family tradition passed on to the next generation. Most perpetrators were abused physically or sexually as children.

Chapter III
Sexual Expressions

TRENDS IN THE AREA OF SEXUAL ABUSE

1. The definition of sexual abuse has been broadened. Sexual abuse includes not only actual harm but *threatened* harm. The range of behaviors which now fall under the category of sexual abuse can vary from exhibitionism to genital contact. The definition of incest has been extended beyond blood relatives to include stepfamily members.

2. The criteria for reportable conditions have been expanded. The recognition that children seldom lie about sexual abuse has encouraged persons to report sexual abuse when "hard evidence" may not be available. Broadened symptoms of possible sexual abuse have been identified. For example, Renshaw (1982) believes that inquiry should be made into possible sexual abuse when adolescents attempt suicide.

3. The list of mandated professionals required to report sexual abuse has been expanded. Generally, the following professionals are considered mandated reporters: school teachers, principals, counselors, nurses, and social workers.

4. There appears to be a trend toward better team work when cases of sexual abuse are reported. Child protective services, police, physicians, schools, the judicial system, and other community agencies seem to be more willing to work together to protect the child victim without as much controversy over maintaining their "turfs."

5. Increased attempts at *prevention* of sexual abuse are being made. Since the intergenerational aspects of sexual abuse have been recognized, trying to stop sexual abuse is critical. Materials—both in written form and through visual media—are available to parents and school personnel.

6. Attempts have been made to minimize the trauma of court procedures on victims. For example, in several states videotaping of the victim's testimony is used in court instead of a court appearance.

7. Another trend in the area of sexual abuse is to seek out treatment for the offender as well as the victim. *Mandating* treatment seems to be the most effective means of assuring help for the offender.

8. A further trend in the area of sexual abuse is attempting to keep the victim in the home whenever possible. Removing the incestuous father is recommended instead of the child who may be in crisis during the disclosure period.

9. Publicity about sexual abuse is on the increase. The news media—television, radio, and newspapers—report incidents of sexual abuse more regularly than ever before.

10. Current pro-incest groups are operational. It was reported in the *FBI Law Enforcement Bulletin* (Barry, 1984) that the author of a master's thesis presented to a group within the American Psychiatric Association

convention considered some incest experiences positive and beneficial. There are pro-incest lobbyists who are attempting to eradicate the taboos surrounding incest. They insist the guilt felt by the perpetrator and the victim is more harmful than the act itself. Other groups such as the René Guyon Society advocate adult-child sex and are working to lower the age for statutory rape.

11. Sexual abuse may be on the increase, according to Kempe and Kempe (1984). The increase of divorce and the loosening of sexual mores may be contributing factors.

FUTURE NEEDS IN THE AREA OF SEXUAL ABUSE

1. More needs to be known about the background of the offender.
2. The subject area needs to be brought out of the "closet."
3. The reasons why some children are more vulnerable to sexual abuse than other children need to be understood.
4. More information on the *male* victim needs to be uncovered.
5. The subject of sexual abuse needs to be incorporated in the school curricula at all levels—elementary, high school, college, and adult education.
6. Research studies need to be undertaken with populations which have experienced sexual abuse within the *immediate* past. Current samples tend to be adult women who give information in retrospect.
7. Research studies need to include a range of victims in a range of settings using different age, sex, and social class variables.
8. Research efforts are needed as to the *effects* of treatment on the child victim.
9. Longitudinal studies need to be undertaken into the effects of treatment on members of the incest family. Relevant questions would be (a) How did each family member fare?, (b) Was there professional treatment?, (c) Did the treatment stop the incest?, (d) Did the family reconstitute?, (e) How is the adult sexual adjustment?
10. Interest not only in the victim but in other family members needs to be shown, since sexual abuse has widespread effects.
11. Additional training in the area of sexual abuse needs to be given to professionals who work with youngsters on a regular basis. Professionals such as teachers and day care workers need such additional training in the identification and support roles they can play.
12. Children need to be more informed as to their rights of body privacy and safety against sexual abuse.
13. Harsher penalties for pornography need to be imposed.
14. More prosecutions of rapists need to occur.

Chapter III
Sexual Expressions

15. More sympathetic attitudes toward rape victims need to be encouraged.

16. More attention to the vulnerability of *boys* for sexual abuse needs to be drawn.

17. Research is needed for exploring better facilitation for boys who disclose sexual victimization.

REFERENCES

Barry, Robert J. 1984. "Incest: The last taboo." *FBI Law Enforcement Bulletin* (January): 1–9.

"California Attorney General's Office." 1980. *Journal of Teacher Education* (September–October): 41.

deYoung, Mary. 1982. *The Sexual Victimization of Children*. Jefferson, N.C.: McFarland.

Finkelhor, D. 1979. *Sexually Victimized Children*. New York: Free Press.

Gagnon, J. H., and W. Simon. 1974. *Sexual Encounters Between Adults and Children*. New York: Behavioral Publications.

Grando, Roy. 1983. "Incest." *The Counseling Interviewer* (December): 32–35.

Groth, A. N., et al. 1978. "Crisis issues for an adolescent-aged offender and his victim," in A. W. Burgess (ed.), *Sexual Assault of Children and Adolescents*. Lexington, Mass.: Heath.

Kempe, C. H., and Ruth S. Kempe. 1984. *The Common Secret: Sexual Abuse of Children and Adolescents*. New York: W. H. Freeman.

Miller, K. H., and E. R. Miller. 1979. "Child abuse and neglect: A framework for identification." *School Counselor* (May): 284–287.

Renshaw, Domeena C. 1982. *Incest Understanding and Treatment*. Boston: Little, Brown.

Rush, Florence. 1980. *The Best Kept Secret*. Englewood Cliffs, N.J.: Prentice-Hall.

Schlesinger, Ben. 1982. *Sexual Abuse of Children: A Resource Guide and Annotated Bibliography*. Toronto: University of Toronto Press.

Stark, Elizabeth. 1984. "The unspeakable family secret." *Psychology Today* (May): 41–46.

Swann, Helen. 1984. Personal communication.

Vander Mey, B. J., and R. L. Neff. 1982. "Adult-child incest: A review of research and treatment." *Adolescence* 717–735.

CHAPTER IV

CRIME AND VIOLENCE

Reading 9
WAREHOUSING CRIMINALS

Donald R. Cressey, *University of California, Santa Barbara*

> *Every prison is a crime factory. By locking criminals into the type of prisons we currently use, we define them as being wild and alien. If we had, instead of such prisons, a penitentiary industry system modeled on a typical factory, chances of rehabilitation would increase.*

Psychiatrists have clinical evidence suggesting that capital punishment causes murder. Some people kill in the hope that their crime will energize the state into killing them.

This psychological fact illustrates the workings of a general principle long ago discovered by sociological criminologists: A nation's program for dealing with criminals is always reflected in the country's crime rates. If a society tries to control crime by rewarding conformity, citizens will keep the crime rate down by rewarding each other for good conduct. If a society tries to control crime by terrorizing its citizenry, the citizens will terrorize each other.

In *Beyond the Punitive Society*, the proceedings of a conference on Skinnerian principles, Harvey Wheeler put the matter succinctly and well:

> Just as prisons teach criminals how to be criminals, not how to be good citizens, so punishment teaches persons how to punish; how to punish themselves by haranguing themselves with guilt feelings, as well as how to punish others retributively. The result is a society characterized by punishing; repressive behavior produces a suppressive society.

The idea that prisons are schools of crime, in the sense that they provide opportunities for naïve youngsters to learn new tricks from old cons, has been overplayed. The damage done by prisons is much more direct, subtle, and devastating. Every prison is a crime factory because it models how all criminals, not just those locked behind its walls, are supposed to behave. The prison, like the police officer's armament, the de-

Published by permission of Transaction, Inc. from SOCIETY, vol. 19, no. 5, copyright © 1982, by Transaction, Inc.

Chapter IV
Crime and Violence

corum of the courtroom, and the dinginess of the county jail, is a symbol of authoritarianism, coercion, condemnation, and rejection. The symbolic message sent by towering walls, razorsharp barbed fences, armed men on catwalks, and cages of reinforced steel suggests that criminals are uncommitted, alien, wild. Because America has increasingly been broadcasting this message, it is not surprising that our criminals have become increasingly violent. Ironically enough, in the last decade legislators and other government officials have responded to the ensuing violence with violence—more and more citizens are being punished by confinement behind walls of concrete and steel.

Americans are strong believers in the idea that the state should hurt criminals by depriving them of their liberty, perhaps because imprisonment as punishment for crime was invented by the radicals of the American Revolution. Today, close to four hundred thousand adults are confined in America's state and federal prisons, up from under two hundred thousand ten years ago. Most will be discharged within a decade, but others will take their places. Altogether, we will imprison over a million people in the next decade, not counting those locked in county jails for short terms. No other Western nation has an imprisonment rate this high.

Despite their love of incarceration, Americans do not want to pay the price of locking up so many citizens. It costs at least $50,000 to build a cell these days, and to keep a prisoner in a cell requires another $1,000 to $2,000 a month. We need a solution to the dilemma that surfaces whenever someone (usually an economist) notes that as the state increases the cost of crime for criminals (longer and harsher prison terms for more offenders), it increases its own economic costs proportionately because it must build, man, and maintain new prisons, pay board-and-room costs of prisoners for longer terms, and pay for increased police and court work as well.

Deterrence policy, long championed by political conservatives, asks that pain be inflicted on criminals as a means of repressing crime—the assumption being that hurting criminals will reduce crime rates both by reforming offenders (specific deterrence) and by terrorizing bystanding citizens so much they will be afraid to violate the law (general deterrence). The psychology underlying this policy, which is the backbone of contemporary criminal law and its administration, has long been discounted by psychologists. Economists, however, like considerable numbers of the general public, continue to subscribe to the hedonistic doctrine that individuals calculate potential costs and benefits in advance of action and regulate their conduct accordingly. The implication is that undesirable acts will not be performed if enough pain is attached to them and if the amount of pain thus attached is made knowable to all, so that prospective criminals can make rational calculations. The upshot, of course, is a tendency to increase punishment (the cost of committing crime) whenever the crime rate seems too high. This tendency now requires more money than even the advocates of deterrence policy are willing to pay.

Influential contemporary liberals (some call them neoconservatives) also have effected policies that are dramatically increasing the costs of punishing criminals. One such policy inflicts the pain of imprisonment on criminals not for its utility but simply because criminals deserve to suffer ("just deserts," "retribution," "vengeance"). Noting that discretionary practices permit discrimination against the poor, liberals also have replaced indeterminate sentences with mandatory, flat, and presumptive sentences. Finally, liberals have begun locking criminals up for purposes of "incapacitation" (warehousing), rather than for either utilitarian or retributive purposes. All three policies, singly and in combination, are being used to imprison more people for longer terms, thus driving state costs out of sight.

It is reasonable, then, to expect economists and others to give their attention to ways of cutting down the costs of punishment while increasing the assumed costs of committing crimes. Some recommend more frequent use of gassing, hanging, and electrocution. Others recommend that we once again banish criminals to a distant land, as Britain once transported criminals first to her American colonies and then, after the Revolution, to her Australian colonies. Still others, like Tom J. Farer, also recommend self-governing distant colonies but with a difference—these colonies would, like the penal colony in French Guiana made famous by Henri Charrie's *Papillon,* be compounds with armed guards at the perimeters.

Transportation of criminals at first cut Great Britain's punishment costs. The Transportation Act of 1718 declared that its purpose was both to deter criminals and to supply colonies with labor. In 1786, after the American colonies had become independent, the policy of transportation to Australia was adopted, and this practice continued until 1867. It was abandoned because it was strenuously opposed by Australians, because it did not seem to produce general deterrence, and because it became too expensive.

Looking back, it cannot be denied that Britain's transportation program was a success. After all, the United States and Australia are now exemplars of democracy, with liberty and justice for all. There is something good about nations whose constitutions were written by the descendants of convicts.

Chapter IV
Crime and Violence

POLICING THE PERIMETERS

But the stories of other penal colonies have no such happy endings. Russia has used Siberia as a penal colony since 1823. Witold Krassowski and I long ago showed, in a 1958 issue of *Social Problems*, that life in Soviet labor camps is not exactly a bean feast, a fact also documented in Alexander Solzhenitsyn's *One Day in the Life of Ivan Denisovich*. These camps, where inmates govern inmates while armed guards patrol the perimeters, seem more like what Farer is proposing than do the Australian and American colonies.

Farer has unwittingly called for more prisons that are run as Attica, San Quentin, and Smokey Mountain are now being run. These and other penitentiaries have the nightmarish character, the hopelessness, the unspeakable humiliations, and the deadly violence Farer mentions. So do Soviet labor camps. Significantly enough, prisons and labor camps have these features precisely because prisoners are left largely alone to conduct their own affairs, as would be the inmates in Farer's guarded compounds.

Until recently, guards in most American prisons functioned like traditional police officers, protecting inmates from each other by arresting and taking misbehaving inmates to disciplinary court for conviction, sentencing, and punishment. In a few prisons, which were said to be "treatment oriented," guards borrowed from the child-rearing techniques of middle-class people and thus controlled inmates by giving love and affection to those who were behaving, and withdrawing love and affection from inmates who were not. Today, guards rarely use either of these control systems, nor have they invented new police methods. They have withdrawn to the walls, as the guards of Farer's compounds would do. As a consequence, inmates are robbing, raping, assaulting, and killing each other as never before.

There are at least four different ways to make sense of the fact that prison guards and their bosses now concentrate on perimeter control, rather than on keeping the prison crime rate down. Each of the four is relevant to Farer's plan for a prison colony "with an easily guarded periphery," a colony that is, like a trust territory, "being prepared for self-determination" through "technical and capital assistance," supervised "democratic elections," and punishment by state officials, not residents, "in case of grave abuse."

The first is to observe that in contemporary prisons, as in Farer's future camps, guards have no obligation to assist inmates. State officials insist only that criminals be warehoused under conditions not constituting cruel and unusual punishment. Accordingly, residents are provided with food, shelter and clothing, an occasional low-paying job, and technical assistance in the form of meager academic and vocational training for those who demand it. That's it. The deterrence policy of conservatives, like the just deserts and incapacitation polices of liberals, insists on nothing more. Guards ignore the needs of inmates because everyone else is ignoring their needs.

Second, haphazard policing in contemporary prisons—the same kind of policing Farer recommends for his compounds—is a way of supplementing the psychological pain stemming from restricted liberty with the bodily pain inflicted by inmates on other inmates. Among unpoliced prisoners, the crime rate is high, but not because the prisoners "are too sick, too emotionally and psychologically crippled to perform necessary social functions." The crime rate is high because most prisoners are bad guys who have track records of violence. Guards are prohibited from beating, choking, cutting, or clubbing inmates, and instances of guard brutality are now rare, despite stories to the contrary. But guards can, and do, retreat to the periphery, thus letting inmates do their dirty work.

Third, poor policing in prisons is valuable to guards and other prison workers because it maximizes inmate divisiveness, thus discouraging inmates from joining forces in attempts to overpower the staff. Armed guards at the perimeters also provide such discouragement, but, if we can believe our Pentagon generals, it is not safe to rely on retaliatory and defensive weapons alone. "If they are fighting each other, they aren't fighting me," a warden told me long ago. They are not banding together to foment revolution either.

The fourth way to make sense of poor prison policing is to recall that a state's crime policies and crime rates are always closely interlaced. Perhaps contemporary guards' withdrawal to the walls is, like proposals for penal colonies whose inmates are to be prepared for "self-determination," a way of encouraging inmates to govern themselves according to the principles underlying the deterrence, incapacitation, and vengeance system of justice dominating official structures in the United States. Using these principles, state officers try to reform offenders by hurting them, try to keep crime rates down by inflicting exemplary punishments, try to give offenders their due by hurting them as much as they have hurt others, and try to incapacitate offenders so they cannot again hurt others, at least for a time. The United States has a high crime rate because many of its citizens, acting as individuals, try to do precisely the same things. American prisons have an even higher crime rate because inmates also ape American criminal justice processes, but do so in the absence of counteracting influences such as humanitarian socialization processes and effective police departments.

Chapter IV
Crime and Violence

PREVENTING CRIME

Crime prevention, whether inside or outside a prison, requires more than merely arresting, convicting, and hurting wrongdoers. There must be preaching and practicing of brotherly love, racial equality, and forgiveness rather than hate. Crime prevention also requires positive programs for cutting the roots of crime and criminality, including programs for giving more and more citizens a larger and larger stake in the economic and political institutions. Penal colonies, whether on the British model (America, Australia), on the Soviet model (labor camps), or on the model used by Howard B. Gill in the Norfolk Prison Colony of Massachusetts during the 1920s (Farer's model), cannot do these things.

Last winter, when federal and state governments were trying to raise about $10 billion for prison construction, Chief Justice Warren Burger recommended that the new prisons should be "factories with fences around them" rather than mere "human warehouses." The rhetoric is right. If prisons would use inmate labor for production, imprisonment costs would go down. For that matter, if we repealed statutes that limit prison industrial production, as the Chief Justice recommended, prisoners might even be persuaded to build their own new prisons, saving even more money. Who knows, an occasional prisoner might even acquire conventional work habits, give up a life of crime, and live happily ever after. As a *Wall Street Journal* editorial put it on December 17, 1981, "On the average, it is probably expecting too much of prisons to do more than segregate criminals as a way of protecting the rest of us. Still, there is always the individual who would benefit from the opportunities Justice Burger has in mind."

A half-dozen years before the Chief Justice gave his speech, Canada introduced a penitentiary industry system modeled on outside industry rather than on traditional prison factories. Only a handful of inmates have been employed, but the plan is to build factories at several prisons and to concentrate on profits rather than on training or rehabilitation. Candidates for jobs must apply in the same manner as they do in private industry, and must be qualified for the position if they are to obtain it. Hours of work are similar to those in private industry. Inmates are paid the federal minimum hourly wage. From their earnings, they pay the prison for room, board, and clothing, and they also pay income taxes as well as fees for unemployment insurance and the Canada Pension Plan (social security).

Maturation of these "factories with fences around them" should be watched closely by U.S. officials. Using inmate labor under fair conditions is a promising way to cut down the costs of punishment. It should be noted, however, that proposals for prison factories, like proposals for penal colonies, do nothing to challenge either our practice of punishing so many citizens or the absurd assumptions on which this practice is based. Every prison and every penal colony, regardless of its program, is a punitive institution. Every prison and every penal colony, no matter how cheap its program, is therefore a symbol of a society's failure to prevent crime by positive, nonpunitive, interventionist means.

Sir Thomas More hurled an angry question at his fellow Englishmen: "What other thing do you do than make thieves and then punish them?" Now, four a half centuries later, too many Americans are responding, "Nothing."

Reading 10

HOW MORAL MEN MAKE IMMORAL DECISIONS

J. Patrick Wright (as told by John Z. DeLorean)

> *John DeLorean relates how a basically immoral and irresponsible business decision was made by men he had perceived generally as having high standards of personal morality. Even though it was known that the basic design of the Corvair made it unsafe, many persons within the General Motors organization fought to keep the car in production.*

...Never once while I was in General Motors management did I hear substantial social concern raised about the impact of our business on America, its consumers or the economy. When we should have been planning switches to smaller, more fuel-efficient, lighter cars in the late 1960s in response to a growing demand in the marketplace, GM management refused because "we make more money on big cars." It mattered not that customers wanted the smaller cars or that a national balance-of-payments deficit was being built in large part because of the burgeoning sales of foreign cars in the American market.

Refusal to enter the small car market when the profits were better on bigger cars, despite the needs of the public and the national economy, was not an isolated case of corporate insensitivity. It was typical. And what disturbed me is that it was indicative of fundamental problems with the system.

General Motors certainly was not more irresponsible than many American businesses. But the fact that the "prototype" of the well-run American business engaged in questionable business practices and delivered decisions which I felt were sometimes illegal, immoral or irresponsible is an indictment of the American business system.

Earlier in my career, I accepted these decisions at GM without question. But as I was exposed to more facets of the business, I came to a real-

---

Reprinted with permission from *On a Clear Day You Can See General Motors: John Z. DeLorean's Look Inside the Automotive Giant* (New York: Avon, 1979), pp. 63–68. Copyright © 1979 by J. Patrick Wright, Wright Enterprises, 1979.

Reading 10
Moral Men—Immoral Decisions

ization of the responsibilities we had in managing a giant corporation and making a product which substantially affected people and national commerce. It bothered me how cavalierly these responsibilities were often regarded.

The whole Corvair case is a first-class example of a basically irresponsible and immoral business decision which was made by men of generally high personal moral standards. When Nader's book threatened the Corvair's sales and profits, he became an enemy of the system. Instead of trying to attack his credentials or the factual basis of arguments, the company sought to attack him personally. This move failed, but, in the process, GM's blundering "made" Ralph Nader.

When the fact that GM hired detectives to follow and discredit Nader was exposed, the system was once again threatened. Top management, instead of questioning the system which would permit such an horrendous mistake as tailing Nader, simply sought to preserve the system by sacrificing the heads of several executives who were blamed for the incident. Were the atmosphere at GM not one emphasizing profits and preservation of the system above all else, I am sure the acts against Nader would never have been perpetrated.

Those who were fired no doubt thought they were loyal employees. And, ironically, had they succeeded in devastating the image of Ralph Nader, they would have been corporate heroes and rewarded substantially. I find it difficult to believe that knowledge of these activities did not reach into the upper reaches of GM's management. But, assuming that it didn't, top management should have been held responsible for permitting the conditions to exist which would spawn such actions. If top management takes credit for a company's successes, it must also bear the brunt of the responsibility for its failures.

Furthermore, the Corvair was unsafe as it was originally designed. It was conceived along the lines of the foreign-built Porsche. These cars were powered by engines placed in the rear and supported by an independent, swing-axle suspension system. In the Corvair's case, the engine was all aluminum and air-cooled (compared to the standard water-cooled iron engines). This, plus the rear placement of the engine, made the car new and somewhat different to the American market.

However, there are several bad engineering characteristics inherent in rear-engine cars which use a swing-axle suspension. In turns at high speeds they tend to become directionally unstable and, therefore, difficult to control. The rear of the car lifts or "jacks" and the rear wheels tend to tuck under the car, which encourages the car to flip over. In the high-performance Corvair, the car conveyed a false sense of control to the driver, when in fact he may have been very close to losing control of the vehicle. The result of these characteristics can be fatal.

113

Chapter IV
Crime and Violence

These problems with the Corvair were well documented inside GM's Engineering Staff long before the Corvair ever was offered for sale. Frank Winchell, now vice-president of Engineering, but then an engineer at Chevy, flipped over one of the first prototypes on the GM test track in Milford, Michigan. Others followed.

The questionable safety of the car caused a massive internal fight among GM's engineers over whether the car should be built with another form of suspension. On one side of the argument was Chevrolet's then General Manager, Ed Cole, an engineer and product innovator. He and some of his engineering colleagues were enthralled with the idea of building the first modern, rear-engine, American car. And I am convinced they felt the safety risks of the swing-axle suspension were minimal. On the other side was a wide assortment of top-flight engineers, including Charles Chayne, then vice-president of Engineering; Von D. Polhemus, engineer in charge of Chassis Development on GM's Engineering Staff; and others.

These men collectively and individually made vigorous attempts inside GM to keep the Corvair, as designed, out of production or to change the suspension system to make the car safer. One top corporate engineer told me that he showed his test results to Cole but by then, he said, "Cole's mind was made up."

Albert Roller, who worked for me in Pontiac's Advanced Engineering section, tested the car and pleaded with me not to use it at Pontiac. Roller had been an engineer with Mercedes-Benz before joining GM, and he said that Mercedes had tested similarly designed rear-engine, swing-axle cars and had found them far too unsafe to build.

At the very least, then, within General Motors in the late 1950s, serious questions were raised about the Corvair's safety. At the very most, there was a mountain of documented evidence that the car should not be built as it was then designed.

However, Cole was a strong product voice and a top salesman in company affairs. In addition, the car, as he proposed it, would cost less to build than the same car with a conventional rear suspension. Management not only went along with Cole, it also told the dissenters in effect to "stop these objections. Get on the team, or you can find someplace else to work." The ill-fated Corvair was launched in the fall of 1959.

The results were disastrous. I don't think any one car before or since produced as gruesome a record on the highway as the Corvair. It was designed and promoted to appeal to the spirit and flair of young people. It was sold in part as a sports car. Young Corvair owners, therefore, were trying to bend their cars around curves at high speeds and were killing themselves in alarming numbers.

It was only a couple of years or so before GM's legal department was

Reading 10
Moral Men—Immoral Decisions

inundated with lawsuits over the car. And the fatal swath that this car cut through the automobile industry touched the lives of many General Motors executives, employees and dealers in an ironic and tragic twist of fate.

The son of Cal Werner, general manager of the Cadillac Division, was killed in a Corvair. Werner was absolutely convinced that the design defect in the car was responsible. He said so many times. The son of Cy Osborne, an executive vice-president in the 1960s, was critically injured in a Corvair and suffered irreparable brain damage. Bunkie Knudsen's niece was brutally injured in a Corvair. And the son of an Indianapolis Chevrolet dealer also was killed in the car. Ernie Kovacs, my favorite comedian, was killed in a Corvair.

While the car was being developed at Chevrolet, we at Pontiac were spending $1.3 million on a project to adapt the Corvair to our division. The corporation had given us the go-ahead to work with the car to give it a Pontiac flavor. Our target for introduction was the fall of 1960, a year after Chevy introduced the car.

As we worked on the project, I became absolutely convinced by Chayne, Polhemus and Roller that the car was unsafe. So I conducted a three-month campaign, with Knudsen's support, to keep the car out of the Pontiac lineup. Fortunately, Buick and Oldsmobile at the time were tooling up their own compact cars, the Special and F-85, respectively, which featured conventional front-engine designs.

We talked the corporation into letting Pontiac switch from a Corvair derivative to a version of the Buick-Oldsmobile car. We called it the Tempest and introduced it in the fall of 1960 with a four-cylinder engine as standard equipment and a V-8 engine as an option.

When Knudsen took over the reins of Chevrolet in 1961, he insisted that he be given corporate authorization to install a stabilizing bar in the rear to counteract the natural tendencies of the Corvair to flip off the road. The cost of the change would be about $15 a car. But his request was refused by the Fourteenth Floor as "too expensive."

Bunkie was livid. As I understand it, he went to the Executive Committee and told the top officers of the corporation that, if they didn't reappraise his request and give him permission to make the Corvair safe, he was going to resign from General Motors. This threat and the fear of the bad publicity that surely would result form Knudsen's resignation forced management's hand. They relented. Bunkie put a stabilizing bar on the Corvair in the 1964 models. The next year a completely new and safer independent suspension designed by Frank Winchell was put on the Corvair. And it became one of the safest cars on the road. But the damage done to the car's reputation by then was irreparable. Corvair sales began to decline precipitously after the waves of unfavorable pub-

Chapter IV
Crime and Violence

licity following Nader's book and the many lawsuits being filed across the country. Production of the Corvair was halted in 1969, four years after it was made a safe and viable car.

To date, millions of dollars have been spent in legal expenses and out-of-court settlements in compensation for those killed or maimed in the Corvair. The corporation steadfastly defends the car's safety, despite the internal engineering records which indicated it was not safe, and the ghastly toll in deaths and injury it recorded.

There wasn't a man in top GM management who had anything to do with the Corvair who would purposely build a car that he knew would hurt or kill people. But, as part of a management team pushing for increased sales and profits, each gave his individual approval in a group to decisions which produced the car in the face of the serious doubts that were raised about its safety, and then later sought to squelch information which might prove the car's deficiences.

The corporation became almost paranoid about the leaking of inside information we had on the car. In April of 1971, 19 boxes of microfilmed Corvair owner complaints, which had been ordered destroyed by upper management, turned up in the possession of two suburban Detroit junk dealers. When the Fourteenth Floor found this out, it went into panic and we at Chevrolet were ordered to buy the microfilm back and have it destroyed.

I refused, saying that a public company had no right to destroy documents of its business and that GM's furtive purchase would surely surface. Besides, the $20,000 asking price was outright blackmail.

When some consumer groups showed an interest in getting the films, the customer relations department was ordered to buy the film, which it did. To prevent similar slip-ups in the future, the corporation tightened its scrapping procedures.

Reading 11
TOMORROW'S THIEVES

Jay S. Albanese

> *As prevention and detection technologies for traditional crimes become more sophisticated, thieves are running ahead of the law and advancing to modern methods of criminality. Computers provide many opportunities for theft. Fraud, larceny by trick, will become the most prevalent forms of theft in the computer age. Legislation and law enforcement agencies still lag behind this form of crime. The relevant laws are so recent that there are many loopholes, and legal tests are needed before enforcement will become effective.*

Perhaps the oldest form of criminal behavior is theft. From biblical times forward, theft has been one of the most common forms of deviant behavior. In fact, the universality of theft as the crime of choice is evident in the crime statistics of all societies of all types.

Given the fact that theft is common and has remained so for much of recorded history, it is likely that stealing will remain popular as long as the incentives and opportunities for it continue. Even though there is no consensus as to why people steal (or steal so frequently), the high rate of theft has remained remarkably stable over time. Perhaps the only exceptional changes in theft have been in its forms and methods.

Criminologists make a living trying to generalize why people steal, although it is clear that few adequate generalizations exist to explain theft. Some people steal to survive, while others steal to improve their social standing. Some steal to acquire material things they don't actually need, whereas others steal for symbolic reasons involving status, frustration, or revenge.

Theft is difficult to predict, despite its frequency, and the explanation of criminal behavior remains largely a mystery. This situation has not deterred social scientists, of course, from generalizing about the causes of

---

Reprinted with permission from *The Futurist*, published by the World Future Society, 4916 St. Elmo Avenue, Bethesda, Md.

crime. Perhaps the only consensus that exists among criminologists is on the fact that crime is strongly related to opportunity. The precise causes of these opportunities, why people choose to exploit them, and what should be done to reduce their incidence are the focus of much of the debate in criminology today.

THE NATURE OF THEFT

The most common form of theft, historically, has been larceny by stealth—that is, stealing by secretive or furtive means. Of course, "theft" requires that property be taken without the consent of the owner. Therefore, it has been important that the owner be unaware of the larceny as it occurs.

Property owners, over the years, have taken great precautions to protect their property. Public police did not exist in England and the United States until the nineteenth century. Prior to that, citizens were responsible for their own property, and they either armed themselves, hired bodyguards, or fashioned "safes" as places to store their valuables. Later in that century, banks became a central repository of valuable private property, when government currency and jewels came to be the primary indicators of wealth and the means for exchange.

The evolution of bank safes offers an interesting example of how theft has changed over time. As sociologist Donald Cressey has pointed out, patterns of theft from banks were strongly related to the available opportunities. During the early twentieth century, safes were locked with a key. Thieves learned how to pick the locks, so the combination lock was invented. Criminals found a way to pry the entire combination spindle from the safe, so sturdier locks were manufactured.

In an apparent response to this move, safecrackers drilled holes in the safes and inserted explosives to open them. Metals were then alloyed to make safes difficult to violate. Some criminals obtained nitroglycerin, which could be inserted into tiny crevices, or used oxyacetylene torches to open safes. Safes soon appeared with perfectly fitted doors that could not be pried, drilled, melted, or penetrated by explosives.

Some criminals turned to kidnapping bankers, forcing them to open the safes, and the time lock was invented to prevent this. In a similar way, some burglars began to cart away the entire safe to be opened later, so safes were enlarged and made too heavy to move. In addition, night depositories were invented to provide businessmen an alternative to keeping cash in their smaller store safes. Safes were later invented that would release gas when disturbed, so criminals equipped themselves with gas masks.

Reading 11
Tomorrow's Thieves: Computer Crime

DUELING TECHNOLOGIES

This "progression" in the organization of thefts from bank safes illustrates an important factor in the history of theft. It appears that there is a relationship between the technology of crime and the technology of prevention. If changes in the nature of safecracking can be generalized to other forms of theft, it may be true that the more sophisicated the prevention technology (e.g., harder metals, time locks, etc.), the more sophisticated criminals must become to maintain acceptable levels of success (e.g., explosives, banker kidnappings, etc.).

British sociologist Mary McIntosh has suggested that the economy, and economic conditions in general (e.g., high unemployment rates), provide the incentive for theft, but it is improvement in crime detection that forces criminals to become more organized to remain successful. As she explains, "Criminals and their opponents are thus engaged in an all-out war which has a tendency to escalate as each side improves its techniques to outwit the other."

Thieves plan and organize their behavior in order to minimize the risk of a direct confrontation with the victim, which may lead to violence. As a result, the primary goal of most thieves is sufficient organization to reduce the possibility of apprehension and, thereby, increase the chances for success.

Rapid changes in technology generate opportunities for theft that can be exploited by criminals for financial gain. Only after thieves experience some success does the government, or private industry, take steps to reduce the opportunities for theft. This improvement in detection and/or prevention technology must then be matched, or surpassed, by criminals if they are to avoid apprehension.

Laws and law enforcement often lag behind the innovative techniques of criminals in exploiting technological change. Consider, for example, that street lighting is often added *after* a number of robberies have taken place on a dark street. The same can be said for steering-column locks on automobiles, burglar alarms in stores, cameras in banks, and secure safes at all-night convenience stores. It appears that the security technology, historically, has been reactionary. Only *after* existing crime-prevention measures have been successfully counteracted (many times) are improvements made to reduce (or at least change) criminal opportunities.

FROM CRACKERS TO HACKERS

The advent and growing popularity of computers have provided the latest opportunity resource for criminal misuse. The invention of the automobile during the early twentieth century has been said to have doubled the number of offenses in the criminal codes of most countries; the invention of the computer will probably have the same impact in the twenty-first century.

Automobiles provided opportunities for misuse through untrained operators, manufacturing shortcuts, numerous rules for road usage, complex registration requirements, repair frauds, storage (parking) problems, as well as theft. Computers will likely have a similar impact as they become ever more sophisticated and popular. Codified offenses will be added to eliminate opportuniites for misuse such as untrained operators, manufacturing shortcuts, unauthorized usage, registration violations, repair frauds, information-storage problems, and theft. Similar to the invention of the automobile, therefore, the invention of the computer will provide abundant opportunities for misuse and theft.

By 1990, there will be one computer for every 50 people in the United States. The incredible number of computers now in circulation, combined with their increasing efficiency and capacity, may produce an impact for law and law enforcement greater than that created by the invention of the automobile. This is largely due to the fact that computers are being employed frequently to provide direct access to cash or merchandise. The vast majority of government computers (85%) are used for payrolls. Likewise, electronic fund transfer (EFT) systems have the greatest potential for abuse due to their ready access to cash or credit.

EFT systems allow for financial transactions via remote terminals. Automatic teller machines (ATM), home banking, and financial transactions among banks and businesses are the most common types of EFT systems now in operation. The opportunities for theft from EFT systems are many, although they generally require more organization than have larcenies in the past. Because the computer system has been given programmed authority to provide access to cash, the thief must deceive the computer. This form of larceny by deception is called *fraud*.

THE GROWTH OF FRAUD

Fraud is, essentially, larceny by trick, and it will likely become the most prevalent form of theft in the computer age. As computers are utilized in banking and for credit, citizens will carry less cash, store less cash, and obtain it upon demand from an ATM. When payment is required for purchases up-front, it will be deducted automatically from the bank account via an EFT.

A thief may certainly steal a victim's ATM card and attempt to gain access to savings and checking accounts—a bigger payoff than the cash a victim usually has on hand. But, in order to succeed, the thief would

Reading 11
Tomorrow's Thieves: Computer Crime

have to obtain the access code, which usually means confronting the victim—something most criminals wish to avoid.

Larceny must change in form if there are fewer opportunities for theft by stealth. Theft by fraud will be necessary, and fraud requires more planning and preparation in its execution. Theft by stealth requires agility and, perhaps, speed. Theft by fraud requires planning.

Crime trends lend support to this view. In the United States, for example, arrests for forgery and fraud have gone up dramatically during the last 20 years. In Canada, frauds reported to the police in recent years have increased as well. When one compares these trends in frauds to trends in larceny by stealth, a shift is apparent.

The rate of reported larcenies in both the United States and Canada increased from 1965 to 1985 by 118% and 123%, respectively. These figures testify to the enduring popularity of larceny, when the rates of other crimes against persons and property have declined in recent years. On the other hand, it can be seen that the rate of frauds reported to police in Canada, and arrests for fraud in the United States, have increased even more dramatically. It appears that fraud rates and arrests have increased faster (264% and 146% in 20 years) than has larceny.

An aggravating factor in this apparent shift toward crimes of fraud is the growing availability of computers and the lack of effective law-enforcement technology to prevent computer frauds. Fewer than half the states in the United States have laws that address computer crime. In Canada, a specific statute against computer crime was not added until 1985. Such laws are needed to address frauds such as unauthorized use of access devices (e.g., identification numbers), insider manipulation (e.g., stolen ID numbers, removal of "holds" on a bad account), and frauds by legitimate card holders (e.g., disclaiming knowledge of withdrawals, merchant collusion).

In addition, typical larceny statutes require "taking of property." The application of these statutes to computer crimes is not clear, where an electronic signal or sequence is generated to alter an account (and no "property" is actually "taken"). In a similar way, fraud statutes usually require a willful "misrepresentation to a person." A computer is not a person under the law; statutes are thus needed to correct these loopholes.

THE FUTURE OF COMPUTER CRIME

Because the laws against crime by computer are so recent, their impact is difficult to determine thus far. It is clear, however, that the laws themselves will have no impact without a significant enforcement effort.

In 1975, for example, there were only 4,000 automated teller machines. By 1982, there were nearly 36,000 ATMs. During this period, the value of transactions processed increased by more than 400% to $2.07 billion per year. Clearly, the opportunities for fraud are increasing dramatically, and they will continue to do so. In the United States, the first interstate ATM network was begun in just 1983. Furthermore, it is predicted that home banking will account for the bulk of all retail bank transactions by the turn of the century.

This large increase in opportunities for fraud has not been overlooked by the criminal element. Losses from credit-card fraud have increased 50% in five years. Also, the growth in reported frauds of all types suggests a relationship between fraud and opportunity.

The enforcement technology has improved in recent years in an effort to reduce computer fraud, but new, better-organized scams continue. As credit cards have become popular during the last 20 years, fewer citizens carry large amounts of cash, and fewer purchases are made with cash. This has resulted in theft of credit cards.

Banks issuing credit cards began to publish regular listings of invalid cards so merchants could make sure a card was not stolen or canceled. Criminals then used stolen cards as many times as possible immediately after stealing them to avoid detection by the published list. Banks responded with magnetic tape readers in stores that communicated with the bank's computer at the point of sale to determine whether a card was valid.

Some thieves decided to take an alternative approach. They would go through store trash bins and retrieve used carbons from credit-card purchases, which contain both the owner's account number and signature. These would be used in forging a duplicate card that would not show up as stolen on the bank computer. Recently, banks have added three-dimensional holograms to credit cards to make them more difficult to forge, and they also have introduced carbonless receipts. Now that many purchases can be made at home with a credit card, via telephone or interactive cable systems, banks intend to issue credit cards without a visible account number in the near future to make theft of credit cards a less attractive criminal opportunity.

It appears that the enforcement technology always will lag behind the criminal technology. Whether it is the technology of bank thefts or credit-card fraud, criminals historically have exploited opportunities for theft in a manner that exceeds the existing law-enforcement technology.

Whether efforts to prevent computer frauds in the twenty-first century will effectively limit criminal opportunities, and also provide quick reactions to changes in the criminal technology, remains to be seen. If history is to be a guide, however, the risk of apprehension must be significantly increased beyond current levels, and the available opportunities more effectively circumscribed.

Reading 12
POLITICAL TERRORISM

Ovid Demaris

> *The definitions of morality governing terrorist activity have changed profoundly over time. Initially, terrorist activities were governed by a "political code" something like the rules of war: only those people who were directly involved should be harmed. Today, there are no innocents.*

Political terrorism is a by-product of the Industrial Revolution, a disorder created by the destruction of the ancient patterns of life. A society that had been largely agrarian was thrust suddenly into a world of machines and factories, of labor and capital. The resulting displacement of populations, the deterioration of the environment, and the disruption of an entire way of life fed the fires already ignited by political repressions and the writings of intellectuals who inspired the violent deeds that have been with us ever since.

Although terrorism's philosophical underpinnings antedate the last two centuries (organized and irregular warfare are almost as old as the human race), religious and economic anarchism are the true antecedents of modern political terrorism.

For example, the Cathari, or Albigensians, and other gnostic heresies held that the universe was totally corrupt, unreal, and without meaning: only the world of the spirit was important, and all authority of a temporal nature was denied. Accused of immorality, devil worship, blood sacrifice, and heresy, they were prosecuted by the Catholics. St. Dominic, the founder of the Dominican Brothers, preached the destruction of Cathari by terror. The wholesale massacre of both heretics and Christians was excused on the theory that "God will know His own."

The Anabaptists believed they belonged to the Community of Saints. They denied the rule of church and state, considering them unnecessary, since they were in direct contact with God. Authority was evil because it stood between man and the divine light within him. The existing society

---

Reprinted with permission from *Brothers in Blood* (New York: 1977), pp. 377–387.

Chapter IV
Crime and Violence

had to be destroyed so that the new order could be established, with its laws revealed by the inner light of the prophet or leader. This was the first time that anarchical philosophy embraced the total leadership of an inspired individual.

Plague, economic disaster, heavy taxation, and religious strife added to the misery of the people of Switzerland, Germany, and the Low Countries. This allowed Jan Mathys and his disciple John of Leiden to arouse the Anabaptists to a fever pitch. The city of Münster was sacked, and all records of contracts and debts were destroyed and all books and manuscripts were burned. They established a communal state, seizing food, clothing, all worldly goods, and placed them in a common store.

After Mathys was killed leading a sortie, John of Leiden instituted a reign of terror accompanied by polygamy and sexual excess. When Münster was retaken in 1535, John of Leiden was tortured to death. The Anabaptist revolt had many features later found in anarchistic movements: belief in the healing properties of violent destruction, the importance of violence as an end in itself, and the belief in the dream of building an entirely new social order on the ruins of the old. As in the cases of the Albigensians and the Peasants' Revolt, Anabaptist terror led not to the desired end but to the destruction of their society, the death of their leaders, and the eradication of their movement by counterterror of unbelievable fury.

The Inquisition and the Dominican order were instruments of organized terror, but the Jesuits provided the closest parallel to today's concept of terrorist groups. Founded by Ignatius Loyola in 1533, the Society of Jesus was called by Loyola "the little battalion of Jesus." Organized to combat the Reformation and to propagate the Roman Catholic faith among the heathen, it grew into one of the largest and best-organized groups of terrorists in history. The Jesuits were the shock troops of the Counter Reformation. Their casuistical principles and the nature of their secret society caused them to be damned and feared by both Protestants and Catholics.

Their belief in the "sovereignty of the people" and "tyrannicide" was anarchical in theory and action. God had vested sovereignty in the people, who voluntarily delegated it to the monarch. The people were free to reassert their prerogatives and depose the monarch whenever he failed to govern in accordance with their wishes. In the Jesuits' judgment, this failure occurred when the sovereign either adopted Protestantism or seemed likely to do so. Under the casuistical principle that the end justifies the means, killing a ruler who had turned away from the church was a sacred duty—not a crime.

Whenever the society deemed it necessary to eliminate a king, prince, or other important personage, the Jesuit assassin was prepared in

*Reading 12
Political Terrorism*

a ceremony called the Blessing of the Dagger. Next to the Dark Chamber where Jesuit novices were initiated was a small room called the Cell of Meditation. A painting was placed in the center of an altar, covered with a veil and surrounded by torches and lamps of a scarlet color. A casket covered with hieroglyphics and bearing a representation of a lamb (symbolic of Christ) on its lid was placed on a table. The brother chosen for the "deed of blood" came here to receive his instructions. When he opened the casket, he found a dagger wrapped in a linen cloth. An officer of the order removed the dagger, kissed it, sprinkled it with holy water, and then handed it to a deacon, who attached it to a rosary and hung it around the neck of the chosen one, informing him that he was the elect of God and telling him the name of his victim.

Then a prayer was offered for his success: "And Thou, invincible and terrible God, who didst resolve to inspire our elect and thy servant with the project of exterminating [the name of the victim], a tyrant and heretic, strengthen him, and render the consecration of our brother perfect by the successful execution of the great work. Increase, O God, his strength a hundredfold, so that he may accomplish the noble undertaking, and protect him with the powerful and divine armor of thine elect and saints. Pour on his head the daring courage which despises all fear, and fortify his body in danger and in the face of death itself."

The veil was then removed from the painting and the elect beheld a portrait of Jacques Clément, the young Dominican monk who had assassinated Henry III of France, surrounded by a host of angels carrying him to celestial glory. The implication was clear; the current elect would also be wafted to the side of a grateful God once his mission was accomplished.

A crown, symbolic of the heavenly crown he was about to win, was placed on his head. "Deign, O Lord of Hosts, to bestow a propitious glance on the servant thou has chosen as thine arm, and for the execution of the high decree of thine eternal justice. Amen."

The technique was not unlike that employed by the Old Man of the Mountain, who used to drug some of his young assassins into a deep sleep and transport them to his secret pleasure garden, persuading them when they awoke that he had brought them to Paradise itself. Drugged again, they would awake in the everyday world, now forever convinced that their master could reward them with eternal Paradise after death if they did his bidding while they were alive. How far removed is all this from today's URA? Kozo Okamoto, the sole surviving terrorist of the Lod Airport massacre, wanted to commit suicide because "we soldiers after we die want to become the three stars of Orion. The revolution will go on, and there will be many stars."

The Jesuits' powers grew quickly and their terrorist methods caused

125

Chapter IV
Crime and Violence

such fear that they came into conflict with civil and religious authorities in most countries where they operated. The Jesuits were driven from France in 1594, from England in 1579, from Venice in 1607, from Spain in 1767, and from Naples in 1768. They were finally suppressed by Pope Clement XIV in 1773 and not revived until they had turned away from terrorist tactics.

Gradually the concept of anarchy moved from the religious realm to the economic. Nineteenth-century pamphleteers exemplified the shift in their demands for social justice. One wrote, "Magistrates, provosts, beadles, mayors—nearly all live by robbery...they all batten on the poor... the stronger robs the weaker." Another said, "I would like to strangle the nobles and the clergy, every one of them....Good working men make the wheaten bread but they never chew it; no, all they get is the sifting from the corn, and from good wine they get nothing but the dregs and from good clothing nothing but the chaff. Everything that is tasty and good goes to the nobles and the clergy."...

There was something romantic about the Russian czar-killers of the late nineteenth century. Unlike the propaganda-conscious terrorist groups of today, who shy away from the word *terrorist*, the members of the Terrorist Brigade were proud of the label. They brought the word *terrorist* into common political usage. They believed that political murder "shakes the whole system to its foundations," but the assassination of Czar Alexander II only meant greater repression. Then the assassination of the czar's uncle, Duke Sergei, followed by the execution of the responsible terrorist led to the October Revolution and its savage repression. The brigade disintegrated in 1908 when it learned that its leader was a member of the secret police.

The Terrorist Brigade was immortalized by Albert Camus in his play *The Just Assassin*. It is the story of a young revolutionary who is chosen to kill the head of the secret police. The plan calls for him to throw a bomb into the target's carriage, but as the carriage draws closer, the terrorist can see that the police official is holding two small children on his lap. Bomb in hand, he turns and runs away, having decided that the deed must be done another day. Agreeing with his decision, his comrades say, "Even in destruction, there's a right way and a wrong way—and there are limits."

There are academicians today who point to this example when they want to show that terrorism has undergone a radical transformation in recent years. Their thesis is that terrorists used to operate under a code of honor, that their murders were strategic and for a cause.

"Until about the middle of the twentieth century, terrorism was most often a modernist version of the older politics of assassination—the killing of particular people thought to be guilty of particular acts." Michael

Reading 12
Political Terrorism

Walzer wrote in the *New Republic* on August 30, 1975. "Since that time terrorism has most often taken the form of random murder, its victims unknown in advance and, even from the standpoint of the terrorists, innocent of any crime. The change is of deep moral and political significance, though it has hardly been discussed. It represents the breakdown of a *political code* worked out in the late 19th century and roughly analogous to the laws of war, developed at the same time."

The code made a distinction between combatants and noncombatants. "In former times," says Walzer, "children, passers-by and sometimes even policemen were thought to be uninvolved in the political struggle, innocent people whom the terrorist had no right to kill. He did not even claim a right to terrorize them; in fact his activity was misnamed—a minor triumph for the forces of order. But today's terrorists earn their title. They have emptied out the category of innocent people; they claim a right to kill anyone; they seek to terrorize whole populations."

Examples to the contrary would fill another book. Bombings during the nineteenth century killed hundreds of "innocent" people. Two incidents come immediately to mind: the Haymarket and the Wall Street bombings. The following sentiment was expressed by French poet Laurent Tailhade: *Qu'importe les victimes si le geste est beau?* ("What do the victims matter if the gesture is fine?")

The best description of a terrorist can be found in Sergei Nechayev's *Revolutionary Catechism:*

> The revolutionary is a dedicated man. He has no personal inclinations, no business affairs, no property, and no name. Everything in his life is subordinated towards a single exclusive attachment, a single thought, and a single passion—the revolution.... He has torn himself away from the bonds which tie him to the social order and to the cultivated world, with all its laws, moralities, and customs.... The revolutionary despises public opinion...morality is everything which contributes to the triumph of the revolution. Immoral and criminal is everything that stands in his way.... Night and day he must have but one thought, one aim,— merciless destruction...he must be ready to destroy himself and destroy with his own hands everyone who stands in his way.

Anarchists who advocate violence, whether Anabaptists or Baader-Meinhof gang members, have spilled a great deal of blood, innocent or otherwise. They preach terrorism for its own sake, the destruction of the old system and the building of the new. "We are not in the least afraid of ruins," said Spanish anarchist leader Buenaventura Durutti. "We are going to inherit the earth. There is not the slightest doubt about it.... We carry a new world, here in our hearts."

The words are representative of the ideal of anarchism and symbolic

Chapter IV
Crime and Violence

of the reality. In the end it was the Fascist who built on the ruins of Spain and the people were subjected to dictatorship.

Anarchist philosophic beliefs and anarchist violent actions are separated by a chasm. The philosophy teaches that man is naturally good and made evil only by laws and governments, that given a stateless condition his reason and primitive sense of right and wrong would assert themselves, permitting all to live peacefully and cooperatively in bliss.

The contradictions of idealism and coercion have caused splits within all anarchical movements. It is perhaps the reason why such movements have never made a successful revolution. Their political theories are based on the false assumption that love and violence are synonymous.

Terrorism also has failed as a tactic because it is ineffective against a ruthless tyranny or strong democracy. Unlike organized revolution, it has never overthrown or even seriously threatened a totalitarian state. What limited success it has achieved has been against parliamentary monarchies and weak democracies. Only in countries like Spain in 1936 and the Weimar Republic has it been possible for unaided terrorism to achieve results commensurate with the effort expended.

The strategy of terrorism is to generate fear, to employ that weapon in a special and complicated sort of way. Terrorism is an illusionist's trick. The power of the terrorist is unreal. Revolution, like war, has been described as the strategy of the strong, while terrorism, being the work of a small elite, is the strategy of the weak. Terrorism is a weapon used by those who lack strength to act directly. The strategy is to achieve its goal not through its acts but through the enemy's response to them. For terrorism is merely the first step in a revolutionary struggle. It is a psychological assault intended to produce a psychological result. It can be fear, frustration, anger, helplessness. Whatever the reaction, the idea is to provoke the government into embarking on a course of action the terrorist desires. In other words, the terrorist is in the peculiar position of having to undertake actions he does not desire, such as hijackings and the murder of innocent people, in order to provoke one he does desire—for example, a brutal police repression. The objective is to reveal the hidden weakness, evil, or corruption of the existing government—to unmask the beast, as it were. In revealing the real face behind the mask, the terrorist hopes to enlist the support of the people, which is the next step toward achieving conditions propitious for revolutionary guerrilla warfare.

The terrorist has been compared to a magician who tricks his mark into watching his right hand while his left hand, unnoticed, makes the switch. The strategy of deliberately killing the innocent is a risky one. The act may appear particularly horrifying to the public because it seems so pointless. The reaction could turn the terrorists into enemies of the people as well as of the government. Che Guevara was opposed to terrorism for precisely this reason. He argued that it hinders "contact with the masses and makes impossible unification for action that will be necessary at a critical moment." In this treatise on guerrilla warfare, he dealt with terrorism in a single paragraph.

On the other hand, Carlos Marighella had much to say about it in his *Mini-Manual of the Urban Guerrilla:* "Terrorism is an arm the revolutionary can never relinquish. Bank assaults, ambushes, desertions, diverting of arms, the rescue of prisoners, executions, kidnapping, sabotage, terrorism and the war of nerves are all cases to point.... The government has no alternative except to intensify repression." The aim, he says, is to escalate the situation so that people "will refuse to collaborate with the authorities and the general sentiment is that the government is unjust." The idea is to show that the capitalist state depends for its continued existence upon the use of violence and its own terror. This is the conventional wisdom of a wide spectrum of terrorist groups—IRA, FLQ, ERP, RAF, ETA, URA, ALN, MIR, FAR, PLO, PFLP, PDFLP, ALF, ELF, TPLA—a veritable alphabet soup of terror, not to mention the separatist movements active all over the globe.

The most successful terrorism is that practiced by governments to sustain their power. Yet even a mild form of repression can boomerang in a colonialist situation, as happened in Ireland and Israel. Great Britain defeated itself, as France did in Algeria. A motley band of Algerian nationalists calling themselves the National Liberation Front (or, by its French initials, FLN) was able to persuade a mixed indigenous population, with no history of its own, to think of itself as the citizenry of a separate nation. The FLN's strategy was to pressure the French into reacting in a way that would demonstrate the unreality of the French claim that there was no distinct Algerian nation, that it was genuinely a part of France. French reaction to random violence was to treat all persons of non-European origin as suspects, even to transferring army units of Muslim Algerian troops into mainland France and replacing them in Algeria by European troops, thereby signaling the end of Algérie Français. When people began to feel excluded from the existing community, their sympathies went to the FLN, which was able to shift from terrorism to organized guerrilla warfare.

The terrorist tactics used in colonial countries seldom succeed against an indigenous government, which is far more reluctant to relinquish its hold than a colonial power with a country of its own to which it can withdraw. The Israelis, who are fighting on home ground, with their backs to the sea, have no place to which to retreat. In Uruguay, once the model democracy of Latin America, the terror of the Tupamaros not only failed but led directly to a repressive military dictatorship.

Chapter IV
Crime and Violence

Despite their inherent weakness, terrorists nonetheless have scored many political successes in the last few decades. They have caused enough damage to intimidate and blackmail powerful governments. Technology—jet travel, satellite communication, lightweight bazookas, plastic bombs, compact automatic weapons—has enabled them to invade the political arena and to express their ideological goals on a more organized level than in the past. Also, world opinion is on their side. Imperialism is not regarded as immoral, even by the United Nations. The colonial empires are dissolving so quickly that it is almost impossible to keep count. This is in part the result of costly wars in Indochina, Indonesia, and Algeria and in part of centrifugal pressures from dissident ethnic minorities. The breakup of large heterogeneous countries into smaller national units has been accelerated by terrorism carried out in the name of oppressed ethnic minorities seeking self-rule.

The United Nations had 51 members in 1945; by 1960 there were 82; there are now 138 and another 20 nations are not members. Indications are that there may be 200 or even 300 politically independent nations in the world by the end of the century.

Brian Jenkins wrote in a Rand Corporation report:

> The resultant international system is likely to resemble the political complexity of Renaissance Italy, in which major kingdoms, minor principalities, tiny states, independent city republics, Papal territories, and bands of *condottieri* engaged in incessant, but low-level, warfare with one another. Medieval Europe, and India in the seventeenth and eighteenth centuries also come to mind.... The world that emerges is an unstable collection of nations, mini-states, autonomous ethnic substates, governments in exile, national liberation fronts, guerrilla groups aspiring to international recognition and legitimacy via violence, and a collection of ephemeral but disruptive terrorist organizations, some of which are linked together in vague alliances, some perhaps the protégé of foreign states. It is a world in which the acronyms of various self-proclaimed revolutionary fronts may take their place in international forums alongside the names of countries. It is a world of formal peace between nations—free of open warfare except, perhaps, for brief periods—but of a higher level of political violence, of increased internal insecurity.

Although most terrorists identify with Mao and Castro, few have the patience to go into the mountains for decades if necessary to wage their revolution. Mao developed the modern theory of guerrilla fighting. He formulated a series of relationships that differed from existing military strategies and earlier Marxist theories of revolution. Contrary to the Marxists, his emphasis was on military power. Political power depends on military power; or, as Mao put it, "political power grows out of the barrel of a gun." Although his forces were initially inferior, Mao reasoned

Reading 12
Political Terrorism

that the superior political motivation of his guerrillas, strengthened by the political support of the Chinese peasants, made it possible for them to survive military reverses. The strategy was to wage a protracted military campaign that would eventually wear down the enemy.

By politicizing and mobilizing people who would be mere bystanders in a conventional conflict, Mao introduced a relationship between military action and propaganda. The effect that any violent action has on the people watching may even exceed the importance of the conflict itself. Terrorism is that principle applied on the grandest scale.

Reading 13
THE EDUCATION OF A TORTURER

Janice T. Gibson, Mike Haritos-Fatouros

> *What type of person could become a torturer? A study of the methods used by the Greek military police to train officers in torture techniques suggests some disturbing answers. Normal, well-adjusted people were trained to blindly obey orders and perform outrageous acts against people defined as "the enemy." Simulated training sessions, using students as subjects in a contrived prison setting, have shown how easy it is to produce abusive behavior.*

Torture—for whatever purpose and in whatever name—requires a torturer, an individual responsible for planning and causing pain to others. "A man's hands are shackled behind him, his eyes blindfolded," wrote Argentine journalist Jacobo Timerman about his torture by Argentine army extremists. "No one says a word. Blows are showered.... [He is] stripped, doused with water, tied.... And the application of electric shocks begins. It's impossible to shout—you howl." The governments of at least 90 countries use similar methods to torture people all over the world, Amnesty International reports.

What kind of person can behave so monstrously to another human being? A sadist or a sexual deviant? Someone with an authoritarian upbringing or who was abused by parents? A disturbed personality affected somehow by hereditary characteristics?

On the contrary, the Nazis who tortured and killed millions during World War II "weren't sadists or killers by nature," Hannah Arendt reported in her book *Eichmann In Jerusalem*. Many studies of Nazi behavior concluded that monstrous acts, despite their horrors, were often simply a matter of faithful bureaucrats slavishly following orders.

Obedience to what we call the "authority of violence" often plays an important role in pushing ordinary people to commit cruel, violent and

---

Reprinted with permission from *Psychology Today* magazine, copyright © 1986 (PT Partners, L.P.).

*Reading 13
Education of a Torturer*

even fatal acts. During wartime, for example, soldiers will follow orders to kill....

We studied the procedures used to train Greek military police as torturers during that country's military regime from 1967 through 1974. We examined the official testimonies of 21 former soldiers in the ESA (Army Police Corps) given at their 1975 criminal trials in Athens; in addition, Haritos-Fatouros conducted in-depth interviews with 16 of them after their trials. In many cases, these men had been convicted and had completed prison sentences. They were all leading normal lives when interviewed. One was a university graduate, five were graduates of higher technical institutes, nine had completed at least their second year of high school and only one had no more than a primary school education.

All of these men had been drafted, first into regular military service and then into specialized units that required servicemen to torture prisoners. We found no record of delinquent or disturbed behavior before their military service. However, we did find several features of the soldiers' training that helped to turn them into willing and able torturers.

The initial screening for torturers was primarily based on physical strength and "appropriate" political beliefs, which simply meant that the recruits and their families were anticommunists. This ensured that the men had hostile attitudes toward potential victims from the very beginning.

Once they were actually serving as military police, the men were also screened for other attributes. According to former torturer Michaelis Petrou, "The most important criterion was that you had to keep your mouth shut. Second, you had to show aggression. Third, you had to be intelligent and strong. Fourth, you had to be 'their man,' which meant that you would report on the others serving with you, that [the officers] could trust you and that you would follow their orders blindly."

Binding the recruits to the authority of ESA began in basic training, with physically brutal initiation rites. Recruits themselves were cursed, punched, kicked and flogged. They were forced to run until they collapsed and prevented from relieving themselves for long stretches of time. They were required to swear allegiance to a symbol of authority used by the regime (a poster of a soldier superimposed on a large phoenix rising from its own ashes), and they had to promise on their knees to obey their commander-in-chief and the military revolution.

While being harassed and beaten by their officers, servicemen were repeatedly told how fortunate they were to have joined the ESA, the strongest and most important support of the regime. They were told that an ESA serviceman's action is never questioned: "You can even flog a major." In-group language helped the men to develop elitist attitudes. Servicemen used nicknames for one another and, later, they used them

Chapter IV
Crime and Violence

for victims and for the different methods of torture. "Tea party" meant the beating of a prisoner by a group of military police using their fists, and "tea party with toast" meant more severe group beatings using clubs. Gradually, the recruits came to speak of all people who were not in their group, parents and families included, as belonging to the "outside world."

The strain of obedience on the recruits was reduced in several ways. During basic training, they were given daily "national ethical education" lectures that included indoctrination against communism and enemies of the state. During more advanced training, the recruits were constantly reminded that the prisoners were "worms," and that they had to "crush" them. One man reported that when he was torturing prisoners later, he caught himself repeating phrases like "bloody communists!" that he had heard in the lectures.

The military police used a carrot-and-stick method to further diminish recruits' uneasiness about torture. There were many rewards, such as relaxed military rules after training was completed, and torturers often weren't punished for leaving camp without permission. They were allowed to wear civilian clothes, to keep their hair long and to drive military police cars for their personal use. Torturers were frequently given a leave of absence after they forced a confession from a prisoner. They had many economic benefits as well, including free bus rides and restaurant meals and job placement when military service was over. These were the carrots.

The sticks consisted of the constant harassment, threats and punishment for disobedience. The men were threatened and intimidated, first by their trainers, then later by senior servicemen. "An officer used to tell us that if a warder helps a prisoner, he will take the prisoner's place and the whole platoon will flog him," one man recalled. Soldiers spied on one another, and even the most successful torturers said that they were constantly afraid.

"You will learn to love pain," one officer promised a recruit. Sensitivity to torture was blunted in several steps. First, the men had to endure it themselves, as if torture were a normal act. The beatings and other torments inflicted on them continued and became worse. Next, the servicemen chosen for the Persecution Section, the unit that tortured political prisoners, were brought into contact with the prisoners by carrying food to their cells. The new men watched veteran soldiers torture prisoners, while they stood guard. Occasionally, the veterans would order them to give the prisoners "some blows."

At the next step, the men were required to participate in group beatings. Later, they were told to use a variety of torture methods on the prisoners. The final step, the appointment to prison warder or chief torturer, was announced suddenly by the commander-in-chief, leaving the men no time to reflect on their new duties.

The Greek example illustrates how the ability to torture can be taught. Training that increases binding and reduces strain can cause decent people to commit acts, often over long periods of time, that otherwise would be unthinkable for them. Similar techniques can be found in military training all over the world, when the intent is to teach soldiers to kill or perform some other repellent act. We conducted extensive interviews with soldiers and exsoldiers in the U.S. Marines and the Green Berets, and we found that all the steps in our training model were part and parcel of elite American military training. Soldiers are screened for intellectual and physical ability, achievement and mental health. Binding begins in basic training, with initiation rites that isolate trainees from society, introduce them to new rules and values and leave them little time for clear thinking after exhausting physical exercise and scant sleep. Harassment plays an important role, and soldiers are severely punished for disobedience, with demerits, verbal abuse, hours of calisthenics and loss of eating, sleeping and other privileges.

Military training gradually desensitizes soldiers to violence and reduces the strain normally created by repugnant acts. Their revulsion is diminished by screaming chants and songs about violence and killing during marches and runs. The enemy is given derogatory names and portrayed as less than human; this makes it easier to kill them. Completing the toughest possible training and being rewarded by "making it" in an elite corps bring the soldiers confidence and pride, and those who accomplish this feel they can do anything. "Although I tried to avoid killing, I learned to have confidence in myself and was never afraid," said a former Green Beret who served in Vietnam. "It was part of the job.... Anyone who goes through that kind of training could do it."

The effectiveness of these techniques, as several researchers have shown, is not limited to the army. History teacher Ronald Jones started what he called the Third Wave movement as a classroom experiment to show his high school students how people might have become Nazis in World War II. Jones began the Third Wave demonstration by requiring students to stand at attention in a unique new posture and follow strict new rules. He required students to stand beside their desks when asking or answering questions and to begin each statement by saying, "Mr. Jones." The students obeyed. He then required them to shout slogans, "Strength through discipline!" and "Strength through community!" Jones created a salute for class members that he called the Third Wave: the right hand raised to the shoulder with fingers curled. The salute had no meaning, but it served as a symbol of group belonging and a way of isolating members from outsiders.

Chapter IV
Crime and Violence

TEACHING TO TORMENT

There are several ways to teach people to do the unthinkable, and we have developed a model to explain how they are used. We have also found that college fraternities, although they are far removed from the grim world of torture and violent combat, use similar methods for initiating new members, to ensure their faithfulness to the fraternity's rules and values. However, this unthinking loyalty can sometimes lead to dangerous actions: Over the past 10 years, there have been countless injuries during fraternity initiations and 39 deaths. These training techniques are designed to instill unquestioning obedience in people, but they can easily be a guide for an intensive course in torture.

1. *Screening to find the best prospects:* normal, well-adjusted people with the physical, intellectual and, in some cases, political attributes necessary for the task.
2. *Techniques to increase binding among these prospects:*
   - Initiation rites to isolate people from society and introduce them to a new social order, with different rules and values.
   - Elitist attitudes and "in-group" language, which highlight the differences between the group and the rest of society.
3. *Techniques to reduce the strain of obedience:*
   - Blaming and dehumanizing the victims, so it is less disturbing to harm them.
   - Harassment, the constant physical and psychological intimidation that prevents logical thinking and promotes the instinctive responses needed for acts of inhuman cruelty.
   - Rewards for obedience and punishments for not cooperating.
   - Social modeling by watching other group members commit violent acts and then receive rewards.
   - Systematic desensitization to repugnant acts by gradual exposure to them, so they appear routine and normal despite conflicts with previous moral standards.

The organization expanded quickly from 20 original members to 100. The teacher issued membership cards and assigned students to report members who didn't comply with the new rules. Dutifully, 20 students pointed accusing fingers at their classmates.

Then Jones announced that the Third Wave was a "nationwide movement to find students willing to fight for political change," and he organized a rally, which drew a crowd of 200 students. At the rally, after getting students to salute and shout slogans on command, Jones explained the true reasons behind the Third Wave demonstration. Like the

Reading 13
Education of a Torturer

Nazis before them, Jones pointed out, "You bargained your freedom for the comfort of discipline."

The students, at an age when group belonging was very important to them, made good candidates for training. Jones didn't teach his students to commit atrocities, and the Third Wave lasted for only five days; in that time, however, Jones created an obedient group that resembled in many ways the Nazi youth groups of World War II (see "The Third Wave: Nazism in a High School," *Psychology Today,* July 1976).

Psychologists Craig Haney, W. Curtis Banks and Philip Zimbardo went even further in a remarkable simulation of prison life done at Stanford University. With no special training and in only six days' time, they changed typical university students into controlling, abusive guards and servile prisoners.

The students who agreed to participate were chosen randomly to be guards or prisoners. The mock guards were given uniforms and nightsticks and told to act as guards. Prisoners were treated as dangerous criminals: Local police rounded them up, fingerprinted and booked them and brought them to a simulated cellblock in the basement of the university psychology department. Uniformed guards made them remove their clothing, deloused them, gave them prison uniforms and put them in cells.

The two groups of students, originally found to be very similar in most respects, showed striking changes within one week. Prisoners became passive, dependent and helpless. In contrast, guards expressed feelings of power, status and group belonging. They were aggressive and abusive within the prison, insulting and bullying the prisoners. Some guards reported later that they had enjoyed their power, while others said they had not thought they were capable of behaving as they had. They were surprised and dismayed at what they had done: "It was degrading.... To me, those things are sick. But they [the prisoners] did everything I said. They abused each other because I requested them to. No one questioned my authority at all."

The guards' behavior was similar in two important ways to that of the Greek torturers. First, they dehumanized their victims. Second, like the torturers, the guards were abusive only when they were within the prison walls. They could act reasonably outside the prisons because the two prison influences of binding and reduced strain were absent.

All these changes at Stanford occurred with no special training, but the techniques we have outlined were still present. Even without training, the student guards "knew" from television and movies that they were supposed to punish prisoners; they "knew" they were supposed to feel superior; and they "knew" they were supposed to blame their victims. Their own behavior and that of their peers gradually numbed their

Chapter IV
Crime and Violence

sensitivity to what they were doing, and they were rewarded by the power they had over their prisoners.

There is no evidence that such short-term experiments produce lasting effects. None were reported from either the Third Wave demonstration or the Stanford University simulation. The Stanford study, however, was cut short when depression, crying and psychosomatic illnesses began to appear among the students. And studies of Vietnam veterans have revealed that committing abhorrent acts, even under the extreme conditions of war, can lead to long-term problems. In one study of 130 Vietnam veterans who came to a therapist for help, almost 30 percent of them were concerned about violent acts they had committed while in the service. The veterans reported feelings of anxiety, guilt, depression and an inability to carry on intimate relationships. In a similar fashion, after the fall of the Greek dictatorship in 1974, former torturers began to report nightmares, irritability and episodes of depression.

"Torturing became a job," said former Greek torturer Petrou. "If the officers ordered you to beat, you beat. If they ordered you to stop, you stopped. You never thought you could do otherwise." His comments bear a disturbing resemblance to the feelings expressed by a Stanford guard: "When I was doing it, I didn't feel regret....I didn't feel guilt. Only afterwards, when I began to reflect...did it begin to dawn on me that this was a part of me I hadn't known before."

We do not believe that torture came naturally to any of these young men. Haritos-Fatouros found no evidence of sadistic, abusive or authoritarian behavior in the Greek soldiers' histories prior to their training. This, together with our study of Marine training and the Stanford and Third Wave studies, leads to the conclusion that torturers have normal personalities. Any of us, in a similar situation, might be capable of the same cruelty. One probably cannot train a deranged sadist to be an effective torturer or killer. He must be in complete control of himself while on the job.

CHAPTER V

ETHNIC AND CLASS DISCRIMINATION

Reading 14

HOW TO KEEP THE POOR ALWAYS WITH US

William Ryan

Our social welfare programs, though attacked as extravagant and useless, are actually a minor part of a two-tiered social policy benefiting the nonpoor more fully than the poor.

Hardly a day goes by on which some expert doesn't remind us smugly that we really can't expect to cure social ills like poverty simply by "throwing federal dollars at them." These experts are apt to go on and explain that we're wasting billions of the taxpayers' dollars on social programs that don't do a damned bit of good. The tax Scrooges among them add the caution that this sentimental waste of good money is threatening to put us all in the poorhouse. In order to engage in any serious consideration of social-welfare and social-policy issues, one must pay some attention to the implications of this rhetoric and, in addition, acquire some knowledge of the relevant facts.

What is it, exactly, that these hard-nosed sophisticates want us to understand by these assertions? Let me try to make their claims a bit more explicit:

- First of all, they expect us to believe that we have been pouring hundreds of billions into social-welfare programs to help the poor. (In the minds of many, the broad term "social welfare" is directly absorbed into the everyday meaning of "welfare" or "relief.")
- They make the further claim that, despite these efforts, the poor remain poor, and their spoken or unspoken explanation is that this is principally because their individual problems or deficiencies cannot be remedied simply by spending money on them.
- Finally, they paint a grim picture for their audience, one showing that all this extravagant generosity to the poor is producing a

From *Equality* by William Ryan. Copyright © 1981 by William Ryan. Reprinted by permission of Pantheon Books, a Division of Random House, Inc.

Chapter V
Ethnic and Class Discrimination

mounting burden of federal taxes, which is bringing the average American to his knees.

What is the reality behind this rhetoric? While it is literally true that about half the federal outlay budget falls under the general rubric of social welfare, we must recognize how inclusive this category is. The fact is that about half of all this money is spent on retirement checks, mostly Social Security payments. The large majority of the recipients of these checks do not belong to the group that most people have in mind when they talk about "the poor." Over twenty million senior citizens receive these checks on the third of every month, the average amount for a retired couple today being something over $500. It must be fairly obvious that the majority of these older persons stay afloat somewhat above the official poverty line precisely because we throw these federal dollars at them.

The two next-largest chunks of the money listed under social welfare are payments to the providers of Medicare services (hospitals, physicians, druggists, and so forth) and grants to the states to help support health, education, and social services—ranging from foster home placement to crippled-children's programs to school lunches.

When we get down to the amount of federal money that goes to welfare recipients, the "poor" in most people's minds, the figure gets quite small. In 1977 it was a bit over $12 billion, out of a total "social welfare" budget of over $250 billion; currently, it is probably about $15 billion. About half of the recipients of this largesse are children in AFDC families, the other half are the aged, blind, and disabled who are not eligible for Social Security. This munificient sum represents, not half the federal budget, but a bit more than 2 percent of it. So, it can be seen that what we call "throwing dollars at poverty" represents only a tiny slice of the budgetary pie. Even during the height of the so-called war on poverty, when the federal budget was racing past the $200 billion mark, the Office of Economic Opportunity, which administered the antipoverty programs, never had an annual budget as large as $2 billion. When it comes to throwing dollars at poverty, there aren't many dollars left, and it doesn't take anyone very long to do the throwing.

Is it true that this spending on social welfare is extravagant and useless? As I argued earlier, some of these programs are effective in reducing inequality somewhat, while others have little or no effect. (Many included under the heading of social welfare are not really relevant to the issue; these include the costs of medical care to members of the armed services, research grants to social scientists, and across-the-board subsidies to medical schools, calculated on the basis of the total number of students enrolled.) The items that are instrumental in reducing inequality to a measurable though relatively small extent are those that I have identified as the relatively "universalistic" social-insurance programs, such as Social Security and unemployment compensation. Cash Social Security benefits to the retired, the disabled, and the surviving spouses and children of breadwinners who died young and weekly compensation checks to the unemployed amounted in 1978 to over $100 billion. Analogous programs—military and civil service retirement, veterans' pensions, railroad retirement pensions, the black-lung program for disabled miners, and the like—add another $30 billion. Medicare accounted for an additional $25 billion. That was almost $160 billion in direct and indirect benefits, going to over 35 million persons. Again, it must be quite obvious that, without this kind of support in the form of social-insurance benefits, most of those 35 million would be in very bad financial trouble indeed. Just considering the elderly, it is beyond the question that there are millions of senior citizens, now supported at some minimal level of dignity and security, who would otherwise be living in unbearable poverty. That is the human meaning of throwing one kind of dollar at social problems. To say that all this has no effect on income inequality and the elimination—or, better, the prevention—of poverty is simply ridiculous.

The exceptionalistic programs, such as welfare and SSI, it is quite true, don't even begin to eliminate poverty. The reason is plain to see: we don't throw enough dollars. To the hapless people dependent on these programs, who number over fifteen million, the majority of them children, we are shamelessly, cruelly stingy.

Of all the individuals who receive benefits from social-welfare programs, a bit more than two-thirds receive some kind of social insurance; the rest receive welfare. We spent ten times as much on social insurance as on welfare. It is rather remarkable, when you come to think of it, that Americans do not appear at all to begrudge the huge amounts we spend on social insurance (essentially to *prevent* poverty) but are brought to the point of outraged frenzy by the relatively small amount we spend on welfare recipients whom we *imprison* in poverty. I say "imprison" advisedly because, obviously, the level of welfare grants guarantees that those who receive them will remain in the lowest depths of poverty.

The grain of truth, then, in the "throwing dollars" charge is that inadequate public assistance—the tiny neglected corner of social welfare—far from solving the poverty problem, is one of its main causes.

The argument that social spending creates spiraling federal taxes, which are bankrupting the average American, is also fallacious. First of all, federal income taxes are not, as we are so frequently told, spiraling up and up. They have remained remarkably stable in relation to income. In absolute figures, of course, taxes go up every year, but they do so at

Chapter V
Ethnic and Class Discrimination

just about the same rate as does gross income. In 1960 federal income taxes were equivalent to 10.5 percent of all personal income; by 1970 the figure had risen to 11.0 percent; by 1977 it had dropped back to 10.6 percent; in 1978 the figure again stood at 11.0 percent; in 1979, at 10.9 percent. In other words, the scarecrow of ballooning federal taxes is a myth.

As for the share of the federal tax burden specifically earmarked for public assistance programs, the average family earning $350 a week spends about $4 a week for all public assistance programs combined (as compared, for example, with $15 a week for national defense). To suggest a more concrete measure of our spending on welfare, for every federal and state tax dollar we spend to support the 7.5 million children on AFDC, we spend over two on liquor and over fifteen on gasoline. This is not to deny that these children are, in fact, a tax burden to the average worker. Many people argue that this is unfair, that it is the responsibility of the natural parents to support these children. But I wonder how long the argument would rage if we all realized how light that burden is. For the average worker, earning $250 a week, the money taken from him for AFDC to support "other men's children," by way of the federal tax deduction, is about fourteen cents a day—the cost of about four cigarettes. All this venom and rage over the cost of four cigarettes a day!

This, then, is the general background. Three questions come to mind:

- How did all this come about?
- What is the purpose of retaining what Alvin Schorr called our two-tiered social-welfare system—universalistic social insurance for the majority and exceptionalistic welfare programs for the despised minority?
- If Americans are ready to support universalistic programs with relatively little grumbling and resentment, why have we not been able to move even further in this direction (as every other industrialized country in the world did long ago)?

The first question can be answered briefly by sketching vignettes of three periods in the history of American social policy—the long period before 1929, the years of the Great Depression in the 1930s, and the decade of the 1960s.

For generations, relief—as it was called—was meager, fragmented, localized, and directed at persons who apparently couldn't make it in the hurly-burly of the free market. Some of these unfortunates were seen as relatively blameless—the ill, widows and orphans, the elderly without families. Others were seen as incompetent and lazy—the drunkard, the malcontent who wanted higher wages than employers were willing to pay, the "town bum," who was found even in the smallest village. The

Reading 14
Keeping the Poor with Us

most basic survival needs of such persons (excluding, whenever possible, the incompetent and lazy) were met primarily by private charities, supplemented by a small amount of local tax money, spent in part for small cash grants, in part to support the grim institutions known as poorhouses or county farms—institutions that remain alive in the memories of many living persons. In 1890 the total amount of tax money spent for such purposes in the entire country was $41 million, mostly by local municipalities.

During these years, the Fair Play ideology was riding high and was closely mirrored in most social arrangements, including philanthropy. The poor, the ill, and the aged, worthy and unworthy alike, were the losers in the great race of life. There were prominent professors and intellectuals who argued that these misfits, nature's marked losers, should simply be allowed to die "for the good of the race," but the great majority of Americans rejected so harsh a solution and made a half-hearted commitment to keep the poor from actually dying of starvation.

It took the Great Depression to bring about a major change both in social-welfare-policy thinking and also in the attitudes and beliefs of the average American. All through those grim years everyone knew many solid, hard-working, righteous people who were unaccountably (and, it began to seem, permanently) impoverished. The able-bodied pauper became commonplace; he was one's uncle or cousin or friend or neighbor and could hardly be branded as improvident or shiftless. There was only one way to distinguish him with certainty from the town bum of one's childhood, and that was to clearly establish a new and more respectable category—the *unemployed*.

In this way the problem of pauperism and idleness—of deviant men who *wouldn't* work—was distinguished from the problem of unemployment—of righteous men who *couldn't find* work. The issue of impoverishment was evaded. The issue of equality never even came up. The issue of jobs was made central, and joblessness was redefined in much more universalistic terms—as a mass phenomenon unrelated to personal characteristics and clearly the result of events external to the individual unemployed person. Programs were rapidly developed that were public, legislated, national in scope, and often directed toward a much larger segment of the population than those traditionally seen as "the poor." The federal government entered for the first time into the arena of cash relief payments. Federally funded programs to provide work were established, such as the Public Works Administration, the Works Progress Administration, and the Civilian Conservation Corps. The implicit *duty* of all to work was becoming something like a *right* to work (for a very low wage, of course).

The Social Security Act of 1935 included near-revolutionary provi-

Chapter V
Ethnic and Class Discrimination

sions for income cushioning that were designed ultimately to protect almost the entire *working* population—social security and unemployment compensation. Both programs were directly related to the experience of work—unemployment insurance if you were laid off from your job, social security pensions based on your having worked most of your life until the age of sixty-five.

For the poor who could not reasonably be defined as able-bodied and eligible for work—again, the traditional widow with small children, the aged, the disabled, the blind—means-tested categorical assistance programs were included, now organized in a more universalistic fashion in some respects, but retaining all the exceptionalistic features of old-fashioned relief.

During the same years, an equally significant piece of legislation, the Wagner Act, guaranteeing labor unions the rights to organize and to engage in collective bargaining, finally gave full legal recognition to the reality that employer-employee relationships were not a series of one-to-one contracts, but that the work force of a firm was a collective entity that could act as such.

The crisis of the Great Depression, then, produced a remarkable upsurge of universalism in thinking about social problems and a dramatic alteration in developments in official social policies. Even the essentially exceptionalistic programs established at that time, and still with us as our public assistance welfare programs, were pushed in the direction of universalism, in that after 1935 the welfare program was national in scope, under federal supervision and with a dramatic increase in public funding.

The next major event, the so-called war on poverty, occurred in the 1960s, following a rediscovery of want in the midst of affluence and the growth of the civil rights movement. The theorizing and the rhetoric accompanying the declaration of war against poverty were, interestingly enough, deeply imbued with universalistic themes. There was a rapid jelling of a consensus about the target to be attacked, namely, the "opportunity structure," the structural barriers built into the fabric of society that kept the poor penned in poverty. But, as the experts translated the rhetoric into actual programs, the target changed subtly but dramatically. All the major poverty programs—Head Start, Adult Education, Manpower Training, Concerted Social Services—were specifically aimed, not at the "opportunity structure," but at the poor themselves. The goal, of course, became the elimination of undesirable internal deficiencies of individuals. The war on poverty was announced in ringing tones with the vow that we would pursue the war to its bitter end. The bitter end was that poverty won.

For forty years now, since our brief romance with openly universalistic programs, we have persisted with our two-tiered social policy, while the rest of the world has far outstripped us in developing social insurance and other universalistic approaches. And it is important to note that variations of this two-tiered system are evident in many other areas of our life. Take housing, for example. Public housing and its alternatives, such as leased housing and rental assistance, are straightforward means-tested programs for the certifiable poor. For middle-income and well-to-do people, we also have housing-assistance programs, but they are almost invisible in their universality—I refer, of course, to income tax exemptions for mortgage interest payments and real estate taxes. These are available to everyone, with no test of eligibility (other than the minor matter of financial capacity to own one's home), and the consequent savings are a direct subsidy to the homeowner from the federal government in precisely the same sense that the relatively low rents in public housing projects are a subsidy to their tenants. The tax deductions that constitute a subsidy to homeowners, however, involve a far greater sum of money than the amount invested in the housing-assistance programs for the poor. But, of course, we homeowners simply take this as our right, our natural entitlement. It never occurs to us that the government is giving us something for nothing.

Transportation offers another example. Public investment in transportation for the poor—that is, public transportation systems—has been minuscule in comparison with the enormous investment in subsidizing interstate highways, airlines, trucking companies, and expressways that conveniently carry commuters to their suburbs.

The general principle seems to be that if a service or social program benefits the well-to-do at least as much as the poor, and preferably a good deal more, it will be organized along universalistic lines. The development of public fire and police departments, of state and national parks and other recreation areas, of polio vaccination, and of sewage disposal systems illustrates this point.

Movement toward universalism, on the other hand, is aborted, transformed, or somehow thwarted and crippled, when it involves any threat of real advance toward greater equalization in the distribution of economic well-being, or even toward the lesser goal of eliminating extreme poverty. I don't believe that public attitudes account for the persistence of exceptionalistic programs. For one thing, as I suggested, the public is dramatically more positive and generous in its attitude toward our universalistic social-insurance programs. In discussions of them we rarely are confronted with the spitefulness that almost always emerges in reaction to any mention of "the poor" or of "welfare people."

Although Americans have been confused and deceived in various ways, they seem almost instinctively committed to universalistic ap-

Chapter V
Ethnic and Class Discrimination

proaches to social policy. Social Security, for example, is now a sacrosanct institution in American life, and any proposal to alter its nature—to make it a voluntary rather than an all-inclusive legislated program, for example—meets with violent disapproval. For as long as there have been records of public opinion on the issue, at least fifty years, Americans have been overwhelmingly in favor of some national program of medical care like federal health insurance.

So true is this that many exceptionalistic programs, designed intentionally or unintentionally to preserve inequality, are set before the public as universalistic schemes. A good example is the Nixon administration's Family Assistance Plan, devised by Daniel P. Moynihan as a substitute for our present public assistance program, and presented to the public under the guise of a "reform" that would institute a "guaranteed annual income." It was, of course, nothing of the kind; it was even more selective than our present system, included provisions for what amounted to forced labor at less than minimum-wage rates, even for mothers of young children, and set income levels far below the government's own poverty line. It was, however, decorated with some universalistic ornaments, such as national administration and standards, the elimination of specific categories, and the inclusion of the working poor, and those universalistic features were its major selling points. The scheme—one of the most insidious attacks on poor people in our history—was narrowly defeated, primarily because of intensive lobbying efforts by poor people's organizations led by George Wiley; yet to this day it is referred to by political columnists and other observers as the progressive Nixon-Moynihan guaranteed-income plan. This probably illustrates why truth-in-labeling laws are so necessary for the protection of consumers.

Nevertheless, gradual movement toward more universalism in social-policy and social-welfare programming contains within itself the seeds of change, the potential leverage for increased equality in our society, depending on the acuteness with which the programs that ultimately emerge are analyzed and explained to the general public. The growing demand for some kind of national health-care program, and the increasing response to this demand on the part of politicians, is a case in point. Such a universalistic program would almost certainly reduce inequality in two ways—it would help to equalize the health *status* of all, and it would reduce the *economic* burden of health care for the great majority of the population.

Reading 15
THE FEMINIZATION OF GHETTO POVERTY

Diana M. Pearce

> *More than fifty percent of the families in poverty are headed by women, and three-quarters of the poor are women and children. This imbalance is the result of a web of inequalities in the economic system and long-term trends in marriage and childbearing practices. Pearce discusses the inadequate policies and the discriminatory biases aimed at women, and particularly Black women, that make it likely that this new form of poverty will continue to grow.*

The "other America" is a changing neighborhood: men are moving out; women and their children are moving in. This dramatic change is not a reaction to recent fluctuations in the economy, but instead reflects long-term structural shifts both in the labor market and in marriage and childbearing practices. Today, three-quarters of the poor are women and children.

The poverty *rate* for female-headed households has remained steady over the past decade, with just under one-third of these families living in poverty. But because a significant number of male-headed households have left poverty, and because the number of households headed by women has increased, the proportion of *poor* families that are maintained by women has risen in the 1970s from 36 percent to more than 50 percent. Moreover, there is evidence that the trend is accelerating. Between 1969 and 1978, there was an annual net increase of 100,000 female-headed families in poverty, but in the two years between 1978 and 1980, the net increase each year was approximately 150,000. Furthermore, according to Reynolds Farley and Suzanne Bianchi, families headed by women have experienced a decline in economic status over the past two decades, with their average income dropping from 77 percent to 62 percent of the average income of white husband-and-wife families, and from 63 percent to 47 percent of black husband-and-wife families.

Reprinted with permission from *Society* (November/December, 1983): 70–74.

Chapter V
Ethnic and Class Discrimination

These trends are appearing even more strongly in the black community. Although the proportion of the poor who are black did not change during the 1970s, the proportion who were in families headed by women increased. Indeed, the decade of the seventies saw a dramatic shift of the burden of poverty among blacks from male-headed to female-headed families. The number of black families in poverty who were maintained by men declined by 35 percent, while the number maintained by women *increased* by 62 percent. In the course of one decade, black female-headed families increased from about one-half to three-fourths of all poor black families.

Some elements of the experience of being poor are common to all women; that is, they are a function of gender. Others, however, are the effect of race, though even these are experienced differently by men and women, as we shall see.

Though poor women share many characteristics in common with poor men (such as low education, lack of market-relevant job skills, or location in job-poor areas), the greater rates of poverty among women can be traced to two distinctly female causes. First of all, women who head their families often bear most or all of the economic burden of raising the children. Secondly, because of sex discrimination, occupational segregation in a segmented labor market, and sexual harassment, women who seek to support themselves and their families through paid work are disadvantaged in the labor market.

If a woman is married, even if she is employed outside the home, she shares substantially in the resources obtained by her husband. That transfer drops off dramatically when the parents no longer live together. In 1975, for example, only 25 percent of the women eligible actually received child support, and for more than half of those, the annual income from child-support payments was less than $1,500. If the parents were never married, the picture is even worse; only 5 percent of these fathers provide child support. Ironically, a woman is better off if her husband is dead, for widows are the best protected against income loss following the loss of a spouse and are therefore least likely to be poor. However, receipt of such transfers is unlikely to provide much of a bulwark against poverty; the average amount as of 1978 was about $1,800, and the duration is generally only a few years.

Accordingly, many women seek income through paid employment. For all too many, this goes against their lifelong expectations and preparations. Although it is true that most women today expect to work or have worked, sex-role socialization in general and vocational preparation in particular do not prepare women to be the *primary* breadwinner. Instead, the traditional emphasis has been on jobs, rather than careers, and on making job choices that emphasize flexibility and adaptability, rather than income potential. Thus, women faced with the necessity of being the sole source of support for themselves and their children are handicapped.

These handicaps are reinforced by a highly discriminatory labor market. Despite increased attention given this problem—including litigation and legislation—continuing high levels of *occupational segregation* of women stand in marked contrast to the decline of racial segregation in employment and education. Women who work full time continue to earn only 59 cents on the dollar earned by men who work full time. And while we do not know with precision the magnitude of the problem, it is increasingly evident that large numbers of women experience sexual harassment and thereby incur heavy economic, as well as personal, costs in lost recommendations, denied promotions, abrupt dismissals, and demotions.

BEING BLACK, FEMALE, AND POOR

The inequality experienced by women in the labor market has been conceptualized by some as confinement to the secondary sector of a dual labor market. According to the dual-economy theory, jobs and industries are readily divided into primary and the secondary sectors, and this division is reinforced by barriers that make it difficult for workers to move from one sector to another. In the primary sector, jobs are characterized by good pay and fringe benefits, job security, a high degree of unionization, good working conditions, and due process in job rights. In contrast, the secondary sector includes work in marginal industries; these jobs are low-paying, often seasonal or sporadic, less likely to be unionized, and offer little protection against the vagaries of either the individual employer or the ups and downs of the marketplace.

The duality of the labor market is complemented and reinforced by a parallel duality in the welfare system. There is a primary welfare sector in which benefits are conferred as a right, often (but not always) because they have been "earned." One is not stigmatized by receipt of these benefits, nor must one demonstrate poverty or suffer degrading, detailed investigations of one's lifestyle. The benefits are more generous, often with minimum or national levels set by the federal government. Not only are benefit levels relatively generous, but one does not have to exhaust one's resources to qualify; nor are benefits reduced in proportion to other income. Examples of primary-welfare-sector benefits include unemployment compensation and social security.

In contrast, the secondary welfare sector is characterized by benefits that are much lower, on the average, and highly variable across states and even across localities within a state. Since such benefits are a privi-

Chapter V
Ethnic and Class Discrimination

lege, not received by right, they may be revoked arbitrarily and for different reasons in different places. They may be, and usually are, reduced in proportion to other income. Receipt of welfare, in the eyes of the public and many recipients, is stigmatizing and demoralizing.

For those in the secondary sector of either the labor market or the welfare system, escape is difficult. This is especially so for women and minorities. For a variety of reasons, the welfare system and related training and jobs programs (such as WIN and CETA) do not overcome the labor-market barriers faced by women. For example, training is often for traditionally female occupations, such as clerical work or food service, occupations that do not pay wages adequate to support a woman and even one child. The stubborn obsession with getting women off welfare and into jobs as quickly as possible, with no attention to their special needs (e.g., for child care or fringe benefits that include adequate health insurance), has long-term results that are counterproductive. Those who accept or are forced to take economically marginal jobs in the secondary sector quickly find that they do not have access to the primary welfare sector when they lose or are laid off from these jobs. They are then forced to depend on impoverished secondary-welfare-sector programs. Thus, the interlocking secondary welfare system and secondary labor market reinforce a vicious circle of welfare dependency and marginal work.

Women and minorities are concentrated in the secondary welfare sector. As shown in Table 1, whereas men are slightly overrepresented and women underrepresented in the primary welfare sector, there is a severe sex discrepancy in the secondary sector. Less than half of white men receive secondary-sector benefits according to their proportion in the population, while three times the number of white women—and six times the number of black women—receive income from the secondary welfare sector according to their proportions in the population.

Many, of course, receive income from earnings as well as from transfer programs, but since the receipt of primary-sector benefits is strongly associated with previously held primary-sector *jobs*, the figures in Table 1 indicate implicitly the effect of differential participation not only in the primary and secondary welfare sectors, but also in the primary and secondary labor markets. (Theoretically, one could receive income from primary as well as from secondary welfare programs, but Census Bureau data show that few actually do.)

If one compares poverty rates across gender and race categories, several conclusions suggest themselves. First, the poverty rate for those receiving benefits (and perhaps, also, earnings) in the secondary sector (67.7%) is more than eleven times the rate for those in the primary sector (5.5%). Second, within each sector, the poverty rates are greater for

Reading 15
Feminization of Ghetto Poverty

Table 1
PRIMARY VERSUS SECONDARY WELFARE SECTORS, 1978

	All Household Heads		Primary Sector [a]		Secondary Sector [b]	
	Percentage	Poverty Rate	Percentage	Poverty Rate	Percentage	Poverty Rate
Men[c]						
white	79.2	4.7	81.5	4.0	30.2	35.7
black	6.2	11.8	7.3	7.2	10.1	36.9
Subtotal	85.4	5.3	88.8	4.3	40.3	36.1
Women[d]						
white	10.4	23.5	8.9	10.4	28.7	66.8
black	4.2	50.6	2.3	32.3	30.9	75.8
Subtotal	14.6	31.4	11.2	15.1	59.6	71.2
Total	100.0		100.0	5.5	100.0	67.7

a. Includes unemployment and workmen's compensation, veterans' benefits
b. Includes all types of cash public assistance (aid to families with dependent children, general assistance, etc.)
c. Both male-only and husband-and-wife households
d. Female householder, no husband

Source: U.S. Census Bureau, *Characteristics of the Population below the Poverty Level: 1978*, Series P-60, No. 124

blacks than for whites, and greater for women than for men; but the gender differentials are greater than the racial ones. In this connection, the differences in poverty rates between black and white men within each sector are quite small, whereas there is a substantial added disadvantage to being both black and female. The "double" disadvantage experienced by black women is actually, in quantitative terms, a geometrically increasing "quadruple" disadvantage.

SPECIAL EFFECTS

It is clear from the data that although much of the economic gulf is accounted for by gender, black women experience considerable further disadvantages associated with race. These disadvantages can be grouped into three areas for purposes of discussion: trends in racial desegregation in various areas, demographic trends, and welfare programs.

Considerable occupational desegregation has been experienced by both men and women. This has meant an exodus from extremely low-paying jobs (often irregular and part-time), particularly in household service, that have been race/sex "occupational ghettoes." But because *sex* segregation levels, which have always been higher than those of race, have remained quite high, and because the wages of women have remained at less than 60 percent of men's wages, black men have benefited more from the racial desegregation of occupations than black women. Thus, statistics purporting to show that black women are closing the gap on white women faster than black men are on white men are misleading. The use of white women as a benchmark is inappropriate, for it eliminates the effects of gender. If one compares the progress of black men and black women to that of white men, then at present rates black men will catch up to white men in 35 years, but it will take black women 135 years to achieve occupational parity with white men.

In other areas, there have been parallel developments. For example, as Robert Crain and Rita Mehard have pointed out, school desegregation has opened up opportunities for black students of both sexes and, therefore, has resulted in increased achievement levels. Continued sex segregation of vocational programs, however, has the consequence of channeling women students into lower-paying occupations. For obvious economic reasons, housing desegregation has been experienced disproportionately by two-parent, two-income black families. In sum, racial desegregation has had a much greater impact on families with a male householder.

More than 40 percent of black families, and more than 50 percent of those with children, are headed by a single parent (almost all of which are women). This is partly related to high divorce rates, but several other factors have contributed to the growth of single-parent homes. One of these is the high ratio of out-of-wedlock births—now at about 55 percent for blacks. Many of these children are born to teenagers. Black women tend to marry or remarry at lower rates than white women, and they tend to remain single longer if they do marry. This is, in part, because of a shortage of black men of marriageable age. For example, the ratio (in the resident population) of black women to men, ages 20 to 49 is 1.16 (the white ratio is 1.01); in other words, there are sixteen "extra" black women for every hundred black men.

This imbalance in the sex ratio is the result of several factors, including higher levels of suicide and homicide among black men and an incredible incarceration rate for young black men—phenomena that are directly related to very high levels of poverty, underemployment, and unemployment. While it is true that *being a single parent* causes poverty, it is also clear that the widespread poverty among young black men, and their less-than-cheerful prospects for future economic stability, is an important *cause* of the formation of single-parent households among blacks.

Reading 15
Feminization of Ghetto Poverty

The converse also holds, so that marriage is as much the result of economic security, well-being, and upward mobility as it is the cause of economic well-being among families. In this connection, Farley and Bianchi find that the black community is not becoming polarized along traditional class lines (such as occupation or education), but that there is a polarization along *marital-status* lines. Two-parent families are increasing their economic status while families headed by women become poorer, opening up a different kind of schism in black America.

All of the factors noted above play a part in the racial differences seen in patterns of welfare use. Keeping in mind that these differences are relative, and that there is high degree of overlap among the factors, I will briefly examine some of the differences between white and black women who are welfare recipients.

White women tend more often to be divorced (as opposed to being single or separated). They also tend to come to welfare with more resources (including education, work experience, and even ownership of a house and/or a more favorable residential location vis-á-vis job opportunities. On the other hand, white women are also less likely to be employed and are more likely to go on welfare as a result of the loss of a husband's earnings. Because of this combination of more immediate need and yet greater "long-run" resources, white women not only tend to be on welfare for shorter periods of time, they are also more fully dependent during the time that they are on welfare. In contrast, more black women come to welfare as a result of unemployment and underemployment. Whereas white women often leave welfare because they have obtained a job or remarried (or both), black women are less likely to find a job—at least one providing sufficient income to support themselves and their family—and are less likely to marry or remarry.

In sum, white women tend more often to use welfare for shorter periods of time, even though welfare accounts for most (if not all) of their income while they are on welfare. Black women who head households, in contrast, are more likely to use welfare for longer periods of time, but in conjunction with earnings and other sources of income (e.g., child support), and are less likely to be totally dependent upon welfare, particularly over a period of years. Again, it should be remembered that these racial differences are relative. It should be emphasized, too, that the differences between women householders who use welfare and those that do not are not all that great. Data reported by Martin Rein and Lee Rainwater show that among those who were heavily dependent on welfare over a seven-year period, almost 30 percent of annual income came from earnings, while among low-income families who did not use welfare during that period, about 70 percent of annual income came from earn-

Chapter V
Ethnic and Class Discrimination

ings. Phillip AuClaire estimates that about 58 percent of the annual income of long-term welfare recipients who were also employed came from earnings.

THE WORKHOUSE WITHOUT WALLS

Black women experience quantitatively more poverty than either black men or white women, no matter what the circumstances or income source. But there is also an important qualitative difference not made explicit by the above discussion. The various causes of white women's poverty can be traced back to a single, fundamental source—sexism, perpetuated mainly by white men. Only in a sexist society can the breakup of a marriage actually improve the economic well-being of the father, cause the mother and children to suffer a large drop in economic status, and permit most fathers to provide little or no support to their children. The low wages afforded women of equal education and experience cannot be explained away as anything except sex discrimination. The poverty of black women, in contrast, is related to more complex factors. Black men are rarely in the position of employers and, therefore, are hardly able to determine the wage scales of women vis-á-vis men. And for many black men, their own high rates of unemployment and low income make the question of sharing income with their children and their children's mothers moot. Thus, in addition to the sources of poverty experienced by all women—the economic burden of children, labor-market discrimination and duality, a welfare system that provides penurious benefits and no training/support system—black women experience directly and, through black men, indirectly the effects or racial discrimination.

A further qualitative difference experienced by black women is that their poverty has a more permanent, or at least, indefinite quality. They, of course, bear the burden of poverty in the black community, a community that as a whole has long had much more poverty than the white community. Thus, because of the greater economic resources in the white community, white women stand a much greater chance of leaving poverty through marriage than black women. Black women are more likely to experience what I have called the "workhouse without walls," in which they support themselves through a combination of earnings, welfare, child support, and other transfers, whether concurrently or serially.

It is evident that, within the black community, there is a growing gulf between two-parent, two-earner families and families headed by women. It is also clear that the high unemployment rates among black youth which contribute to the formation of single-parent families, together with the sexism in the labor/welfare system which locks women householders into poverty, are resulting in increasing proportions of black children being born into and/or growing up in families that must struggle every day with poverty.

SUGGESTED READINGS

AuClaire, Phillip A. 1979. "The mix of work and welfare among long-term AFDC recipients." *Social Service Review* (December): 586–606.

Crain, Robert L., and Mehard, Rita E. 1981. "Minority achievement: Policy implications of research," in Willis D. Hawley (ed.), *Effective School Desegregation*. Beverly Hills, Calif.: Sage.

Farley, Reynolds, and Bianchi, Suzanne M. 1982. "Social and economic polarization: Is it occurring among blacks?" Paper presented at the annual meeting of the American Sociological Association, San Francisco, August.

Pearce, Diana M. 1978. "The feminization of poverty: Women, work and welfare." *The Urban and Social Change Review* 11: 28–36.

Piore, Michael J. 1971. "The dual labor market: Theory and implications," in David M. Gordon (ed.), *Problems in Political Economy: An Urban Perspective*. Lexington, Mass.: Heath, 1971.

Reagan, Barbara. 1974. "Comments on Ashenfelter and Heckman Paper." Prepared for the MIT Research Workshop on Equal Employment Opportunity, January.

Rein, Martin, and Rainwater, Lee. 1978. "Patterns of welfare use." *Social Service Review* (December): 511–34.

Schulman, Joanne. 1981. "Poor women and family law." *Clearinghouse Review* (February).

U.S. Bureau of the Census. 1981. *Child Support and Alimony: 1978*. Special Studies, series P-23, no. 112. Washington, D.C.: U.S. Government Printing Office.

Reading 16
RACE-SPECIFIC POLICIES AND THE TRULY DISADVANTAGED

William Julius Wilson

> *It has been incorrectly assumed that race-specific programs would help all Blacks. The policies developed during the civil rights movement were primarily beneficial to more advantaged Blacks. The truly disadvantaged have benefited very little. Wilson proposes a new direction for preferential treatment toward all people who are defined as disadvantaged by their lack of competitive resources due to their economic-class background.*

In the period following the thirtieth anniversary of the 1954 Supreme Court decision against racial separation, Brown v. the Board of Education of Topeka, Kansas, and the twentieth anniversary of the 1964 Civil Rights Act, a troubling dilemma confronts proponents of racial equality and social justice. The dilemma is that while the socioeconomic status of the most disadvantaged members of the minority population has deteriorated rapidly since 1970, that of advantaged members has significantly improved. This is perhaps most clearly seen in the changes that have occurred within the American black population in recent years.

In several areas, blacks have not only improved their social and economic positions in recent years, but have made those improvements at a relatively faster rate than the reported progress of comparable whites. The most notable gains have occurred in professional employment, income of married-couple families, higher education, and home ownership. The number of blacks in professional, technical, managerial, and administrative positions increased by 57 percent (from 974,000 to 1,533,000) from 1973 to 1982, while the number of whites in such positions increased by only 36 percent (U.S. Department of Labor, 1983). The

---

From William Julius Wilson, *The Truly Disadvantaged: The Inner City, The Underclass and Public Policy,* Chicago: University of Chicago Press, 1987, pp. 109–120. Reprinted with permission.

Reading 16
Race-Specific Policies and the Disadvantaged

median annual income for black married-couple families in 1982 was $20,586, compared to $26,443 for white married-couple families. The gap was even narrower in households where both husband and wife were employed; this was especially true for couples between the ages of twenty-four and thirty-five, where the difference in annual income between blacks and whites was less than $3,000. And the fraction of black families earning $25,000 or more (in 1982 dollars) increased from 10.4 percent in 1960 to 24.5 percent in 1982. Meanwhile, the number of blacks enrolled full time at American colleges and universities nearly doubled between 1970 and 1980 (going from 522,000 to over 1 million) (Puckrein, 1984). Blacks recorded a 47 percent increase in home ownership during the 1970s (from 2.57 million to 3.78 million), compared to a 30 percent increase for whites (U.S. Bureau of the Census, 1983).

But for millions of other blacks, most of them concentrated in the ghettos of American cities, the past three decades have been a time of regression, not progress.... These low-income families and individuals are, in several important respects, more socially and economically isolated than before the great civil rights victories, particularly in terms of high joblessness and the related problems of poverty, family instability, and welfare dependency.

These changes are reflected in a growing economic schism between lower-income and higher-income black families.... The percentage of total black family income attributable to the lowest two-fifths of black families declined from 15.8 percent in 1966 to 13.4 percent by 1981; the upper two-fifths of black families contributed 67.3 percent of the total in 1966, but 70.6 percent in 1981. The lowest two-fifths of white families, on the other hand, contributed 18.2 percent to the total white family income in 1966, and 17.1 percent in 1981; the upper two-fifths of white families contributed 64 percent in 1966, and 65.4 percent in 1981. The index of income concentration (a statistical measure of income inequality ranging from zero, which indicates perfect equality, to one, which reveals perfect inequality) reveals that income inequality is greater and has increased at a faster rate among black families than among white families from 1966 to 1981.

...The factors associated with the growing woes of low-income blacks are exceedingly complex and go beyond the narrow issue of contemporary discrimination. Indeed, it would not be unreasonable to contend that the race-specific policies emanating from the civil rights revolution, although beneficial to more advantaged blacks (i.e., those with higher income, greater education and training, and more prestigious occupations), do little for those who are truly disadvantaged. The Harvard black economist Glenn Loury (1984) has argued in this connection that

Chapter V
Ethnic and Class Discrimination

It is clear from extensive empirical research on the effect of affirmative action standards for federal contractors, that the positive impact on blacks which this program has had accrues mainly to those in the higher occupations. If one examines the figures on relative earnings of young black and white men by educational class, by far the greater progress has been made among those blacks with the most education. If one looks at relative earnings of black and white workers by occupation going back to 1950, one finds that the most dramatic earning gains for blacks have taken place in the professional, technical, and managerial occupations, while the least significant gains have come in the lowest occupations, like laborer and service worker. Thus a broad array of evidence suggests, at least to this observer, that better placed blacks have simply been able to take more advantage of the opportunities created in the last twenty years than have those mired in the underclass.

The crucial point is not that the deteriorating plight of the ghetto underclass is associated with the greater success enjoyed by advantaged blacks as a result of race-specific programs, but rather that these programs are mistakenly presumed to be the most appropriate solution to the problems of all blacks regardless of economic class. In the following sections this argument is explored in some detail, beginning with a critical discussion of the basic assumptions associated with two liberal principals that underlie recent, but entirely different, policy approaches to problems of race, namely, equality of individual opportunity, which stresses the rights of minority individuals, and equality of group opportunity, which embodies the idea of preferential treatment for minority groups.

EGALITARIAN PRINCIPLES OF RACE AND DISADVANTAGED MEMBERS OF MINORITIES

The goals of the civil rights movement have changed considerably in the last fifteen to twenty years. This change has been reflected in the shift in emphasis from the rights of minority individuals to the preferential treatment of minority groups. The implementation of the principle of equality of group rights results in the formal recognition of racial and ethnic groups by the state, as well as economic, educational, and political rewards based on formulas of group membership (Gordon, 1981). Although many of the proponents of this principle argue that preferential treatment is only a temporary device to overcoming the effects of previous discrimination, this shift in precepts has long divided the civil rights movement, which, in the early 1960s, was unified behind the principle of equality of individual opportunity.

However, neither programs based on equality of individual opportu-

Reading 16
Race-Specific Policies and the Disadvantaged

nity nor those organized in terms of preferential group treatment are sufficient to address the problems of truly disadvantaged minority group members. Let us consider, first of all, the principle of equality of individual rights which dominated the early phases of the civil rights movement.

At mid-twentieth century, liberal black and white leaders of the movement for racial equality agreed that the conditions of racial and ethnic minorities could best be improved by an appeal to the conscience of white Americans to uphold the American creed of egalitarianism and democracy. These leaders directed their efforts to eliminating Jim Crow segregation statutes through Supreme Court litigation, pressing for national legislation to outlaw discrimination in employment and housing, and breaking down the extralegal obstacles to black voting in the South (Gordon, 1975).

It was assumed that the government could best protect the rights of individual members of minority groups not by formally bestowing rewards and punishments based on racial or ethnic categories, but by using antidiscrimination legislation to enhance individual freedom of choice in education, employment, voting, and public accommodations. The individual, therefore, was "the unit of attribution for equity considerations" (Gordon, 1981), and the ultimate goal was to reward each citizen based on his or her merits and accomplishments. In short, equality of opportunity meant equality for citizens.

Thus, from the 1950s to 1970, emphasis was on the equality of individual opportunity, or freedom of choice; the approved role of government was to ensure that people were not formally categorized on the basis of race. Antidiscrimination legislation was designed to eliminate racial bias without considering the actual percentage of minorities in certain positions. These actions upheld the underlying principle of equality of individual rights, namely, that candidates for positions stratified in terms of prestige or other social criteria should be judged solely on individual merit and therefore ought not be discriminated against on the basis of race or ethnic origin.

It would be ideal if programs based on this principle were sufficient to address problems of inequality in our society because they are consistent with the prevailing ideals of democracy and freedom of choice, do not call for major sacrifices on the part of the larger population, and are not perceived as benefiting certain groups at the expense of others. The "old" goals of the civil rights movement, in other words, were more in keeping with "traditional" American values, and thus more politically acceptable than the "new" goals of equal opportunity for groups through a system of collective racial and ethnic entitlements. However, programs based solely on the principle of equality of individual opportu-

Chapter V
Ethnic and Class Discrimination

nity are inadequate to address the complex problems of group inequality in America.

More specifically, as James Fishkin (1983) appropriately points out, this principle does not address the substantive inequality that exists at the time the bias is removed. In other words, centuries or even decades of racial subjugation can result in a system of racial inequality that may linger on for indefinite periods of time after racial barriers are eliminated. This is because the most disadvantaged minority group members, who have been crippled or victimized by the cumulative effects of both race and class subordination (including those effects passed on from generation to generation), are disproportionately represented among that segment of the total population that lacks the resources to compete effectively in a free and open market. The black columnist William Raspberry recognized this problem when he stated: "There are some blacks for whom it is enough to remove the artificial barriers of race. After that, their entry into the American mainstream is virtually automatic. There are others for whom hardly anything would change if, by some magical stroke, racism disappeared from America. Everyone knows this of course. And yet hardly anyone is willing to say it. And because we don't say it, we wind up confused about how to deal with the explosive problems confronting the American society, confused about what the problem really is" (Raspberry, 1980).

It is important to recognize that in modern industrial society the removal of racial barriers creates the greatest opportunities for the better-trained, talented, and educated segments of the minority population—those who have been crippled the least by the weight of past discrimination. This is because they possess the resources that allow them to compete freely with dominant group members for valued positions. In this connection, as Leroy D. Clark and Judy Trent Ellis (1980) have noted,

> there must be a recognition that civil rights legislation can only benefit those in a position to take advantage of it. To the extent that some members of minority groups have been denied education and certain work experience, they will be able to compete for only a limited number of jobs. Certain disabilities traceable in general to racism may deprive some minority members of the qualifications for particular jobs. Title VII, however, protects only against arbitrary use of race or its equivalents as a barrier to work; it does not assure one of employment or promotion if legitimate qualifications are lacking.

In short, the competitive resources developed by the advantaged minority members—resources "resulting from the income, family stability, peer groups, and schooling that their parents can make available to

*Reading 16
Race-Specific Policies and the Disadvantaged*

them" (Fishkin, 1983: 92)—result in their benefiting disproportionately from policies that promote the rights of minority *individuals,* policies that remove artificial barriers and thereby enable individuals to compete freely and openly for the more desirable and prestigious positions in American society.

However, since 1970, government policy has tended to focus on the equitable distribution of *group* rights, so that people have been formally categorized or recognized on the basis of race or ethnicity. Formal programs have been designed and created not only to prevent discrimination, but also to ensure that minorities are adequately represented in certain positions. Thus emphasis has shifted from equality of opportunity, stressing individual rights, to equality of condition, emphasizing group rights. Between the mid-1950s and 1970, the elimination of existing discrimination was the sole concern of liberal policymakers; since 1970, however, serious attention has also been given to negating the effects of past discrimination. This has resulted in a move from the simple investigation and adjudication of complaints of racial discrimination by fair employment practices commissions and civil rights commissions to government-mandated affirmative action programs designed to ensure minority representation in employment, in public programs, and in education (Raspberry, 1980).

Nonetheless, if the more advantaged minority members profit disproportionately from policies built on the principle of equality of individual opportunity, they also reap disproportionate benefits from policies of preferential treatment based solely on their group membership. I say this because minority individuals from the most advantaged families are likely to be disproportionately represented among the minority members most qualified for preferred positions—such as higher-paying jobs, college admissions, promotions, and so forth. Accordingly, if policies of preferential treatment for such positions are conceived not in terms of the actual disadvantages suffered by individuals but rather in terms of race or ethnic group membership, then these policies will further enhance the opportunities of the more advantaged without addressing the problems of the truly disadvantaged. In other words, programs such as affirmative action "can be very effective in increasing the rate of progress for minorities who are doing reasonably well" (Raspberry, 1980). Special admission programs that enlarge the number of minorities in law schools and medical schools, and special programs that increase minority representation in high-level government jobs, in the foreign service, and on university faculties not only favor minorities from advantaged backgrounds but require a college education to begin with. To repeat: programs of preferential treatment applied merely according to racial or

Chapter V
Ethnic and Class Discrimination

ethnic group membership tend to benefit the relatively advantaged segments of the designated groups. The truly deprived members may not be helped by such programs.

Nonetheless, as William L. Taylor has argued, "the focus of much of the [affirmative action] effort has been not just on white collar jobs, but also on law enforcement, construction work, and craft and production jobs in large companies—all areas in which the extension of new opportunities has provided upward mobility for less advantaged minority workers." Taylor also notes that "studies show that of the increased enrollment of minority students in medical schools during the 1970s, significant numbers were from families of low income and job status, indicating that the rising enrollments of minorities in professional schools stemming from affirmative action policies reflects increased mobility, not simply changing occupational preferences among middle-class minority families (Taylor, 1986). However, although affirmative action programs do in fact create opportunities for some less advantaged minority individuals, ghetto underclass individuals are severely underrepresented among those who have actually benefited from such programs. In other words, upon close examination what we really see is a "creaming" process in the sense that those with the greatest economic, educational, and social resources among the less advantaged individuals are the ones who are actually tapped for higher paying jobs and higher education through affirmative action.

It has been argued, however, that group preferential treatment based on race, although more directly beneficial to advantaged minority members, will "trickle down" to the minority poor. Thus, a government policy favoring minority business would ultimately lead to greater employment opportunities for the black poor. Affirmative action programs designed to increase the number of blacks in medical schools would thus ultimately result in improved medical care for low-income blacks. Indeed, these programs are often justified on the ground that they would improve the black poor's chances in life. "The question should be raised though as to how the black poor are to be benefited by the policy actions extracted from the system in their name," observes Glenn Loury. "The evidence of which I am aware suggests that, for many of the most hotly contested public policies advocated by black spokesmen, not much of the benefit 'trickles down' to the black poor. There is no study, of which I am aware, supporting the claim that set-asides for minority businesses have led to a significant increase in the level of employment among lower class blacks" (Loury, 1984: 14).

But what about the argument, often heard during the heated debate over the *Bakke* decision, that increasing the percentage of blacks in medical schools will result in improvements in medical care for lower-income

Reading 16
Race-Specific Policies and the Disadvantaged

blacks? Although there is virtually no definitive research on this question, I believe that we would not improve the health of the ghetto underclass, in either the long or the short run, even if we tripled the number of black physicians in our large central cities.

This is not to say that a sharp increase in the number of black physicians would have no impact in the black community. Blacks who can afford to pay for adequate medical care would certainly have more black physicians to choose from, and poor blacks would undoubtedly witness the opening of more clinics, staffed by black physicians, in their neighborhoods. But the ultimate determinant of black access to medical care is not the supply of black physicians, even if an overwhelming majority choose to practice in the black community,[1] but the availability of programs such as Medicaid, Medicare, National Health Insurance, or other benefits designed, regardless of race, to give people who lack economic resources access to expensive medical care. There are plenty of doctors for those who can afford them.

However, there does exist a third liberal philosophy concerned with equality and social justice, namely, what Fishkin has called the principle of equality of life chances. According to this principle, if we can predict with a high degree of accuracy where individuals will end up in the competition for preferred positions in society "merely by knowing their race, sex, or family background, then the conditions under which their talents and motivations have developed must be grossly unequal." Supporters of this principle believe that a person "should not be able to enter a hospital ward of healthy newborn babies and, on the basis of class, race, sex, or other arbitrary native characteristics, predict the eventual positions in society of those children." In other words, it is unfair that some individuals "are given every conceivable advantage while others never really have a chance in the first place, to develop their talents" (Fishkin, 1983: 4).

Proponents of equality of life chances recognize not only that those from higher social strata have greater life chances or more-than-equal opportunities, but that "they also have greater than equal influence on the political process and greater than equal consideration from the health

---

[1]There is a question as to whether black physicians actually prefer to practice medicine within the black community, especially the poor black community. It is reasonable to assume that the typical black physician, like the typical white physician, would seek out the areas of practice providing the greatest financial and professional rewards. Accordingly, the more opportunities a black physician has to practice in attractive areas, the less likely that he or she will choose to serve poor blacks.

Of course, racial barriers have restricted the movements of many black physicians. It is ironic that the removal of racial barriers would result in a decrease in the percentage of the most qualified black physicians practicing medicine in the black community.

Chapter V
Ethnic and Class Discrimination

care and legal systems." The major factor that distinguishes the principle of equality of life chances from the principles of equality of individual opportunity and equality of group opportunity is the recognition that the problems of truly disadvantaged individuals—class background, low income, a broken home, inadequate housing, poor education, or cultural or linguistic differences—may not be clearly related to the issue of previous discrimination. Nevertheless, "children growing up in homes affected by these disadvantages may be deprived of an equal life chance because their environments effectively inhibit the development of their talents as aspirations" (Fishkin, 1983: 17).

Accordingly, programs based on this principle would not be restrictively applied to members of certain racial or ethnic groups but would be targeted to truly disadvantaged individuals regardless of their race or ethnicity. Thus, whereas poor whites are ignored in programs of reverse discrimination, based on the desire to overcome the effects of past discrimination, they would be targeted along with the truly disadvantaged minorities for preferential treatment under programs to equalize life chances by overcoming present class disadvantages.

Under the principle of equality of life chances, efforts to correct family background disadvantages through such programs as income redistribution, compensatory job training, compensatory schooling, special medical services and the like would not "require any reference to past discrimination as the basis for justification" (Fishkin, 1983: 17). All that would be required is that the individuals targeted for preferred treatment be objectively classified as disadvantaged in terms of the competitive resources associated with their economic-class background.

Ironically, the shift from preferential treatment for those with certain racial or ethnic characteristics to those who are truly disadvantaged in terms of their life chances would not only help the white poor, but would also address more effectively the problems of the minority poor. If the life chances of the ghetto underclass are largely untouched by programs of preferential treatment based on race, the gap between the haves and have-nots in the black community will widen, and the disproportionate concentration of blacks within the most impoverished segments of our population will remain. As Fishkin appropriately points out, programs based on the principle of equality of life chances would not be mistargeted to those who are already relatively affluent (Fiskin, 1983: 17).

TARGETED PROGRAMS AND THE PROBLEMS OF POLITICAL SUPPORT

Despite the emphasis placed on helping disadvantaged members of minority groups through programs based on the principle of equality of in-

Reading 16
Race-Specific Policies and the Disadvantaged

dividual opportunity and those based on the principle of equality of group opportunity (as brought out in the previous section), only programs based on the principle of equality of life chances are capable of substantially helping the truly disadvantaged. Nonetheless, even these, however comprehensive and carefully constructed, may not represent the most efficacious or viable way to lift the truly disadvantaged from the depths of poverty today.

...An important consideration in assessing public programs targeted at particular groups (whether these groups are defined in terms of race, ethnicity, or class) is the degree of political support those programs receive, especially when the national economy is in a period of little growth, no growth, or decline. Under such economic conditions, the more the public programs are perceived by members of the wider society as benefiting only certain groups, the less support those programs receive. I should like to deal with the implications of this argument by briefly contrasting the institutionalization of the programs that emanated from the New Deal legislation of the Roosevelt administration with the demise of the Great Society programs of the Johnson administration, bearing in mind that Johnson's Great Society program was the most ambitious effort in our nation's history to implement the principle of equality of life chances.[2]

In 1932 Franklin D. Roosevelt received a popular mandate to attack the catastrophic economic problems created by the Great Depression. He then launched a series of programs—such as Social Security and unemployment compensation—designed to protect all citizens against sudden impoverishment. One of these programs was Aid to Families with Dependent Children (AFDC), the current symbol of income-tested public welfare programs. Aid to Families with Dependent Children, however, was conceived not as a permanent alternative to working but as a temporary means of support for families that were, at the time they applied for aid, clearly unemployable. Indeed the "safety net" of Roosevelt's New Deal emphatically included the creation of public works projects designed to forestall the formation of a permanent welfare class. It was not necessary to satisfy a means test to work in these projects; the only requirement was that the applicant be unemployed, want a job, and be able to work. Furthermore, no one was denied eligibility for these jobs as a result of being either overskilled or underskilled; the programs attempted to match jobs with individual abilities (Fishkin, 1983: 17).

Thus, jobs for able individuals, Social Security, and unemployment compensation for the unemployed were to provide a modicum of secu-

---

[2]In drawing this comparison I have benefited from Toby Cohen's insightful article, "Reagan's New Deal," *New York Times*, August 19, 1981, p. 23.

Chapter V
Ethnic and Class Discrimination

rity for all. Economic stability was not tied to the dole. By contrast, nearly all of the Great Society programs *were* tied to the dole. Job training, legal aid, and Medicaid levied income tests. In effect, one had to be on welfare to be eligible. Unlike the New Deal programs, the Great Society programs were modeled on the English poor laws. Although these programs improved the life chances of many of their recipients—because job-training programs enabled many long-term welfare recipients to find their first jobs, Medicaid enabled many to receive decent medical care for the first time, and legal aid gave many access to capable lawyers—the programs were increasingly perceived in narrow terms as intended for poor blacks. In the cities, especially, the Great Society programs established what amounted to separate legal and medical systems—one public and predominantly black, the other private and predominantly white. The real problem, however, was that the taxpayers were required to pay for legal and medical services that were provided to welfare recipients but not to the taxpayers—services many taxpayers could not afford to buy for themselves. In other words, this system amounted to taxation to pay for programs that were perceived to benefit mostly minorities, programs that excluded taxpayers perceived to be mostly white (Fishkin, 1983: 17). Thus, these programs were cut back or phased out during the recent periods of recession and economic stagnation because they could not sustain sufficient political support.[3]

From the New Deal to the 1970s, the Democrats were able to combine Keynesian economics and prosperity for the middle class with social welfare programs and pressures for integrating the poor and minorities into the mainstream of American economic life. The MIT economist Lester Thurow reminds us that "in periods of great economic progress when [the incomes of the middle classes] are rising rapidly, they are willing to share some of their income and jobs with those less fortunate than themselves, but they are not willing to reduce their real standard of living to help either minorities or the poor" (Thurow, 1981).

In the face of hard economic times, Pres. Ronald Reagan was able to persuade the middle classes that the drop in their living standards was attributable to the poor (and implicitly, minorities), and that he could restore those standards with sweeping tax and budget cuts. In short, the

---

[3] A number of political activists have argued against considering seriously potential political resistance on the grounds that it is better to press for the adoption of certain programs, even when it is clear that they are doomed to failure, than to bow to political pressures. But it is one thing to ignore political realities because certain programs are noble; it is quite another thing to channel scarce energy into programs that could have significant long-term payoffs for the truly disadvantaged. The question is not the abandonment of noble programs because of political realities, but the shaping of those programs so that they can achieve noble goals while still receiving vital political support.

Reading 16
Race-Specific Policies and the Disadvantaged

New Deal coalition collapsed when Reagan was elected. In 1980 the only groups that did not leave the Democratic party in significant numbers were blacks, Hispanics, and the poor—groups that constitute only a quarter of the American population, hardly enough to win a national election (Thurow, 1981), and certainly not enough to sustain programs, incorrectly perceived as benefiting only the minority poor, based on the principle of equality of life chances. What is interesting, however, is that the Reagan administration has shown far less willingness to cut significantly the much more expensive universal programs such as Social Security and Medicare, programs that are not income tested and therefore are available to people across class lines. In this connection, one of the reasons why western European social welfare programs enjoy wide political support (especially in countries such as the Federal Republic of Germany, France, Austria, Sweden, the Netherlands, Belgium, and Norway) is that they tend to be universal—applied across class and racial/ethnic lines—and therefore are not seen as being targeted for narrow class or racially identifiable segments of the population (Kamerman and Kahn, 1981).

I am convinced that, in the last few years of the twentieth century, the problems of the truly disadvantaged in the United States will have to be attacked primarily through universal programs that enjoy the support and commitment of a broad constituency. Under this approach, targeted programs (whether based on the principle of equality of group opportunity or that of equality of life chances) would not necessarily be eliminated, but would rather be deemphasized—considered only as offshoots of, and indeed secondary to, the universal programs. *The hidden agenda is to improve the life chances of groups such as the ghetto underclass by emphasizing programs in which the more advantaged groups of all races can positively relate.* . . .

REFERENCES

Clark, Leroy D., and Judy Trent Ellis. 1980. "Affirmative action in recessionary periods: The legal structure," *Adherent: A Journal of Comprehensive Employment Training and Human Resources Development* 7 (December):64.

Fishkin, James S. 1983. *Justice, Equal Opportunity, and the Family, 1983*. New Haven, Conn.: Yale University Press.

Gordon, Milton M. 1975. "Toward a general theory of racial and ethnic group relations," pp. 84–110 in Nathan Glazer and Daniel P. Moynihan (eds.), *Ethnicity: Theory and Experience*. Cambridge, Mass.: Harvard University Press.

———. 1981. "Models of pluralism: The new American dilemma." *Annals of the American Academy of Political and Social Sciences* 454(March):183.

Chapter V
Ethnic and Class Discrimination

Kamerman, Shelia, and Alfred J. Kahn. 1981. "Europe's innovative family policies." *Transatlantic Perspectives* 2(March):9–12.

Loury, Glenn C. 1984. "On the need for moral leadership in the Black community." Paper presented at the University of Chicago, sponsored by the Center for the Study of Industrial Societies and the John M. Olin Center, Chicago, April 18, pp. 13–14.

Puckrein, Gary. 1984. "Moving up." *Wilson Quarterly* 8(Spring):74–87.

Raspberry, William. 1980. "Illusion of Black progress." *Washington Post*, May 18:A19.

Taylor, William L. 1986. "*Brown,* equal protection, and the isolation of the poor." *Yale Law Journal* 95(July):1714.

Thurow, Lester C. 1981. "Recession plus inflation spells statis." *Christianity and Crisis* March 30:91–92.

U.S. Bureau of the Census. 1983. "Statistical Abstract of the United States, 1982–1983." Washington, D.C.: U.S. Government Printing Office.

U.S. Department of Labor. 1983. *Handbook of Labor Statistics*. Washington, D.C.: U.S. Government Printing Office (December).

Reading 17

SHATTERING MYTHS ABOUT THE HOMELESS

David Whitman

> *Though the homeless are very apparent in media reports and on urban streets, their numbers are not overwhelming, and help is possible. The popular notion that they are so numerous that it would be too expensive to do anything about them is just one of many myths about the homeless. The media often focus on displaced families when in fact relatively few families are homeless. Studies show that correcting the lack of housing is not a sufficient cure for the problems of the homeless. Community centers offering various forms of treatment would provide a better solution.*

When homeless men and women started crowding urban America's back alleys seven years ago, a sloppy debate began over just how many people were homeless and where they came from. Republicans like Ronald Reagan minimized the problem, claiming a "large" percentage of the homeless were former mental patients. Democrats and liberal activists like Washington's Mitch Snyder countered that "millions" of Americans were homeless and warned that only "the grace of God" kept more middle-class families out of the gutter. In the absence of any reliable national statistics, these competing visions of the homeless persistently crippled attempts to help the country's most destitute citizens.

Now, three new national surveys of the urban homeless indicate that nearly everyone in the debate was mistaken about the homeless. The new data indicate that most homeless are neither mental patients nor members of the family next door and there are far fewer of them than most people believed. The surveys, including one scheduled to be released this week by the U.S. Department of Housing and Urban Development, also refute a host of other popular myths that led to well-intentioned but ineffective programs for helping the homeless. A sampling:

Copyright March 20, 1989, *U.S. News & World Report*.

Chapter V
Ethnic and Class Discrimination

MYTH 1. THERE ARE TEEMING MILLIONS.

Democrats like Michael Dukakis and House Speaker Jim Wright, as well as countless news reports, have claimed that 3 million Americans are huddled in streets, doorways and shelters each night. Wrong. A 1988 study by the nonpartisan Urban Institute, based in part on interviews with 1,700 homeless individuals in 20 large cities, concludes that at most 600,000 Americans were living in shelters or on the streets on a given night in 1987. That means the homeless are quite rare among urban dwellers or even among the poor. Less than 2 percent of the poor, for instance, are homeless.

Homeless advocates counter that one homeless American, let alone 600,000, is too many. Mitch Snyder has gone so far as to dismiss the "gnawing curiosity" for more precise numbers as the work of "Western little minds." Still, even a Zen master can see that the homeless problem is far more manageable if it is, say, five times smaller than previously advertised. As Martha Burt, the author of the Urban Institute study, put it: "We don't, in fact, need to build 3 million units to house tonight's homeless—and then turn around and build 3 million more tomorrow night."

MYTH 2. THEY ARE BAG-LADY BRIGADES.

George Bush said last year that mental illness was the "principal cause" of homelessness. Yet both the HUD survey and a 19-city health-care demonstration project funded largely by the Robert Wood Johnson Foundation show that only a third of homeless adults are mentally ill. Moreover, deinstitutionalization, the wholesale release of mental patients from hospitals, did little to create the homeless problem of the 1980s. In the forthcoming book *Address Unknown,* Tulane University Prof. James Wright reports that fewer than 5 percent of the 83,000 homeless men and women treated at the Robert Wood Johnson clinics were in a mental institution immediately prior to becoming homeless.

MYTH 3. THEY ARE PEOPLE LIKE US.

Equally erroneous are emotionally appealing arguments by homeless advocates and liberal Democrats that the homeless are ordinary, middle-class folks down on their luck. As Representative Charles Schumer (D-N.Y.), chairman of a congressional task force that deals with housing issues, said not long ago: "The vast majority of homeless are like you and me; they simply cannot afford housing." Numerous media reports, particularly those on television, have furthered this sanitizing of the homeless. To take one example, in an NBC special last year, Tom Brokaw traveled to rural Iowa to find white two-parent homeless families. The homeless, Brokaw informed viewers, are "people you know."

Not quite. While most of the homeless are not mentally ill, and their ranks vary considerably from city to city, about two thirds of homeless adults have at least one serious personal problem that helps put them on the streets and in shelters. The recent studies show that 33 percent to 38 percent of homeless adults are alcoholics, 13 percent to 25 percent are drug abusers and 21 percent to 24 percent either have had a felony conviction or have served time in state and federal prisons. Besides being extremely poor, homeless men and women are also sadly isolated from their own families and mainstream American institutions. On the average, they have been out of work for almost four years.

MYTH 4. THE OKIES HAVE RETURNED.

Perhaps the most misleading impressions about the homeless have centered on homeless families, the most poignant newcomers to the nation's streets and shelters. Numerous media reports have depicted these families as the new Okies, displaced working-class Americans who can no longer find inexpensive rental apartments. An egregious example of this genre was last year's critically acclaimed made-for-TV movie "God Bless the Child," which starred Mare Winningham as a white, separated mom who lost her job and then abandoned her little girl so the child would not be raised in horrid shelters.

The truth, however, is that most homeless parents with children are black or Hispanic single women on welfare, and many have little job experience. All told, women with children account for a quarter of those in shelters and on the streets. And while the new studies show they are not nearly as likely as single homeless adults to be alcoholics, mentally ill individuals or ex-convicts, they sadly are far more likely to have ended up in shelters because they were driven from their homes by domestic violence.

MYTH 5. MORE CHARITY IS THE ANSWER.

The new surveys also weaken the case for two popular solutions to the homeless crisis. On the political right, President Bush and others have warned that there needs to be "an enormous awakening" to the homeless by charities and religious groups, the so-called thousand points of light. But the HUD shelter survey reveals the private sector has already mounted a phenomenal effort to help the homeless. Last year, roughly 9 out of 10 shelters for the homeless were operated by community groups and churches. It is difficult to see, moreover, how the thousand points of light can put out much more wattage. Last year, a whopping 80,000 volunteers worked in shelters, nearly quadruple the number that helped out five years ago.

As might be expected, the public sector has also substantially boosted its financial support for shelters since 1984, paying about $1 billion or two thirds of their operating costs last year. Yet federal aid for fighting this nationwide problem is modest, particularly when matched against the contributions of many state and local governments. In this fiscal year, New York City alone will spend about $475 million on direct aid to the homeless, not that much less than the federal government will spend in all 50 states.

MYTH 6. ALL THEY NEED IS HOUSING.

Many liberals and homeless advocates subscribe to what Robert Hayes of the National Coalition for the Homeless has put forth as a three-word solution to the homeless crisis: "Housing, housing, housing." Yet recent studies suggest that roughly half of the urban homeless have been homeless more than once, indicating that a roof over the head of an alcoholic, a mentally ill person or an addict might not keep him off the street indefinitely. Unfortunately, most shelters are too preoccupied with short-term emergency needs, such as providing hot meals and beds, to offer adequate rehabilitative care. The HUD survey shows that fewer than a third of the nation's shelters provide treatment for substance abuse or mental illness, and just as few offer child care or health care.

One conclusion to be drawn from the new studies is that the homeless may need transitional services and interim housing tailored to their needs even more than a new public-housing complex. Most of the homeless require treatment at a community mental-health center, a stay at an alcohol-free halfway home, classes in parenting, help with getting disability benefits or even a bed in a safe and clean flophouse. The danger, of course, is that once the public accepts the fact that the majority of homeless adults have persistent personal problems, they may also dismiss them as the undeserving poor. Yet the homeless, as Hayes puts it, "are not a different species of human beings." And even though some Americans will deem them undeserving, the ranks of homeless show no signs of dissipating. The issue now is not whether the homeless will continue to cost billions in emergency food and shelter aid but whether those billions in the years ahead will be spent more sensibly.

Reading 18
ADDITIVE MULTICULTURALISM: A SPECIFIC PROPOSAL

Harry C. Triandis, *University of Illinois*

> *Rather than integration, we need additive multiculturalism, where we recognize and appreciate cultural differences, so that both sides gain cultural features instead of one side's losing theirs.*

Rather than integration, as it is conceived by the popular press, we need *additive multiculturalism*. I hope that the future of pluralism is additive multiculturalism. I borrowed the idea, by analogy, from Lambert's[1] discussion of additive and subtractive bilingualism. Lambert argues that when an English Canadian learns French he adds to his capacities; when a French Canadian learns English there is danger of assimilation into the vast North American culture and loss of the French identity. Whites who learn about black subjective culture and learn to appreciate the positive features of black culture become enriched. Asking blacks to become culturally white is subtractive multiculturalism. As Taylor (1974) wrote, perhaps too strongly, integration as advocated today is a white idea about how blacks would become psychologically white. That conception is *subtractive multiculturalism*. The way to reduce conflict is not for one side to lose what the other side gains, but for both sides to gain.

Some of the negative features of American society—including anxiety over achievement, which results in much "Type A behavior" and a third of a million deaths from heart attacks each year—might be reduced if we adopt a more relaxed outlook, often found among blacks. (I am personally in need of reform, in this respect, as much as anyone else.) The pace is frantic. Too often we are in the situation of the passenger on an

---

Reprinted with permission from "The future of pluralism," *Journal of Social Issues* 32 (1976):179–208.

[1] W. E. Lambert, "Culture and language as factors in learning and education," paper presented at the Symposium on Cultural Factors in Learning, Bellingham, Washington, 1973.

Chapter V
Ethnic and Class Discrimination

airplane who hears the pilot say, "I have excellent news: our speed is breaking all records. Now for the bad news: we are lost." Perhaps we should contemplate whether our crime, pollution, suicide, and divorce rates are where they should be. In any case, we need to understand the feelings associated with each kind of multiculturalism. Desirable pluralism permits everyone to have additive multiculturalist experiences. Ideally, pluralism involves enjoyment of our ability to switch from one cultural system to another. There is a real sense of accomplishment associated with the skill to shift cultures. The balanced bilingual/bicultural person, or even more, the multicultural person, gets kicks out of life that are simply not available to the monolingual/monocultural person. There is a thrill associated with the competence to master different environments, to be successful in different settings. The person who delights in different social settings, different ideologies, different life-styles, simply gets more out of life. There are now effective ways to train people to appreciate other cultures (Brislin and Pedersen, 1976). We must use these procedures in our schools to broaden the perspective of most students.

At the simplest level, we find this broadening in the appreciation of different foods. Contrast the meat and potatoes diet of some people with the diet of those who have the means to explore the multinational cuisine of a large city. The ability to appreciate the full range of music produced in different parts of the world is another example. But, food and music appreciation are not as difficult to learn as the subtle ways of human interaction, and particularly intimacy. To be able to become intimate with many kinds of people who are very different is a great accomplishment. This should be the goal of a good education, and the essential step forward to a pluralist society.

A good education also means an education which is adjusted to the needs of the minority as well as the majority groups. Castañada, James, and Robbins (1974) outlined some of the ways in which schools must change to provide the best learning environments for Latin-background, black, and Native American children. Castañada, for instance, points out that frequently teachers punish behaviors that are learned in the child's home, thus making the school environment noxious. The Spanish-American emphasis on family, the personalization of interpersonal relations, the clear-cut sex-role differentiation, and so on create a particular way of thinking, feeling, and learning. A teacher who is not aware of these cultural influences can easily lose contact with a child. For example, teaching a Spanish-background child may be improved if the teacher sits close to the child, touches a lot, hugs, smiles, uses older children to teach younger children, involves the children in group activities, sends work to the child's home so the parents can get involved, arranges for Mexican foods to be cooked in class, teaches Spanish songs to all children, and so on. Similarly, if monocultural American children under-

*Reading 18
Additive Multiculturalism*

stood why Native Americans have values stressing harmony with nature rather than its conquest, a present rather than a future time orientation, giving one's money away rather than saving it, respect for age rather than emphasis on youth, such children would broaden their perspective. The dominant American culture will profit from inclusion of such conceptions in its repertoire of values: Harmony with nature is much more conducive to the respect that ecology imposes on technology in the postindustrial era, respect for old age may be much more functional in a nation where the majority is old as it will be soon, a present orientation may be more realistic in a society that can no longer afford to grow rapidly because of energy and resource limitations, and so on. The majority culture can be enriched by considering the viewpoints of the several minority cultures that exist in America rather than trying to force these minorities to adopt a monocultural, impoverished, provincial viewpoint which may in the long run reduce creativity and the chances of effective adjustment in a fast-changing world.

Such goals are equally viable for minority and majority members provided we respect each other's cultural identity. We must not ask blacks to become culturally white. We must not ask them to lose their identity. Integration in the form of becoming like us implies by definition that their culture is inferior. Rather, what we want is to find more common superordinate goals and methods of interdependence that give self-respect to all. We need to be creative if we are to discover such methods.

In his 1969 presidential address to SPSSI Tom Pettigrew (1969) asked whether we should be racially separate or together. After almost ten years I still find his analysis compelling. Yet I also sympathize with black writers who, like Taylor (1974), disagree with Pettigrew's position. Taylor has argued that dependent people cannot be integrated in an equalitarian society. Integration, he argued, can imply loss of identity and inferiority. He insists that only after power is equalized can we have racial justice. Similarly, Ron Katanga has stated: "We can't be independent unless we have something to offer; we can live with whites interdependently once we have black power" (cited by Pettigrew in Epps, 1974). Taylor (1974) is optimistic and gives us some examples of power shifting to blacks: He tells us that in Atlanta the NAACP agreed to the busing of only 3000 instead of 30,000 students in exchange for 9 out of 17 administrative positions in the school system, including the positions of superintendent and assistant superintendent of instruction. The argument is that power can lead to decisions that will improve the quality of education of the black children of Atlanta and that is better than mere integration. Taylor[2] is also impressed by discussions among administrators of the Massachusetts Institute of Technology to transfer a substantial por-

---

[2]D. A. Taylor, personal communication, 1976.

Chapter V
Ethnic and Class Discrimination

tion of the M.I.T. group life insurance from a white-controlled to two black-controlled insurance companies. His argument is that only when the power gap between the races is made much smaller is contact likely to lead to harmony. Thus, as a first step toward pluralism, he visualizes what he calls "empowerment strategies" for blacks to acquire power. He also emphasizes the importance of institutional racism much more than individual prejudice, as a barrier to pluralism.

I agree with Taylor, I see no good reason to expect more integration as advocated today to lead to additive multiculturalism. To reach additive multiculturalism I see the need for a three-pronged strategy.

1. Blacks and other minorities must seek power. They need to develop a flexible, imaginative approach to acquiring it. To get power they need resources. They do have one important resource—a common fate. If they manage to communicate within each community the importance of concerted action for improving their position in American society, they will be able to engage in balance-of-power politics and thus acquire more resources than they now have.

2. To learn about another culture one must be secure in one's own identity. The essence of additive multiculturalism is that those who have a firm identity— the well-established mainstream of America—must do the learning. And they should learn not only about blacks, but also about Spanish-speakers, Native Americans, and other ethnic minorities that exist in significant numbers in the U.S. To be educated in this country should mean that one is able to have good, effective, and intimate relationships with the ten or more important cultural groups that exist here. Specifically, whites must learn to interact effectively with blacks. Right now, given the status of blacks and whites in this country, whites have no good reasons to learn how to get along with blacks. Unlike the American who if he is to visit Paris should learn a bit of French, since otherwise he may not get much champagne or perfume, whites have little motivation to get along with blacks.

Note that I am emphasizing that learning to get along means learning new interaction skills. But this is exactly what additive pluralism is all about. It is being able to get along not only with one's own group but also with other groups. New techniques for culture learning (Seelye, 1975; Triandis, 1975, 1976; Brislin and Pedersen, 1976; Landis, Day, McGrew, Thomas, and Miller, 1976) are becoming available. These techniques can train people to engage in interactions where the rewards exceed the cost for both persons, with a large variety of ethnic groups. By extension some of these techniques can be used to improve relationships between men and women, old and young, and so on. In short, whenever the life experiences of a group are sufficiently different from the experience of another group, the gap in subjective cultures requires an effort to reduce

*Reading 18
Additive Multiculturalism*

misunderstandings. Each group must learn more about the perspective of the other groups than happens now.

3. *There is an urgent need for programs that guarantee jobs to every American who is capable of working.* Our data show the largest gap in subjective culture not between blacks and whites but between unemployed blacks and employed blacks. Current estimates of unemployment rates among young black males exceed 50 percent. This is a totally unacceptable rate. A program of guaranteed jobs for those who can work, negative income tax for those who earn too little, job supportive services (such as public nurseries), and welfare payments for the old and disabled, may eventually cost less than the $200 billion spent on various forms of welfare ("Progress Against Poverty," 1976). Such a program can benefit both whites and blacks (though blacks will be helped proportionately more), the costs can be diffused through the income tax structure, and it is consistent with the dominant values of this society—it puts people to work (Rothbart, 1976). I would add one more most important benefit: It creates the preconditions for successful contact. Given the importance of having a job within the American status system, the elimination of the unequal rates of unemployment via elimination of most unemployment would immediately reduce one of the important dissimilarities that make successful interracial contact difficult. I must emphasize that our evidence (Triandis, 1976), as well as that of Feldman (1974), suggests that working class blacks are very similar in their subjective cultures to working class whites; the discrepancies in subjective culture occur among the unemployed. Thus, by eliminating this category we would move toward another precondition of successful contact. Finally, by integrating the unemployed into the economy, we would create some commitment to the successful operation of the whole economic system, and a variety of superordinate goals.

For the guaranteed jobs plan to have the desired effects, however, these jobs must be identified not as government-jobs-specially-made-to-take-care-of-the-unemployment-problem but as legitimate jobs. This means that a variety of avenues toward full employment must be created simultaneously—stimulation of the private sector, identification of activities that have national priority (such as conservation projects), job training, and other programs.

WE NEED MORE RESEARCH

Consider a theoretical model that describes black/white contact. There might be n dimensions on which two groups might be different. In the case of assimilated blacks, n tends to be close to zero; they differ little

Chapter V
Ethnic and Class Discrimination

from whites. In the case of blacks with ecosystem distrust, it may be a very large number.

Now consider m dimensions specifying the conditions under which contact is likely to lead to "successful" interpersonal relationships, that is, relationships where the rewards exceed the costs for *both* blacks and whites. It is likely that in the case of work relationships (one of the m dimensions) this would be the case, while in the case of other relationships it may not be the case.

One of the research projects urgently needed is one that specifies how the n dimensions of difference are related to the m dimensions of successful contact. For example, a difference in trust in the American system of government might have strong implications for cooperation between a white and a black person in a business venture, while it may have little relevance for an intimate relationship; conversely, a difference in trust in the reliability of friends may have little significance in a relationship which is specified by a written contract but very large significance for an intimate relationship. We need to develop much greater understanding of how differences in subjective culture between blacks and whites have implications for some interpersonal relationships but not for others.

There is already enough research to indicate that acceptance in formal settings is more likely than acceptance in informal settings (Triandis and Davis, 1965; Goldstein and Davis, 1974; Pettigrew, 1969). We also know that when superordinate goals can be made salient, when contact receives institutional support, and when contact is associated with pleasurable events, it is more likely to lead to successful interpersonal relationships. In short, we already know some of the m dimensions. But there might be others that we still need to discover.

On the antecedent side of the coin we know that certain characteristics of the groups in contact help to predispose successful interpersonal relationships. When two groups have similar status and know each other's subjective cultures, there is a high probability of successful interpersonal relationships in those social situations which induce cooperation. This is not so when people are of different status or do not know each other's subjective culture.

It follows from this discussion that contact without the preconditions of similarity in status, knowledge of the other group's subjective culture, and similarity of goals may have undesirable consequences. Yet much of the current thinking on integration proposes exactly that kind of contact.

In addition we must learn a great deal more than we know now about successful intergroup contact. The aim should be to create in the shortest time the largest number of what we defined above as "successful interpersonal relationships." We must become an experimenting society (Campbell, 1969). As research on this topic gives usable answers, we might be able to create a new group of professionals—applied social psychologists—whose job it would be to counsel people on how to achieve successful interpersonal relationships in the shortest time. Such people might be called human relations catalysts. In situations where people with different subjective cultures must interact they would act as consultants to provide the kind of training and perspective needed to establish a successful interpersonal relationship. The human relations catalysts would know what skills, knowledge, and attitudes are needed to be successful in particular job settings, in schools, or in community activities. We already know much about this kind of problem (Brislin and Pedersen, 1976) but we still have too many research gaps to be able to train such professionals well today. However, after only a few years of successful research I am confident we could do a very good job.

A VISION OF THE FUTURE

What kind of society would emerge from such activities? As I see it, it would be one in which people would have more choices and their choices would be more acceptable to others. I see few situations that are more confining than unemployment. The unemployed person is forced to seek other avenues to gain status or income—crime is a common one. Yet that is often imposed by outside circumstances rather than a matter of free choice. Furthermore, a person with a steady job can seek better housing and better schools. This does not mean, in my view, that all blacks will want to live in white neighborhoods. Nor does it mean that all will want to send their children to integrated schools. But note the large difference between having to be segregated and deciding to be segregated. What I am advocating is increasing the number of times when people decide to adopt a particular life-style rather than have the life-style imposed on them via ideology, legal action, or economic pressure.

The situation I visualize is that some blacks will go to all black schools, some will work in all black companies, and some will live in all black neighborhoods, but they will do so as a matter of free choice. The catalysts, who will often be black, after careful examination of each case might conclude that integration of a particular individual is premature or unlikely to lead to successful interpersonal relationships. They would so advise a client, giving reasons for that advice. Then the client might voluntarily choose to go to an all-black school, or what not. Hopefully, over time, fewer and fewer persons would receive such advice. My emphasis is on dealing with individuals and recognizing that there are individual differences. I can see the law as giving everyone the right to integrate, but it may not be to everybody's advantage to exercise this right immediately. A child with low self-esteem who is placed in a school where failure is guaranteed is not served well.

One of the ways in which the catalysts might operate would be the analysis of the subjective culture of various groups of clients in relation to the known subjective cultures of various mainstream groups. Then, by identifying the smallest existing gaps in subjective culture they would advise their clients about the right move, and would train them to be successful in the new social setting in which they will have to work, live, or learn. Broadening the client's perspective concerning various subjective cultures seems to be an effective way to train for intercultural behavior (Triandis, 1976). It does increase cognitive complexity and makes a person more flexible in different kinds of social environments (Triandis, 1975). Thus, as I see it, the catalysts will keep constantly abreast of changes in the subjective culture, job requirements, specially needed skills, and so on of different job settings and will advise their clients to move into those situations in which their clients are likely to be most successful.

All of this discussion, however, does have a very strong overtone which I wish to dispel. All along I have been talking about contact across small gaps and what will happen over time. There are a few dimensions on which homogeneity is desirable. Total status is one of them. But in general I think homogeneity is undesirable. We need to learn to value different life-styles and assign equal status to them, in spite of the fact that they are different. Just as a Nobel-prizewinner in physics is different from a Nobel-prizewinner in literature yet one is not different in status from the other, so we must learn that different life-styles are perfectly viable. I suspect that we need cultural heterogeneity in order to have an interesting life, but also in order to invent the new life-styles needed in a fast-changing culture. What we do not need is the "different is inferior" viewpoints that so frequently have characterized humankind's interpersonal relations.

CONCLUSION

Pluralism, then, is the development of interdependence, appreciation, and the skills to interact intimately with persons from other cultures. It involves learning to enter social relationships where the rewards exceed the costs for both sides of the relationship. To achieve this state we need more understanding of social psychological principles and experimentation with new forms of social institutions, such as the catalysts.

My argument has been that our current attempts at integration, based on a legal framework, disregard individual differences and are attempts to eliminate cultural differences. I am advocating a shift from that perspective to one that provides for a marriage of the legal framework with our understanding of social psychological principles. Rather than integration, as conceived today, or assimilation, which involves the elimination of cultural differences, I am advocating *additive multiculturalism* where people learn to be effective and to appreciate others who are different in culture. Additive multiculturalism is by its very nature something that needs to be developed in the majority rather than the minority of the population. As more members of the minority learn to integrate in jobs and are given a chance to do so, the majority must learn to relate to the minorities with the perspective of additive multiculturalism. Within that framework and over a period of many years, we should develop a pluralism that gives self-respect to all, appreciation of cultural differences, and social skills leading to interpersonal relationships with more rewards than costs. Thus, when those who will celebrate our tricentennial look back they will be able to say: Those people 100 years ago had many difficulties making their society a good one but they tried many creative solutions, one or two of these solutions worked, and they finally succeeded in creating a truly good society.

REFERENCES

Brislin, R. W., and P. Pedersen. 1976. *Cross-cultural Orientation Programs.* New York: Gardner Press, 1976.

Campbell, D. T. 1969. "Reforms as experiments." *American Psychologist* 24:409–429.

Catañada, A., R. L. James, and W. Robbins. 1974. *The Educational Needs of Minority Groups.* Lincoln, Neb.: Professional Educators Publishers.

Epps. E. G. 1974. *Cultural Pluralism.* Berkeley, Calif.: McCatchan Press.

Feldman, J. 1974. "Race, economic class and the intention to work: Some normative and attitudinal correlates." *Journal of Applied Psychology* 59:179–186.

Goldstein, M., and E. E. Davis. 1973. "Race and belief: A further analysis of the social determinants of behavioral intentions." *Journal of Personality and Social Psychology,* 26:16–22.

Landis, D., H. R. Day, P. L. McGrew, J. A. Thomas, and A. B. Miller. 1976. "Can a black 'culture assimilator" increase racial understanding?" *Journal of Social Issues* 32(2):169–183.

Pettigrew, T. F. 1969. "Racially separate or together?" *Journal of Social Issues* 25(1):43–69.

"Progress against poverty: 1964–74." 1976. *Focus on Poverty Research* 8–12.

Rothbart, M. 1976. "Achieving racial equality: An analysis of resistance to social reform," in P. A. Katz (ed.), *Toward the Elimination of Racism.* New York: Pergamon.

Seelye, H. N. 1975. *Teaching Culture.* Skokie, Ill.: National Textbook Co.

Chapter V
Ethnic and Class Discrimination

Taylor, D. Q. 1974. "Should we integrate organizations?" in H. Fromkin and J. Sherwood (eds.), *Integrating the Organization*. New York: Free Press.

Triandis, H. C. 1975. "Culture training, cognitive complexity and interpersonal attitudes, in R. Brislin, S. Bochner, and W. Lonner (eds.), *Cross-cultural perspectives on learning*. New York: Halsted/Wiley.

——— (ed.). 1976. *Variations in Black and White Perceptions of the Social Environment*. Urbana: University of Illinois Press.

———, and E. E. Davis. 1965. "Race and belief as determinants of behavioral intentions." *Journal of Personality and Social Psychology* 2:715–725.

CHAPTER VI

SEXISM AND PROBLEMS OF THE AGING

Reading 19
Sexual Harassment on a University Campus: The Confluence of Authority Relations, Sexual Interest and Gender Stratification

Donna J. Benson, Gregg E. Thomson, *University of California, Berkeley*

> *Thirty percent of Berkeley undergraduate women reported receiving unwanted sexual attention from a male instructor. Even if it never happens to the individual female, the possibility of sexual harassment shapes and colors women's experiences in the male-dominated college world.*

Female workers have always been vulnerable to sexual abuse by male employees.[1] It wasn't until *Redbook* published a survey in 1976, however, that sexual harassment began to be recognized as a social problem (Safran, 1976). Since then, numerous newspapers and magazines have contained accounts of female workers subject to disruptive and coercive sexual harassment by male supervisors and coworkers. In non-random surveys (e.g., Silverman, 1976) as many as 70 percent of respondents report harassment on the job. In Gutek et al.'s (1980) random survey in Los Angeles, 11 percent of the women experienced such non-verbal sexual behaviors as looks, gestures, and touching. Women in various occupations and institutions have taken legal action in response to sexual harassment or the repercussions of failing to comply with the sexual demands of male superiors.

As with rape (Rose 1977a,b), feminists have been instrumental in promoting the awareness that sexual harassment on the job is a serious

---

Reprinted with permission from *Social Problems*, 29 (3) (February 1982): 236–251, abridged by The Society for the Study of Social Problems and by the authors.

[1]For observations on indentured servants and private household workers, see, Morris (1946), Lerner (1972), and Katzman (1978). Sexual exploitation of working girls and women as they were drawn into the industrial labor force is described by Sanger (1858), Bularzik (1978), Hymowitz and Weissman (1978), Farley (1978), and Backhouse and Cohen (1979).

Chapter VI
Sexism and Problems of the Aging

social problem, and have encouraged victims to seek legal redress for their grievances. Administrators, responding to public pressure, have begun to acknowledge the prevalence of the problem.

The key to this recognition has been the conceptualization and labelling of a broad class of behaviors as sexual harassment.[2] MacKinnon (1979:27) notes: "Until 1976, lacking a term to express it, sexual harassment was literally unspeakable, which made a generalized, shared and social definition of it inaccessible." What heretofore have often been viewed as largely unrelated and in many instances inconsequential behaviors are now viewed as part of a single pattern:

> Sexual harassment can be any of or all of the following: verbal sexual suggestions or jokes, constant leering or ogling, "accidentally" brushing against your body, a "friendly" pat, squeeze, pinch or arm around you, catching you alone for a quick kiss, the explicit proposition backed by threat of losing your job, and forced sexual relations. (WWUI, 1978: 1)

Observable differences between the sexes, previously viewed as social differentiation, are now recognized as reflecting social inequality. Sexual behaviors once treated as part of this differentiation—and indeed as manipulative behavior on the part of women—can be seen as an aspect of this inequality. All of the above behaviors therefore represent the unwarranted intrusion of male sexual prerogative into the work setting.

MacKinnon (1979) provided a persuasive sociological and legal argument that sexual harassment constitutes illegal sex discrimination. In 1980, the Equal Employment Opportunity Commission (EEOC, 1980) issued guidelines which made explicit the liability for sexual harassment under Title VII of the Civil Rights Act of 1964 which prohibits discrimination on the basis of race, sex, religion and national origin. Moreover, the guidelines specified that sexual harassment occurs whenever sexual behaviors substantially interfere with an employee's work performance or create an intimidating, hostile or offensive work environment. Employers are required to "take all steps necessary" to prevent sexual harassment.[3]

Legally, then, harassment is not limited to direct sexual assault, bribery, or retaliation for refusing to comply with sexual demands. It can also be distinguished from flirting, come-ons, and office romances (Quinn, 1977), in that harassment is unwanted and potentially coercive or disrup-

---

[2] The term apparently was first defined in May 1975 in a survey developed by the women's section of the Human Affairs Program, Cornell University.

[3] In August, 1981, U.S. Vice-President George Bush said the existing regulations on sexual harassment were unworkable and indicated the Reagan administration intended to reverse the Equal Employment Opportunity Guidelines.

Reading 19
Sexual Harassment on Campus

tive, though in practice even a supposedly friendly come-on by a male superior may have an element of implicit coercion.

It is easy to see why the concept of sexual harassment has been applied to instructor-student relationships as well as those of employer-employee. Male teachers have the authority to evaluate the performance of female students and, accordingly, the opportunity to affect that performance by initiating sexual demands or behaviors. The Association of American Colleges' Project on the Status and Education of Women (1978) identified sexual harassment as a serious and widespread "hidden issue" on campus.

Surveys and reports of harassment corroborate both the seriousness of the issue and its growing visibility (Benson, 1977; Munich, 1978; Nelson, 1978; Lesser, 1979). Pope, Levenson, Shover (1979) found that one in four recently trained women psychologists reported having had sexual contact with their professors (see also Fields, 1979). Pope, Shover, and Levenson (1980) highlighted the *ethical* implications of such behavior while plaintiffs in university sexual harassment cases have stressed, as do their counterparts in the workplace, the *illegal sex discrimination* involved. Sexual harassment is now recognized as a violation of Title IX of the Education Amendments Act prohibiting sex discrimination in federally assisted programs.[4] The National Advisory Council on Women's Education (Till, 1980) released a survey showing reports of sexual harassment were increasing. The council recommended that sexual harassment be explicitly established as sex discrimination and urged all U.S. colleges and universities to reduce tolerance for sexual harassment on the campus....

METHOD

In the spring of 1978, we placed an advertisement in the University of California student newspaper inviting students to discuss experiences of "unwanted sexual attention" received from an instructor while at Berkeley. Informal interviews with the 20 women who responded helped us construct the seven-page questionnaire used for the present study.

In June, 1978, we mailed the questionnaire to a random sample of 400 female students in their senior year at Berkeley. A week later the

---

[4]In 1977, several women at Yale University initiated the lawsuit (*Alexander* v. *Yale University*, 1977) which established this principle. In 1979, 29 students at the University of California, Berkeley, filed a complaint with the Department of Health, Education and Welfare on similar grounds. Women Organized Against Sexual Harassment (WOASH, 1979) has helped coordinate charges of sexual harassment against a University of California professor as well as publicize the issue generally. Field (1981) discusses more recent developments, including a case involving a countersuit by the alleged harasser.

sample was reminded of the survey by both telephone and mail. Despite the concurrence of final examinations and graduation ceremonies, 269 women (67 percent) returned the questionnaire.

A letter accompanying the questionnaire explained the purpose of the study and presented an inclusive definition of sexual harassment formulated by the Working Women United Institute (WWUI, 1978): "Any unwanted sexual leers, suggestions, comments or physical contact which you find objectionable in the context of a teacher-student relationship." Purposely broad, we used this definition so that we could assess the full range of unwanted sexual attention from the ostensibly trivial to the obviously extreme....

RESULTS

Awareness of Sexual Harassment on Campus

Our respondents estimated how frequently women students are sexually harassed at Berkeley and how serious a problem it is for those who are harassed. A majority (59 percent) estimated that sexual harassment occurs "occasionally," 9 percent thought it occurred "frequently," and less than 2 percent said it "almost never" happens. There was a high degree of consensus, therefore, that sexual harassment is not an isolated or rare phenomenon and indeed is likely to be at least an occasional occurrence. Our respondents were divided on whether the problem of harassment is "very serious" (37.9 percent), "moderately serious" (34.4 percent), and only "mildly serious" or less (27.7 percent). As the accounts of actual sexual harassment indicate, there is a considerable range in the degree of difficulty which sexual harassment presents for individual women. Results for our entire sample, however, suggest an overall perception that sexual harassment is a problem.

Confirmation that an awareness of sexual harassment is at least relatively widespread among our sample can be found in the fact that 93 women—more than one in three of the respondents—said they knew personally at least one woman who had been harassed at Berkeley. Because transfer students (59 percent of the sample) were not asked about acquaintances at previous institutions and, one assumes, minor harassment episodes may not be shared even among friends, this figure may be conservative. It certainly suggests that consciousness of harassment is part of the female university experience, even as the issue remains "hidden" from official recognition by a predominantly male faculty and administration.

Reading 19
Sexual Harassment on Campus

SELF-REPORTS OF SEXUAL HARASSMENT

Thirty-one of 111 non-transfer students (27.9 percent) reported that they had been sexually harassed by at least one male instructor at Berkeley. Twenty-four of 158 transfer students (15.2 percent) also reported that they had been harassed after transferring to Berkeley. An additional 25 of the transfer students (15.9 percent) indicated that harassment had occurred at their previous college or university but not at Berkeley. Thus, a total of 80 out of 269 respondents (29.7 percent), or precisely one of every five women in our original sample of 400, reported at least one incident of sexual harassment at some point during their college career. We can estimate, therefore, that between 20 and 30 percent of the women in the senior class we sampled had been harassed.

Each of the 55 women who reported sexual harassment at Berkeley indicated the number of different male instructors who had harassed them. Thirty reported harassment by a single instructor, 15 by two, six by three, and two each by four and five or more instructors, respectively. Most of the women who reported harassment adopted strategies to minimize opportunities for future harassment. Nonetheless, nearly one hundred instances of harassment from different instructors were reported.

We made no attempt to estimate the degree to which the numerous separate reports of harassment may have reflected the behavior of a smaller number of individual faculty. We note, however, that those who reported harassment represented a wide diversity in majors and that, typically, the incident occurred while the student was enrolled in a course in her major. Based on respondents' estimates, the male instructors involved came from all age groups. Eleven of the instructors were identified as teaching assistants, seven as lecturers and the remainder as regular faculty. On the basis of this profile and descriptions of individual experiences, male instructors whom our respondents identified as harassers appeared to be widely dispersed among the faculty.

TYPES OF HARASSMENT

Of the 55 students who reported sexual harassment, 50 provided sufficiently detailed descriptions of their experiences to be useful for analysis. Examples are also drawn from the experiences of those who responded to our newspaper advertisement. The 50 incidents varied in form and degree of severity. Most typical were intrusive expressions of sexual and personal interest which respondents found objectionable.

Sexual propositions ranged from vague to blatant; invitations ranged from a dinner date to a weekend at a mountain resort. Sometimes a sex-

Chapter VI
Sexism and Problems of the Aging

Table 1
TYPES OF UNWANTED SEXUAL ATTENTION INITIATED BY MALE INSTRUCTORS AT THE UNIVERSITY OF CALIFORNIA, BERKELEY, AS REPORTED BY FIFTY SENIOR WOMEN

Behavior	Examples	No. of Students
Verbal advances	Explicit sexual propositions, expressions of sexual interest	17
Invitations	For dates, to one's apartment, for weekend at cabin	17
Physical advances	Touching, kissing, fondling breasts	10
Body language	Leering, standing too close	9
Emotional come-ons	Talking about personal problems; writing long letters	7
Undue attention	Obsequiously friendly; too helpful	5
Sexual bribery	Grade offered in exchange for affair; sexual pressure-*cum*-evaluation	3
Total		68[a]

[a]Total is greater than 50 because some reports specified more than one type of behavior.

ual advance or invitation was made only once, especially when the woman avoided subsequent contact with the instructor. In many other cases, categorizing the harassment experience as simply a sexual advance or invitation does not convey adequately the persistence of the instructor's objectionable behavior. A number of respondents reported that the instructor would "call and call" or "not take 'no' for an answer."

Ten of the 50 respondents reported direct physical advances. Instructors frequently touched and occasionally kissed students in an objectionable and sexually provocative manner. More severe harassment occurred only once among our sample, but was described by three of the women in other exploratory interviews. The following example from the interviews is typical of all three experiences:

> I needed help with an assignment so I went to the professor's office hours. He was staring at my breasts....It made me uncomfortable and confused....He reached over, unbuttoned my blouse and started fondling my breasts.

Not as physically aggressive, but nonetheless irritating and sometimes anxiety-arousing, were incidents of leering and suggestive body language. Seven respondents described "emotional come-ons" which, though not directly sexually aggressive, were experienced as intrusive and containing obvious implications for sexual involvement. Some instructors confided, in person or by letter, details of problems with their marriage or loneliness, and pressed for emotional involvement with the student.

Reading 19
Sexual Harassment on Campus

In contrast to reports of sexual harassment at the workplace, *overt* sexual bribery was rarely reported by our sample of female students. There were a handful of examples, however, of explicit offers of academic reward for sexual favors. Sometimes the possibility of punishment for refusing such "bargains" was also communicated:

> He would make verbal expressions of his desires and would often give me a choice of having an affair and doing well in his class without hardly any effort, or refusing him and suffering in the course. He often made excuses to detain me after class and graded my papers very hard to force me to come to his office. I was tense and uneasy in his presence.

At the workplace, where a single supervisor often has the power of evaluation, promotion and even firing, the terms of sexual exchange are likely to be explicit and obvious. Explicit demands can also happen on campus, as illustrated by the following anonymous account written by a woman at Berkeley in 1978 and given to Women Organized Against Sexual Harassment (WOASH). Having politely refused a direct sexual proposition on a previous encounter with the explanation that she was happily married and did not do that kind of thing, the student wrote:

> In response to my question about which of the two grades appearing on the midterm would be recorded, he asked me which one I wanted, the higher grade or the lower one. (He was towering over me, peering down my blouse.) I said I wanted the grade I deserved. It appeared that he was trying to barter for my "affections"; he acted as though he was giving me something out of the goodness of his heart and whether or not I deserved it didn't matter. Obviously he was trying to make me feel obligated to return the "favor." How are students supposed to get a fair assessment of their work when professors use their power to give grades to get sexual favors? (WOASH, 1978)

More typically, however, an instructor's inducements were more gradual and less overtly linked to either concrete rewards (e.g., a higher grade) or immediate sexual obligation. Friendliness, extra help, flexibility in grading and extended deadlines were seen by respondents as means by which instructors tried to accumulate credit for potential sexual exchange. Similarly, attention and friendliness obviously unwarranted by the particular teacher-student relationship were recognized as reflecting sexual and not academic interest.

Instances of selective help given by men to covertly "press their pursuits" of attractive female students (Goffman, 1977) need not be blatant, however. The bluntness of a direct proposition can be avoided through manipulation of the authority and latitude of the faculty role. Indeed, one male faculty member who volunteered his perception of sexual harassment in response to our newspaper advertisement described some of his colleagues as fundamentally "dishonest" in this regard: they falsely praised female students' work to render them more vulnerable to future sexual advances. Sexual propositions and invitations, therefore, do not necessarily "come out of the blue." Male instructors may have laid the groundwork for such overtures through patterns of selective attention and reward.

MANAGING THE TROUBLE

Once a male instructor tries to "come on" to a female student, he is perceived as "trouble" if the attention is unwanted (Emerson and Messinger, 1977). The student must then *manage the trouble* and renegotiate her status as a student. As our study indicates, managing the trouble for many women in our sample meant not expressing their true feelings when harassed. Once an instructor had begun obvious and even highly objectionable sexual advances, the "power-dependence" (Emerson, 1962) aspect of the teacher-student relationship severely inhibited the initial attempts of many women to remedy the situation:

> I tried to let him know I wasn't interested in a personal relationship with him. I couldn't be as rude as I would have liked to have been. At the time I felt I had to put up with it because I was trying to get into the honor's program.
>
> I ignored it; I didn't want to make a scene and possibly jeopardize my student standing.
>
> I didn't say anything because I thought being outspoken might affect my grade.
>
> I didn't say anything, but I wanted to tell him to fuck off. But I needed the recommendation and I'm too polite—I didn't want to be totally rude.

Students used several indirect tactics to forestall escalation of the sexual harassment. These included ignoring or "tuning out" sexual innuendoes and directing disclosures of personal matters (e.g., marital dissatisfaction, "my wife and I have an open marriage," loneliness) back to academic discussion. Physical actions, such as bringing a friend to the instructor's office, pointedly leaving the office door open upon entering, and sitting at a safe distance, were techniques which carried an implicit message that the instructor's behavior had been troublesome.

Students often mentioned their boyfriends or husbands to instructors, both in relatively ambiguous situations and those which had reached the point at which acknowledging an instructor's sexual interest could no longer be avoided. In both instances, apparently, students believed that calling attention to a boyfriend—whether explicitly or implicitly—was the one effective means to "keep him at a distance."

Reading 19
Sexual Harassment on Campus

> I had my boyfriend pick me up after class to make it clear to the professor that I was involved with someone.
>
> I just told him I was living with a man and was not interested in seeing anyone else.
>
> I told him I had a boyfriend, which I did not.

It is easy to understand why this tactic was used so frequently. Direct complaint would make sexuality the focus of the instructor-student relationship and make the trouble a "fully interpersonal matter" (Emerson and Messinger, 1977:125). Mention of a boyfriend both legitimates, rather than contests or sanctions, the introduction of sexual interest and simultaneously isolates the instructor's sexuality, denying it any connection with the student's. The tactic remains one of compromise.

STUDENT STATUS

Only occasionally did the students in our sample directly complain to an instructor about his behavior; the risks may have been too great. Thirty percent of the respondents did not even communicate their displeasure directly to the instructor. This did not prove to be an effective way of managing the harassment, for in 13 of these 15 instances the unwanted sexual attention persisted. Predictably, the 70 percent of the respondents who communicated in various ways to the instructor that his sexual attention was not acceptable were more successful in stopping it. That instructors did not always honor even fairly direct appeals to desist may be attributed to the combination of their superior power and the belief (or perhaps rationalization) that a woman's "no" really means "yes."

There is evidence in our study that this may have been the case. Using Emerson's (1962) definition of power as "implicit in the other's dependency," we examined the effects of three likely indicators of an instructor's power: (1) tenured status of the professor; (2) student and professor in the same field; and (3) student aspirations for graduate school. When less than all three of these conditions were present, sexual harassment ceased in 21 of 24 cases when the student expressed her displeasure. However, when all three conditions were present, the harassment stopped in only five of 11 cases.

Even when an instructor stopped harassing a student, the strategies adopted to manage the trouble still may not have been entirely effective. In a few cases, women successfully "talked out" the problem with their instructor and re-established a mutually satisfying student-teacher exchange. Much more often, however, respondents said that faculty members inflicted punishment for not reciprocating sexual attention. Perceived reprisals included withdrawing intellectual support and encouragement, sharp and often sarcastic criticism of work once praised, and low grades. One woman felt she had successfully managed a professor's sexual interest by making her boyfriend highly visible, only to be caught by surprise at the end of the term:

> He wasn't so nice to me after I didn't show interest. I didn't think anything of the incident until I got my grade, then I realized that the grade I got was due to my reaction to him. I knew another woman in the class who did terrible work but got a higher grade than I. Since then, I've heard notorious stories about him.

More severe repercussions occurred where students had more interaction with instructors. A student who was also employed part-time by her professor reported:

> Up until the time of our conflict he repeatedly told me that the work I was doing for him was good and that he was pleased with it. During the conflict period I was told the complete opposite: that my work was lousy, that I was lazy.... He tried to make me feel inept and incompetent. He then proceeded to prevent me from obtaining another job in the department. When the sexual conflict arose, my position was suddenly terminated and no explanation was given. As an employee and a student in the department my credibility was completely ruined. For a while, I really worried about the quality of my work. I questioned whether it was good or not, even though I knew it was.

In summary, a student's ability to monitor her instructor's behavior and to renegotiate her student status varied with the degree of power dependence in the teacher-student relationship. Thus, students frequently refrained from direct complaints for fear of reprisal; when direct complaints were made, they were sometimes not heeded and occasionally punished, despite attempts to avoid a confrontation.

THE TACTIC OF SELECTIVE AVOIDANCE

Kirkpatrick and Kanin (1957) found that women whose male dates had attempted forced sexual relations avoided situations where the act might be repeated. We, too, found that women used this tactic. Twenty-two students said they had no contact whatsoever with the instructor after the incident of sexual harassment. Twenty-four of the descriptions of harassment contained examples of avoidance:

> I avoided situations where we would have to converse. In short, I tried to have as little interaction with the person as possible.
>
> When he didn't respond to my hints and continued to give me unwanted attention, I avoided him.
>
> I never went to his office hours.

> I no longer went to section because of the uncomfortable situation.
>
> I never spoke to him alone again. He was an ignorant, insensitive person and I just avoided having to say anything to him.

Both non-verbal harassment, including various forms of "checking out" a student, and more direct come-ons were experienced as irritating and annoying in themselves. Yet they were also indicators that there might be more to come. Hence, selective avoidance was often used as a means to preclude the possibility of escalated harassment:

> I believe it started through the eyes: staring at my breasts, looking me up and down.... He was being overly helpful.... [As a result] I didn't trust the man and, thus, discontinued seeing him as my advisor.... I had the opportunity to work with this professor during the summer, but because of his reputation, not only regarding me, but others, I did not take advantage of the opportunity.

Anticipated sexual harassment, then, was also a factor in teacher-student relationships, and students sometimes adopted a "better safe than sorry" course of action. But as a woman in Benson's (1977) survey of the Berkeley campus recognized, this tactic may mean foregoing a potentially valuable *academic* relationship:

> My academic relationships with particular professors have been inhibited by a sexual factor. I have not gotten too friendly with one professor who could help me with my academic work, because I feared he would be interested in some kind of sexual relationship. So, I avoided him, missing out on his academic support. (Benson, 1977: 6)

THE DIRECT COSTS OF SEXUAL HARASSMENT

Students who had little prior involvement with an instructor who harassed them often simply tried to withdraw from future interaction, wherever possible. Missed opportunities was the most obvious price paid for this management behavior. When the teacher-student relationship was more established, however, the costs tended to be more direct. Unlike the typical employer-employee relationship, a young woman in college is in the process of intellectual development and identity formation. Successful completion of this process may depend, at least in part, on interaction with, and evaluation by, faculty members.

Loss of Self-confidence

The abrupt surfacing of intrusive sexual interest in a relationship where there had been considerable interaction caused confusion and uncer-

Chapter VI
Sexism and Problems of the Aging

tainty among our respondents. Standards of performance became cloudy as the professor's sexual intent became clear:

> It became difficult to know whether I was doing a good job.
>
> I worried that he had given me an "A" on the midterm to convince me to go to bed with him. I could not make a clear decision about the quality of my work in the class for this reason.
>
> I wondered what my real status in the class was—my real ability.

Eighteen students experienced self-doubt and loss of confidence in their academic ability after harassment. This occurred when students were unable to avoid their instructor. Typically, they had extensive previous interaction with him and likely did not find it easy to simply blame him for the trouble and withdraw from the situation (Emerson and Messinger, 1977):

> As this particular professor knew me and my work better than anyone else, I came away feeling very insecure about my academic work—[afraid] that his support of me was skewed by his sexual attraction.
>
> All of a sudden I had an anxiety attack about my intelligence....I wondered if all these years I had only gotten good grades because of my looks.
>
> For sometime afterwards I felt I had no ability in my major field; I couldn't analyze effectively or write clearly.

DISILLUSIONMENT WITH MALE FACULTY

With only a single exception, students who reported loss of academic self-confidence also became disillusioned and cautious about male faculty in general.

> I was so disillusioned with academia....[The experience] lessened my confidence on whether I felt it was worth going through with it all.
>
> I had just entered college....After dealing with him I never took an in-depth study again.

Even women whose self-confidence was not shaken reported that they became suspicious of male instructors. Behavior which previously had appeared natural and helpful was thereafter perceived as calculated and sexually motivated, and subsequent interactions became constrained by a sense of distrust:

> I became disillusioned and suspicious of people I'd otherwise responded naturally to. I'm more cautious of male faculty in general.
>
> [With male faculty, I am] more cautious about being open and friendly.

Two respondents volunteered comments about the composition of the faculty:

> I wish there were more female teachers and faculty members on campus so I wouldn't have to face a similar situation. I became doubtful and fearful of male faculty; I thought they must all be the same.
>
> I'm much more guarded in relating to my professors and male [teaching assistants]. I'm so relieved if I find out they're gay.

THE CUMULATIVE EFFECTS OF HARASSMENT ON CAMPUS

Theoretically, women now compete on the same terms as men for training and the credentials required for professional careers. But to the extent that male instructors perceive that female students are not, or should not be, as talented or committed as male students, they can act or fail to act in a number of ways—often minor or subtle in themselves, but nonetheless accumulating to produce a "discriminatory environment" (Bourne and Wikler, 1978; Coser and Rokoff, 1971; Rowe, 1977). The pattern of sexual harassment that we have documented is an integral part of this phenomenon.

Changes in sexual attitudes and practices have led to a greater acceptance of both casual and intimate relationships between faculty and students. At one time college officials, acknowledging the very real danger of improper sexual advances by male instructors, often required that office doors remain ajar during consultation with female students (Bernard, 1964). The seduction of a coed may have been sufficiently scandalous to threaten dismissal at some point in the past; but casual and comradely sexual interaction between faculty and students is now fully tolerated.[5]

It is important, therefore, to clarify that the issue of sexual harassment does not derive from a moralistic concern with sexual expression per se. Rather, the problem of sexual harassment on campus is significant because of the specific—and at times highly ambiguous—manner in which the formal teacher-student relationship overlaps with the pursuit of sexual interest. In a setting where an overwhelmingly male faculty determines to a considerable degree academic rewards (and punishments), intellectual self-esteem, and the possibility of a professional career, individual instructors also have the power to initiate or impose sexual relationships with female students.

---

[5]Professor Elizabeth Scott, in a personal communication (March 1979), recalled that custodians at Berkeley were once instructed to enforce a university policy which forbade daybeds, cots and covered doors in faculty offices.

Chapter VI
Sexism and Problems of the Aging

A faculty member's power to force compliance with his sexual interest doubtlessly varies. It is frequently the case with graduate training that a single faculty member has as much influence over a student's career prospects as an employer does over an employee's. In such contexts, one readily imagines, the coercive effects of sexual intrusion can be quite consequential.

Individual professors and teaching assistants typically have less direct power over the lives of undergraduate women. But in a society where few women have received support for intellectual accomplishment, an instructor's ability to manipulate both academic validation and his own sexual self-interest is hardly innocuous. The unexpected intrusion of sexual harassment alone can threaten self-confidence and commitment to academic pursuits.

Similarly, the direct costs of actual reprisals (e.g., lower evaluations, withdrawal of support, termination of employment) are obvious, though they apply to only some of those harassed. More subtle, and more common, are the effects inherent in the implicit threat when a student rejects her instructor's sexual overtures. And because sexual harassment continues to be a prevalent institutional practice, no actual reprisals are necessary to reinforce the belief that women should be sexually and personally accommodating to male authority. The male prerogative to define the terms of the relationship—to use sexual rather than official criteria to evaluate a woman's worth in academia—remains unchecked.

Women continually confronted with the possibility of sexual harassment are put in a double-bind situation. Responding to unwanted sexual attention, many women in our study adopted individual ad hoc management strategies which, ironically, further removed them from opportunities for professional advancement. Avoiding and mistrusting male faculty—the logical and practical reaction of many women in our study—hinders the formation of serious mentor relationships. Without comfortable access to the informal channels of professional socialization, women ultimately experience less control over their academic lives.

Telling an instructor that one has other emotional/sexual commitments ("I have a boyfriend") only confirms that a woman is defined in relation to a man rather than as an independent scholar or professional. Historically, sexual or gender-specific definitions have been used to disqualify women from positions of responsibility (Cott, 1978). And, as Bourne (1977) has suggested, pre-professional or professional women today who are categorized as "sexy" find their competence and authority devalued.

The experience of sexual harassment is, after all, only the most conclusive indicator that many male instructors continue to impose a sexual and gender-specific definition on their female students. Women learn that even simple friendliness and academic enthusiasm are often misinterpreted as an invitation for sexual advances and are forced to change their behavior accordingly. Men, on the other hand, interpret a wary stance adopted to forestall sexual harassment and stereotyping as an indication of coldness and a difficult emotional disposition (Wikler, 1976). Women who do not conform to the appropriate feminine stereotype may be perceived as technically competent but, lacking moral psychological "goodness," devoid of real authority (Bourne, 1977).

CONCLUSION

The practice of sexual harassment both reflects and reinforces the devaluation of women's competence and helps erode their commitment to competitive careers. Approached as the confluence of male formal authority and sexual interest, sexual harassment should not be seen as an isolated or deviant phenomenon. Rather, attention to harassment should be routine in any study of authority and gender in male-dominated institutions. For, as our research suggests, sexual harassment may be endemic to the university, and women must bear the costs of the latitude and ambiguity operating between a male-dominated system of formal authority and the sexual interests of numerous individual male instructors.

REFERENCES

Acker, Joan R. 1980. "Women and stratification: A review of recent literature." *Contemporary Sociology* 9 (January):25–35.

Backhouse, Constance, and Leh Cohen. 1979. *Secret Oppression: Sexual Harassment*. Toronto: Macmillan.

Benson, Donna J. 1977. "The sexualization of the teacher-student relationship." Unpublished paper, Department of Sociology, University of California, Berkeley.

Bernard, Jessie. 1964. *Academic Women*. University Park: Pennsylvania State University Press.

Blau, Peter. 1964. *Exchange and Power in Social Life*. New York: John Wiley.

_____. 1973. *The Structure and Organization of Academic Work*. New York: Academic Press.

Bourne, Patricia. 1977. " 'You can't use it, but don't lose it': Sex in medical school." *Proceedings of the Conference on Women's Leadership and Authority in the Health Professions*. Washington, D.C.: Department of Health, Education and Welfare, Health Resources Administration, Office of Health Resources Opportunity.

_____, and Norma Juliet Wikler. 1978. "Commitment and the cultural mandate: Women in medicine." *Social Problems* 25 (April):430–440.

Chapter VI
Sexism and Problems of the Aging

Coser, Rose, and Gerald Rokoff. 1971. "Women in the occupational world: Social disruption and conflict." *Social Problems* 18 (Spring):535–554.

Cott, Nancy. 1978. "Passionlessness: An interpretation of Victorian sexual ideology, 1790–1850." *Signs* 4 (Winter):219–236.

EEOC (Equal Employment Opportunity Commission). 1980. "Discrimination because of sex under Title VII of the Civil Rights Act of 1964, as amended: Adoption of interim interpretive guidelines." *Federal Register* 29 (March 11):1604. Washington D.C.: U.S. Government Printing Office.

Emerson, Richard. 1962. "Power-dependence relations." *American Sociological Review* 27 (February):31–41.

_____, and Sheldon Messinger. 1977. "The micro-politics of trouble." *Social Problems* 25 (December):121–134.

Fields, Cheryl M. 1979. "One-fourth of women psychologists in survey report sexual contacts with their professors." *Chronicle of Higher Education* 11 (September 17):1, 10.

Goffman, Erving. 1977. "The arrangements between the sexes." *Theory and Society* 4 (Fall):301–331.

Gutek, Barbara, Charles Y. Nakamura, Martin Gahart, Inger Handschumacher, and Dan Russell. 1980. "Sexuality and the workplace." *Basic and Applied Social Psychology* 1 (October):255–265.

Kirkpatrick, Clifford, and Eugene Kanin. 1957. "Male sex aggression on a university campus." *American Sociological Review* 22 (February):52–58.

Lesser, Ellen. 1979. "Sexus et veritas: Yale sued for sexual harassment." *Seven Days* 3 (February):25–26.

MacKinnon, Catherine. 1979. *Sexual Harassment of Working Women: A Case of Sex Discrimination*. New Haven, Conn.: Yale University Press.

Munich, Adrienne. 1978. "Seduction in academe." *Psychology Today* 11 (February):82–84, 108.

Nelson, Anne. 1978. "Sexual harassment at Yale." *Nation* 226 (January 7–14):7–10.

Pope, Kenneth S., Hanna Levenson, and Leslie R. Shover. 1979. "Sexual intimacy in psychology training: Results and implications of a national survey." *American Psychologist* 34 (August):682–689.

Quinn, Robert E. 1977. "Coping with Cupid: The formation, impact, and management of romantic relationships in organizations." *Administrative Science Quarterly* 22 (March):30–45.

Rose, Vicki McNicle. 1977a. "Rape as a social problem: A by-product of the feminist movement." *Social Problems* 25 (October):75–89.

_____. 1977b. "The rise of the rape problem," pp. 167–195 in Armand L. Mauss and Julie C. Wolfe (eds.), *Our Land of Promises: The Rise and Fall of Social Problems in America*, Philadelphia: J. B. Lippincott.

Rowe, Mary P. 1977. The Saturn's rings phenomenon: Micro-inequities and unequal opportunity in the American economy." *Proceedings of the Conference on Women's Leadership and Authority in the Health Professions*. Washington, D.C.: Department of Health, Education and Welfare, Health Resources Administration, Office of Health Resources Opportunity.

Safran, Claire. 1976. "What men do to women on the job: A shocking look at sexual harassment." *Redbook* (November):148–149.

Silverman, Dierdre. 1976–77. "Sexual harassment: Working women's dilemma." *Quest: A Feminist Quarterly* 3 (Winter):15–24.

Till, Frank J. 1980. "Sexual harassment: A report on the sexual harassment of students." Report of the National Advisory Council on Women's Educational Programs. Washington, D.C.: U.S. Department of Education.

Wikler, Norma. 1976. "Sexism in the classroom." Paper presented at the annual meeting of the American Sociological Association, New York, September.

WOASH (Women Organized Against Sexual Harassment). 1978. Anonymous personal communication. Unpublished.

———. 1979. "Sexual harassment: What it is, what to do about it." Pamphlet available from WOASH, University of California, Berkeley.

WWUI (Working Women United Institute). 1978. *Sexual Harassment on the Job: Questions and Answers.* New York: WWUI.

Reading 20
THE INVISIBLE HANDS: SEX ROLES AND THE DIVISION OF LABOR IN TWO LOCAL POLITICAL PARTIES

Diane Rothbard Margolis, *The University of Connecticut, Stamford Branch*

> *Contrary to appearances, women are politically active, but they are segregated into the support activities that the public never sees. Margolis describes the grass-roots, entry-level experience of most women in political life and shows why women will not achieve power until this role is changed.*

Women make up a majority of the U.S. electorate, yet they hold few high-ranking positions in government. Classic studies of the American political system, if they mention women at all, generally limit their analyses to a note on the insignificance of women's participation (e.g., Duverger, 1972; Key, 1948; Lazarsfeld et al., 1944; Lipset, 1960). Recently, the women's movement has turned attention to women's role in politics and several reports have been published (e.g., Chamberlin, 1974; Kirkpatric, 1974; Tolchin and Tolchin, 1974; Diamond, 1977; Githens and Prestage, 1977). Most of these, however, concentrate on the few women who do achieve political standing, overlooking the many who take the first step beyond the ballot box into their local political organization, but who seldom advance further. Yet it is at the base of the political system, in the local organization, that many political careers are spawned while others are aborted (Almond and Verba, 1963; Kornhauser, 1959). We know little about what happens to women there.

The objective of this paper is to begin to fill this gap. It is based on a study examining in detail the day-to-day workings of two local political organizations. It seeks to reveal the social patterns and interpersonal behaviors by which the process of equality at the base of the political system yields to increasing inequalities as political hierarchies are ascended.

Reprinted with permission from *Social Problems* 26 (February 1979):314–324, abridged by The Society for the Study of Social Problems and by the author.

Reading 20
Sex Roles and Division of Labor in Politics

BACKGROUND AND METHODS

The thirteen female and twenty-three male respondents were the members of the Republican and Democratic Town Committees of Fairtown, Connecticut.[1] There, as in most other New England states, affairs of both political parties are conducted at the grassroots level by Town Committees. These bodies serve as a kind of personnel department for their towns. They interview and recommend candidates for appointive offices and they endorse candidates for elective offices. In addition, they run local political campaigns, serve as links to the state party organizations and determine the local party's position on issues.

Fairtown is an affluent, almost entirely (98.9 percent) white community of about 18,000. In 1970 the median years of education for Fairtowners was thirteen; the median family income was close to $17,000; almost 60 percent of the employed men (only 1.6 percent of the men were unemployed) worked as professionals, technicians, managers or proprietors; and over half of them worked out of town. Of the 10,000 voters registered in 1973, more than half were registered Republicans, the rest splitting almost evenly between Democrats and unaffiliated voters. The actual political divisions, however, were most complicated. Both parties were split between conservative and liberal or moderate factions, the latter having gained a bare majority on both party's Town Committees shortly before the study began.

The group under study was small and not statistically representative of the American population, nor even of grassroots political organizations, and therefore generalizations must be made with caution. Nevertheless, because the focus was on those ordinary, taken-for granted acts that are part of the everyday fabric of our culture, intensive and detailed data collection techniques, impossible to perform with large samples, were necessary.

Members of the two Town Committees were interviewed frequently and observed at meetings and other political gatherings from September through December, 1974. In addition, at the initial interview all respondents were given a form on which to record all of their daily political activities. Although each committee member was asked to record *all* conversations that had any political content, and *all* the work each subject had done for the party, there were variations in the completeness of the logs. In general, the men were slightly better log-keepers than the women. This may exaggerate the amount of activity of the males and minimize that of the females, a possible bias in a direction opposite from the findings. Thus differences between the men and women might have

---

[1] All names of persons and places are fictitious.

AMOUNT AND LOCATION OF ACTIVITY

Men outnumbered women on both Town Committees—thirteen to six on the Republican Town Committee and ten to seven on the Democratic—but the women were far more active than the men. Of the 1,832 interactions recorded, 1,185, or about two-thirds, were performed by women. The average number of interactions per man was thirty-one, while the average for the women was three times that, or one hundred. This was an unexpected finding because men had seemed to be as frequently present as women at meetings, fund-raisers and work sessions.

The location of their activities helps explain why women seemed less busy than they actually were. Whatever the men and women were doing politically could range from the highly noticeable to the invisible. Public speeches were probably the most noticeable activity, while work done alone was the least noticed. In between were attendance at meetings, fund-raisers or group work sessions at which one would be seen by several others, and phone conversations which would be noticed by only one other. Women's activities tended to take place in situations where they would not be widely observed; the reverse was true of men's activities. . . .

SOCIAL NETWORKS

Although women were more likely to work alone or with just one other person, the range of their associations was greater than men's. Women's communications were not as restricted to members of their Town Committees as were men's. Forty-nine percent of women's interactions were within their own Town Committees as opposed to 58 percent of men's. Moreover, the average woman interacted with a greater number of other persons (18) than the average man (10). On the other hand, especially when venturing beyond their own Town Committees, women were much more likely than men to restrict their interactions to persons of their own gender. Clearly, then, all members of the Town Committees were parochial, interacting almost exclusively with others of their own party, if not necessarily with their Town Committee colleagues, and predominantly with persons of their own gender. However, men showed a somewhat greater tendency to be ideocentric—restricting their interactions to persons of the same political *persuasion;* women showed a greater tendency towards sexocentrism—restricting their communications more to persons of the same *gender* (72.4 percent compared to 63.2 percent for men.)

Reading 20
Sex Roles and Division of Labor in Politics

TOPICS OF TALK AND KINDS OF WORK

What were all those communications about? When we look at the subjects that men and women discussed and the tasks they worked on, patterns emerge which further explain the invisibility of women and also indicate differences in the roles assumed by men and women....

WOMEN'S TALK

Women's talk most often involved an exchange of information. When an extra meeting was called or when the time or place of a regular meeting was changed, women would spread that information. If facts had to be gathered, such as the rulings on absentee ballots, a woman would call some authority to find out. Not infrequently, if a man needed some information he would ask a woman to get it for him. (For example, a sample woman's log showed that Joe, a candidate, asked her to get information about absentee ballots from Janet, the town clerk.)

Women also talked about arrangements for work tasks. Whether it was a mailing that had to be sent out, a fund-raiser that had to be arranged, or some other task, women were almost invariably the ones who took upon themselves the responsibility of organization and management. They usually did this in committees or teams, and sometimes men were included. Profuse communications were generated in the coordination of every task and it often took far more separate interactions, if not more time, to get any job set up than it took to actually do the work. (For instance, a sample female log showed that it took six communications to arrange for absentee ballots to be sent to voters.)

Third, women talked—mostly among themselves, but sometimes with men—about the campaign. When a candidate issued a statement, or a speech was made, or some decision was needed about how to run a campaign, women sought out each other's opinion; and they discussed and analyzed the virtues and shortcomings of candidates and their campaigns—frequently and at some length.

The fourth most common topic of women's talk was problems on their own Town Committees.

Finally, women more often than men ranged from one topic to another. For example, nine of the twenty-two items on a woman's sample log covered more than one subject.

MEN'S TALK

The most common item on the men's logs was an attempt to influence another person. Most male talk about specific issues took place just before a vote was scheduled. Women's talk about most topics, even those

Chapter VI
Sexism and Problems of the Aging

on which a vote was eventually held, was usually spread over a protracted period before the issue came to a decision.

In addition to conversations aimed at influencing others, men's logs included more mentions of large group functions at which attendance would be noticed by many others—parties, fund-raisers, rallies and openings of campaign headquarters....

To summarize: The subjects women talked about tended to be general and far-ranging, and they often covered several topics in a single conversation. Commonly when women wished a change of some sort they casually initiated issues to test for support. Men's talk, on the other hand, covered just a single subject; normally it arose at the moment when some issue was about to be decided; and generally it had a specific goal—to garner support for some position. Where women's talk was specific, it had as its goal not so much the influencing of another as an exchange of information or the organization of a work task.

Women took care of what needed to be done for the day-to-day maintenance of the Town Committees. Tasks which normally must be done on a regular monthly or yearly basis were more likely to be undertaken by women, especially if those chores were not attached to an official role. In contrast, men did only that work which was assigned to them by virtue of the official positions they held, and whatever they then did beyond that was usually a special or nonrecurring job. Women worked behind the scene; men worked in public.

THE UNOFFICIAL ROLES WOMEN PLAY

Up until now items in the logs have been grouped by gender as if all the men and all the women contributed equally to the work and talk of their parties. They didn't. Some men and some women were hardly doing a thing while others were working and talking prodigiously. In fact, thirteen men, more than two-thirds of the men keeping logs,[2] recorded less than forty interactions; three recorded between forty and sixty; and another three between sixty and one hundred. No man recorded more than one hundred interactions. The balance shifts in the opposite direction on the distaff side. Four women recorded more than one hundred interactions; one logged between sixty and one hundred; three between forty and fifty-nine; and three others logged less than forty.

What accounts for these differences in activity? Without exception those who recorded more than forty interactions were playing a special

---

[2] Two of the men and one of the women who did not keep a log resigned from their Town Committees before the study was completed. In addition two men and one woman refused to keep a log.

Reading 20
Sex Roles and Division of Labor in Politics

role. There was, however, a strategic difference between the roles played be men and those played by women. Only men who had titular status recorded more than fifty interactions, while most of the roles women played were parts without title or acknowledgment.

Party chairpersons were the most active men. The Republican logged eighty-two interactions and the Democrat sixty-seven. The Republican treasurer, a man, logged precisely the same number, fifty-two, as his Democratic counterpart, a woman. Two other men logging more than forty interactions were the former chairpersons of the party clubs. They continued to lead their factions after they were elected to the Town Committee by assuming the unofficial role of "Advisor-to-the-Majority." The sixth man with more than forty interactions was a Republican who assisted his party's Advisor-to-the-Majority.

All other unofficial roles were played by women.[3] There was no regular position for a person who would spread news throughout the Town Committee and keep the Committee in touch with other groups in town, and yet both parties had such a woman, whom we shall call the "Communicator-in-Chief." As has already been noted, there was a great deal of routine work especially related to getting out the vote and raising money which by unwritten rule was to have been shared equally by all the Town Committee members. It wasn't. Each Town Committee had a woman, whom we shall call the "Drudge," who assumed much of that burden. Again, when a Town Committee vote was nearing, someone had to call members to make sure they attended the meeting and voted with their faction. Only the moderate Republicans and liberal Democrats seemed to have such a person, a woman, whom we shall call the "Majority Whip." But the Majority Whip did not decide how her faction should act; for that she turned to the man we call the "Advisor-to-the Majority." Most notable was the fact that, different as the parties were, almost identical roles appeared in both, and the gender of the persons filling parallel roles was the same in both parties.

THE COMMUNICATOR-IN-CHIEF

The role that called for the most interactions was that of Communicator-in-Chief. It was played on the Republican Town Committee by Sophie

---

[3]Three of the women who played unofficial roles also held a titular position. However, the unofficial role was not a part of their official role. Thus the Republican "Whip" was her party's secretary, while it was the Vice-chairperson of the Democratic party who played that role. The "Communicator-in-Chief" of the Republican party was also the Vice-chairperson, but the "Communicator-in-Chief" for the Democrats had no official role. No man holding an official position assumed an unofficial one as well.

Chapter VI
Sexism and Problems of the Aging

Morelli, and on the Democratic Town Committee by Janie Brown. They acted as intermediaries between the factions in their parties; carried information and other communications between the Town Committee and other groups in town; and even on occasion linked the two Town Committees. Although her political activities were extensive, they were but a small part of the Communicator-in-Chief's community participation—she was active in several organizations and this brought her into acquaintanceships with persons all over town.

Sophie Morelli, an eighty-year-old woman who had been active in Fairtown's Republican party for close to a half-century, ambled through Town Hall each day having a word with her relatives (a daughter and a grandchild) and others who worked there, picking up and spreading bits and pieces of the news of the day. She often lunched at a local diner whose clientele was made up mostly of conservative Republicans. They interspersed gossip about weddings, births, children and divorces with discussion of candidates and political issues. When there was an important development, Morelli would call her party chairperson. Whatever there was to say, she talked with several members of her Town Committee daily.

Although Janie Brown was clearly a liberal Democrat she worked hard to maintain her ties in other groups. Her party chairperson, a conservative, spoke with her more than with anyone else in the liberal faction. Indeed, of all the members on both Town Committees, Janie Brown was the one with the broadest network of contacts. The average woman on a Town Committee talked with only twenty other persons; in Brown's log there was mention of almost twice that number, thirty-eight.

Majority Whips

To get out the faction's vote there was in each majority faction a Whip. The Majority Whip usually notified the Advisor-to-the-Majority when concerted action was needed and then, after she and the Advisor had decided what was to be done, called others in their faction. Before an important vote was taken, Barbara Weatherton conferred with her two Advisors-to-the-Majority and then canvassed the Republican moderates.

Several times during that autumn the liberal Democrats decided to caucus. When they did they usually met at Marjorie Hasting's house and it was she who called the others to the meeting. Many additional meetings were also held at her house; it was usually she who acted as the unofficial moderator. The Whip had two other functions. If a position was open and no one to the liking of the faction came forward, the Whip would try to find a candidate. (In the Democratic party Hastings shared this job with Brown.) She also filled in whenever a male failed to carry out his assignment. For instance, the Democratic campaign manager took a trip to Europe two weeks before the election: Hastings than ran the campaign.

The role of Whip involved a large number of communications. Hastings listed 121 interactions with thirty-two different persons, and she was listed in other persons' logs forty-nine times. Weatherton was somewhat less active; she listed eighty-two separate interactions with twenty-six different persons and was mentioned in the logs of others only seven times.

DRUDGES

Another unofficial role that involved many interactions and was performed exclusively by women was that of "Drudge." The Drudge made most of the arrangements for fund-raisers; prepared more than her share of the food; decorated the room in which the fund-raisers were held; cleaned up afterwards; made arrangements for mailings and addressed more envelopes than anyone else. Unlike others on the Town Committee, a large percentage of the Drudge's work was done alone. Edna Halsey, the Democratic Drudge, logged a modest forty-six items, but for thirty-six percent of those items she was working alone preparing food, ironing tablecloths for a fund-raiser square dance and addressing envelopes. The Republican Drudge was Mary Kelley. Her log does not show such a high percentage of work done alone because she was also an assistant Communicator-in-Chief for Morelli. Also, as the Republican treasury was ample, most of their fund-raisers were catered, requiring many arrangements but not much solitary preparation.

Mary Kelley and Edna Halsey handled the role of Drudge differently. Halsey was assigned tasks by other women who organized the affairs at which she worked. Kelley was self-directed. She organized the tasks and tried to get others to help out, but then did most of the work herself. Both women were appreciated for what they did, but only Kelley was respected for it. A number of Republican men lauded her with the same words: "What we need in this party is more women like Kelley." And Kelley, fully a year before nominations were in order, was being urged to run for Selectperson or even for "First."

Edna Halsey was strictly a Drudge. A feminist Democratic woman said of her:

> I don't know why she was ever put on that Town Committee. She's a sweet lady, she does all the cooking and baking and fussing at parties, but political philosophy is beyond her.

Chapter VI
Sexism and Problems of the Aging

CONCLUSIONS

Women who enter politics tend to be motivated either by a service orientation or by what Elazar has called a "moralistic" political orientation—belief that politics is "one of the great activities of man in his search for the good society" (1972:96-98). The service orientation lends itself to the role of Drudge, and women who view politics as a locale for giving are welcome in any political party. The idealistic orientation is not so welcome. Women who view politics as an opportunity to help bring forth a better world are likely to find their way into politics only where the system is open. Politics in Fairtown was open, but not so open that individuals filled roles by virtue for their talents rather than their gender.

This is, of course, not the first time a study has uncovered unofficial divisions of labor by gender where the rules called for equality. Rosabeth Moss Kantor (1977), for example, found that women in business corporations played special roles not unlike those played by Fairtown's Town Committee women. There were few ranking women in the corporation she studied, and she attributed their seemingly sex-linked roles and behaviors to their token status. In this study, the women, though a minority, were not tokens. Numbers seemed to have little to do with the situation. The proportion of women on the two Town Committees differed—thirty-two percent of the Republicans and forty-one percent of the Democrats—yet the roles played on both committees were linked to gender. Ideology was apparently not relevant. Four of the Democratic women were outspoken feminists; none of the Republicans was. Yet women played the same unofficial roles in both parties; indeed, the Democratic Majority Whip was a staunch feminist.

In her study of state legislatures, Diamond found that the women there, like the women in Fairtown, were extraordinarily conscientious, and she asks:

> Is that conscientiousness...a response to the expectation that women are incompetent unless they prove otherwise? Is it their way of adapting to their "marginal man" status in the legislature? Or is it an outgrowth of sex-role training, a manifestation of the "tidy housewife" syndrome?... [Or could it be] that these women actually have fewer outside conflicts in the allocation of their time than male breadwinners? (1977:95)

She does not answer, noting that "the question needs further exploration."

I would like to suggest that the overriding reason men and women take on the roles they do is that these are the roles they play in our culture wherever men and women come together in any sort of social organization, the prototypical one being the family. With only minor

Reading 20
Sex Roles and Division of Labor in Politics

transformations, the roles the Fairtown men and women were playing on their Town Committees were the same ones men and women play in households. Men are thought to be the "heads" of their families; and men were the chairpersons of the Town Committees. Men have specific and narrow functions in the family—primarily to provide its income and sometimes to act as its public spokesperson. So, too, on the Town Committees they did only what was specifically required of them. Women, on the other hand, handle the day-to-day maintenance of the household, performing a plethora of tasks, some precisely defined such as preparing food, but many amorphous, such as bonding the nuclear family to others through social contacts. Similarly, on the Town Committees all the regular, official maintenance-type functions and also all tasks which could not be specifically defined fell to women. Another role women played in both the family and on the Town Committees was that of standby. They were there to step in whenever a man failed to accomplish his appointed task.

Women, then, take care of the maintenance of institutions and fill in the gaps. They are also the ones to *spot* gaps, bringing to the attention of men situations that call for a decision, and monitoring the early stages in decision making—gathering the necessary information and garnering support. But when it is time to settle an issue, to make a final decision, men come to the fore. The analogy between the family and the political party is so close that even when it comes to the selection of persons to fill official positions on the Town Committees and in town government, patterns characteristic of the family are followed—i.e., men aggressively seek positions, but women wait to be wooed.

The tendency among women to work in seclusion (while men seek to capture center stage) also has antecedents in the family. The women in this study, as in Kantor's (1977) and Diamond's (1977), were of the middle class. It is a class that has, over the past half-century, suffered some ambivalence towards work—especially the work that women do.

The Protestant ethic places a high value on work, but as Thorstein Veblen (1953) noted: "To be leisured is a sign of success while manual work is *declassé*." Before World War II, it was a point of honor with the middle class that men did not do menial labor and women did not labor at all. Housework was done by paid help. After the war, household help rose in cost beyond the reach of most families, so that women who are now past forty (an age most common among the women on the Town Committees and in state legislatures) had to take on the menial work their mothers had spurned. Their situation changed, but their values did not. So, with the help of tips from women's magazines, they learned to do their housework in secret. The mark of a well-run household was freshly vacuumed carpets, gourmet meals, shinyfaced children and a neatly dressed wife-mother who was never seen cooking, cleaning or washing, not even by her husband.

When there is political work to do, the same women who learned to work this magic at home take pains to repeat it in the political arena. They are task-oriented, measuring their political performance by completed projects. The men, on the other hand, garner their self-esteem, not from tasks accomplished but from being included in decision making. For them, to be seen in a place where decisions are being made is more important than accomplishing any task. Carrying this orientation over to the Town Committees the men did little alone. The significant part of their political involvement was to *appear* to be running things, to *appear* to be part of the process, to be seen.

These differences have implications for the political careers of men and women. When work needs to be done, the women who in the past have so reliably performed tasks for their party are called upon again. But when ranking positions are to be filled, it is the men—ever conspicuous and desirous of titles—who usually get the nod.

REFERENCES

Almond, Gabriel A., and Sidney Verba. 1963. *The Civic Culture*. Boston: Little, Brown.
Chamberlain, H. 1974. *A Minority of Members: Women in the U.S. Congress*. New York: Praeger.
Diamond, Irene. 1977. *Sex Roles in the State House*. New Haven, Conn.: Yale University Press.
Duverger, Maurice. 1972. *The Study of Politics*. New York: Thomas Y. Crowell.
Elazar, Daniel. 1972. *American Federalism*. 2nd ed. New York: Thomas Y. Crowell.
Githens, Marianne, and Jewel L. Prestage. 1977. *A Portrait of Marginality: The Political Behavior of the American Woman*. New York: David McKay.
Kantor, Rosabeth Moss. 1977. *Men and Women of the Corporation*. New York: Basic Books.
Key, V. O. 1948. *Politics, Parties and Pressure Groups*. New York: Thomas Y. Crowell.
Kirkpatric, Jean. 1974. *Political Woman*. New York: Basic Books.
Kornhauser, William. 1959. *The Politics of Mass Society*. Glencoe, Ill.: Free Press.
Lazarsfeld, Paul, Bernard Berelson, and Hazel Gaudet. 1944. *The People's Choice*. New York: Columbia University Press.
Lipset, Seymour Martin. 1960. *Political Man*. Garden City, N.Y.: Doubleday.
Tolchin, Susan, and Martin Tolchin. 1974. *Clout: Women in the Mainstream*. New York: Coward, McCann and Geoghegan.
Veblen, Thorstein. 1953. *The Theory of the Leisure Class*. New York: Mentor Books.

Reading 21
SEXUAL TERRORISM

Carole J. Sheffield, *William Paterson College*

> *Sexual terrorism is a built-in support of the patriarchal system. Like other forms of terrorism practiced by a majority group, its purpose is to dominate and control people in minority positions by keeping them continuously frightened. Sexual and political terrorism are similar in four of five main components (ideology, propaganda, arbitrary unpredictability, and voluntary compliance by the terrorists). Sexual terrorism is more devastating in a fifth main characteristic: We sympathize with the innocent victims of political terrorism; in sexual terrorism we blame the victims.*

> *No two of us think alike about it, and yet it is clear to me, that question underlies the whole movement, and our little skirmishing for better laws, and the right to vote, will yet be swallowed up in the real question, viz: Has a woman a right to herself? It is very little to me to have the right to vote, to own property, etc., if I may not keep my body, and its uses, in my absolute right. Not one wife in a thousand can do that now.*
>
> Lucy Stone,
in a letter to Antoinette Brown,
July 11, 1855

The right of men to control the female body is a cornerstone of patriarchy. It is expressed by their efforts to control pregnancy and childbirth and to define female health care in general. Male opposition to abortion is rooted in opposition to female autonomy. Violence and the threat of vi-

---

Copyright © 1984 by Carole J. Sheffield. Reprinted with permission. Due to the historical and theoretical significance of this ground-breaking piece, it is being reprinted in its original form. The author acknowledges that as a result of considerable activism, more states have eliminated the marital rape exemption and are working on improving police training and procedures. Most importantly, the author is rethinking the relationship between violence and sex. She believes that for men, acts of sexual terrorism are a fusion of aggression, domination, and sexuality but that women experience sexual terrorism as violence.

Chapter VI
Sexism and Problems of the Aging

olence against females represent the need of patriarchy to deny that a woman's body is her own property and that no one should have access to it without her consent. Violence and its corollary, fear, serve to terrorize females and to maintain the patriarchal definition of woman's place.

The word *terrorism* invokes images of furtive organizations of the far right or left, whose members blow up buildings and cars, hijack airplanes, and murder innocent people in some country other than ours. But there is a different kind of terrorism, one that so pervades our culture that we have learned to live with it as though it were the natural order of things. Its targets are females—of all ages, races, and classes. It is the common characteristic of rape, wife battery, incest, pornography, harassment, and all forms of sexual violence. I call it *sexual terrorism* because it is a system by which males frighten and, by frightening, control and dominate females.

The concept of terrorism captured my attention in an "ordinary" event. One afternoon I collected my laundry and went to a nearby laundromat. The place is located in a small shopping center on a very busy highway. After I had loaded and started the machines, I became acutely aware of my environment. It was just after 6:00 P.M. and dark; the other stores were closed; the laundromat was brightly lit; and my car was the only one in the lot. Anyone passing by could readily see that I was alone and isolated. Knowing that rape is a crime of opportunity, I became terrified. I wanted to leave and find a laundromat that was busier, but my clothes were well into the wash cycle, and, besides, I felt I was being "silly," "paranoid." The feeling of terror persisted, so I sat in my car, windows up, and doors locked. When the wash was completed, I dashed in, threw the clothes into the drier, and ran back out to my car. When the clothes were dry, I tossed them recklessly into the basket and hurriedly drove away to fold them in the security of my home.

Although I was not victimized in a direct, physical way or by objective or measurable standards, I felt victimized. It was, for me, a terrifying experience. I felt controlled by an invisible force. I was angry that something as commonplace as doing laundry after a day's work jeopardized my well-being. Mostly I was angry at being unfree: a hostage of a culture that, for the most part, encourages violence against females, instructs men in the methodology of sexual violence, and provides them with ready justification for their violence. I was angry that I could be victimized by being "in the wrong place at the wrong time." The essence of terrorism is that one never knows when is the wrong time and where is the wrong place.

Following my experience at the laundromat, I talked with my students about terrorization. Women students began to open up and reveal terrors that they had kept secret because of embarrassment: fears of jogging alone, dining alone, going to the movies alone. One woman recalled feelings of terror in her adolescence when she did child care for extra money. Nothing had ever happened and she had not been afraid of anyone in particular, but she had felt a vague terror when being driven home late at night by the man of the house.

The men listened incredulously and then demanded equal time. The harder they tried the more they realized how very different—qualitatively, quantitatively, and contextually—their fears were. All agreed that, while they experienced fear in a violent society, they did not experience terror; nor did they experience fear of rape or sexual mutilation. They felt more in control, either from a psychophysical sense of security that they could defend themselves or from a confidence in being able to determine wrong places and times. All the women admitted fear and anxiety when walking to their cars on the campus, especially after an evening class or activity. None of the men experienced fear on campus at any time. The men could be rather specific in describing when they were afraid: in Harlem, for example, or in certain parts of downtown Paterson, New Jersey—places that have a reputation for violence. But these places could either be avoided or, if not, the men felt capable of self-protective action. Above all, male students said that they *never* feared being attacked simply because they were male. They *never* feared going to a movie or to dinner alone. Their daily activities were not characterized by a concern for their physical integrity.

As I read the literature on terrorism it became clear that both sexual violence and nonviolent sexual intimidation could be better understood as terrorism. For example, although an act of rape, an unnecessary hysterectomy, and the publishing of *Playboy* magazine appear to be quite different, they are in fact more similar than dissimilar. Each is based on fear, hostility, and a need to dominate women. Rape is an act of aggression and possession, not of sexuality. Unnecessary hysterectomies are extraordinary abuses of power rooted in man's concept of woman as primarily a reproductive being and in his need to assert power over reproduction. *Playboy*, like all forms of pornography, attempts to control women through the power of definition. Male pornographers define women's sexuality for their male customers. The basis of pornography is men's fantasies about women's sexuality.

COMPONENTS OF SEXUAL TERRORISM

The literature on terrorism does not provide a precise definition (Alexander, 1979; Evans, 1979; Johnson, 1978; Thornton, 1964; Walter, 1969; Watson, 1976; Wilkinson, 1974). Mine is taken from Hacker (1976), who says that "terrorism aims to frighten, and by frightening, to dominate and

Chapter VI
Sexism and Problems of the Aging

control." Writers agree more readily on the characteristics and functions of terrorism than on a definition. This analysis will focus on five components to illuminate the similarities of and distinctions between sexual terrorism and political terrorism. The five components are: ideology, propaganda, indiscriminate and amoral violence, voluntary compliance, and society's perception of the terrorist and the terrorized.

An *ideology* is an integrated set of beliefs about the world that explains the way things are and provides a vision of how they ought to be. Patriarchy, meaning the "rule of the fathers," is the ideological foundation of sexism in our society. It asserts the superiority of males and the inferiority of females. It also provides the rationale for sexual terrorism. The taproot of patriarchy is the masculine/warrior ideal. Masculinity must include not only a proclivity for violence but also all those characteristics necessary for survival: aggression, control, emotional reserve, rationality, sexual potency, etc. Marc Feigen Fasteau (1974), in *The Male Machine*, argues that "men are brought up with the idea that there ought to be some part of them, under control until released by necessity, that thrives on violence. This capacity, even affinity, for violence, lurking beneath the surface of every real man, is supposed to represent the primal untamed base of masculinity."

Propaganda is the methodical dissemination of information for the purpose of promoting a particular ideology. Propaganda, by definition, is biased or even false information. Its purpose is to present one point of view on a subject and to discredit opposing points of view. Propaganda is essential to the conduct of terrorism. According to Francis Watson (1976:15), in *Political Terrorism: The Threat and the Response*, "Terrorism must not be defined only in terms of violence, but also in terms of propaganda. The two are in operation together. Violence of terrorism is a coercive means for attempting to influence the thinking and actions of people. Propaganda is a persuasive means for doing the same thing." The propaganda of sexual terrorism is found in all expressions of the popular culture: films, television, music, literature, advertising, pornography. The propaganda of sexual terrorism is also found in the ideas of patriarchy expressed in science, medicine, and psychology.

The third component, which is common to all forms of political terrorism, consists of "indiscriminateness, unpredictability, arbitrariness, ruthless destructiveness and amorality" (Wilkinson, 1974:17). Indiscriminate violence and amorality are also at the heart of sexual terrorism. Every female is a potential target of violence—at any age, at any time, in any place. In her study of rape, Susan Brownmiller (1975) argues that rape is "nothing more or less than a conscious process of intimidation by which all men keep all women in a state of fear." Further, as we shall see, amorality pervades sexual violence. Child molesters, incestuous fathers, wife beaters, and rapists often do not understand that they have done anything wrong. Their views are routinely shared by police officers, lawyers, and judges, and crimes of sexual violence are rarely punished in American society.

The fourth component of the theory of terrorism is "voluntary compliance." The institutionalization of a system of terror requires the development of mechanisms other than sustained violence to achieve its goals. Violence must be employed to maintain terrorism, but sustained violence can be costly and debilitating. Therefore, strategies for ensuring a significant degree of voluntary compliance must be developed. Sexual terrorism is maintained to a great extent by an elaborate system of sex-role socialization that in effect instructs men to be terrorists in the name of masculinity and women to be victims in the name of femininity.

Sexual and political terrorism differ in the final component, perception of the terrorist and the victim. In political terrorism we know who is the terrorist and who is the victim. We may condemn or condone the terrorist depending on our political views, but we sympathize with the victim. In sexual terrorism, however, we blame the victim and excuse the offender. We believe that the offender either is "sick" and therefore in need of our compassion or is acting out normal male impulses.

TYPES OF SEXUAL TERRORISM

Many types of sexual terrorism are crimes. Yet when we look at the history of these acts we see that they came to be considered criminal not so much to protect women as to adjust power relationships among men. Rape was originally a violation of a father's or husband's property right; consequently, a husband by definition could not rape his wife. Wife beating was condoned by the law and still is condemned in name only. The pornographic presentation of sexual violence serves to direct male violence against women and girls and to contain male violence toward other men (Chesler, 1980). Although proscriptions against incest exist, society assumes a more serious posture toward men who sexually abuse other men's daughters. Sexual harassment is not a crime, and only recently has it been declared an actionable civil offense. Crimes of sexual violence are characterized by ambiguity and diversity in definition and interpretation. Because each state and territory has a separate system of law in addition to the federal system, crimes and punishments are assessed differently throughout the country.

RAPE

The most generally accepted definition of rape is "sexual intercourse with a female, not the wife of the perpetrator, without the consent of the female" (Russell, 1975). Seventeen states punish rape within marriage (National Clearinghouse on Marital Rape).

Because rape is considered a sexual act, evidence of force and resistance (that is, nonconsent) plays a major role in the conviction or acquittal of rapists. Proof of nonconsent and resistance is not demanded of a victim of any other crime. If one is stopped on the street and robbed one never has to justify nonresistance or prove resistance and nonconsent. Females are expected to resist rape as much as possible, otherwise "consent" is assumed.

John M. MacDonald (1975), in *Rape Offenders and Their Victims,* offers the following advice to law enforcement officials: "To constitute resistance in good faith it must have been commenced at the inception of the advances and continued until the offense was consummated. Resistance by mere words is not sufficient, but such resistance must be by acts, and must be reasonably proportionate to the strength and opportunities of the woman." Passive resistance or compliance, even in a situation that is perceived to be life-threatening, is not, to many prosecutors, clear evidence that the rape was against one's will.

WIFE ASSAULT

For centuries it has been assumed that a husband had the right to punish or discipline his wife with physical force. The popular expression, "rule of thumb," originated from English common law, which allowed a husband to beat his wife with a whip or stick no bigger than his thumb. The husband's prerogative was incorporated into American law. Several states had statutes that essentially allowed a man to beat his wife without interference from the courts (*Bradley v. State*).

In 1871, in the landmark case of *Fulgham v. State,* an Alabama court ruled that "the privilege, ancient though it be, to beat her with a stick, to pull her hair, choke her, spit in her face or kick her about the floor or to inflict upon her other like indignities, is not now acknowledged by our law." The law, however, has been ambiguous and often contradictory on the issue of wife assault. While the courts established that a man had no right to beat his wife, it also held that a woman could not press charges against her abusive husband. In 1910, the U.S. Supreme Court ruled that a wife could not charge her husband with assault and battery because it "would open the doors of the courts to accusations of all sorts of one spouse against the other and bring into public notice complaints for assaults, slander and libel" (*Thompson v. Thompson*). The courts virtually condoned violence for the purpose of maintaining peace.

Laws and public attitudes about the illegality of wife assault and the rights of the victim have been slowly evolving, and attempts are being made to resolve the contradictions. Only three states (California, Hawaii, and Texas) define wife abuse as a felony (Langley and Levy, 1977). In other states, laws applicable to wife battery include assault, assault and battery, aggravated assault, intent to assault or to commit murder, and possession of a deadly weapon with intent to assault.

SEXUAL ABUSE OF CHILDREN

Defining sexual abuse of children is very difficult. The laws are complex and often contradictory. Generally, sexual abuse of children includes statutory rape, molestation, carnal knowledge, indecent liberties, impairing the morals of a minor, child abuse, child neglect, and incest. Each of these is defined and interpreted differently in each state. Convictions run the gamut from misdemeanors to various degrees of assault and felony. Punishments vary widely from state to state as well.

The philosophy underlying statutory rape laws is that a child below a certain age—arbitrarily fixed by law—is not able to give meaningful consent. Therefore, sexual intercourse with a female below a certain age, with or without the use of force, is a criminal act of rape. Punishment for statutory rape, although rarely imposed, can be as high as life imprisonment. Coexistent with laws on statutory rape are laws on criminal incest. Incest is generally interpreted as sexual activity, most often intercourse, with a blood relative. The difference, then, between statutory rape and incest is the relation of the offender to the child. Statutory rape is committed by someone outside the family; incest, by a member of the family. The penalty for incest, also rarely imposed, is usually no more than ten years in prison. This contrast suggests that sexual abuse of children is tolerated when it occurs within the family and that unqualified protection of children from sexual assault is not the intent of the law.

SEXUAL HARASSMENT

"Sexual harassment" is a new term for an old phenomenon. The research on sexual harassment, as well as the legal interpretation, centers on acts of sexual coercion or intimidation on the job and at school. Lin Farley (1978), in *Sexual Shakedown: The Sexual Harassment of Women on the Job,* describes sexual harassment as "unsolicited nonreciprocal male behavior that asserts a woman's sex role over her function as a worker. It can be any or all of the following: staring at, commenting upon, or touching a woman's body; requests for acquiescence in sexual behavior; repeated nonreciprocated propositions for dates; demands for sexual intercourse; and rape."

Sexual harassment is now considered a form of sex discrimination under some conditions and is therefore a violation of Title VII of the 1964 Civil Rights Act, which prohibits sex discrimination in employment, and of Title IX of the 1972 Education Amendments, which prohibits sex-based discrimination in education.

CHARACTERISTICS OF SEXUAL TERRORISM

Those forms of sexual terrorism that are crimes share several common characteristics. Each will be addressed separately, but in the real world these characteristics are linked together and form a vicious circle, which functions to mask the reality of sexual terrorism and thus to perpetuate the system of oppression of females. Crimes of violence against females (1) cut across socioeconomic lines; (2) are the crimes least likely to be reported; (3) when reported, are the crimes least likely to be brought to trial or to result in conviction; (4) are often blamed on the victim; (5) are generally not taken seriously; and (6) are not really about sex.

Violence against Females Cuts across Socioeconomic Lines

The question "Who is the typical rapist, wife beater, incest offender, etc?" is constantly raised. The answer is simple: men. Even among those who commit incest, women are exceedingly rare. The men who commit acts of sexual terrorism are of all ages, races, and religions; they come from all communities, income levels, and educational levels; they are married, single, separated, and divorced. The typical sexually abusive male does not exist.

One of the most common assumptions about sexual violence is that it occurs primarily among the poor, uneducated, and predominately nonwhite populations. Instead, violence committed by the poor and nonwhite is simply more visible because they lack the resources to ensure the privacy that the middle and upper classes can purchase. Most rapes, indeed most incidents of sexual assault, are not reported, and therefore the picture drawn from police records must be viewed as very sketchy.

The data on sexual harassment in work situations indicates that it occurs among all job categories and pay ranges (Farley, 1978:18). Sexual harassment is committed by academic men, who are among the most highly educated members of society.

All of the studies on wife battery testify to the fact that wife beating crosses socioeconomic lines. Wife beaters include high government officials, members of the armed forces, businessmen, policemen, physicians, lawyers, clergy, bluecollar workers, and the unemployed (Langley and Levy, 1977:43). According to Maria Roy, founder and director of New

Reading 21
Sexual Terrorism

York's Abused Women's Aid in Crisis: "We see abuse of women on all levels of income, age, occupation, and social standing. I've had four women come in recently whose husbands are Ph.D.s—two of them professors at top universities. Another abused woman is married to a very prominent attorney. We counseled battered women whose husbands are doctors, psychiatrists, even clergymen" (Langley and Levy, 1977: 44).

Similarly, in Vincent De Francis's (1969) classic study of 250 cases of sexual crimes committed against children, a major finding was that incidents of sexual assault against children cut across class lines.

Since sexual violence is not "nice," we prefer to believe that nice men do not commit these acts and that nice girls and women are not victims. Our refusal to accept the fact that violence against females is widespread on all levels of society strongly inhibits our ability to develop any meaningful strategies toward the elimination of sexual violence. Moreover, because of underreporting, it is difficult to ascertain exactly how widespread it is.

CRIMES OF SEXUAL VIOLENCE ARE THE LEAST LIKELY TO BE REPORTED

The underreporting issue, often called the "tip-of-the-iceberg theory," is common to all crimes against females. The FBI recognizes that rape is the most frequently committed violent crime and is seriously underreported. According to FBI data for 1981, 81,536 rapes were reported (U.S. Department of Justice, 1987). The FBI and other criminologists suggest that this figure be multiplied by at least a factor of ten to compensate for underreporting. The FBI *Uniform Crime Report* for 1981 estimates that a forcible rape occurs every six minutes (Ibid: 6). This estimate is based on reported cases; to account for the high rate of underreporting the FBI estimates that a rape occurs every two minutes. The number of forcible rapes reported to the police has been increasing every year. Between 1977 and 1981, there has been a 29 percent increase in reported forcible rapes (Ibid: 14). It is estimated that one-half of all rape victims are under eighteen years of age and 25 percent of rape victims are under twelve years of age (Rush, 1980).

The FBI's *Uniform Crime Report* indexes 10 million reported crimes a year but does not collect statistics on wife abuse. Since statutes in most states do not identify wife beating as a crime, incidents of wife beating are usually classified under "assault and battery" and "disputes." However, the FBI estimates that wife abuse is three times as common as rape. Estimates that 50 percent of American wives are battered are not uncommon in the literature (Langley and Levy, 1977:3).

"The problem of sexual abuse of children is of unknown national dimensions," according to Vincent De Francis (1969), "but findings strongly point to the probability of an enormous national incidence many times larger than the reported incidence of physical abuse of children." He discussed the existence of a wide gap between the reported incidence and the actual occurrence of sexual assault against children and suggested that "the reported incidence represents the top edge of the moon as it rises over the mountain."

Incest, according to author and researcher Florence Rush (1980), is the *Best Kept Secret*. The estimates, however speculative, are frightening. Alfred Kinsey (1953), in a study involving 4,441 female subjects, found that 24 percent had been approached sexually by an adult male prior to their adolescence; in 23 percent of the cases that adult male was a relative. Significantly, all the respondents in the Kinsey study were white and predominately middle class. The Child Sexual Abuse Project in San Jose, California, estimates that there are approximately 26,000 cases of father–daughter incest each year. This estimate excludes incestuous behavior by grandfathers, uncles, brothers, cousins. Cases reported to the Santa Clara Child Sexual Abuse Treatment Program increased from 31 in 1974 to 269 in 1976, suggesting that the incidence of incest may be grossly underestimated. Child-protection organizations estimate that the number of reported incidents of child sexual abuse ranges from one hundred thousand to 1 million and that the majority of sexual assaults against children are not reported (*New York Times*, 1982).

Accurate data on the incidence of sexual harassment is impossible to obtain. Women have traditionally accepted sexual innuendo as a fact of life and only recently have begun to report and analyze the dimensions of sexual coercion in the workplace. Research indicates that sexual harassment is pervasive. Lin Farley (1978:31) found that accounts of sexual harassment within the federal government, the country's largest single employer, are extensive and that surveys of working women in the private sector indicate "a dangerously high rate of incidence of this abuse."

In 1976, over nine thousand women responded to a survey on sexual harassment conducted by *Redbook* magazine. More than 92 percent reported sexual harassment as a problem; a majority of the respondents described it as serious; and nine out of ten reported that they had personally experienced one or more forms of unwanted sexual attentions on the job (Farley, 1978:20). The Ad Hoc Group on Equal Rights for Women attempted to gather data on sexual harassment at the United Nations. The questionnaire was confiscated by UN officials, but 875 staff members had already responded; 73 percent were women, and more than half of them said that they had personally experienced or were aware of incidents of sexual harassment at the UN (Farley, 1978:21). In May 1975, the Women's Section of the Human Affairs Program at Cornell University,

Ithaca, New York, distributed the first questionnaire on sexual harassment. Of the 155 responses, 92 percent identified sexual harassment as a serious problem; 70 percent had personally experienced some form of sexual harassment; and 56 percent reported incidents of physical harassment (Farley, 1978:20).

A pilot study conducted by the National Advisory Council on Women's Educational Programs on Sexual Harassment in Academia concluded:

> The sexual harassment of postsecondary students is an increasingly visible problem of great, but as yet unascertained, dimensions. Once regarded as an isolated, purely personal problem, it has gained civil rights credibility as its scale and consequences have become known, and is correctly viewed as a form of illegal sex-based discrimination. (Till, 1980)

CRIMES OF VIOLENCE AGAINST FEMALES HAVE THE LOWEST CONVICTION RATES

The common denominator in the underreporting of all sexual assaults is fear. Females have been well trained in silence and passivity. Early and sustained sex-role socialization teaches that women are responsible for the sexual behavior of men and that women cannot be trusted. These beliefs operate together. They function to keep women silent about their victimization and to keep others from believing women when they do come forward. The victim's fear that she will not be believed and, as a consequence, that the offender will not be punished is not unrealistic. Sex offenders are rarely punished in our society.

Rape has the lowest conviction rate of all violent crimes. On a national average, one rapist in twenty is arrested, one out of thirty prosecuted, and one in sixty is convicted (Geiser, 1979). In *Forcible Rape: The Crime, the Victim, and the Offender*, the authors report that the conviction rate for Los Angeles County is less than 10 percent (Chappell, Geis, and Geis, 1977: 266) and that "in no recent year have more than eight percent of rape arrests resulted in rape convictions" in New York City. The authors conclude that rapists in New York City have enjoyed "almost complete immunity" from prosecution (Ibid: 245–246).

Data on prosecution and conviction of wife beaters are practically nonexistent. According to Roger Langley and Richard Levy (1977:173), authors of *Wife-Beating: The Silent Crisis*, "the vast majority of wife-beaters are never prosecuted. In fact, they are seldom even charged. The battered wife has to overcome an incredible array of roadblocks and detours built into the legal system before she can prosecute her husband."

The roadblocks are both technical and attitudinal. The laws on wife

Chapter VI
Sexism and Problems of the Aging

beating are confusing and vary from state to state. Their application varies with the attitudes and beliefs of law-enforcement personnel. Police indifference to wife beating has been extensively documented by victims.

> Dee Zurbrium of Laurel, Maryland, says she called police for help and was told, "We can't get involved in a domestic quarrel, Lady. The best thing you can do is get out of there because next time you may be dead."
>
> The *Detroit Free Press,* in an article headlined "Emergency Number Still Has Kinks," reports: "A near-breathless woman, beaten by her husband, dialed 911 to ask for police assistance. 'Does he have a weapon?' the operator asked.
> "She answered he did not.
> 'Then I am sorry. We won't be able to help you,' the operator said to the dismayed woman."
>
> One woman called the police after her husband broke her nose. They took her to the hospital, bleeding and with both eyes swelling shut, but they refused to arrest her husband. "You don't want to do that, honey," said the cop, reassuringly. "It's something that happens in every man's life." (Langley and Levy, 1977:160, 171-172).

It is routine policy for police officers and lawyers to discourage women from filing charges against an abusive husband. The instructors at the Police Training Academy in Michigan use the following guidelines in teaching police officers how to convince a woman not to press charges:

> a. Avoid arrest if possible. Appeal to their vanity.
> b. Explain the procedure of obtaining a warrant.
>   (1) Complainant must sign complaint.
>   (2) Must appear in court.
>   (3) Consider loss of time.
>   (4) Cost of court.
> c. State that your only interest is to prevent a breach of the peace.
> d. Explain that attitudes usually change by court time.
> e. Recommend a postponement.
>   (1) Court not in session.
>   (2) No judge available.
> f. Don't be too harsh or critical. (Martin, 1977)

It is also common practice for police officers and lawyers to use outright intimidation to convince battered women not to pursue the matter legally. Battered wives are confronted with statements or questions such as these: "You know he could lose his job." "Who will support you if he is locked up?" "Why don't you just kiss and make up?" "What did you do to make him hit you?" "Lady, why do you want to make trouble?" (Langley and Levy, 1977:171).

It is ironic that police officers do not view what they call a "domestic

*Reading 21
Sexual Terrorism*

disturbance," "lover's quarrel," or "family spat" as serious. The category of answering family disturbance calls accounts for about 20 percent of the incidents of police killed on duty (Langley and Levy, 1977:165).

According to Detroit Police Commander James Bannon (Martin, 1977:115):

> The attrition rate in domestic violence cases is unbelievable. In 1972, for instance, there were 4,900 assaults of this kind which had survived the screening process long enough to at least have a warrant prepared and the complainant referred to the assault and battery squad. Through the process of conciliation, complainant harassment and prosecutor discretion, fewer than 300 of these cases were ultimately tried by a court of law. And in most of these the court used the judicial process to attempt to conciliate rather than adjudicate.

Mr. Bannon argues: "You can readily understand why the women ultimately take the law into their own hands or despair of finding relief at all. *Or why the male feels protected by the system in his use of violence*" (emphasis mine).

In his study of child sexual abuse, Vincent De Francis (1969:190–191) found that plea-bargaining and dismissal of cases were the norm. The study sample consisted of 173 cases brought to prosecution. Of these, 44 percent (seventy-six cases) were dismissed; 22 percent (thirty-eight cases) voluntarily accepted a lesser plea; 11 percent (six cases) were found guilty of a lesser charge; and 2 percent (four cases) were found guilty as charged. The remaining thirty-five cases were either pending (fifteen); terminated because the offender was committed to a mental institution (five) or because the offender absconded (seven); or no information was available (eight).

Of the fifty-three offenders who were convicted or pleaded guilty, thirty offenders escaped a jail sentence. Twenty-one received suspended sentences and were placed on probation; seven received suspended sentences without probation; and two were fined a sum of money. The other 45 percent, twenty-three offenders, received prison terms from under six months to three years; five were given indeterminate sentences—that is, a minimum term of one year and a maximum term subject to the discretion of the state board of parole.

Most of the victims of sexual harassment in the Cornell University study were unwilling to use available procedures, such as grievances, to remedy their complaints, because they believed that nothing would be done. Their perception is based on reality; of the 12 percent who did complain, over half found that nothing was done in their cases (Farley, 1978:22). The low adjudication and punishment rates of sexual harassment cases are particularly revealing in light of the fact that the offender

Chapter VI
Sexism and Problems of the Aging

is known and identifiable and that there is no fear of "mistaken identity," as there is in rape cases. While offenders accused of familial violence—incest and wife abuse—are also known, the courts' posture is heavily in favor of keeping the family intact, or so they say. There is no such motivation in cases of sexual harassment.

Blaming the Victim of Sexual Violence Is Pervasive

The data on conviction rates of men who have committed acts of violence against females must be understood in the context of social/political attitudes about women. The male-dominated society has evoked powerful myths to justify male violence against females and to ensure that these acts will rarely be punished. Victims of sexual violence are almost always suspect. We have developed an intricate network of beliefs and attitudes that perpetuate the idea that "victims of sex crimes have a hidden psychological need to be victimized" (Dullen, 1979). We tend to believe either that the female willingly participated in her victimization or that she outright lied about it. Either way, we blame the victim and excuse or condone the offender.

Consider, for example, the operative myths about rape, wife battery, incest, and sexual harassment.

Rape

All woman want to be raped.

No woman can be raped if she doesn't want it (you-can't-thread-a-moving-needle argument).

She asked for it.

She changed her mind afterwards.

When she says no she means yes.

If you are going to be raped you might as well enjoy it.

Wife Battery

Some women need to be beaten.

A good kick in the ass will straighten her out.

She needs a punch in the mouth every so often to keep her in line.

She must have done something to provoke him.

Incest

The child was the seducer.

The child imagined it.

Sexual Harassment

She was seductive.

She misunderstood, I was just being friendly.

Underlying all the myths about victims of sexual violence is the belief that the victim causes and is responsible for her victimization. Underlying the attitudes about the male offender is the belief that he could not help himself; that is, he was ruled by his biology and/or he was seduced. The victim becomes the offender and the offender becomes the victim. Clearly, two very important processes are at work here: blaming the victim and absolving the offender. These serve a vital political purpose: to protect our view of the world as orderly and just and to help us make sense of sexual violence. The rationale is that sexual violence against an innocent female is unjustifiable; therefore, she must have done something wrong or it would not have happened. Making a victim believe she is at fault erases not only the individual offender's culpability but also the responsibility of the society as a whole. Sexual violence becomes an individual problem, not a sociopolitical one.

One need only read the testimony of victims of sexual violence to see the powerful effects of blaming the victim. From the National Advisory Council on Women's Educational Programs Report on Sexual Harassment of Students:

> I was ashamed, thought it was my fault, and was worried that the school would take action against me (for "unearned" grades) if they found out about it.
>
> This happened seventeen years ago, and you are the first person I've been able to discuss it with in all that time. He's still at ____, and probably still doing it.
>
> I'm afraid to tell anyone here about it, and I'm just hoping to get through the year so I can leave. (Till, 1980:28)

From *Wife-Beating: The Silent Crisis,* Judge Stewart Oneglia comments:

> Many women find it shameful to admit they don't have a good marriage. The battered wife wraps her bloody head in a towel, goes to the hospital, and explains to the doctor she fell down the stairs. After a few years of the husband telling her he beats her because she is ugly, stupid, or incompetent, she is so psychologically destroyed that she believes it. (Langley and Levy, 1977:117)

A battered woman from Boston relates:

> I actually thought if I only learned to cook better or keep a cleaner house, everything would be okay. I put up with the beatings for five years before I got desperate enough to get help. (Ibid: 115)

Chapter VI
Sexism and Problems of the Aging

Another battered woman said,

> When I came to, I wanted to die, the guilt and depression were so bad. Your whole sense of worth is tied up with being a successful wife and having a happy marriage. If your husband beats you, then your marriage is a failure, and you're a failure. It's so horribly the opposite of how it is supposed to be. (Ibid: 116)

Katherine Brady (1981) shared her experience as an incest survivor in *Father's Days: A True Story of Incest*. She concluded her story with the following:

> I've learned a great deal by telling my story. I hope other incest victims may experience a similar journey of discovery by reading it. If nothing else, I would wish them to hear in this tale the two things I needed most, but had to wait years to hear: "You are not alone and you are not to blame."

SEXUAL VIOLENCE IS NOT TAKEN SERIOUSLY

Another characteristic of sexual violence is that these crimes are not taken seriously. Society manifests this attitude by simply denying the existence of sexual violence, denying the gravity of these acts, joking about them, and attempting to legitimate them.

Many offenders echo the societal norm by expressing genuine surprise when they are confronted by authorities. This seems to be particularly true in cases of sexually abused children, wife beating, and sexual harassment. In her study of incest, Florence Rush found that child molesters very often do not understand that they have done anything wrong (Rush, 1980:14). This is true as well for men who beat their wives. Many men still believe that they have an inalienable right to rule "their women." Batterers, for example, often cite their right to discipline their wives; incestuous fathers cite their right to instruct their daughters in sexuality. Clearly, these men are acting on the belief that women are the property of men.

The concept of females as property of men extends beyond the family unit, as the evidence on sexual harassment indicates. "Are you telling me that this kind of horsing around may constitute an actionable offense?" queried a character on a recent television special on sexual harassment (Till, 1980:4). This represents the typical response of a man accused of sexual harassment. Men have been taught that they are the hunters, and women—all women—are fair game. The mythology about the workaday world abounds with sexual innuendo. Concepts of "sleazy" (read "sexually accessible") nurses and dumb, big-breasted, blond secretaries are standard fare for comedy routines. When the existence of sexual violence can no longer be denied, a common response is to joke about it in order to belittle it. "If you are going to be raped, you might as well enjoy it" clearly belittles the violence of rape. The public still laughs when Ralph threatens Alice with "One of these days, POW—right in the kisser." Recently, a television talk-show host remarked that "incest is a game the whole family can play." The audience laughed uproariously.

Sexual Violence Is Not about Sex

The final characteristic common to all forms of violence against females is perhaps the most difficult to comprehend. Sexual assault, contrary to popular belief, is not about sex. The research that has been done in every area of sexual assault suggests that while the motivation is complex, it is not rooted in sexual frustration or sexual prowess. Rather, the motivation for the violent abuse of women has to do with the need to assert a masculine image or a masculine privilege as defined by the culture. In an article in *Ms.* magazine, "I Never Set Out to Rape Anybody," a rapist talked about his motivation to rape. He said that the image of men (masculinity) as hypersexual, violent, and dominant and the image of women (femininity) as liking tough men made him feel compelled to live up to this standard.

A rapist is usually regarded as either a healthy male who was the victim of a seductive and vengeful woman, a sexually frustrated man who was no longer able to control his desires, or a "pervert" or "sex fiend." These views all suggest that the rapist's behavior is motivated by sexual desire. The assumption that rape, forceful and often violent, is about the satisfaction of sexual need or desire is entirely false. In his study *Men Who Rape: The Psychology of the Offender,* A. Nicholas Groth (1979) reports that "careful clinical study of offenders reveals that rape is in fact serving primarily nonsexual needs. It is the sexual expression of power and anger."

Men do not rape for sexual pleasure. They rape to assert power and dominance. Jack Fremont's interviews of several rapists revealed the notion of masculine privilege as a dominant motive. For example:

> *Interviewer:* Do you think many men commit rape?
>
> *Jimmy:* Oh, yes, I know damn well they do! With no more feeling involved and no more neurosis than just, I want you, and I can't have you, so I'll take you. (Russell, 1975:13)

David Finkelhor (1979), in his study *Sexually Victimized Children,* argues that the sexual exploitation of women and children is made easier in a society that is dominated by men. "Sex in any society is a valuable commodity, and a dominant group—such as men—will try to rig things to maximize their access to it." He maintains that "the cultural beliefs

Chapter VI
Sexism and Problems of the Aging

that underpin the male-dominated system contribute to making women and children sexually vulnerable. For example, to the extent that family members are regarded as possessions, men can take unusual and usually undetected liberties with them." Research by Robert Geiser (1979:52) supports the conclusion that sexual gratification is not the dominant motive in the abuse of children. A daughter asked her father, "Why did you do it to me?" He replied, "You were available and you were vulnerable." Research on offenders suggests that men turn to children because their adult relationships are complicated, unsatisfying, stressful, or anxiety-laden. According to Geiser (1979:34), child molesters need to exercise authority and avoid rejection: "The child's vulnerability and helplessness make her easier to overpower and dominate."

Husbands who batter their wives are often trying to prove their superiority. Del Martin (1977:46) found that wife beating is unquestionably an example of power abuse. Martin characterized the battering husband this way:

> He is probably angry with himself and frustrated by his life. He may put up a good front in public, but in the privacy and intimacy of his home he may not be able to hide, either from himself or his wife, his feelings of inadequacy and low self-esteem. The man who is losing his grip on his job or his prospects may feel compelled to prove that he is at least the master of his home. Beating his wife is one way for him to appear a winner.

Sexual harassment is also not about sex but about power. Farley (1978:208) argues that the sexual harassment of women at work arose from men's need to maintain control of women's labor. Sexual harassment serves to keep women (individually and collectively) economically inferior and ensures the system of male dominance (Ibid: xvi).

CONCLUSION

Sexual terrorism is a system that functions to maintain male supremacy through actual and implied violence. Violence against the female body (rape, battery, incest, and harassment) and the perpetuation of fear of violence form the basis of patriarchal power. Both violence and fear are functional. Without the power to intimidate and to punish, the domination of women in all spheres of society—political, social, and economic—could not exist.

REFERENCES

Alexander, Yonah. 1979. "Terrorism and the mass media: Some considerations," p. 159 in Yonah Alexander, David Carlton, and Paul Wilkinson (eds.), *Terrorism: Theory and Practice.* Boulder, Colo.: Westview Press.

Reading 21
Sexual Terrorism

Brady, Katherine. 1981. *Father's Days: A True Story of Incest.* New York: Dell Publishing Co., 1981.
Bradley v. State, 1 Miss. (7 Walker) 150 (1824); *State v. Black,* 60 N.C. (Win.) 266 (1864).
Brownmiller, Susan. 1975. *Against Our Will: Men, Women and Rape.* New York: Simon and Schuster, p. 5.
Chappell, Duncan, Robley Geis, and Gilbert Geis (eds.). *Forcible Rape: The Crime, the Victim, and the Offender.* New York: Columbia University Press, p. 266.
Chesler, Phyllis. 1980. "Men and pornography: Why they use it," in Laura Lederer (ed.), *Take Back the Night: Women on Pornography.* New York: William Morrow and Co.
De Francis, Vincent. 1969. *Protecting the Child Victim of Sex Crimes Committed by Adults.* Denver: American Humane Society, p. vii.
Dullea, Georgia. 1979. "Child prostitution: Causes are sought." *New York Times* September 4:C11.
Evans, Ernest. 1979. *Calling a Truce to Terrorism: The American Response to International Terrorism.* Westport, Conn.: Greenwood Press, p 3.
Farley, Lin. 1978. *Sexual Shakedown: The Sexual Harassment of Women on the Job.* New York: McGraw-Hill Book Co., pp. 14–15.
Fasteau, Marc Feigen. 1974. *The Male Machine.* New York: McGraw-Hill Book Co., p. 144.
Finkelhor, David. 1979. *Sexually Victimized Children.* New York: Free Press, p. 29.
Fulgham v. State, 46 Ala. 143 (1871).
Geiser, Robert L. 1979. *Hidden Victims: The Sexual Abuse of Children.* Boston: Beacon Press, p. 24.
Groth, A. Nicholas. 1979. *Men Who Rape: The Psychology of the Offender.* New York: Plenum Press, p. 2.
Hacker, Frederick F. 1976. *Crusaders, Criminals and Crazies: Terrorism in Our Times.* New York: W. W. Norton and Co., p. xi.
Kinsey, Alfred C., and Paul H. Gebhard. 1953. *Sexual Behavior in the Human Female.* Philadelphia: W. B. Saunders Co., p. 121.
Johnson, Charmers. 1978. "Perspectives on terrorism," p. 273 in Walter Laquer (ed.), *The Terrorism Reader.* Philadelphia: Temple University Press.
Langley, Roger, and Richard C. Levy. 1977. *Wife-Beating: The Silent Crisis.* New York: E. P. Dutton, p. 153.
MacDonald, John M. 1975. *Rape Offenders and Their Victims.* Springfield, Ill.: Charles C Thomas, p. 266.
Martin, Del. 1977. *Battered Wives.* New York: Pocket Books, p. 94.
Ms. 1972. "I never set out to rape anybody." *Ms.* (December):22–23.
National Clearinghouse on Marital Rape, 2325 Oak Street, Berkeley, Calif. 94708 (send stamped, self-addressed envelope for more information).
New York Times. 1982. "Studies find sexual abuse of children is widespread." *New York Times* May 13:C10.
Rush, Florence. 1980. *The Best Kept Secret.* Englewood Cliffs, N.J.: Prentice-Hall, p. 5.
Russell, Diana E. H. 1975. *The Politics of Rape.* New York: Stein and Day Publishers, 1975, p. 13.
Thompson v. Thompson, 218 U.S. 611 (1910).

Chapter VI
Sexism and Problems of the Aging

Thornton, Thomas P. 1964. "Terror as a weapon of political agitation," p. 73 in H. Eckstein (ed.), *The Internal War.* New York: Free Press.

Till, Frank J. 1980. *Sexual Harassment: A Report on the Sexual Harassment of Students.* Washington, D.C.: National Advisory Council on Women's Educational Programs, p. 3.

U.S. Department of Justice, Federal Bureau of Investigation. 1987. *Crime in the United States,* Uniform Crime Reports 1987. Washington, D.C.: U.S. Government Printing Office, p. 13.

Walter, Eugene. 1969. *Terror and Resistance.* New York: Oxford University Press, p. 6.

Watson, Francis M. 1976. *Political Terrorism: The Threat and the Response.* Washington, D.C.: R. B. Luce Co., p. 15.

Wilkinson, Paul. 1974. *Political Terrorism.* New York: John Wiley and Sons, p. 11.

Reading 22
ELDERS UNDER SIEGE

Peggy Eastman

> *Elder abuse, sometimes called "gram-slamming," is just beginning to be discovered as a problem. It seems to be a pattern much like child abuse or abuse of females and reflects our society's devaluation of the aged.*

She is 79 and frail, a widow living with her married daughter. She has bruises on her arms and legs and is fearful and uncommunicative. Most of the time she stays locked in her room, afraid her daughter will come in and kick her, call her names, empty out her bureau drawers and throw her possessions all over. She is a victim of elder abuse.

According to estimates from Senate and House committees on aging, the number of cases of abused, neglected or exploited elderly in the United States ranges from 600,000 up to 1 million, or 4 percent of the elderly population. And the number appears to be growing.

One explanation for the increase in elder abuse could be the increase in the number of people older than 65: from 16.6 million in 1960 to 25.6 million in 1980 and a predicted 35 million by 2000. And among these, the 75-plus age group, the most vulnerable to abuse and exploitation, is the fastest-growing segment of the population.

Who would abuse a vulnerable older person? According to the profile that emerged in 1981 from a year-long investigation by the House Select Committee on Aging, an elder abuser is usually a relative, such as a son or daughter. Some studies suggest that not only are abused children more likely than others to become child abusers when they grow up, they have a one-in-two chance of abusing their dependent parents.

Researchers have also found that elder abuse is a recurring problem, not a one-time offense, and that stress aggravates it. In a survey conducted in Massachusetts, for instance, 63 percent of abusers perceived their elders as a source of stress because they needed extra care and were

---

Reprinted with permission from *Psychology Today* (January 1984):30. Copyright © 1984, P. T. Partners, L. P.

Chapter VI
Sexism and Problems of the Aging

DAUGHTER DEAREST

My husband died 10 years ago. The house where we lived became mine exclusively. My younger daughter, who had two unfortunate marriages, was welcomed by us with her children. This began more than 18 years ago. The past three years, things have gotten steadily worse. My daughter locked me in the garage and left me there for more than an hour. She always parked her car behind mine in the garage so I could not get my car out except by her permission.

Whenever I tried to cook a meal, she would appear and turn the gas off and remove the grills so the only way I could cook was to hold the pan over the flame. If she found me using the electric toaster oven, my food was thrown on the floor and the toaster oven was removed and hidden for several days.

My daughter's treatment of me kept getting worse. Always hurting me physically and mentally; kicking me, pushing me, grappling with me, telling me to get out, at one time throwing a drawer down the stairs at me, calling me names, telling me I belonged in a nursing home and why didn't I go to one.

I was warned many times to get out of the house by my doctor, my lawyer, my protective counselor and my adviser at the Mental Health Association. They all knew my life was in danger while staying under the same roof with this emotionally very sick 45-year-old person. She is a well-educated woman, having graduated from college, continued in graduate school and gotten a master's degree in no less than social service.

From testimony by Mrs. X, a 79-year old Massachusetts resident, before a joint hearing of the Senate Special Committee on Aging and the House Select Committee, June 1980.

---

a financial burden on the family. Other pressures—poverty, alcoholism, drug abuse or marital fights—can push a potential elder abuser into that role.

Elder abuse can be physical, exploitative (confiscating a parent's savings, say), neglectful (failing to give food or medication) or psychological (name-calling). Abusers also often threaten to put their parents out on the street or to commit them to a mental institution or a nursing home if they complain about the abuse.

Most victims don't complain. They simply endure. Most are women, physically disabled and dependent. They fear abandonment, placement in an institution or further punishment if they attempt to get help.

Reading 22
Elders under Siege

Experts say tough laws are needed, requiring people who suspect cases of elder abuse to report them to state protective services agencies—exactly the kind of law to protect children from abuse that Congress passed in January 1974.

Representative Mary Rose Oaker of Ohio recently introduced a bill in Congress that would create the National Center on Adult Abuse and provide money to states for prevention and treatment programs—if those states have "immunity statutes" to protect reporting individuals from lawsuits. Slightly more than half the states have adult-protective service laws, but there is little uniformity among them. And not all of the states with protective statutes require mandatory reporting of elder abuse.

CHAPTER VII

THE DISRUPTED FAMILY

Reading 23
THE LOVE LOST IN CLICHÉS

Robert C. Solomon, *University of Texas at Austin*

> *Achieving romantic love is an important goal in our society. The figures of speech that lovers use to describe this love tell us how they feel it should be expressed. Is it a "fair exchange," something to "work at," or "just one of those things"? When behavior matches the definition of both partners, a successful relationship results.*

We'd known each other for years; and for months, we were—what?—"seeing each other" (to choose but one of so many silly euphemisms for playful but by no means impersonal sex). We reveled in our bodies, cooked and talked two or three times a week, enjoying ourselves immensely, but within careful bounds, surrounded by other "relationships" (another euphemism), cautiously sharing problems as well as pleasures, exorcising an occasional demon and delighting each other with occasional displays of affection, never saying too much or revealing too much or crossing these unspoken boundaries of intimacy and independence.

Then, we "fell in love." What happened?

There was no "fall," first of all. Why do we get so transfixed with that Alice-in-Wonderland metaphor, and not just that one but a maze of others, obscuring everything; what is a "deep" relationship, for example? And why is love "losing" yourself? Is "falling for" someone really "falling for"—that is, getting *duped*? Where do we get that imagery of tripping, tumbling, and other inadvertent means of getting *in*-volved, *im*mersed, and *sub*-merged in love, "taking the plunge" when it really gets serious? If anything, the appropriate image would seem to be openness rather than depth, flying rather than falling. One makes love (still another euphemism, this one with some significance), but our entire romantic mythology makes it seem as if it happens, as if it is something

---

Adapted from *Love: Emotion, Myth & Metaphor* (New York: Doubleday, 1981). Reprinted with permission of the author.

Chapter VII
The Disrupted Family

someone suffers (enjoying it as well), as if it's entirely natural, a need and something all but unavoidable.

We look at love, as we look at life, through a series of metaphors, each with its own language, its own implications, connotations, and biases. For example, if someone says that love is a game, we already know much of what is to follow: relationships will tend to be short-lived. Sincerity will be a strategy for winning and so will flattery and perhaps lying ("all's fair..."). The person played with is taken seriously only as an opponent, a challenge, valued in particular for his or her tactics and retorts, but quickly dispensable as soon as someone has won or lost. Playing hard to get is an optional strategy, and being "easy" is not immoral or foolish so much as playing badly, or not at all.

On the other hand, if someone sees love as God's gift to humanity, we should expect utter solemnity, mixed with a sense of gratitude, seriousness, and self-righteousness that is wholly lacking in the "love-is-a-game" metaphor. Relationships here will tend to be long-lasting, if not forever fraught with duties and obligations dictated by a gift that, in the usual interpretations, has both divine and secular strings attached.

The game metaphor is, perhaps, too frivolous to take seriously. The gift-of-God metaphor, on the other hand, is much too serious to dismiss frivolously. Not suprisingly, these love metaphors reflect our interests elsewhere in life—in business, health, communications, art, politics, and law, as well as fun and games and religion. But these are not mere figures of speech; they are the self-imposed structures that determine the way we experience love itself. For that reason, we should express reservations about some of them.

LOVE AS A FAIR EXCHANGE

One of the most common love metaphors, now particularly popular in social psychology, is the economic metaphor. The idea is that love is an exchange, a sexual partnership, a trade-off of interests and concerns and, particularly, of *approval*. "I make you feel good about yourself and in return you make me feel good about myself." Of course exchange rates vary—some people need more than others—and there is a law of diminishing returns; that is, the same person's approval tends to become less and less valuable as it becomes more familiar. (This law of diminishing returns, which we experience as the gradual fading of romantic love, has been explored by the psychologist Elliot Aronson of the University of California at Santa Cruz. His theory has been aptly named by the students "Aronson's Law of Marital Infidelity.") In some relationships, the balance of payments may indeed seem extremely one-sided, but the assumption is, in the words of the Harvard sociologist George Homans, that both parties must believe they are getting something out of it or they simply wouldn't stick around.

The economic model has much to offer, not least the fact that it gives a fairly precise account of the concrete motivation for love, which is left out of more pious accounts that insist that love is simply good in itself and needs no motives. But the problem is that it too easily degenerates into a most unflattering model of mutual buying and selling, which in turn raises the specter that love may indeed be, as some cynics have been saying ever since Marx and Engels, a form of covert prostitution, though not necessarily—or even usually—for money. "I will sleep with you and think well of you or at least give you the benefit of the doubt if only you'll tell me good things about myself and pretend to approve of me."

It may be true that we do often evaluate our relationships in this way, in terms of mutual advantage and our own sense of fairness. The question "What am I getting out of this, anyway?" always makes sense even if certain traditional views of love and commitment try to pretend that such selfishness is the very antithesis of love. But the traditional views have a point to make as well, which is simply that such tit-for-tat thinking inevitably undermines a relationship based on love, not because love is essentially selfless, but because the bargaining table is not the place to understand mutual affection. Love is not the exchange of affection, any more than sex is merely the exchange of pleasure. What is left out of these accounts is the "we" of love, which is quite different from "I and thou." This is not to say that fairness cannot be an issue in love, nor is it true that all's fair in love. But while the economic exchange model explains rather clearly some of the motives for love, it tends to ignore the experience of love almost altogether, which is that such evaluations seem at the time beside the point and come to mind only when love is already breaking down. It is the suspicion, not the fact, that "I'm putting more into this than you are" that signals the end of many relationships, despite the fact that, as business goes, there may have been "a good arrangement."

LOVE AND ELECTRONICS

A powerful metaphor with disastrous consequences that was popular a few years ago was a communication metaphor, often used in conjunction with a relating metaphor, for obvious reasons. Both were involved with the then-hip language of media and information theory: "getting through" to each other and "we just can't communicate any more" gave lovers the unfortunate appearance of shipwrecked survivors trying to keep in touch over a slightly damaged shortwave radio. The information-processing jargon ("input," "feedback," "tuning in," and "turning off")

Chapter VII
The Disrupted Family

was typically loaded with electronic-gadget imagery, and good relationships, appropriately, were described in terms of their "good vibrations." But, like all metaphors, this one revealed much more than it distorted, namely, an image of isolated transmitters looking for someone to get their messages. It was precisely this milieu that gave birth to Rollo May's *Love and Will* and his concern that people had rendered love impossible. Love was thought to be mainly a matter of self-expression—largely but not exclusively verbal expression. Talk became enormously important to love; problems were talked over, talked through, and talked out. The essential moment was the "heavy conversation," and talk about love often took the place of love itself. Confession and openness (telling all) became the linchpins of love, even when the messages were largely hostility and resentment.

Psychotherapist George Bach wrote a number of successful books, including *The Intimate Enemy* (with Peter Wyden), that made quite clear the fact that it was expression of feelings, not the feelings themselves, that made for a successful relationship. On the communications model, sex, too, was described as a mode of communication, but more often sex was not so much communicating as the desire to be communicated with. Sex became, in McLuhan's jargon, a cool medium. And, like most modern media, the model put its emphasis on the medium itself (encounter groups and the like), but there was precious little stress on the content of the programming. Not surprisingly, love became an obscure ideal, like television commercials full of promise of something fabulous yet to come, hinted at but never spoken of as such. The ultimate message was the idea of the medium itself.

LOVE AS WORK

A very different model is the work model of love. The Protestant ethic is very much at home in romance. (Rollo May calls love the Calvinist's proof of emotional salvation.) And so we find many people who talk about "working out a relationship," "working at it," "working for it," and so on. The fun may once have been there but now the real job begins, tacking together and patching up, like fixing up an old house. This is, needless to say, a particularly self-righteous model, if for no other reason than that it begins on the defensive and requires considerable motivation just to move on. Personal desires, the other person's as well as one's own, may be placed behind "the relationship," which is conceived of as the primary project. Love, according to the work model, is evaluated above all on its industriousness, its seriousness, its success in the face of the most difficult obstacles. Devotees of the work model not infrequently choose the most inept or inappropriate partners, rather like buying a run-down shack—for the challenge. They will look with disdain at people who are merely happy together (something like buying a house from a tract builder). They will look with admiration and awe at a couple who have survived a dozen years of fights and emotional disfigurements because "they made it work...."

THE BLAND LEADING THE BLAND

Blandness can be just as significant as excitement, and a metaphor may be intentionally noncommittal as well as precise. Thus we find the word "thing" substituted for everything from sexual organs (a young virgin gingerly refers to her first lover's "thing") to jobs, hangups, and hobbies (as in "doing your own thing"). Where love is concerned, the most banal of our metaphors is the word "relating," or "relationship" itself. There's not much to say about it, except to ponder in amazement the fact that we have not yet, in this age of "heavy relationships," come up with anything better. There is a sense, of course, in which any two people (or two things) stand in any number of relationships to one another (being taller than, heavier than, smarter than, more than 15 feet away from...and so forth). The word "relations" was once, only a few years ago, a polite and slightly clinical word for sex (still used, as most stilted archaisms tend to be, in law). People "relate" to each other as they "relate a story," perhaps on the idea that what couples do most together is to tell each other the events of the day, a less-than-exciting conception of love, to be sure. The fact that this metaphor dominates our thinking so much (albeit in the guise of a *meaningful* relationship) points once again to the poverty of not only our vocabulary but our thinking and feeling.

ESCAPE FROM ALONENESS

In our extremely individualistic society we have come to see isolation and loneliness as akin to the human condition, instead of as by-products of a certain kind of social arrangement that puts mobility and the formation of new interpersonal bonds at a premium. This individualistic metaphor, which I call the "ontology of loneliness," because it implies some kind of coherent law in the human organism's development, is stated succinctly by Rollo May: "Every person, experiencing as he [or she] does his [or her] own solitariness and aloneness, longs for union with another."

This viewpoint has been developed by the philosopher Ayn Rand into an argument for selfishness: "Each of us is born into the world alone, and therefore each of us is justified in pursuing our own selfish interests." But the premise is false, and the inference is insidious.

Chapter VII
The Disrupted Family

Not only in our infancy but also in adulthood we find ourselves essentially linked to other people, to a language that we call our own, to a culture and, at least legally, to a country as well. We do not have to find or "reach out" to others; they are, in a sense, already *in us*. Alone in the woods of British Columbia, I find myself still thinking of friends, describing what I see as if they were there—and in their language. The idea of the isolated self is an American invention—reinforced perhaps by the artificially isolated circumstances of the psychiatrist's office and our fantasies about gunfighters and mountain men—but it is not true of most of us. And this means that love is not a refuge or an escape, either. Our conception of ourselves is always as a social self (even if it is an antisocial or rebellious self).

Our language of love often reflects the idea of natural isolation, for example in the communication metaphor in which isolated selves try desperately to get through to each other. But this picture of life and love is unnecessarily tragic, and its result is to make love itself seem like something of a cure for a disease, rather than a positive experience that already presupposes a rather full social life. Indeed, it is revealing that, quite the contrary of social isolation, romantic love is usually experienced only *within* a rather extensive social nexus. "Sure, I have lots of friends and I like my colleagues at work but, still, I'm lonely and I want to fall in love." But that has nothing to do with loneliness. It rather reflects the tremendous importance we accord to romantic love in our lives, not as a cure for aloneness, but as a positive experience in its own right, which we have, curiously, turned into a need.

MADE FOR EACH OTHER?

Standing opposed to the "ontology of loneliness" is an ancient view which takes our unity, not our mutual isolation, as the natural state of humanity. Our own image of two people "being made for each other" is also an example of the metaphysical model, together with the idea that marriages are "made in heaven" and that someone else can be your "better half." The metaphysical model is based not on the idea that love is a refuge from isolated individualism but that love is the realization of bonds that are already formed, even before one meets one's "other half."

The ontology of loneliness treats individuals as atoms, bouncing around the universe alone looking for other atoms, occasionally forming more or less stable molecules. But if we were to pursue the same chemical metaphor into the metaphysical model, it would more nearly resemble what physicists today call "field theory." A magnetic field, for instance, retains all of its electromagnetic properties whether or not there is any material there to make them manifest. So, too, an individual is already a network of human relationships and expectations, and these exist whether or not one finds another individual whose radiated forces and properties are complementary. The old expression about love being a matter of "chemical attraction" is, scientifically, a century out of date; attraction is no longer a question of one atom affecting another but the product of two electromagnetic fields, each of which exists prior to and independent of any particular atoms within its range. So, too, we radiate charm, sexiness, inhibition, intelligence, and even repulsiveness, and find a lover who fits in. The problem with this view is that it leaves no room for the development of relationships, but makes it seem as if love has to be there in full, from the very beginning. . . .

THE ARTISTIC MODEL

Perhaps the oldest view of love, the pivot of Plato's *Symposium*, is an aesthetic model: love as the admiration and the contemplation of beauty. The emphasis here is on neither relating nor communicating (in fact, unrequited love and even voyeurism are perfectly in order). On this model, it is not particularly expected that the lover will actually do much of anything, except, perhaps, to get within view of the beloved at every possible opportunity. It is this model that has dominated many of our theories about love, though not, luckily, our practices.

It is this model about which women rightly complain when they accuse men of putting them up on a pedestal, a charge that too often confuses the idealization that accompanies it with the impersonal distancing that goes along with the pedestal. The objection is not the fact that it is a pedestal so much as that it is usually a very tall pedestal; any real contact is out of the question. Or else it is a very small pedestal, "and like any small place," writes Gloria Steinem, "a prison."

THE CONTRACT MODEL

What is crucial to the contract model is that emotion plays very little part in it. One accepts an obligation to obey the terms of the contract (implicit or explicit) whether or not one wants to. The current term for this ever-popular emasculation of emotion is commitment. In fact there seems to be an almost general agreement among most of the people I talk with that commitment constitutes love. (The contrast is almost always sexual promiscuity.) But commitment is precisely what love is not, though one can and often does make commitments on the basis of whether one loves someone. A commitment is an obligation sustained *even if the emotion that originally motivates it no longer exists.* And the sense of obligation isn't love.

Chapter VII
The Disrupted Family

THE BIOLOGICAL METAPHOR

The idea that science itself can be but a metaphor strikes us as odd, but much of what we believe about love, it seems, is based on wholly unliteral biological metaphors. For example, we believe that love is natural, even an instinct, and this is supported by a hundred fascinating but ultimately irrelevant arguments about "the facts of life": the fact that some spiders eat their mates, that some birds mate for life, that some sea gulls are lesbians, that some fish can't mate unless the male is clearly superior, that chimpanzees like to gang-bang and gorillas have weenies the size of a breakfast sausage, that bats tend to do it upside down, and porcupines do it "carefully." But romantic love is by no means natural; it is not an instinct but a very particular and peculiar attitude toward sex and pair-bonding that has been carefully cultivated by a small number of people in modern aristocratic and middle-class societies.

Even sex, which would seem to be natural if anything is, is no more mere biology than taking the holy wafer at high Mass is just eating. It, too, is defined by our metaphors and the symbolic significance we give to it. It is not a need, though we have certainly made it into one. Sex is not an instinct, except in that utterly minimal sense that bears virtually no resemblance at all to the extremely sophisticated and emotion-filled set of rituals that we call—with some good reason—making love. And where sex and love come together is not in the realm of nature either, but in the realm of expression, specific to a culture that specifies its meaning.

There is one particular version of the biological metaphor, however, that has enjoyed such spectacular scientific acceptance, ever since Freud at least, that we tend to take it as the literal truth instead of, again, as a metaphor. It is the idea that love begins in—or just out of—the womb, and that our prototype of love—if not our one true love—is our own mother.

Our models and prototypes of love include not only our parents but also brothers, sisters, teachers in junior high school, first dates, first loves, graduating-class heroes and heroines, hundreds of movie stars and magazine pictures, as well as a dozen considerations and pressures that have nothing to do with prototypes at all. Indeed, even Freud insisted that it is not a person's actual parent who forms the romantic prototype but rather a phantom, constructed from memory, which may bear little resemblance to any real person. But if this is so, perhaps one's imagined mother is, in fact, a variation on one's first girlfriend, or a revised version of Myrna Loy. Why do we take the most complex and at times most exquisite emotion in our lives and try to reduce it to the first and the simplest?...

Reading 23
Love Lost in Cliches

LOVE AS A LESS-THAN-PERFECT FIT

So what, after all, is love? It is, in a phrase, an emotion through which we create for ourselves a little world—the love-world—in which we play the roles of lovers and create our selves as well. Thus love is not, as so many of the great poets and philosophers have taken it to be, any degree of admiration or worship, not appreciation or even desire for beauty, much less, as Erich Fromm was fond of arguing, an "orientation of character" whose object is a secondary consideration. Even so-called unrequited love is shared love and shared identity, if only from one side and thereby woefully incomplete.

In love we transform ourselves and one another, but the key is the understanding that the transformation of selves is not merely reciprocal, a swap of favors like "I'll cook you dinner if you'll wash the car." The self transformed in love is a shared self, and therefore by its very nature at odds with, even contradictory to, the individual autonomous selves that each of us had before. And yet at the same time, romantic love is based on the idea of individuality and freedom. This means, first of all, that the presupposition of love is a strong sense of individual identity and autonomy that exactly contradicts the ideal of "union" and "yearning to be one" that some of our literature has celebrated so one-sidedly. And second, the freedom that is built in includes not just the freedom to come together but the freedom to go as well. Thus love is always in a state of tension, always changing, dynamic, tenuous, and explosive.

Love is a dialectic, which means that the bond of love is not just shared identity—which is an impossible goal—but the taut line of opposed desires between the ideal of an eternal merger of souls and our cultivated urge to prove ourselves as free and autonomous individuals. No matter how much we're in love, there is always a large and nonnegligible part of ourselves that is not defined by the love-world, nor do we want it to be. To understand love is to understand this tension, this dialectic between individuality and the shared ideal. To think that love is to be found only at the ends of the spectrum—in that first enthusiastic discovery of a shared togetherness or at the end of the road, after a lifetime together—is to miss the love-world almost entirely, for it is neither an initial flush of feeling nor the retrospective congratulations of old age, but rather, a struggle for unity and identity. And it is this struggle—neither the ideal of togetherness nor the contrary demand for individual autonomy and identity—that defines the dynamics of romantic love.

Reading 24

THE SOCIAL CONSTRUCTION OF DEVIANCE: EXPERTS ON BATTERED WOMEN

Donileen R. Loseke, Spencer E. Cahill, *Skidmore College*

> *The question most often asked by "experts" about battered women is: "Why do they stay?" The assumption is that the natural response would be to leave. By definition, those who stay are treated as if they are in need of "support services." The "experts" have thereby created a clientele to serve.*

SOCIOLOGICAL IMPLICATIONS OF THE QUESTION

The question "why do they stay?" implicitly defines the parameters of the social problem of battered women. By asking this question, the experts imply that assaulted wives are of two basic types: those who leave their mate and those who do not. Not only are possible distinctions among assaulted wives who remain with their mates implicitly ignored, but so too are the unknown number of assaulted wives who quickly terminate such relationships. By focusing attention on those who stay, the experts imply that assaulted wives who remain with their mates are more needy and deserving of public and expert concern than those who do not. In fact, some of the experts have explicitly defined battered women as women who *remain* in relationships containing violence (Ferraro and Johnson, 1983; Pizzey, 1979; Scott, 1974; Walker, 1979).

Moreover, the experts' common and overriding concern with the question of why assaulted wives stay reveals their shared definition of the normatively expected response to the experience of battering. To ask why assaulted wives remain with their mates is to imply that doing so requires explanation. In general, as Scott and Lyman (1968) have noted, normatively expected behavior does not require explanation. It is norma-

---

Reprinted with permission from *Social Problems* 31(3) (February 1984):296–310, abridged by The Society for the Study of Social Problems and by the authors.

Reading 24
Experts on Battered Women

tively unanticipated, untoward acts which require what Scott and Lyman term an "account." By asking why battered women stay, therefore, the experts implicitly define leaving one's mate as the normatively expected response to the experience of wife assault. Staying, on the other hand, is implicitly defined as deviant, an act "which is perceived (i.e., recognized) as violating expectations" (Hawkins and Tiedeman, 1975:59).

In other words, once the experts identify a woman as battered, normative expectations regarding marital stability are reversed. After all, separated and divorced persons are commonly called upon to explain why their relationships "didn't work out" (Weiss, 1975). It is typically marital stability, "staying," which is normatively expected and marital instability, "leaving," which requires an account. However, as far as the experts on battered women are concerned, once wife assault occurs, it is marital stability which requires explanation.

In view of the experts' typifications of relationships within which wife assault occurs, this reversal of normative expectations seems only logical. Although research indicates that the severity and frequency of wife assault varies considerably across couples (Straus et al., 1980), the experts stress that, *on the average*, wife assault is more dangerous for victims than is assault by a stranger (U.S. Department of Justice, 1980). Moreover, most experts maintain that once wife assault has occurred within a relationship it will become more frequent and severe over time (Dobash and Dobash, 1979), and few believe that this pattern of escalating violence can be broken without terminating the relationship.[1] It is hardly surprising, therefore, that the experts on battered women define "leaving" as the expected, reasonable, and desirable response to the experience of wife assault.[2] Staying, in contrast, is described as "maladaptive choice behavior" (Waites, 1977-78), "self-destruction through inactivity" (Rounsaville, 1978), or, most concisely, "deviant" (Ferraro and Johnson, 1983). For the experts, battered women who remain with their mates pose an intellectual puzzle: Why are they so unreasonable? Why do they stay?

To ask such a question is to request an account. Experts who provide answers to this question are, therefore, offering accounts on behalf of battered women who remain with their mates. According to Scott and Lyman (1968), two general types of accounts are possible: justifications

---

[1] There has been little systematic study of the possibility of change in relationships. Walker (1979) reports that her pessimism is based on clinical experience. See Coleman (1980) for a more optimistic prognosis.

[2] Of course, this commonsense deduction is also based on the common, although often unspoken, assumption that humans are "rational actors." If the basis of human motivation is a desire to maximize rewards and minimize costs, then why would a battered woman remain in such an obviously "costly" relationship?

and excuses. A justification is an account which acknowledges the actor's responsibility for the behavior in question but challenges the imputation of deviance ("I did it, but I didn't do anything wrong"). An excuse, on the other hand, acknowledges the deviance of the behavior in question but relieves the actor of responsibility for it ("I did something wrong, but it wasn't my fault").

Clearly, these different types of accounts elicit different kinds of responses. If the behavior in question is socially justifiable, then the actor was behaving reasonably, as normatively expected. The actor's ability or competence to manage everyday affairs without interference is not called into question (Garfinkel, 1967:57). In contrast, excusing behavior implies that the actor cannot manage everyday affairs without interference. Although the behavior is due to circumstances beyond the actor's control, it is admittedly deviant. By implication, assistance from others may be required if the actor is to avoid behaving similarly in the future. In order to fully understand the experts' responses to battered women who remain with their mates it is necessary, therefore, to determine which type of account they typically offer on behalf of such women.

THE EXPERTS' ACCOUNTS

Experts on battered women are a diverse group. This diversity is reflected in the emphasis each expert places on various accounts, in the number of accounts offered, and in how series of accounts are combined to produce complex theoretical explanations. Despite such diversity, however, there is a sociologically important similarity among the experts' accounts. None of the experts argues that "staying" is justifiable. "Staying" is either explicitly or implicitly defined as unreasonable, normatively unexpected, and, therefore, deviant. By implication, the accounts offered by the experts are excuses for women's deviant behavior, and they offer two basic types.[3] Battered women are said to remain with their mates because of external constraints on their behavior or because of internal constraints. In either case, the accounts offered by the experts acknowledge the deviance of staying but relieve battered women of responsibility for doing so.

---

[3] A third type of explanation for why victims of wife assault remain with their mates is seldom found in the literature on battered women and, therefore, will not be reviewed here. This type of explanation is based on a systems theory analysis of family interactions. Straus (1974) suggests the empirical applicability of such an approach, and Denzin (1983) provides a phenomenological foundation. Erchak (1981) used this approach to explain the maintenance of child abuse, and Giles-Sims (1983) has used this to explain the behavior of battered women.

Reading 24
Experts on Battered Women

EXTERNAL CONSTRAINTS

Almost all contemporary experts on battered women maintain that staying is excusable due to external constraints on women's behavior (Dobash and Dobash, 1979; Freeman, 1979; Langley and Levy, 1977; Martin, 1976; Pagelow, 1981a,b; Pizzey, 1979; Ridington, 1977-78; Roy, 1977; Shainess, 1977).

> Why does she not leave? The answer is simple. If she has children but no money and no money and no place to go, she has no choice. (Fleming, 1979:83)

Clearly, such accounts are based on the assumption that battered women who stay are economically dependent upon their mates. If a woman has no money and no place to go, she cannot be held responsible for the unreasonable act of staying. She has no choice.

Although this excuse is the most prevalent in the literature on battered women, further elaboration is necessary. In its simplest form, such an account can be easily challenged: What about friends, family, the welfare system, and other social service agencies? In response to such challenges, experts must offer accounts which will excuse women for not taking advantage of such assistance. Experts meet these challenges with at least two further accounts of external constraints. First, experts claim that most battered women are interpersonally isolated. Even if they are not, family and friends are said to typically blame women for their problems instead of providing assistance (Carlson, 1977; Dobash and Dobash, 1979; Fleming, 1979; Hilberman and Munson, 1977-78; Truninger, 1971). Second, experts claim that social service agencies typically provide little, if any, assistance. In fact, experts maintain that the organization of agencies (bureaucratic procedures and agency mandates to preserve family stability) and the behavior of agency personnel (sexism) discourage battered women who attempt to leave (Bass and Rice, 1979; Davidson, 1978; Dobash and Dobash, 1979; Higgins, 1978; Martin, 1976, 1978; McShane, 1979; Pizzey, 1979; Prescott and Letko, 1977; Truninger, 1971). In other words, the experts maintain that battered women can expect little assistance in overcoming their economic dependency. According to the experts, the excuse of economic dependency should be honored given the additional excuses of unresponsive friends, family, and social service agencies.

Although the external constraint type of excuse acknowledges that staying is unreasonable, it relieves battered women of the responsibility for doing so. Battered women who remain with their mates are portrayed as "more acted upon than acting" (Sykes and Matza, 1957:667). The implication, of course, is that women would leave (i.e., they would be rea-

Chapter VII
The Disrupted Family

sonable) if external constraints could be overcome. The experts provide a warrant, therefore, for intervention in battered women's everyday affairs. In order to act reasonably and leave, battered women must overcome the external constraint of economic dependency which they cannot do without the assistance of specialized experts.

Despite the prevalence of external constraint accounts in the literature on battered women, most experts consider such excuses insufficient. Instead of, or in addition to, such accounts, the experts maintain that battered women face a second type of constraint on their behavior. Although few contemporary experts argue that women stay because they enjoy being the objects of abuse, that they are masochistic, the experts do maintain that battered women face various "internal constraints."[4]

INTERNAL CONSTRAINTS

Some experts have proposed that biographically accumulated experiences may lead women to define violence as "normal" and "natural" (Ball, 1977; Gelles, 1976; Langley and Levy, 1977; Lion, 1977). Likewise, according to some experts, women define violence as a problem only if it becomes severe and/or frequent "enough" (Carlson, 1977; Gelles, 1976; Moore, 1979; Rounsaville and Weissman, 1977-78).[5] If violence is not subjectively defined as a "problem," then women have no reason to consider leaving.

For the most part, experts have focused their attention on documenting internal constraints which are said to prevent women from leaving their mate *even when* violence is subjectively defined as a problem. Experts suggest two major sources of such internal constraints: femininity and the experience of victimization.

To many experts, the primary source of internal constraints is the femininity of battered women. Attributes commonly regarded as "feminine" are automatically attributed to battered women, especially when these characteristics can conceivably account for why such women might remain with their mates. For example, women who stay are said to be emotionally dependent upon their mates (Dobash and Dobash, 1979;

---

[4]Theories focusing on feminine masochism have been proposed by Snell et al. (1964) and Gayford (1975). Waites (1977-78) suggested that the "appearance" of masochism results from "enforced restriction of choice." Most experts argue that the concept of masochism is not applicable to battered women (Breines and Gordon, 1983).

[5]Empirical testing of the association between leaving and childhood experiences has not confirmed this theory (Pagelow, 1981a; Star, 1978; Walker, 1977-78). Likewise, empirical testing of the association between leaving and "severity/frequency" has also not supported theory. See Pagelow (1981b) for a complete discussion.

*Reading 24
Experts on Battered Women*

Fleming, 1979; Freeman, 1979; Langley and Levy, 1977; Moore, 1979; Pizzey, 1979; Roy, 1977); to have a poor self-image or low self-esteem (Carlson, 1977; Freeman, 1979; Langley and Levy, 1977; Lieberknecht, 1978; Martin, 1976; Morgan, 1982; Ridington, 1977-78; Star et al., 1979; Truninger, 1971); and to have traditional ideas about women's "proper place."[6] In isolation or in combination, these so-called feminine characteristics are said to internally constrain women's behavior. According to the experts, women find it subjectively difficult to leave their mates even when violence is defined as a problem.

Internal constraints are also said to follow from the process of victimization itself. According to the experts, battered women not only display typically feminine characteristics, but they also develop unique characteristics due to the victimization process. For example, some experts have argued that once a woman is assaulted she will fear physical reprisal if she leaves (Lieberknecht, 1978; Martin, 1979; Melville, 1978). Other physical, emotional, and psychological after-effects of assault are also said to discourage battered women from leaving their mates (Moore, 1979; Roy, 1977). Indeed, battered women are sometimes said to develop complex psychological problems from their victimization. These include the "stress-response syndrome" (Hilberman, 1980), "enforced restriction of choice" (Waites, 1977-78), "learned helplessness" (Walker, 1979), or responses similar to those of the "rape trauma syndrome" (Hilberman and Munson, 1977-78). A symptom common to all such diagnostic categories is that sufferers find it subjectively difficult to leave their mates.

As with external constraint excuses, these internal constraint accounts also acknowledge the deviance of remaining in a relationship containing violence while, at the same time, relieving battered women of responsibility for doing so. They function in this way, as excuses, because the various internal constraints attributed to battered women are identified as beyond their personal control. Clearly, battered women are not responsible for their gender socialization or for the physical violence they have suffered. In other words, both external and internal constraint accounts portray battered women who stay with their mates as more acted upon than acting. What women require, "for their own good," is assistance in overcoming the various barriers which prevent them from acting reasonably. Thus, both types of accounts offered by the experts on behalf of battered women who stay provide grounds for expert intervention in these women's everyday affairs.

---

[6]"Traditional ideology" includes such beliefs as: divorce is a stigma (Dobash and Dobash, 1979; Langley and Levy, 1977; Moore, 1979; Roy, 1977); the children need their father (Dobash and Dobash, 1979); the woman assumes responsibility for the actions of her mate (Fleming, 1979; Langley and Levy, 1977; Martin, 1976); or feels embarrassed about the family situation (Ball and Wyman, 1977-78; Fleming, 1979; Hendrix et al., 1978).

Chapter VII
The Disrupted Family

As Scott and Lyman (1968) have pointed out, the criteria in terms of which accounts are evaluated vary in relation to the situation in which they are offered, the characteristics of the audience, and the identity of the account provider. In the present context, the identity of the account provider is of particular interest. When experts provide accounts which implicitly serve to promote their right to intervene in others' affairs, an important evaluative criterion is the quality of supportive evidence they offer. Experts who speak on behalf of others are expected to do so on the basis of uncommon knowledge. If, therefore, the evidence which the experts offer in support of their accounts for why battered women stay fails to confirm the expectation of uncommon knowledge, then their claim to be speaking and acting on such women's behalf is open to question.

THE EVIDENCE FOR EXPERTS' ACCOUNTS

How do experts obtain their knowledge about the experiences and behavior of battered women? In order to explore the experts' claim to uncommon knowledge, we address three questions: From whom is evidence obtained (the issue of generalizability)? By what means is evidence obtained (the issue of validity)? How consistently does the evidence support the accounts offered (the issue of reliability)?

GENERALIZABILITY

Experts on battered women claim to have knowledge of the experiences and behavior of women who remain in relationships containing violence. Yet, while there is general agreement that many battered women suffer in silence, with few exceptions the experts have studied only those assaulted wives who have come to the attention of social service agencies, many of whom have already left their mates.[7] Women who contact social service agencies have decided that they require expert intervention in their private affairs, and there is good reason to believe that such women differ from women who have *not* sought assistance.

The decision to seek professional help is typically preceded by a complex process of problem definition, and this process is invariably more difficult and of longer duration when the problem involves the behavior of a family member (Goffman, 1969; Schwartz, 1957; Weiss, 1975; Yarrow et al., 1955). Regardless of the nature of the problem, this defini-

---

[7]Exceptions are Gelles (1976), Hofeller (1982), and Rosenbaum and O'Leary (1981), who included matched samples of persons not receiving services, and Prescott and Letko (1977) who used information from women who responded to an advertisement in *Ms.* magazine.

tional process seems to follow a fairly predictable pattern. Only as a last resort are professional helpers contacted (Emerson and Messinger, 1977; Kadushin, 1969; Mechanic, 1975). Since it is primarily the experiences of women who have reached the end of this help-seeking process which provide evidence for experts' accounts, the generalizability of this evidence is questionable.

VALIDITY

When not simply stating their own perceptions of battered women, experts obtain their evidence in one of two ways. They sometimes question other experts and they sometimes directly question women. Clearly, others' perceptions, whether expert or not, are of uncertain validity. However, even the evidence based on battered women's responses to the question "why do you stay?" is of doubtful validity.

To ask a battered woman to respond to this question is to request that she explain her apparently deviant behavior. This leaves her two alternatives. She can either justify her staying ("I love him;" "he's not all bad;" "the kids need him") or she can excuse her behavior. Since experts have predefined staying as undeniably deviant, it is unlikely that they will honor a justification. Indeed, some experts on battered women have explicitly characterized justifications for staying as "rationalizations," accounts which are self-serving and inaccurate (Ferraro and Johnson, 1983; Waites, 1977–78). Given the experts' presuppositions about the behavior of "staying" and the typical desire of persons to maintain "face" (Goffman, 1955), it is likely that the only accounts the experts will honor—excuses—are subtly elicited by the experts who question battered women. If this is so, then the experts, by asking women why they remain with their mates, have merely constructed an interactional situation which will produce evidence confirming the accounts they offer on women's behalf.[8]

It is hardly surprising, therefore, that the experts on battered women offer remarkably similar accounts of why women stay. This is particularly visible in the evidence which supports the external constraint accounts. By almost exclusively interviewing women who turn to inexpensive or free social service agencies and then constructing an interactional situation which is likely to elicit a particular type of account, experts practi-

---

[8]The situation is more complicated when women who have left are asked why *did* you stay? Or, as Dobash and Dobash (1979:147) asked: "Why do you think you stayed with him as long as you did?" In such situations, the question asks women to retrospectively reconstruct their personal biographies based on their current circumstances and understandings.

Chapter VII
The Disrupted Family

cally ensure that their presuppositions about external constraints are confirmed.[9] In brief, the validity of the experts' evidence is doubtful.

RELIABILITY

Relying primarily on evidence from interviewing and observation, the experts on battered women offer amazingly similar accounts of why women remain. There are, however, many ways to obtain evidence. The question at hand is whether evidence gained from interviewing and observation is similar to evidence obtained using other methods.

If the economic dependency (external constraint) excuse is to avoid challenge, it must be supplemented by the additional excuses of unresponsive friends, family members, and social service agencies. Yet, evidence to support these supplementary external constraint excuses is less than overwhelming. In fact, some evidence undermines the excuse that social service agencies and providers discourage battered women from leaving their mates. Pagelow (1981a) found little relationship between her measures of "agency response" and the amount of time battered women had remained with their mates. Hofeller (1982) found that many battered women self-reported being either "completely" or "somewhat" satisfied with the efforts of social service agencies on their behalf.[10]

As with the excuse of unresponsive social service agencies, available evidence conflicts with various internal constraint accounts offered by the experts. For example, available evidence does not support assertions that battered women hold traditional beliefs about "women's proper place," or that these beliefs internally constrain women from leaving their mates. Walker (1983) reports that battered women perceive themselves to be *less* traditional than "other women," and the results of experimental studies conducted by Hofeller (1982) and Rosenbaum and O'Leary (1981) indicate that women who have *not* been victims of wife assault hold more traditional attitudes than women who are victims. Moreover, Pagelow (1981a) reports that her measures of "traditional ideology" did not help explain the length of time battered women remained with their mates.

The experts have also maintained that the low self-esteem assumed to be common to women in general is exacerbated by the process of victimization, producing a powerful internal constraint on the behavior of battered women. Yet in their now classic review of research evidence re-

---

[9] However, Rounsaville (1978) found that "lack of resources" did not distinguish between women who had left and women who had not left.

[10] The "satisfaction" of victims with social services varies considerably by the type of agency (Hofeller, 1982; Prescott and Letko, 1977).

garding sex differences in self-esteem, Maccoby and Jacklin (1974:15) labelled as a popular myth the commonsense deduction that "women, knowing that they belong to a sex that is devalued...must have a poor opinion of themselves." Contrary to this commonsense deduction, sex differences in self-esteem have rarely been found in experimental studies, and when they have, women's self-esteem is often higher than men's. In addition, at least two studies contained in the literature on battered women refute the statement that battered women have lower self-esteem than women who have not experienced assault. Walker (1983) found that battered women reported their self-esteem has higher than that of "other women," and Star (1978) found that shelter residents who had *not* experienced wife assault scored lower on an "ego-strength" scale than residents who had been assaulted.

In short, the evidence provided to support expert claims about battered women is, by scientific standards, less than convincing. In fact, it appears as if the experts' accounts are presupposed and then implicitly guide both the gathering and interpretation of evidence. In constructing their accounts, the experts have employed the commonsense practice of automatically attributing to individual women (in this case, battered women) sets of traits based on their sex. As females, battered women are automatically assumed to be economically and emotionally dependent upon their mates, to have low self-esteem, and to hold traditional attitudes and beliefs. Methodologies which might yield conflicting evidence are seldom used, and when seemingly conflicting evidence is uncovered it is often explained away. For example, Walker (1983:40) implicitly argues that battered women have an inaccurate perception of themselves. She interprets the finding that battered women consider themselves to be in control of their own behavior as a "lack of acknowledgment that her batterer *really* is in control" (emphasis added). Likewise, Pagelow (1981a) discredits seemingly conflicting evidence by challenging her own measures; the presupposed accounts are not questioned. In other words, the interpretive force of the "master status" of sex "overpowers" evidence to the contrary (Hughes, 1945:357). What the experts on battered women offer in support of their accounts for why women remain is not uncommon knowledge, therefore, but professional "folklore" which, however sophisticated, remains folklore (Zimmerman and Pollner, 1970:44).

This does not mean that evidence which conflicts with the experts' accounts is itself above question. On the contrary, the generalizability, reliability, and validity of conflicting evidence is also problematic. For example, both Pagelow (1981a) and Star (1978) used paper and pencil tests, and both studies were primarily concerned with residents of shelters in urban southern California. Likewise, Walker's (1979, 1983) findings are based primarily on clinical records of an unrepresentative group of

Chapter VII
The Disrupted Family

women, and evidence regarding self-esteem is primarily derived from experimental studies involving only college students.

The sociologically intriguing issue is not, however, the "truthfulness" of accounts. In a diverse society, a variety of different vocabularies of motive (Mills, 1940) are available for making sense out of the complex interrelationships between actor, biography, situation, and behavior. Under such circumstances, "what is reason for one man is mere rationalization for another" (Mills, 1940:910). Any attempt to ascertain battered women's "true" motives would therefore be an exercise in what Mills termed "motive-mongering." What is of sociological interest is that the experts' accounts are not based upon uncommon knowledge but upon commonsense deductions best described as folklore. Clearly, this should raise questions about both the experts' claim to be speaking on battered women's behalf and their claim to have the right to intervene in such women's private affairs.

Given the experts' claim to be speaking and acting in battered women's "best interests," the sociologically important issue is the relative plausibility of the particular vocabulary of motive used by the experts. According to the experts, their primary concerns are the condemnation and elimination of wife assault, tasks which are likely to require specialized expertise. The vocabulary of motive which supports this agenda is one of highlighting "constraints" on women's behavior which must be overcome in order for them to behave reasonably—that is, in order for them to leave. But such a vocabulary is not the only plausible way to make sense of women's behavior.

AN ALTERNATIVE VOCABULARY OF MOTIVE

Prior to the 1970s, the problems of battered women received little attention. In contrast, the contemporary experts have portrayed women as little more than victims. The tendency has been to define both battered women and their relationships with their mates almost exclusively in terms of the occurrence and effects of physical and emotional assault. Battered women are simply defined as assaulted wives who remain with assaultive mates (Ferraro and Johnson, 1983; Pizzey, 1979; Scott, 1974; Walker, 1979), and their relationships are portrayed as no more than victimizing processes. Such a focus leads to what Barry (1979) has termed "victimism," knowing a person only as a victim. One effect of the victimism practiced by the experts on battered women is that possible experiential and behavioral similarities between battered women and other persons are overlooked. It is simply assumed that the occurrence and experience of assault clearly distinguishes battered women and their relationships from individuals in cross-sex relationships which do not contain violence. However, even a cursory review of the sociological literature on marital stability and instability suggests that, at least in regard to their reluctance to leave their mates, battered women are quite similar to both other women and to men.

This literature consistently indicates that marital stability often outlives marital quality. Goode (1956) found that such stability was only sometimes due to the obvious, objective costs of terminating the relationship ("external constraints"). Contrary to predictions that relationships will terminate when apparent "costs" outweigh apparent "benefits," it is not at all unusual for relationships to be sustained even when outsiders perceive costs to be greater than benefits. Although experts on battered women have argued that leaving a relationship means that a woman's status will change from "wife" to "divorcee" (Dobash and Dobash, 1979; Truninger, 1971), a variety of family sociologists have noted that terminating a relationship is far more complex than is suggested by the concept of "status change." Over time, marital partners develop an "attachment" to one another (Weiss, 1975), a "crescive bond" (Turner, 1970), a "shared biography" (McLain and Weigert, 1979). As a result, each becomes uniquely irreplaceable in the eyes of the other. Such a personal commitment to a specific mate has been found to persist despite decreases in marital partners' liking, admiration, and/or respect for one another (Rosenblatt, 1977; Weiss, 1975). Battered women who remain in relationships which outsiders consider costly are not, therefore, particularly unusual or deviant.

Moreover, the sociological literature on marital stability and instability suggests that the process of separation and divorce, what Vaughan (1979) terms "uncoupling," is typically difficult. One indication of the difficulty of this process is the considerable time uncoupling often takes (Cherlin, 1981; Goode, 1956; Weiss, 1975). It is also typical for a series of temporary separations to precede a permanent separation (Lewis and Spanier, 1979; Weiss, 1975; Vaughan, 1979). In brief, the lengthy "leaving and returning" cycle said to be characteristic of battered women is a typical feature of the uncoupling process. Further, the guilt, concern, regret, bitterness, disappointment, depression, and lowered perception of self attributed to battered women are labels for emotions often reported by women and men in the process of uncoupling (Spanier and Castro, 1979; Weiss, 1975).

Although the experts attribute unusual characteristics and circumstances to battered women who remain with their mates, the reluctance of battered women to leave can be adequately and commonsensically expressed in the lyrics of a popular song: "Breaking up is hard to do." It can also be expressed in the more sophisticated vocabulary of sociological psychology: Individuals who are terminating intimate relationships "die

Chapter VII
The Disrupted Family

one of the deaths that is possible" for them (Goffman, 1952). The sociological literature on marital stability and instability does suggest, therefore, an alternative to the vocabulary of battered women's motives provided by the experts on battered women. Because a large portion of an adult's self is typically invested in their relationship with their mate, persons become committed and attached to this mate as a uniquely irreplaceable individual. Despite problems, "internal constraints" are experienced when contemplating the possibility of terminating the relationship with the seemingly irreplaceable other. Again, if this is the case, then women who remain in relationships containing violence are not unusual or deviant; they are typical.

Some experts on battered women have reported evidence which supports this alternative characterization of the motives of women who remain. Gayford (1975) reports that half of his sample of battered women claimed to be satisfied with their relationships, and Dobash and Dobash (1979) note that, apart from the violence, battered women often express positive feelings toward their mates. Moreover, Ferraro and Johnson (1983) report that battered women typically believe that their mates are the only person they could love, and Walker (1979) reports that battered women often describe their mates as playful, attentive, exciting, sensitive, and affectionate. Yet, because of the victimism they practice, experts on battered women often fail to recognize that such findings demonstrate the multi-dimensionality of battered women's relationships with their mates. Indeed, some of these experts have explicitly advised that battered women's expressions of attachment and commitment to their mates not be believed:

> The statement that abused wives love their husbands need not be taken at face value. It may represent merely a denial of ambivalence or even unmitigated hatred. (Waites, 1977–78:542)

> The only reasons the woman does not end the marriage are dependence—emotional or practical—and fear of change and the unknown. These are often masked as love or so the woman deludes herself. (Shainess, 1977:118)

Such expressions of commitment and attachment are *justifications* for why a person might remain with [her] mate. To honor such a justification would be to acknowledge that staying in a relationship which contains violence is not necessarily deviant. In order to sustain their claim to expertise, therefore, the experts on battered women cannot acknowledge the possible validity of this alternative, "justifying" vocabulary of motive even when it is offered by battered women themselves. In other words, the experts discredit battered women's interpretations of their own experiences. The justifications offered by battered women are reinterpreted by the experts as merely "symptoms" of the Stockholm Syndrome (Ochberg, 1980), of an "addiction" which "must be overcome" (Waites, 1977-78), or as the "miracle glue" which "binds a battered woman to her batterer" (Walker, 1979:xvi). By reinterpreting the justifications of battered women in these ways, the experts sustain their claim that such women require this assistance of specialized experts.

CONCLUSIONS

This case study of the social construction of deviance by a group of experts illustrates how members of the knowledge class create a new clientele for their services. In effect, experts discredit the ability of a category of persons to manage their own affairs without interference. The actors in question are portrayed as incapable of either understanding or controlling the factors which govern their behavior. In order for them to understand their experiences and gain control over their behavior, by implication, they require the assistance of specialized experts. Because the category of actors which compose such a clientele are characterized as unreasonable and incompetent, any resistance they offer to the experts' definitions and intervention is easily discredited. For example, battered women's attempts to justify staying with their mates are often interpreted by the experts as further evidence of such women's unreasonablenesss and incompetence. Experts are able to sustain their claims to be speaking and acting on others' behalf, therefore, despite the protests of those on whose behalf they claim to be speaking and acting.

We do not mean to suggest that experts' potential clientele do not benefit from experts' efforts. For example, the experts on battered women have played a major role in focusing public attention on the plight of the victims of wife assault. In doing so, they have helped to dispel the popular myth that these women somehow deserved to be assaulted. In turn, this has undoubtedly encouraged the general public, the police, the courts, and various social service agencies to be more responsive and sensitive to the needs of such women. Yet, battered women may pay a high price for the assistance.

The experts on battered women define leaving one's mate as the normatively expected, reasonable response to the experience of wife assault. By implication, staying with one's mate after such an experience requires explanation. In order to explain this unreasonable response, the experts have provided accounts, that is, ascribed motives to battered women which excuse such deviance. As Blum and McHugh (1971:106) have noted, "observer's ascription of motive serves to formulate...persons." In offering accounts on behalf of battered women who stay, the experts propose a formulation of the type of persons such women are. For example, the experts characterize this type of person as "oversocialized into feminine identity" (Ball and Wyman, 1977–78), "bewildered and helpless" (Ball, 1977), "immature" and lacking clear self-identities (Star et al., 1979), "overwhelmingly passive" and unable to act on their own behalf (Hilberman and Munson, 1977–78), and cognitively, emotionally, and motivationally "deficient" (Walker, 1977–78). Moreover, these women are described as suffering from either the "battered wife syndrome" (Morgan, 1982; Walker, 1983) or the "adult maltreatment syndrome" in Section 995.8 of the International Classification of Diseases. They are "society's problem" (Martin, 1978). Clearly, the categorical identity of battered women is a deeply discrediting one. As Hawkins and Tiedeman (1975) have noted, such typifications of persons by experts often have significant, practical consequences. The experts' descriptions of such "types" often serve as "processing stereotypes" which influence the perceptions and responses of social service providers. Indeed, Loseke (1982) documented how the experts' typifications of battered women served as a processing stereotype which influenced workers' perceptions and service provision at a shelter for battered women.

In summary, once a woman admits that she is a victim of wife assault, her competence is called into question if she does not leave. She is defined as a type of person who requires assistance, a person who is unable to manage her own affairs. As a result, the experts on battered women have constructed a situation where victims of wife assault may lose control over their self-definitions, interpretations of experience, and, in some cases, control over their private affairs. In a sense, battered women may now be victimized twice, first by their mates and then by the experts who claim to speak on their behalf.

REFERENCES

Ball, Patricia G., and Elizabeth Wyman. 1977–78. "Battered wives and powerlessness: What can counselors do?" *Victimology* 2(3, 4):545–552.

Barry, Kathleen. 1979. *Female Sexual Slavery.* New York: Avon.

Bass, David, and Janet Rice. 1979. "Agency responses to the abused wife." *Social Casework* 60 (June):338–342.

Breines, Wini, and Linda Gordon. 1983. "The new scholarship on family violence." *Signs* 8 (Spring):490–531.

Carlson, Bonnie E. 1977. "Battered women and their assailants." *Social Work* 22 (November):455–460.

Cherlin, Andrew J. 1981. *Marriage, Divorce, Remarriage.* Cambridge, Mass.: Harvard University Press.

Coleman, Karen Howes. 1980. "Conjugal violence: What 33 men report." *Journal of Marital and Family Therapy* 6 (April):207–214.

Davidson, Terry. 1978. *Conjugal Crime.* New York: Hawthorne.

Denzin, Norman K. 1983. "Towards a phenomenology of family violence." Paper presented at the meetings of the American Sociological Association. Detroit, August.

Dobash, R. Emerson, and Russell Dobash. 1979. *Violence Against Wives: A Case Against the Patriarchy.* New York: Free Press.

Emerson, Robert M., and Sheldon L. Messinger. 1977. "The micro-politics of trouble." *Social Problems* 26 (December):121-134.

Erchak, Gerald M. 1981. "The escalation and maintenance of child abuse: A cybernetic model." *Child Abuse and Neglect* 5:153-157.

Ferraro, Kathleen J., and John M. Johnson. 1983. "How women experience battering: The process of victimization." *Social Problems* 30 (February):325-339.

Fleming, Jennifer Baker. 1979. *Stopping Wife Abuse.* New York: Garden City, N.Y.: Anchor.

Freeman, M. D. A. 1979. *Violence in the Home.* Westmead, England: Saxon House.

Garfinkel, Harold. 1967. *Studies in Ethnomethodology.* Englewood Cliffs, N.J.: Prentice-Hall.

Gaylord, J. J. 1975. "Wife battering: A preliminary survey of 100 cases." *British Medical Journal* 1:194-197.

Gelles, Richard J. 1976. "Abused wives: Why do they stay?" *Journal of Marriage and the Family* 38(4):659-668.

Giles-Sims, Jean. 1983. *Wife Battering: A Systems Approach.* New York: Guilford Press.

Goffman, Erving. 1952. "On cooling the mark out: Some aspects of adaptation to failure." *Psychiatry* 15 (November):451-463.

_____. 1969. "Insanity of place." *Psychiatry* 32 (November):352-388.

Goode, William J. 1956. *After Divorce.* Glencoe, Ill.: Free Press.

Hawkins, Richard, and Gary Tiedeman. 1975. *The Creation of Deviance, Interpersonal and Organizational Determinants.* Columbus, Ohio: Charles E. Merrill.

Hendrix, Melva Jo, Gretchen E. LaGodna, and Cynthia A. Bohen, 1978. "The battered wife." *American Journal of Nursing* 78 (April):650-653.

Higgins, John G. 1978. "Social services for abused wives." *Social Casework* 59 (May):266-271.

Hilberman, Elaine. 1980. "Overview: The 'Wife-beater's wife' reconsidered." *American Journal of Psychiatry* 137 (November):1336-1346.

_____, and Kit Munson. 1977-78. "Sixty battered women." *Victimology* 2(3, 4):460-470.

Hofeller, Kathleen H. 1982. *Social, Psychological, and Situational Factors in Wife Abuse.* Palo Alto, Calif.: R. and E. Associates.

Hughes, Everett. 1945. "Dilemmas and contradictions of status." *American Journal of Sociology* 50 (March):353-359.

Kadushin, Charles. 1969. *Why People Go to Psychiatrists.* New York: Atherton.

Langley, Roger, and Richard C. Levy. 1977. *Wife Beating: The Silent Crisis.* New York: Pocket Books.

Lewis, Robert A., and Graham B. Spanier. 1979. "Theorizing about the quality and stability of marriage," pp. 268-294 in Wesley R. Burr, Reuben Hill, F. Ivan Nye, and Ira L. Reiss (eds.), *Contemporary Theories About the Family,* Vol. 1. New York: Free Press.

Chapter VII
The Disrupted Family

Lieberknecht, Kay. 1978. "Helping the battered wife." *American Journal of Nursing* 78 (April):654–656.

Lion, John R. 1977. "Clinical aspects of wifebattering," pp. 126–136 in Maria Roy (ed.), *Battered Women: A Psychosociological Study of Domestic Violence*. New York: Van Nostrand Reinhold.

Maccoby, Eleanor Emmons, and Carol Nagy Jacklin. 1974. *The Psychology of Sex Differences*. Stanford, Calif.: Stanford University Press.

McLain, Raymond, and Andrew Weigert. 1979. "Toward a phenomenological sociology of family: A programmatic essay," pp. 160–205 in Wesley R. Burr, Reuben Hill, F. Ivan Nye, and Ira L. Reiss (eds.), *Contemporary Theories About the Family*, Vol. 2. New York: Free Press.

McShane, Claudette. 1979. "Community services for battered women." *Social Work* 24 (January):34–39.

Martin, Del. 1976. *Battered Wives*. San Francisco: Glide Publications.

———. 1978. "Battered women: Society's problem," pp. 111–142 in Jane Roberts Chapman and Margaret Gates (eds.), *The Victimization of Women*. Beverly Hills, Calif.: Sage Publications.

———. 1979. "What keeps a woman captive in a violent relationship? The social context of battering," pp. 33–58 in Donna M. Moore (eds.), *Battered Women*. Beverly Hills, Calif.: Sage Publications.

Mechanic, David. 1975. "Sociocultural and social-psychological factors affecting personal responses to psychological disorder." *Journal of Health and Social Behavior* 16(4):393–404.

Melville, Joy. 1978. "Women in refuges," pp. 293–310 in J. P. Martin (ed.), *Violence and the Family*. New York: John Wiley.

Mills, C. Wright. 1940. "Situated actions and vocabularies of motive." *American Sociological Review* 5 (December):904–913.

Moore, Donna M. 1979. "An overview of the problem," pp. 7–32 in Donna M. Moore (ed.), *Battered Women*. Beverly Hills, Calif.: Sage Publications.

Morgan, Patricia A. 1981. "From battered wife to program client; The state's shaping of social problems." *Kapitalistate* 9:17–40.

Morgan, Steven M. 1982. *Conjugal Terrorism: A Psychological and Community Treatment Model of Wife Abuse*. Palo Alto: Calif.: R. and E. Associations.

Ochberg, F. M. 1980. "Victims of terrorism." *Journal of Clinical Psychiatry* 41:73–74.

Pagelow, Mildred Dailey. 1981a. *Woman-Battering: Victims and Their Experiences*. Beverly, Hills, Calif.: Sage Publications.

———. 1981b. "Factors affecting women's decisions to leave violent relationships." *Journal of Family Issues* 2 (December):391–414.

Pizzey, Erin. 1979. "Victimology interview: A refuge for battered women." *Victimology* 4(1):100–112.

Prescott, Suzanne, and Carolyn Letko. 1977. "Battered women: A social psychological perspective," pp. 72–96 in Maria Roy (ed.), *Battered Women: A Psychosociological Study of Domestic Violence*. New York: Van Nostrand Reinhold.

Ridington, Jillian. 1977-78. "The transition process: A feminist environment as reconstructive milieu." *Victimology* 2(3, 4):563–575.

Rosenbaum, Alan, and K. Daniel O'Leary. 1981. "Marital violence: Characteristics of abusive couples." *Journal of Consulting and Clinical Psychology* 49(1):63–71.

Reading 24
Experts on Battered Women

Rosenblatt, Paul C. 1977. "Needed research on commitment in marriage," pp. 73–86 in George Levinger and Harold L. Raush (eds.), *Close Relationships: Perspectives on the Meaning of Intimacy*. Amherst: University of Massachusetts.

Rounsaville, Bruce J. 1978. "Theories in marital violence: Evidence from a study of battered women." *Victimology* 21(1, 2):11–31.

Rounsaville, Bruce, and Myrna M. Weissman. 1977–78. "Battered women: A medical problem requiring detection." *International Journal of Psychiatry in Medicine* 8(2):191–202.

Roy, Maria. 1977. "A current survey of 150 cases," pp. 25–44 in Maria Roy (ed.), *Battered Women: A Psychosociological Study of Domestic Violence*. New York: Van Nostrand Reinhold.

Schwartz, Charlotte Green. 1957. "Perspectives on deviance: Wives' definitions of their husbands' mental illness." *Psychiatry* 20(3):275–291.

Scott, Marvin B., and Stanford, M. Lyman. 1968. "Accounts." *American Sociological Review* 33 (December):46–62.

Scott, P. D. 1974. "Battered wives." *British Journal of Psychiatry* 125 (November):433–441.

Shainess, Natalie. 1977. "Psychological aspects of wifebattering," pp. 111–118 in Maria Roy (ed.), *Battered Women: A Psychosociological Study of Domestic Violence*. New York: Van Nostrand Reinhold.

Snell, John E., M. D. Richard, J. Rosenwald, and Ames Robey. 1964. "The wifebeater's wife." *Archives of General Psychiatry* 11 (August):107–112.

Spanier, Graham, and Robert F. Castro. 1979. "Adjustment to separation and divorce: An analysis of 50 case studies." *Journal of Divorce* 2 (Spring):241–253.

Star, Barbara. 1978. "Comparing battered and non-battered women." *Victimology* 3(1, 2):32–44.

_____, Carol G. Clark, Karen M. Goetz, and Linda O'Malia. 1979. "Psychosocial aspects of wife battering." *Social Casework* 60 (October):479–487.

Stark, Evan, and Anne Flitcraft. 1983. "Social knowledge, social policy, and the abuse of women: The case against patriarchal benevolence," pp. 330–348 in David Finkelhor, Richard J. Gelles, Gerald T. Hotaling, and Murray A. Straus (eds.), *The Dark Side of Families*. Beverly Hills, Calif.: Sage Publications.

Straus, Murray A. 1974. "Forward," pp. 13–17 in Richard J. Gelles, *The Violent Home*. Beverly Hills, Calif.: Sage Publications.

_____, Richard J. Gelles, and Suzanne Steinmetz. 1980. *Behind Closed Doors: Violence in the American Home*. Garden City, N.Y.: Anchor.

Sykes, Gresham, and David Matza. 1957. "Techniques of neutralization: A theory of delinquency." *American Sociological Review* 22 (December):664–669.

Truninger, Elizabeth. 1971. "Marital violence: The legal solutions." *Hastings Law Journal* 23 (November):259–276.

Turner, Ralph. 1970. *Family Interaction*. New York: John Wiley.

Vaughan, Diane. 1979. "Uncoupling: The process of moving from one lifestyle to another." *Alternative Lifestyles* 2 (November):415–442.

Waites, Elizabeth A. 1977–78. "Female masochism and the enforced restriction of choice." *Victimology* 2(3, 4):535–544.

Walker, Lenore E. 1977–78. "Battered women and learned helplessness." *Victimology* 2(3, 4):525–534.

_____. 1979. *The Batttered Woman*. New York: Harper & Row.

Chapter VII
The Disrupted Family

———. 1983. "The battered woman syndrome study," pp. 31-48 in David Finkelhor, Richard J. Gelles, Gerald T. Hotaling, and Murray A. Straus (eds.), *The Dark Side of Families*. Beverly Hills, Calif.: Sage Publications.

Wardell, Laurie, Dair L. Gillespie, and Ann Leffler. 1983. "Science and violence against wives," pp. 69-84 in David Finkelhor, Richard J. Gelles, Gerald T. Hotaling, and Murray A. Straus (eds.), *The Dark Side of Families*. Beverly Hills, Calif.: Sage Publications.

Weiss, Robert. 1975. *Marital Separation*. New York: Basic Books.

Yarrow, Marian Radke, Charlotte Green Schwartz, Harriet S. Murphy, and Leila Calhoun Desy. 1955. "The psychological meaning of mental illness in the family." *Journal of Social Issues* 11(4):12-24.

Zimmerman, Don, and Melvin Pollner. 1970. "The everyday world as a phenomenon," pp. 80-104 in Jack Douglas (ed.), *Understanding Everyday Life*. Chicago: Aldine.

Reading 25
DIVORCE AND STIGMA

Naomi Gerstel, *University of Massachusetts and Rutgers University*

> *As many different forms of family structures come to be defined as societally acceptable, the general level of disapproval of divorce has declined. Nevertheless, interviews with a sample of separated and divorced respondents show that many of the divorced still stigmatize or devalue themselves. They maintain that to be married is "normal" and that divorce is only acceptable under special circumstances. Divorced people also feel they are subjected to a number of informal but powerful sanctions in their day to day social relations.*

By most accounts, tolerance of variation in family life has increased dramatically in the United States. Public opinion polls over the last two decades reveal declining disapproval of extended singlehood (Veroff et al., 1981), premarital sex and pregnancy (Gerstel, 1982), employment of mothers with young children (Cherlin, 1981), and voluntary childlessness (Huber and Spitze, 1983). Divorce resembles these other situations; in fact public tolerance of divorce appears to have increased especially dramatically over the last few decades (Veroff et al., 1981).

In the mid-1950's, Goode (1956:10) could still observe: "We know that in our own society, divorce has been a possible, but disapproved, solution for marital conflict." However, comparing attitudes in 1958 and 1971, McRae (1978) found an increasing proportion of adults believing that divorce was only "sometimes wrong" while a decreasing proportion felt that it was "always wrong." These data, he claimed, indicated attitudes toward divorce had shifted "from moral absolutism to situational ethics" (1978:228). In an analysis of panel data collected between 1960 and 1980, Thornton (1985) found that changes in attitudes toward divorce were not only large but pervasive: all subgroups—whether defined by age, class, or even religion—showed substantial declines in disapproval of marital separation.

Reprinted with permission from *Social Problems* 34(1987): 172-180m, 182m-183 by the Society for the Study of Social Problems and the author.

Chapter VII
The Disrupted Family

What are the implications of declining disapproval of divorce? In historical perspective, it is clear that the divorced are no longer subject to the moral outrage they encountered centuries, or even decades, ago. Certainly, divorce is no longer treated as a sin calling for repressive punishment, as it was in theological doctrine and practice (be it Catholic or Protestant) until the beginning of the twentieth century (Halem, 1980; O'Neil, 1967). In electing a divorced president and many divorced senators and governors, U.S. citizens seem to have repudiated the idea that divorce is grounds for exclusion from public life. With the recent passage of no-fault divorce laws in every state, U.S. courts no longer insist on attributing wrongdoing to one party to a divorce (Weitzman, 1985).

Most recent commentators on a divorce even argue that it is no longer stigmatized. For example, Spanier and Thompson (1984:15) claim that "the social stigma associated with divorce has disappeared" and Weitzman (1981:146) suggests that "the decline in the social stigma traditionally attached to divorce is one of the most striking changes in the social climate surrounding divorce."

However, I argue in this paper that the stigma attached to divorce has disappeared in only two very limited senses. First, although other studies have shown a clear decline in disapproval of divorce as a general category, disapproval of divorced individuals persists contingent on the specific conditions of their divorce. Thus, as I show below, some divorced people experience disapproval and at least one party to a divorce often feels blamed.

Second, while many of the formal, institutional controls on divorce—imposed in the public realm of church or state—have weakened, the individual who divorces suffers informal, relational sanctions. These are the interpersonal controls that emerge more or less spontaneously in social life. I will present evidence indicating that the divorced believe the married often exclude them and that the divorced themselves frequently pull toward, yet devalue, others who divorce.

In these two senses, I argue that the divorced are still subject to the same social processes and evaluations associated with stigmatization more generally. As in Goffman's (1963:3) classic formulation—which stresses both the conditional and relational aspects of stigma—my findings suggest that the divorced come to be seen (and to see themselves) as "of a less desired kind...reduced in our minds from a whole and usual person to a tainted, discounted one."

METHODS

My data come from interviews with 104 separated and divorced respondents: 52 women and 52 men. Based on a conception of marital dissolution as a process rather than a static life event, the research team sampled respondents in different stages of divorce: one-third of the respondents were separated less than one year; one-third separated one to two years; one-third separated two or more years. To obtain respondents, we could not rely on court records alone, for most couples who have filed for a divorce have already been living apart for at least a year. Thus, 61 percent of the respondents were selected from probate court records in two counties in the Northeast; the others came from referrals. Comparisons between the court cases and referred respondents show no statistically significant differences on demographic characteristics.

A team of three interviewers conducted household interviews, using a schedule composed of both open- and closed-ended items. Each interview, lasting from two to seven hours (an average of three hours), was taped and transcribed in full. My analysis is based primarily on the extensive information collected on social ties. Using measures adapted from Fischer (1982), interviewers asked each respondent to name all those individuals with whom, in the last month, they had a series of common exchanges: engaged in social activities, discussed personal worries, received advice in decisions, etc. Respondents were also asked to name those individuals with whom interaction had become difficult since the separation. To complete the network list, the interviewer compiled a list of those named, gave it to the respondent, and asked: "Is there anyone important to you who doesn't show up on this list?" Any new names were then added to the network list. Respondents (both women and men) named a mean of 18 people (with a minimum of 8 and a maximum of 35). Using the list, the interviewer asked the respondents a series of questions about each person named including, for example, the person's marital status, how long they had known the person, and whether or not he or she disapproved of the divorce. Respondents were also asked to expand on these close-ended items, to answer a number of open-ended questions about how their relationships had changed since the divorce, and to discuss their participation in organized groups (including sports, cultural, religious, and service groups as well as those "singles groups" set up by and for the divorced—e.g., Parents Without Partners.) In addition, two measures of mental health status were included: the Center for Epidemiological Studies Depression Scale (CES-D) and a generalized emotional distress or demoralization scale (PERI).

SAMPLE CHARACTERISTICS

In contrast to the samples in most previous research on separation and divorce, the respondents are a heterogeneous group. They include people in the working class as well as in the middle class whose household incomes ranged from under $4,000 to over $50,000, with a median of $18,000 (with women's significantly lower than men's.) Levels of educa-

Chapter VII
The Disrupted Family

tion varied widely: about one-fourth had less than a high school degree, and slightly less than one-fourth had four or more years of college. The sample also includes significant numbers whose primary source of income came from public assistance and from manual, clerical, and professional jobs. Only 11 percent were not currently employed while another 9 percent were working part-time. The median age of the respondents was 33 years, and the mean number of years married was nine. Finally, 30 percent of the sample had no children, 19 percent had one child, and 51 percent had more than one child.

FINDINGS

Disapproval of Divorce

When asked whether people they knew disapproved of their divorce, 34 percent of the respondents named no one and another 21 percent named only one person (out of a total of eight to thirty-five people in their networks), although the number named as disapproving did range from zero to nine. If we consider just respondents' perceptions of friends (or non-kin), only 18 percent (of the total) said more than one friend disapproved while fully 60 percent said no friend disapproved. The respondents were somewhat more likely to suggest that relatives disapproved. However, only 23 percent named more than one relative who disapproved while just over half (51 percent) named none. Moreover, although the respondents perceived more criticism from relatives than friends—perhaps because one of the privileges accorded kin in our society is to remark on things friends might think better left unsaid—the divorced nonetheless often dismissed their few critical relatives as "outdated," "old farts," or "living in the past."

...In sum, the circumstances of divorce, rather than the mere fact, are now the subject of disapproval. The conditions associated with the experience of disapproval vary for women and men, reflecting a gender-based ideology of divorce—and marriage. If a "bad" man is a cavalier home-wrecker, a "bad" woman is one who does not (or cannot) sacrifice for her children. While McRae's (1978) longitudinal data suggest divorce has been removed from the realm of absolute moral condemnation or categorical blame, these findings indicate that the specific conditions of the divorce may nonetheless generate disapproval.

The Experience of Blame

Even though categorical disapproval of divorce has declined, individuals may still feel they are held accountable and blamed for their divorce. Evidence for this can be seen in the "splitting of friends." Numerous studies show that ex-spouses often split friends they shared while married (e.g., see Spanier and Thompson, 1984; Weiss, 1975). Among those interviewed in this study, over half of the men (55 percent) and close to half (43 percent) of the women spoke spontaneously and sadly of dividing friends—e.g., finding "our friends polarized" (C007, male), "our social group split down the middle" (C035, female). Many divorced people lose friends who feel loyal to their ex-spouse and, *consequently*, are estranged from them as well.

To be sure, the respondents reported that this process of splitting friends is complicated: one spouse keeps particular friends because she or he brought those friends to the marriage—from childhood, from work, or from independent leisure activities. That spouse then "owns" those friends and receives them almost as if they were property when the marriage ends. But this pattern of splitting also indicates ways the divorced individual comes to experience social devaluation. In the splitting of friends, we discover processes that provoke others to at least act as if they blame one party to a divorce.

Feeling hurt or angry, the divorced themselves may put pressure on friends to take sides. One woman said it quite emphatically:

> I am furious at Ted [her ex-spouse]. I can't stand him being with my friends. I don't want him to have anything (N004, female).

To be supportive to one ex-spouse, a friend may have to agree to attribute blame (or at least act as if they do) to the other. As one young mother of two put it:

> Things have become difficult with friends. He [her ex-husband] has tried to put friends in the middle (N013, female).

When asked, "what do you mean?", she replied:

> He tries to get them to choose sides or to, I think, feel sorry for him. To turn them against me.

Her response suggests that friends and kin are pushed to define one ex-spouse as "guilty," the other as "innocent." They may feel pressured to blame at least one spouse in order to justify their detachment from that one and attachment to the other.

...In his study of the divorced, Weiss (1975:15) argues that "developing the story" or the "account" of the divorce is a "device of major psychological importance not only because it settles the issue of who was responsible but because...it organizes the events into a conceptual, manageable unity." I would argue that the development of accounts is not simply a psychological mechanism but a social device. As Scott and Lyman (1968:46) observe, "accounts" are "statements made by a social

Chapter VII
The Disrupted Family

actor to explain unanticipated or untoward behavior." The development of accounts is a means by which the divorced justify their actions not only to themselves but to others as well. That the divorced feel the need to develop such accounts suggests that divorce is neither experienced nor greeted neutrally. Rather, it is an aspect of biography that must be managed and negotiated socially. In the splitting of friends, then, others often are pressured to "blame" one ex-spouse. And, by offering "accounts" for their actions, the divorced not only share but sustain the notion that blame should and will be allocated.

SOCIAL EXCLUSION: REJECTION BY THE MARRIED

Partners to a divorce not only split friends; they are often excluded from social interaction with the married more generally. Many ex-husbands and ex-wives found they could not maintain friendships with married couples: about one-half of both men (43 percent) and woman (58 percent) agreed with the statement: "Married couples don't want to see me now." Moreover, less than one-fourth (23 percent) of the women and men agreed: "I am as close to my married friends as when I was married." By getting a divorce, then, they became marginal to at least part of the community on which they had previously relied.

One man summed up the views of many when he spoke of the "normal life" of the married:

> One of the things I recognized not long after I was separated is that this is a couple's world. People do things in couples, normally (C043, male).

Remembering his own marriage, he now recognized its impact:

> We mostly went out with couples. I now have little or no contact with them.

Discovering "they don't invite me anymore" or "they never call," many of the divorced felt rejected:

> The couples we shared our life with, uh, I'm an outsider now. They stay away. Not being invited to a lot of parties that we was always invited to. It's with males and females. It sucks (C030, male).

The divorced developed explanations for their exclusion. Finding themselves outsiders, some simply thought that their very presence destabilized the social life of couples: "I guess I threaten the balance" (N004, female). They found themselves social misfits in that world, using terms like "a third wheel" (N010, female; N027, male) and "odd person out" (N006, male) to describe their newly precarious relationship with the married.

*Reading 25
Divorce and Stigma*

Some went further, suggesting that those still in couples felt threatened by the divorce or were afraid it would harm their own marriages. "They say, 'My God, it's happening all over.' It scares them" (N019, male). Men and women expressed this form of rejection in terms of "contagion" (C027, male) and "a fear it's going to rub off on them" (N010, female). Because the difficulties of marriage are often concealed, others found their divorce came as a surprise to married friends. That surprise reinforced the idea "it can happen to anyone" and "so they tend to stay away" (C027, male)....

The exclusion of the divorced from the social life they had enjoyed while married constitutes a negative sanction on divorce. This is not simply a functional process of friendship formation based on homogamy (cf. Lazarsfeld and Merton, 1964): it involves conflict, producing a sense of devaluation on the part of one group (the divorced) who feel rejected by another group still considered normal (the married).

The divorced try to come to terms with their experience by talking to others who share it. Together they develop a shared understanding similar to what Goffman (1963:5) calls a "stigma theory": the married feel uncomfortable, even threatened by them, and act as if divorce, as a "social disease," is contagious. Or divorce poses a threat because of the desired freedom and sexuality it (perhaps falsely) represents. Finally, divorced people mutually develop a broader explanation for the modern response to them: they are avoided because the dissolution of marriage is so common, so possible, that it becomes a real threat both to any given couple and to the social world built on, and routinized by, groups consisting of couples.

COLLEAGUES AND DEMORALIZATION

The separation of the divorced from the married is even more clearly apparent in the social life developed by the divorced themselves. The divorced pull away from the married and into the lives of others like them. Goffman (1963:18) argues that the stigmatized turn to others like them in anticipation that "mixed social contact will make for anxious, unanchored interaction." Accordingly, many of the divorced said they felt "uncomfortable" (C042, female), "strained" (C003, male; N014 and C029, females), "strange" (C034, female), and "awkward" (C019, male) in a world composed of couples. And some abandoned the married: "I've been pulling way from my coupled friends" (C026, female).

Drawing together with other divorced, they can develop as well as share their "sad tales" (Goffman, 1963:19) and learn how to behave. In fact, over half of the people with whom these divorced men (52 percent) and women (62 percent) socialized were other divorced individuals, a far

Chapter VII
The Disrupted Family

higher proportion than is found in the general population (U.S. Bureau of the Census, 1983). The divorced used many well-worn phrases to talk about others who shared their marital status: "birds of a feather flock together" (N021, male) and "likes attract likes" (N025, female)....

THE DEVALUATION OF SELF

Perhaps the most striking evidence that the divorced devalue their own condition is found in their assessment of organizations established for the divorced. Only 10 percent of the respondents were in such groups. In fact, most of the divorced—male as well as female—explicitly rejected such formal mechanisms of integration set up by and for others like them.

For the relatively small number of people who did join, such groups provided both a source of entertainment for their children as well as an opportunity to meet other adults. However, in explaining why they joined, the divorced typically stressed child care. Thus, children were not simply a reason for joining; they provided legitimation for membership. By explaining membership in instrumental rather than expressive terms, and in terms of children rather than themselves, the divorced distanced themselves from the potentially damaging implications of membership for their own identity. In this sense, children provide a "face saving device," much like those inventoried by Berk (1977) among people who attended singles dances.

The notion that groups for the divorced—and therefore those who join them—are stigmatized is substantiated still further by the comments of those who did not join. They gave a number of reasons for their reluctance. Some attributed their lack of participation to a lack of knowledge. Others simply felt they did not have the time or energy. When asked why she had not joined any divorce group, one 25-year-old saleswoman said:

> I've thought about it, but I have just never done anything about it. I know it is not getting me anywhere by not doing anything. Basically I am a lazy person (C024, female).

But while she first blamed herself for non-participation in these groups, she then went on to add a more critical note: "I think I would feel funny walking into a place like that." Her second thought reiterated a common theme—an attitude toward divorce and membership in organizations for them—which came through with compelling force. Many imagined that people who joined such groups were unacceptable in a variety of ways, or even that to join them was somehow a sign of weakness. For example:

These people really don't have somebody to turn to. I guess that's the main reason for them belonging and I do have someone to turn to, matter of fact, more than one. They're really not sure of themselves, they're insecure (N013, female).

Such comments reveal that respondents saw divorce as a discredit, at least insofar as it became the axis of one's social life. Consequently, to join such groups was to reinforce the very devaluation they hoped to avoid....

CONCLUSION

...To argue that the divorced are no longer stigmatized is to misunderstand their experience. To be sure, divorce is now less deviant in a statistical sense than it was a decade ago. As a group, the divorced are not categorized as sinful, criminal, or even wrong. Moreover, even though the divorced lose married friends and have smaller networks than the married, they do not become completely ghettoized into subcultures of the divorced (Gerstel et al., 1985; Weiss, 1979). Finally, as I have shown here, the divorced themselves do not think that most of their kin and friends disapprove.

However, a decrease in statistical deviance, a relaxation of institutional controls by church or state, or a decline in categorical disapproval is not the same as the absence of stigmatization. Although a majority of Americans claim they are indifferent in principle to those who make a "personal decision" to leave a "bad" marriage, this indifference does not carry over into the social construction of private lives. The divorced believe they are the targets of informal relational sanctions—exclusion, blame, and devaluation. If we understand stigma as referring not simply to the realm of public sanctions but rather see it as emerging out of everyday experience, then we can see that the divorced continue to be stigmatized.

REFERENCES

Becker, Howard S. 1963. *Outsiders: Studies in the Sociology of Deviance.* New York: Free Press.

Berk, Bernard. 1977. "Fact saving at the singles dance." *Social Problems* 24:530–544.

Best, Joel, and David Luckenbill. 1980. "The social organization of deviants." *Social Problems* 28:14–31.

Chapter VII
The Disrupted Family

Caplan, Gerald. 1974. *Social Supports and Community Mental Health.* New York: Behavioral Publications.

Cherlin, Andrew. 1981. *Marriage, Divorce and Remarriage.* Cambridge, Mass.: Harvard University Press.

Conrad, Peter, and Joseph W. Schneider. 1980. *Deviance and Medicalization: From Badness to Sickness.* St. Louis: C. V. Mosby.

Ephron, Nora. 1983. *Heartburn.* New York: Pocket Books.

Fischer, Claude. 1982. *To Dwell Among Friends.* Chicago: University of Chicago Press.

Foucault, Michel. 1967. *Madness and Civilization.* London: Tavistock.

Furstenberg, Frank P. 1982. "Conjugal succession: Reentering marriage after divorce," pp. 107–146 in Paul B. Bates and Orville G. Brim (eds.), *Life-Span Development and Behavior,* Volume 4. New York: Academic Press.

Gerstel, Naomi. 1982. "The new right and the family," pp. 6–20 in Barbara Haber (ed.), *The Woman's Annual.* New York: G. K. Hall.

Gerstel, Naomi, Catherine Kohler Riessman, and Sarah Rosenfield. 1985. "Explaining the symptomatology of separated and divorced women and men: The role of material resources and social networks." *Social Forces* 64:84–101.

Goffman, Erving. 1963. *Stigma.* Englewood Cliffs. N.J.: Prentice-Hall.

Goode, William. 1956. *Women in Divorce.* New York: Free Press.

Gove, Walter R., and Michael Geerkin. 1977. "The effect of children and employment on the mental health of married men and women." *Social Forces* 56:66–76.

Halem, Lynne Carol. 1980. *Divorce Reform.* New York: Free Press.

Hetherington, E.M., M. Cox, and R. Cox. 1976. "Divorced fathers." *The Family Coordinator* 25:417–428.

Hochschild, Arlie Russell. 1983. "Attending to, codifying and managing feelings: Sex differences in love," pp. 250–262 in Laurel Richardson and Verta Taylor (eds.), *Feminist Frontiers.* Reading, Mass.: Addison-Wesley.

Huber, Joan, and Glenna Spitze. 1983. *Stratification: Children, Housework, and Jobs.* New York: Academic Press.

Kessler, Ronald D. 1982. "A disaggregation of the relationship between socioeconomic status and psychological distress." *American Sociological Review* 47:752–764.

Kitson, Gay, and Marvin Sussman. 1982. "Marital complaints, demographic characteristics and symptoms of mental distress in marriage." *Journal of Marriage and the Family* 44:87–101.

Krause, Harry D. 1986. *Family Law.* Second Edition. St. Paul, Minn.: West.

Lazarsfeld, Paul, and Robert K. Merton. 1964. "Friendship as a social process: A substantive and methodological analysis," pp. 18–66 in Monroe Berger, Theodore Abel, and Charles Page (eds.), *Freedom and Control in Modern Society.* New York: Van Norstrand.

Lopata, Helena. 1979. *Women as Widows.* New York: Elsevier.

McRae, James A. 1978. "The secularization of divorce," pp. 227–242 in Beverly Duncan and Otis Dudley Duncan (eds.), *Sex Typing and Sex Roles.* New York: Academic Press.

Miall, Charlene E. 1986. "The stigma of involuntary childlessness." *Social Problems* 33:288.

O'Neil, William L. 1967. *Divorce in the Progressive Era.* New Haven, Conn.: Yale University Press.

Riessman, Catherine, and Naomi Gerstel. 1986. "It's a long story: Women and men account for marital failure." Paper presented at the World Congress of Sociologists, New Delhi, India.

Rosenberg, Morris. 1979. *Conceiving the Self.* New York: Basic Books.

Schneider, Joseph W., and Peter Conrad. 1980. "In the closet with illness: Epilepsy, stigma potential and information control." *Social Problems* 28:32–44.

Scott, Marvin B., and Stanford M. Lyman. 1968. "Accounts." *American Sociological Review* 33:46–62.

Simmel, Georg. 1950. *The Sociology of Georg Simmel.* Kurt H. Wolff, translator. New York: Free Press.

Spanier, Graham, and Linda Thompson. 1984. *Parting.* Beverly Hills, Calif.: Sage.

Stein, Peter (ed.) 1981. *Single Life.* Englewood Cliffs, N.J.: Prentice-Hall.

Thornton, Arland. 1985. "Changing attitudes toward separation and divorce: Causes and consequences." *American Journal of Sociology* 90:856–872.

U.S. Bureau of Census. 1983. "Marital status and living arrangements: March, 1983." Current Population Reports, Series P-20, no. 389. Washington, D.C.: U.S. Government Printing Office.

Veroff, Joseph, Elizabeth Douvan, and Richard A. Kulka. 1981. *The Inner American: A Self-Portrait from 1957–1976.* New York: Basic Books.

Wallerstein, Judith S., and Joan B. Kelly. 1980. *Surviving the Breakup.* New York: Basic Books.

Weiss, Robert. 1975. *Marital Separation.* New York: Basic Books.

———. 1979. *Going It Alone.* New York: Basic Books.

Weitzman, Lenore. 1981. *The Marriage Contract.* New York: Free Press.

———. 1985. *The Divorce Revolution: The Unexpected Social and Economic Consequences for Women and Children in America.* New York: Free Press.

Zola, Irving. 1983. *Sociomedical Inquiries: Recollections, Reflections and Reconsiderations.* Philadelphia: Temple University Press.

CHAPTER VIII

EDUCATIONAL PROBLEMS

Reading 26
EXPECT AND YE SHALL RECEIVE

William Ryan

> *Before each student can perform up to his or her ability, we must get rid of the self-fulfilling prophecy produced by the expectations and definitions of teachers. Bias toward middle-class children has encouraged their best performance but has penalized children from poorer backgrounds.*

There is an apocryphal story about an energetic teacher who was quite convinced that she gave her very best to every member of her classes and, in turn, got the very best out of each one of them. She was satisfied that this was so because, every year when school began, she would diligently collect information about the aptitudes of all of her pupils and keep their IQs—individual by individual—under the glass top of her desk, until she had virtually memorized them. At the end of every year, when she compared the achievements and grades of the students with their IQs, she found an almost perfect match—those with high aptitudes, with high IQs, did best; those with low IQs did worst. Every single child was performing to his capacity.

When a new principal came to the school, the teacher explained her system to him and demonstrated it in the classroom. She called on a pupil with a high IQ and he gave the right answer, and then on one with a low IQ, who gave the wrong answer. The principal was very interested and asked to borrow her list of IQs. The next day he came back to give it to her and said, "You're certainly right about the kiddoes performing just about the way these numbers say they should. I must tell you one thing, though. Instead of copying down your pupil's IQs, you've copied down their *locker numbers*."

This story illustrates the central mechanism in the classroom by which the miracles of sorting and labeling...are accomplished: human beings, and particularly children, act the way we *expect* them to act, be-

---

Reprinted with permission from *Equality* (New York: Vintage, 1981), pp. 130-135 by Random House, Inc.

Chapter VIII
Educational Problems

cause we unconsciously convey to them what those expectations are. The teacher in the story expected children with high locker numbers to perform well, and those with low numbers to perform poorly, and they did.

This process has now been demonstrated rather thoroughly in real life. Kenneth Clark and his associates in the HARYOU project, for example, concluded that Harlem schools were doing a poor job of educating Harlem children because the teachers in those schools *expected* the children to learn very little, and, naturally, they got what they expected. A few years later, Rosenthal and Jacobson demonstrated this point in their dramatic "Pygmalion in the Classroom" experiment.

This study has become very well known over the past few years, but I will summarize it very briefly. The experimenters were looking for the effects of expectations on behavior, the so-called self-fulfilling prophecy, and they tested it in the classrooms of an elementary school in San Francisco. At the end of one year, they administered a newly developed intelligence test to all the children in the school, but they gave it a meaningless high-sounding name, the "Test of Inflected Acquisition," and described it to the teachers as a new kind of test that would pick out children who were likely to show sudden intellectual improvement—"spurters" who would abruptly start to do much better in their school work. The test was obviously nothing of the sort, and they didn't use it for that purpose; rather, they just randomly selected 20 percent of the children—about five from each class—and casually informed the teachers that these were the ones the test had selected as potential "spurters." There was no intervention beyond this. At the beginning of the next year, they gave this false information to teachers in the hope of setting up expectations in their minds, before they even had a chance to see the children or get to know anything about them. Then they sat back to see the effect, which they measured by retesting the children later in the year and by getting personality and behavior ratings of the children from the teachers.

The results were striking. Most of the children who had been randomly picked out and labeled as potential "spurters" did in fact "spurt," particularly the younger children in the early grades, who showed tremendous gains on their tests. In addition, these children were seen by the teachers much more favorably than were their classmates; they appeared more curious and better adjusted, among other things. Finally, and in some ways most interesting of all, children *not* labeled as "spurters" who spurted anyway—who went *against* the expectations that had been set up in the teachers' minds—were viewed much more negatively, as showing undesirable behavior, being poorly adjusted, and so on.

*Reading 26
Teachers' Self-Fulfilling Prophecies*

Ray Rist followed up the Pygmalion experiment with a study in which he tried to find out more about how expectations form in teachers' minds in the ordinary classroom situation without any experimental intervention. He focused his attention on a single class in a ghetto school, all black children, starting with them in kindergarten and following them into the second grade, stopping along the way for frequent formal and informal observations of the classroom goings-on and for interviews with teachers. Again, the results are rather startling.

On the eighth day of school, the kindergarten teacher was prepared to divide thirty children into three distinct ability groups. Two and one-half years later, in the second grade, ten of the thirty were still in the same building (others had moved, had not been promoted, or were in other second-grade classes in an annex). Of the ten, six had been in the top-ability group in kindergarten. All six were in the top group in second grade. The other four had been in the middle and low groups in kindergarten. All were the middle group in second grade. (By the second grade, the lowest group was made up predominantly of children who were repeating the year.) What an incredible evaluating and prognosticating ability that kindergarten teacher had! Think of it: after eight days of school with thirty little five-year-olds she had never seen before—that is, after an acquaintance of not much more than thirty hours—this teacher was able to sort them out precisely in terms of their academic abilities in a manner that would hold up for at least two and one-half years (and, as we know from other studies, would hold up almost as well for the full twelve years of school).

Rist watched the teachers and the children very closely during that first year of kindergarten, and he found some interesting relationships. It was quite clear in the teacher's own mind how she went about dividing up the children: the nine children at table one, she explained, were her "fast learners," the other twenty-one, at tables two and three, "had no idea of what was going on in the classroom." How could she spot the "fast learners" so quickly? Rist did notice a number of objective characteristics and behavior that differentiated the "fast learners" from the others. First of all, the "fast learners," as she labeled them, were all neatly dressed in clean clothes; this was true of only one of the twenty-one other children. Second, the table-one elite all interacted readily with the teacher and each other. Third, they were more verbal and used standard middle-class English almost all the time; the others were much less responsive verbally and tended to use the phrases and syntax of so-called Black English. Finally, the children differed in a number of background characteristics that were known to the teacher from preschool registration: the parents of the table-one children had much better educations,

Chapter VIII
Educational Problems

jobs, and incomes than had the parents of the others. None of these families were on welfare, whereas six of the twenty-one others were. Only one-third of the table-one children did not have both parents living in the home, whereas the great majority of the others—sixteen out of the twenty-one—came from one-parent families. These and similar social-class characteristics sharply differentiated the three groups, even more than did relative cleanliness and verbal skills. Somehow, then, the teacher's estimation of a five-year-old's academic ability, whether or not he was a fast learner, coincided precisely with whether or not he was a neat, clean, verbal kid from a middle-class family.

At this point, we can consider three possible explanations of this uncanny course of events. The first is that the kindergarten teacher had an eerie, almost clairvoyant capacity to sense the abilities of five-year-olds and that the remarkable correlation between her judgments and the background of the children was purely coincidental.

The second explanation involves what might be termed the Coleman-Herrnstein hypothesis—that, because of either genetic or cultural differences, middle-class children do indeed have greater verbal skill, greater learning potential, and that an accurate prediction of who the fast learners will be inevitably means picking out the middle-class children.

The third explanation is that the teacher has a preconceived idea of what "fast learners" look and act like (namely, like the teacher herself), that her expectations are based on these preconceived ideas, and that her teaching style is such that she treats children from different class groups differently, conveys to them her own evaluations and expectations, and thereby produces the anticipated results.

Rist's observations tend to support the last explanation. For example, although the three tables faced a blackboard that ran along the entire length of the wall, the teacher consistently tended to stand in front of table one and to write on the board directly in front of her "fast learners." She gave the overwhelming majority of her attention to the table-one children and usually called on them to respond to questions, to tell what they did on Halloween, to take attendance, and to act as monitors. In one classroom hour that Rist observed, the teacher communicated exclusively with the children at table one, except for two commands of "Sit down!" directed at children seated at the other tables. To sum up the year, it is quite clear that the teacher *taught* the children at table one, and either ignored, belittled, or disciplined the other children. At the end of the year, of course, the table-one children had finished all of their kindergarten work, and were ready for the first grade and the great adventure of learning to read. The teacher was still persuaded that these were the children who were most capable and interested in school and that the others were "off in another world" and basically "low achievers." The latter were, in fact, already behind, and when they went to the first grade, they were not *permitted* to start the first-grade reading lessons until they had finished up the kindergarten work that their teacher had neglected to teach them the previous year. The process continued into the second grade, the gap widened, and the differences among the children became more pronounced. As Rist put it, "The child's journey through the early grades of school at one reading level and in one social grouping appeared to be preordained from the eighth day of kindergarten."

In addition, he noted that the belittling of the lower-track children was imitated by the high-track children, who gradually began to verbalize their own sense of superiority over those in the lower tracks. The labeling process was made quite manifest in the second grade, where the three different tables—instead of being called one, two, and three, as in kindergarten, or A, B, and C, as in the first grade—received characterizing labels that left no doubt in anyone's mind: the top group were the "Tigers," the middle group the "Cardinals," and the lowest group the "Clowns."

Other recent studies have discovered, with much more reliability and precision, the specific details of what Rist had been able to see so clearly at a more general level. Brophy and Good, and others, have developed detailed procedures for observing and coding interactions in the classroom between teacher and pupils and have shown that, even when there is no substantial difference in the *quantity* of interaction between high-expectancy and low-expectancy groups, the *qualitative* differences are enormous. With students of whom they hold high expectations, teachers more often praise correct answers, or "sustain" the interaction if the answer is incorrect—that is, they repeat or rephrase the question, give a clue, and in general try to get the student to continue to work toward a correct response. With pupils of whom they expect little, teachers are more inclined to accept correct answers with minimal praise and to criticize incorrect answers. In addition, the teacher is much more likely to limit her interactions with these students to matters of class organization and discipline.

The summated data of all these recent studies appear to explain quite clearly how the tracking process works, mediated by teacher expectations. First of all, teachers always assume that some students will learn and that others will not. Second, they tend to take for granted that it is the children of middle-class background and characteristics who will be the fast learners, and that those of working-class background will do poorly. The teachers make their expectations come true—apparently not consciously—by their grossly different treatment of the children. Oversimplifying the vast array of available data, one might say that teachers

Chapter VIII
Educational Problems

instruct and praise the middle-class and upper-class children, making them feel superior, and that they discipline and criticize the working-class children, making them feel inferior. The result is that the former gain confidence, tend to like school, develop high educational aspirations, and act out the expectations conveyed to them; the latter also act out the expectations they perceive, by coming to believe in their own lack of aptitude, by disengaging from school, and by dropping out as soon as they decently can.

The saddest part of the whole process is the destruction visited upon the spirits and self-esteem of the poor and working-class children, many of whom are gradually convinced—by the behavior of the teachers and administrators, as well as by that of their peers who are labeled good students—that they are dumb, incompetent, unfit for intellectual activity, destined to be on the bottom of the heap in real life as they are in the classroom as little children. Sennett and Cobb, in *The Hidden Injuries of Class*, have documented this ravaging of the spirit, which is one of the major functions of the school system.

Reading 27

CLASS OF 2000: THE GOOD NEWS AND THE BAD NEWS

Marvin J. Cetron

> *"The class of 2000 will need a far better education simply to get a decent job." The occupational growth areas, such as information processing, health, and legal services, all demand special study. Schools are able to make extra efforts and provide superior preparation. This has been proven. What is still under debate is society's and parents' willingness to adjust to the necessary new teaching formats that Cetron outlines.*

The year 2000 is still more than a decade into the future, but the high-school graduating class of 2000 is with us already; its members entered kindergarten in September 1987. The best of them are bright, inquiring, and blessed with all the benefits that caring, attentive parents can provide. They will need all those advantages and more. The class of 2000, and their schools, face educational demands far beyond those of their parents' generation. And unless they can meet those demands successfully, the United States could be nearing its last days as a world power.

No one had to tell Ben Franklin or Thomas Jefferson that their new country would live or die with its school system. In a democracy, citizens must be able to read, so they can learn about the issues on which they are voting. (No, television and radio have not made reading unnecessary.) They must know history so that they can develop political judgments and not be taken in by the false promises of unscrupulous candidates. Today, they must also understand basic science so that they can make informed decisions about such issues as the space program, nuclear power, computer technology, and genetic engineering.

Reprinted, with permission, from *The Futurist*, published by the World Future Society, 4916 St. Elmo Avenue, Bethesda, MD.

Chapter VIII
Educational Problems

PREPARING FOR 2000

The class of 2000 will need a far better education simply to get a decent job. In part, this is because today's fast-growing employment areas—the ones where good jobs can be found—are fields such as computer programming, health care, and law. They require not only a high-school diploma, but advanced schooling or job-specific training.

By contrast, less than 6% of workers will find a place on the assembly lines that once gave high-school graduates a good income; the rest will have been replaced by robots. Instead, service jobs will form nearly 90% of the economy. A decade ago, about 77% of jobs involved at least some time spent in generating, processing, retrieving, or distributing information. By the year 2000, that figure will be 95%, and that information processing will be heavily computerized.

Traditional jobs also call for more familiarity with technology; even a department store sales clerk must be "computer literate" enough to use a computerized inventory system. Approximately 60% of today's jobs are open to applicants with a high-school diploma; among new jobs, more than half require at least some college. By the year 2010, virtually every job in the country will require some skill with information-processing technology.

Beyond that, simply living in modern society will raise the level of education we all need. By the year 2000, new technology will be changing our working lives so fast that we will need constant retraining, either to keep our existing jobs or to find new ones. Even today, engineers find that half of their professional knowledge is obsolete within five years and must go back to school to keep up; the rest of us will soon join them in the classroom. Knowledge itself will double not once, not twice, but four times by the year 2000! In that single year, the class of 2000 will be exposed to more information and knowledge than their grandparents experienced in a lifetime.

THE CHALLENGE FOR SCHOOLS

Schools will have to meet these new demands. Today, schools offer adult education as a community service or in hope of earning sorely needed revenue. In the future, they will be teaching adults because they haven't any choice. Many public schools will be open 24 hours a day, retraining adults from 4 P.M. to midnight and renting out their costly computer and communications systems to local businesses during the graveyard shift.

Fortunately, American schools can provide top-quality education when they make the effort to do so. The proof can be seen not only in affluent suburbs, but in some cities. In Fairfax, a community of about

350,000, Mantua Elementary School principal Joe Ross has made this effort. His "school for all reasons, school for all seasons" seems quite ordinary on the outside. But enter its tiled halls and you will find yourself surrounded by multicolored posters depicting cultural highlights of Kuwait—all written in Arabic. Other posters appear in languages ranging from German to Vietnamese—and all are readily understood by children who are eight or nine years old. Children learn sign language as early as kindergarten, when basic consonants are taught. The school is stocked with desktop computers, and there is video equipment for every room.

Specialized classes are a major feature of Mantua's educational program. There are classrooms filled with high-technology devices to aid handicapped students. Advanced students hone their thinking skills in programs designed for the gifted and talented. At one end of the building, a school-age-child-care center continues the educational process long after traditional schools hours have ended. There are also programs for the hearing impaired, the learning disabled, preschool handicapped, and English as a Second Language students.

Mantua's educational system works. Its average students rank far higher than the national average, and all the specialized programs manage to extract top grades from students who in many cases might be expected to fail. Perhaps more importantly, the Mantua Elementary children are exposed to and work with the students in the special programs mentioned above and know they are an integral part of a pluralistic society. These children will better accept each person, whatever his or her gift or handicap, as an individual and not as someone to be stared at.

PARENTAL GUIDANCE SUGGESTED

Parental involvement is the key to making the system work. At Mantua, teachers have long emphasized this need. According to my wife, Gloria, who teaches kindergarten at the school, it is very simple: "When the parents get involved, the kids do better." In an effort to get the parents involved, Gloria and her aide, Lynn Curran, asked parents of the kindergartners in the class of 2000 what they are doing to prepare their children for the year 2000. Jason Hovell's parents answered, "To prepare a child for the year 2000, we think a child needs a first-rate education and strong family relationships." The parents of Sarah Crutchfield believe that "exposing [her] to the avenues of learning...[through] library trips, museums, nature walks, and the theater" will be the best preparation.

Many of the parents expressed concern about the moral fabric of America. Heather Goodwin's parents are "trying to rear her in a manner that leads to upright moral conduct and ethical practices, to teach her to

Chapter VIII
Educational Problems

believe in herself and stand up for what is right, and to respect the views and beliefs of others." The parents go to the head of the class. They are at the first critical stage of awareness.

THE STATE OF EDUCATION TODAY

Programs similar to those at Mantua Elementary are available—and successful—all over the country. Unfortunately, these remain rare bright spots in a bleak educational picture. There is all too much evidence that American schools are failing many students. In 1982, American eighth-graders taking a standardized math test answered only 46% of the questions correctly, which put them in the bottom half of the 11 nations participating. (Japanese children got 64% correct.) That same year, the top 5% of twelfth-graders from nine developed countries, the ones who had taken advanced math courses, took standardized tests of algebra and calculus. America's best and brightest came in dead last.

The failure is not limited to tough subjects like math. Other studies have shown that only one high-school junior in five can write a comprehensible note applying for a summer job; that among high-school seniors, fewer than one-third know to within 50 years when the Civil War took place, and one in three does not know that Columbus discovered America before 1750.

More than 500,000 children drop out of school each year; in some school districts, the dropout rate exceeds 50%. Perhaps 700,000 more students in each class finish out their 12 years hardly able to read their own diplomas. Among young adults, one government-sponsored study found, well under 40% can understand an average *New York Times* article or figure out their change when paying for lunch, and only 20% have mastered the weighty intellectual challenge of reading a bus schedule.

The results of this endemic ignorance can already be seen throughout American society. The sad condition of America's once-great space program is a heartrending comment on the state of science education in the country; as a nation, we simply are not qualified to manage large, demanding technological problems. And listen to the National Restaurant Association, which estimates that by the year 1995 a million jobs in their industry will go unfilled because too many entry-level job hunters are too poorly educated to succeed even as waiters, cashiers, and hamburger flippers. By the year 2000, according to one estimate, the literacy rate in America will be only 30%.

TRAINING FOR THE FUTURE

Solving the problems of conventional education is only one half of the task. America will also need a much stronger system of vocational education if it is to meet the challenge of the years to come. On average, the next generation of workers will have to make no fewer than five complete job changes in a lifetime, not counting the multiple tasks (which will also be changing) associated with each respective job. This is a mandate for continuous retraining.

In the future, vocational training will be just as crucial as traditional education. If schools fail to turn out well-educated high-school and college graduates, more and more young people will find themselves unqualified for any meaningful career, while millions of jobs go begging for trained people to fill them. If schools and businesses fail to retrain adults for the growing technical demands of their jobs, millions of conscientious workers will find their careers cut short, and the skilled work they should have done will be exported to countries like Japan and Taiwan, where educational systems definitely are up to the task.

EDUCATION FOR THE CLASS OF 2000

America's school system today is clearly overburdened, even by the traditional demands placed on it. How can the school system be strengthened to bring high-quality education to all members of the class of 2000? And what can be done about the growing demand for adult education in the years to come? Over half a dozen measures come to mind, most of them embarrassingly simple:

- Lengthen the school day and year. In any field, you can get more work done in eight hours than in six, in 10 days than in seven. Japan's school year consists of 240 eight-hour days. America's averages 180 days of about 6.5 hours. So let's split the difference: Give us 210 seven-hour school days a year.

- Cut the median class size down from 17.8 to 10 students. Naturally, this means hiring more teachers. This will give teachers more time to focus on the *average* student.

Not too long ago, schools were just beginning to recognize the needs of special students with learning disabilities or exceptional talents. Now there are programs for the learning disabled and the gifted and talented, as there should be. But, in focusing attention and resources on the needs of the minority at the extremes, the nation's schools have neglected the needs of the majority in the middle. American students' dismal performance on standardized tests attests to this.

Inadequate attention at school is exacerbated by inadequate attention at home for the average student. The big advantage that schools like Mantua enjoy over less-successful institutions is not their specialized programs, but the fact that their students are drawn largely from traditional families where parents are available and are actively interested in the child's education. Where one-parent homes are the rule, teachers

Chapter VIII
Educational Problems

must provide the individual attention that parents cannot. In crowded classrooms, they simply can't do it. The answer is to cut class size.

• Computerize. Computer-aided learning programs are already replacing drill books; as software improves, they will begin to replace some kinds of textbooks as well. More teachers should be actively involved in writing the software. The best computerized learning programs already include primitive forms of artificial intelligence that can diagnose the student's learning problems and tailor instruction to compensate for them.

"We can put 30 computers in a room, and they will go as fast or as slow as each child needs; the child controls it," observes Representative James Scheuer (Democrat, New York). "He has an equal and comfortable relationship, building his morale and self-esteem, which can only enhance the learning process."

The result may not be as good as having highly skilled, caring teachers give hours of personal attention to each student, but computerization is a lot easier to achieve, and it's a big improvement over today's situation. This should be an easy notion to sell to taxpayers; in a survey of parents of Mantua kindergartners, fully two-thirds cited computers as one of the most important topics their children should learn in school.

But making this transition won't be cheap. By 1990, the United States will already have spent $1 billion on computerized learning, but two-thirds of that will have been spent by affluent parents for their own children. If public school systems fail to develop their own programs, the less-affluent students could suffer an irreparable educational disadvantage.

• Tailor courses to the needs of individual students. Individualized education programs (IEPs) are already used in many schools; they suggest which skills the student should practice and recommend ways of testing to make sure they have been learned. But far more is possible.

In the future, IEPs will look at the students' learning style; whether they learn best in small groups or large classes; whether they learn best from reading, lectures, or computer programs; how much supervision they need; and so on. Teachers will be evaluated in the same way and assigned to large or small classes, good readers or good listeners, as best suits them. These programs may not be adopted in time to help the class of 2000, but the sooner the better.

• Promote students based on performance, not on time served in class. Students starting school in 2000 will move up not by conventional grade levels, but by development levels, ensuring that each child can work on each topic until it's mastered.

• Recruit teachers from business and industry, not just university educational programs. Get chemists to teach chemistry, accountants to teach arithmetic, and so on. These specialists could become teachers in areas where teachers are scarce. Give them the required courses in education necessary to meet teaching standards. But start by making sure that would-be teachers actually know something worth teaching.

- Set new priorities for school systems that today are overregulated and underaccountable. In many communities, the curriculum is so standardized that teachers in any given course on any given day will be covering the same material. It's time to cut through that kind of red tape and give teachers the right to do the job they supposedly were trained for. Then make teachers and their supervisors responsible for the performance of their students. Teachers who turn out well-educated students should be paid and promoted accordingly. If students don't advance, neither should their would-be educators.

- Bring business and industry into the public school system. Corporations must train and retrain workers constantly, and that requirement will grow ever more pressing. The obvious answer is for them to contract with schools to do the teaching. The money earned from such services can go toward teachers' salaries and investments in computers, software, and such things as air conditioning needed to keep schools open all year.

For students not headed toward college, businesses may also provide internships that give high-school students practical experience in the working world they are about to enter. When public schools turn out graduates who haven't mastered reading, writing, or math, business suffers.

- Finally, if Americans really want quality education, they must be willing to pay for it. Since the National Commission on Excellence in Education published its landmark report, *A Nation at Risk*, in 1983, the Reagan administration has never asked for a significant increase in federal aid to education. In fact, since 1984, the White House has attempted to cut the national education budget by more than $10 billion. Though Congress has always restored most of those proposed cuts, the federal government is actually spending, after inflation, about 14% less for education than it did five years ago.

Teachers are still dramatically underpaid compared with other professions that require a college education. In 1987, the average starting salary for an accountant was $21,200, new computer specialists received $26,170, and engineers began at $28,500. The average starting salary for teachers was only $17,500.

Today's education system cannot begin to prepare students for the world they will enter on graduation from high school. By 2030, when the class of 2000 will still be working, they will have had to assimilate more inventions and more new information than have appeared in the last 150

Chapter VIII
Educational Problems

years. By 2010, there will be hardly a job in the country that does not require skill in using powerful computers and telecommunications systems.

America needs to enact all the reforms outlined above, and many others as well. It is up to concerned citizens, parents, and teachers to equip our children with the knowledge and skills necessary to survive and thrive in the twenty-first century. In this election year, education should be a major political issue, for time is running out: The class of 2000 is already with us.

CHAPTER IX

CONCENTRATIONS OF ECONOMIC AND POLITICAL POWER

Reading 28
THE BUREAUCRATIC ETHOS

Arthur Vidich, Joseph Bensman, *New School for Research*

> *The American bureaucratic structure seems to be informal and friendly, yet respectful of authority. To survive, however, translations must be made of many common expressions; for example, you must hear, "That's an interesting idea that needs further developing," as "Let's not discuss it now."*

One important aspect of the New Society is the ever-increasing growth of the administrative structure of bureaucracy and of the scale of large organizations. Government, industry, education, trade unions, and churches carry out the internal and external operations of the society by use of the bureaucratic mechanism. It is critical to note that the exact counterpart of the growth of the middle class is the growth of the administrative structure of bureaucracy which administers this enormous productive and service-oriented society.

In describing the characteristics of bureaucracies and especially European political bureaucracies, Max Weber provided the foundations for the technical description of large-scale business organization. The key theme in Weber's description of bureaucracy is the separation of the administrator from the means of administration, just as the soldier in an earlier epoch had been separated from the ownership of his weapons, and the worker from the means of production. Bureaucracies are characterized by relatively fixed hierarchies and spheres of competence (jurisdictions), and they depend on files and legalistic regulations for specifying their operations. The entire bureaucracy depends on technical experts who are engaged in a lifelong career and who are dependent on their jobs as their major means of support. Thus discipline, obedience, loyalty, and impersonal respect for authority tend to become psychological characteristics of the bureaucrat.

Even more important, however, is the bureaucrat's habit of making

---

Reprinted with permission from *The New American Society* (Chicago: Quadrangle Books, 1971), pp. 21–25. Copyright by the authors.

standardized categorical decisions which are rationally calculated—in form if not in content—to administer thousands of cases which become revelant because they fall into a category predescribed by administrative regulation and procedure. Weber describes bureaucracy as a giant machine in which all individuals, both administrators and subjects, are cogs. This Weberian nightmare is so awesome and horrifying in its portrayal of the dehumanization of men and the disenchantment of society that it has been hard to swallow in all its implications. It is only Weber's academic style that has prevented him from being treated as another George Orwell.

For Weber, bureaucracy did not arise out of a devilish plot. Rather it was a dominant institution emerging from the administrative efficiency that results from size, scope, and categorical application of cases. Bureaucracy is adaptive to large-scale enterprises in all areas of society, as governmental and private activities expand in response to the growth of societies from localistic (feudal) and small units to giant large-scale enterprises that are national and international in scope. In many respects, Weber saw bureaucracy as almost self-generating, with one important qualification: the desire of leaders of large-scale enterprises to extend their own freedom, autonomy, and opportunity for rational decision-making by limiting the assertiveness, the interference, the power, and the irrationality of others within their sphere of administration. Thus those who control large-scale institutions limit the freedom of others in order to maximize their own freedom. Seen from the point of view of leadership, bureaucracy must always be something more than a technical system of administration. It is also a system for the organization and distribution of power and the formulation of policy within institutions, between institutions, and within societies. From this perspective, bureaucracy, in its full form, is diametrically opposed to the Jeffersonian and Jacksonian image of a viable democracy.

American social and political scientists did not find it easy to accept Weber's discussion of bureaucracy. For the most part they reacted against the image of the officious, legalistic bureaucrat and criticized Weber for universalizing the image of the uniform-happy, tyrannical German bureaucrat, later overdrawn in the image of the Prussian Junker or the Nazi official. Americans contrasted the German stereotype to the oft-perceived style of the American official, who appeared to be easygoing, equalitarian, breezy, friendly, personal, and nonofficious, even though a bureaucratic official. What they failed to realize was that the American tradition, stemming as it does from the Jeffersonian and Jacksonian frontier style, causes the power holder to conceal his power in proportion to its growth. The Weberian bureaucrat does not look like the American manager because the *cultural* style surrounding bureaucracy is different in America. As a result of this mask, the subordinate in any organization has at subliminal levels the ability to make precise estimates of the actual power positions of each officeholder in the organization. With this as his framework, the formal, equalitarian, personal, and friendly responses of co-workers are based on these estimates. In the American system the official knows how to be informal and friendly without ever intruding into the office of the superior, and the superior knows how to be equalitarian without ever losing his authority. Thus bureaucracy functions in the classical Weberian way while retaining an air of American friendliness and informality.

This special bureaucratic by-product of Jeffersonian and Jacksonian democracy creates a bureaucratic style in which it becomes a major requirement to mask authority relations. As a result, very substantial changes have taken place in the ideology of the social worker, the human relations specialist, the psychological counselor, the personnel officer, and in interpersonal relations in almost all bureaucratic job situations. In the United States a whole range of bureaucratic sub-specialties have been created in welfare, government, and business bureaucracies for the express purpose of concealing bureaucratic authority. In American bureaucracy it is possible to sustain a rhetoric of agreement, respect for the individual personality, and rewards for technical ability as the critical factors governing the relationship between boss and subordinate.

In actual bureaucratic practice the subordinate is expected to agree voluntarily with his superior and to suggest the conditions for his subordination without ever openly acknowledging the fact of his subordination. The rhetoric of democracy has become the sine qua non of bureaucratic authoritarianism.

So complex is this masking process that in a literal sense a linguistic revolution has taken place that allows us to conceal from ourselves the inequalitarianism of bureaucratic social relations. Bureaucracy, like any dominant institution, has developed a structure of linguistic euphemisms which allow the retention of an equalitarian, friendly, personal ideology while concealing the authoritarianism and at times the harshness of bureaucracy. The following expressions, placed opposite their euphemisms, are intended only to suggest some of the possibilities.

Euphemism	**Real Meaning**
Obedience	
We expect your cooperation.	Obey.
I'd like to have consensus on this issue.	I expect you to repress all differences.
Obligation and duty require this.	My job and responsibilities require your obedience.

Chapter IX
Economic and Political Power

Euphemism	**Real Meaning**
Being reminded of one's place	
It's a wonderful idea, but at the present we don't have the time to give your idea the attention and consideration it needs.	Drop it.
You're kidding, aren't you.	You're out of line.
That's an interesting idea that needs further developing.	Let's not discuss it now.
We must respect the autonomy and individual rights of others.	You're overstepping your authority.
You can do that if you want to, but I'll take no responsibility for it if it gets out of hand.	You do it at your own risk, but I'll take the credit for it if it's successful.
With some development and elaboration, the germ of your idea could be useful.	I'm stealing your idea; forget it, the idea is no longer yours.
That was a good idea you had at our meeting yesterday.	I'm giving it back to you.
Ways to get fired	
You've been late three times in the past month.	Warning of forthcoming dismissal.
Your work is not up to your usual standards.	Warning of forthcoming dismissal.
You haven't reached your full potential in this job.	You're not fired, but don't expect a raise or promotion.
We feel that this organization can do no more to further your career.	You're fired.
We can't stand in the way of your growth.	You're fired.
You're too well trained for this job.	You're fired.
We'll give you excellent references.	Please leave without making a scene.
We'll give you an extra month's severance pay.	Please leave and forget you ever worked here.
At other levels	
Free lunch	A small, somewhat ambiguous bribe setting the stage for bigger bribery.
Fringe benefits	Fairly serious bribery.
Hanky-panky	Serious bribery.

Euphemism	Real Meaning
A preliminary meeting	Setting out to rig a forthcoming meeting.
A well-organized meeting	A rigged meeting.
An informal coffee meeting	An incipient plot.
A private meeting	A plot.

Although this whole area of linguistic usage is central to the functioning of society, few writers apart from George Orwell, Hannah Arendt, and Shepherd Mead have emphasized it. The bureaucratic aspects of the New Society could well be studied through the revolution in linguistics of which we have suggested only a few examples.

Reading 29

THE LIMITS TO COMPLEXITY: ARE BUREAUCRACIES BECOMING UNMANAGEABLE?

Duane S. Elgin, Robert A. Bushnell

> The bureaucracies in modern society were originally created to increase efficiency, but they are now so large and complex that they may soon no longer function at all. Elgin and Bushnell give us 16 reasons why this is a very serious problem. They also give us some possible solutions that would help to maintain the existing form of these bureaucracies.

Modern society must face up to the prospect that we may be reaching the limits of our capacity to manage exceedingly large and complex bureaucracies. Already there is considerable agreement regarding the details of bureaucratic malfunction, such as massive but ineffective urban governments and huge but wasteful governmental programs. Indeed, there is growing concern whether many of the largest bureaucracies can survive.

Consider a sampling of recent statements by opinion leaders:

> Ten years ago government was widely viewed as an instrument to solve problems; today government itself is widely viewed as the problem.
> Charles Schultze and Henry Owen,
> *Setting National Priorities.* 1976

> We're frantically trying to keep our noses above water, racing from one problem to the next.
> U.S. Senator Adlai Stevenson,
> *U.S. News and World Report.*
> November 10, 1975

> The demands on democratic government grow while the capacity of democratic government stagnates. This, it would appear, is the central di-

---

Reprinted with permission from *The Futurist*, published by the World Future Society, 4916 St. Elmo Avenue, Bethesda, MD.

*Reading 29
Bureaucracies—Too Large and Complex?*

lemma of the governability of democracy which has manifested itself in Europe, North America, and Japan in the 1970s.
Report to the Trilateral Commission on the Governability of Democracies.
1975

These statements raise the possibility that, with an enormous increase in our technological capacity, we have rushed to create bureaucracies of such extreme levels of scale, complexity, and interdependence that they now begin to exceed our capacity to comprehend and manage them. We are discovering that the power to create large, complex social bureaucracies does not automatically confer the ability to control them.

Recognition of the growing complexity of social systems as a problem worthy of attention in its own right emerged during a recent study, conducted by the Center for the Study of Social Policy, a division of SRI, Inc., in Menlo Park, California, which was seeking to identify important future problems that now are receiving insufficient attention.

PROBLEMS OF LARGE, COMPLEX SYSTEMS

After an extensive review of literature pertaining to the problems of bureaucracies, 16 propositions were selected as a useful sample of the problems associated with the growth of social systems. (See list.)

These propositions are not necessarily problems per se, but they become problematical in accordance to the relative *speed* of systems growth, its relative *size* (the absolute number of elements grouped together), its *complexity* (the number and diversity of elements in the system), and *interdependence* (tightness of coupling among elements both within and between bureaucracies). Thus, although the size of a social system is not the exclusive consideration in formulating these propositions, it is the primary point of reference from which the patterns of growth of large, complex systems are explored.

This article focuses on problems of large social bureaucracies as exemplified by the welfare system, the Medicare-Medicaid programs, and major metropolitan governments. These bureaucracies are very large and complex, highly interdependent, and concerned primarily with the delivery and consumption of public services. They are further characterized by high levels of human interaction and by ambiguous and sometimes conflicting objectives.

Although this article is directed principally to the problems of bureaucracies in the public sector, it also has relevance for private sector bureaucracies (such as large corporations). Crucial differences between these two categories of bureaucracies, however, prevent the direct application of this discussion to private sector bureaucracies.

Chapter IX
Economic and Political Power

PROBLEMS OF LARGE, COMPLEX SYSTEMS

It is hypothesized that if a social system grows to extreme levels of scale, complexity, and interdependence, the following characteristics will *tend* to become manifest:

1. Diminishing relative capacity of a given individual to comprehend the overall system.
2. Diminishing level of public participation in decision-making.
3. Declining public access to decision-makers.
4. Growing participation of experts in decision-making.
5. Disproportionate growth in costs of coordination and control.
6. Increasingly de-humanized interactions between people and the system.
7. Increasing levels of alienation.
8. Increasing challenges to basic value premises.
9. Increasing levels of unexpected and counterintuitive consequences of policy action.
10. Increasing system rigidity.
11. Increasing number and uncertainty of disturbing events.
12. Narrowing span of diversity of innovation.
13. Declining legitimacy of leadership.
14. Increasing system vulnerability.
15. Declining overall performance of the system.
16. Growing deterioration of the overall system unlikely to be perceived by most participants in that system.

The 16 problems are as follows: (Note: Each problem should be read as if it began with "When a bureaucracy grows to extreme levels of scale, complexity, and interdependence, then....)

1. *The relative ability of any individual to comprehend the system will tend to diminish.* This proposition applies both to the public that is served by the social system and to the decision-makers who run it. To manage a social system effectively, a decision-maker must acquire knowledge at a rate at least equal to the pace at which decisions become more numerous and complex.

As a system grows in scale, the parts of the system will increase generally in an arithmetic progression but the interrelationships between the parts will tend to increase in a geometric progression. Hence, the *knowledge required* to comprehend both the discrete parts and their interrelationships will tend to increase geometrically, but due to the decision-maker's biological, mechanical, and temporal limitations, the *knowledge available* is likely to grow relatively slowly.

Reading 29
Bureaucracies—Too Large and Complex?

The importance of this problem is stated succinctly by seasoned bureaucrat Elliot Richardson in his book, *The Creative Balance* (New York: Holt, Rinehart and Winston, 1976):

> For a free society, the ultimate challenge of the foreseeable future will consist not simply in managing complexity but in keeping it within the bounds of understanding by the society's citizens and their representatives in government.

Thus the size and complexity of social systems may jeopardize representative democracy itself. There is evidence to suggest that the relative levels of the public's comprehension of social systems may be declining significantly. For example, over a number of years, the Survey Research Center in the University of Michigan has asked people if they agreed or disagreed with the following statement: "Sometimes politics and government seem so complicated that a person like me can't really understand what's going on." In 1960, 40 percent of those responding disagreed with this statement and in 1974 only 26 percent disagreed.

The fact is that the stuff of public life seems to elude the grasp of many people. Bureaucratic processes have become specialized and professionalized. Yet, many of the larger bureaucracies are plagued with the unspoken but undeniable feeling among management and staff that no one truly is in control, that the dynamics of the organization are beyond the comprehension of any one individual.

Nor does the mere aggregation of information necessarily contribute to the understanding of the system. Although the computer revolution has vastly increased the amount of information at our disposal, it has exacerbated the difficulty of decision-making by confronting the manager with a mountain of information that he has no hope of ever assimilating given the crisis management that prevails in many of the largest bureaucracies. Thus, the ability to collect massive amounts of information does not automatically assure that it will be used or be useful in the management of large systems. It is possible to be information-rich and knowledge-poor as a manager or consumer of public services.

2. The capacity and motivation of the public to participate in decision-making processes will tend to diminish. As discussed in Proposition 1, the relative capacity of all constituents of a social bureaucracy to participate knowledgeably in decision-making may diminish as the system grows. At larger scales, the perceived significance of an individual's participation in systems governance, especially through the act of voting, is impaired by the participation of large numbers of people in the process.

At smaller scales there is much greater opportunity for an individual citizen to have a discernible impact, but these small-scale decisions are likely to be relatively inconsequential. Robert Dahl, in an article on "The City in the Future of Democracy," concludes:

Chapter IX
Economic and Political Power

> Thus for most citizens, participation in very large units becomes minimal and in very small units it becomes trivial.

To the extent that the cost (in time or money) of informing oneself for participation in the system is substantial and the perceived return from that information is trivial, then a rational response is to remain ignorant and passive. In his book, *Inside Bureaucracy,* urbanist Anthony Downs explains:

> Therefore, we reach the startling conclusion that it is irrational for most citizens to acquire political information for the purpose of voting....Hence, ignorance of politics is not a result of unpatriotic apathy; rather it is a highly rational response to the facts of political life in a large democracy.

An initially diminished capacity to participate as a result of mounting complexity is thus coupled with incentives that further reinforce the diminished capacity. As part of a self-fulfilling pattern, the power and willingness to make decisions are shifted from the public to the systems managers.

3. *The public's access to decision-makers will tend to decline.* Regardless of the size of his constituency, there is only one mayor, one governor, one Secretary of Health, Education and Welfare, and one President. As the number of persons under his jurisdiction grows, an inevitable consequence is a reduction in the amount of time that a manager can spend with any one person. Beyond some threshold size, general access to the leader will, for all practical purposes, be eliminated.

In his discussion of the effects of scale upon a political system, Robert Dahl states:

> The essential point is that nothing can overcome the dismal fact that as the number of citizens increases the proportion who can participate *directly* in discussions with their top leaders must necessarily grow smaller and smaller.

Certainly the actual degree of public access to its leaders has steadily declined as the scale of institutions has increased.

Despite this gradual erosion of access, the perception of this process by the public seems relatively recent. A 1975 Louis Harris survey reveals substantial changes in citizen perceptions of distance from their leadership during the period of 1966 to 1975. Although this period included the unusual events surrounding Watergate and the Viet Nam War (which exacerbated the feeling of distance between the American people and their leaders), the statistics, nonetheless, are striking.

> The feeling that "What I think doesn't really count much any more" has risen from 37% to 67% since 1966; the view of the "People with power are

THE "RATCHET EFFECT": REASONS WHY BUREAUCRACIES GROW TOO LARGE

Imprecise means of measurement. The "rule of profit" may be harsh, but for business firms it is a relatively certain yardstick against which to measure the efficiency of a given scale of activity. In contrast, governmental bureaucracies and other social systems must attempt to measure efficiency via a number of qualitative, multidimensional, often conflicting, and ambiguous measures and objectives. With virtually no measures of system health, bureaucracies can conceivably grow to excessive scales of social organization.

Responding to the needs of a given population. A business firm can choose its scale of operation so as to maximize efficiency. However, many government bureaucracies are obliged by law and/or by egalitarian principles to attempt to respond to the needs of an entire population or population segment (e.g., all old people, all school-age children, all poor people who are in ill health). There may be little choice as to the size of the bureaucracy if it is largely dictated by the size of system needed to respond to a given population segment.

Bureaucratic imperative. If the size of a system or subsystem is considered an important source of status and power to the managers of that system, then systems managers may attempt to foster the growth of a system in order to secure greater benefit for themselves—even at the cost of a decline in overall systems efficiency. This "tragedy of the commons" behavior within a bureaucracy may be prompted by the search for a larger staff, a larger budget, greater responsibility, and so on. If many bureaucrats pursue this behavior, the collective effect could be considerable in producing an inefficient scale of activity in social bureaucracies.

Technological imperative. Technology provides the possibility to vastly expand the scale of social systems, and this possibility often seems to be translated into a necessity. Social systems may be designed so as to reap the maximum benefits from potent technologies (ranging from computers to photocopying machines) only to find that the overall system (which includes the human element) now exceeds its most efficient scale. Thus, uncritical adoption of technologies may push a system to excessive scales of social organization.

Growth is good. A central value premise in the industrial world view has been that growth is good. This has created a climate in which a concern for the bigness of our social bureaucracies would be less likely to be questioned.

Something for everyone. Political bureaucracies employ the art of compromise in an attempt to provide "something for everyone" so that no important constituency will be alienated or angered. The bureaucracy defends its own interest group and draws support from the many persons who depend on its continued existence. Intrinsic to democratic political processes, then, is a pattern of expectations and demands which tends to inhibit the reduction of bureaucratic activity which, once instituted, becomes the norm.

Chapter IX
Economic and Political Power

out to take advantage of me" has jumped from 33% to 58% over the same period; the notion that "People running the country really don't care what happens to me" has gone up from 33% to 63%.

As our bureaucracies burgeon, they recede from the comprehension, the familiarity, and the control of the public.

4. *Participation of experts in decision-making will tend to grow disproportionately, but this expertise will only marginally counteract the effects of geometrically mounting knowledge requirements for effective management of the bureaucracy.* It seems reasonable for a decision-maker faced with a large number of complex problems to seek expert advice in trying to grapple with those problems. Yet, as Elliot Richardson has warned in *The Creative Balance*, this apparently rational response to complexity may reduce the ability of the public to participate in decision-making:

> Unless we in America can succeed in [managing complexity]...we shall lose our power to make intelligent—or at least deliberate—choices. We shall no longer be self-governing. We shall instead be forced to surrender more and more of our constitutional birthright—the office of citizenship—to an expert elite. We may hope it is a benevolent elite. But even if it is not, we shall be dependent on it anyway. Rather than participating in the process of choice, we shall be accepting the choices made for us.

Moreover, it is possible that exponentially growing needs for knowledge in decision-making will eventually overwhelm the expert as well as the decision-maker. The expert ultimately faces the same human limitations to his acquisition of knowledge as does the decision-maker and the general public.

Further, there appear to be intrinsic limits to the assistance that experts can render to decision-makers. Expert knowledge may be so fragmented, as a result of specialization, that it is below the necessary threshold of aggregation to be useful to the decision-maker. Also, the information may be exceedingly complex and difficult to transmit efficiently from expert to decision-maker. Accordingly, expert information may be ignored for very rational reasons.

5. *The costs of coordinating and controlling the system will tend to grow disproportionately.* Initial increases in scale allow greater efficiency by facilitating specialization and division of labor and by allowing the use of more advanced technologies (which may only become cost-effective for larger organizations). Yet, at some scale of activity, the number of units in the system will grow so large that the costs of coordinating and controlling those units will more than offset any increases in efficiency that accrue from the larger scale.

As the bureaucracy grows and top management becomes increasingly divorced from day-to-day functioning of the system, decision-making responsibility and authority must be delegated to successively lower levels within the system. This, however, requires increases in staff, paper work, travel budgets, and communication costs if the plans and decisions of a vast number of separate decision-making units are going to mesh. Beyond some critical threshold of size, then, the costs of coordination grow disproportionately.

6. *An attempt may be made to improve efficiency by depersonalizing the system.* Since human diversity adds enormously to a system's complexity, a potential means of coping with complexity is to reduce the diversity of human interactions within the system. Rational management techniques may attempt to depersonalize the system by standardizing human responses within the organization.

To the extent that efficiency is valued over human diversity, the human interaction with the system must acquire attributes that increasingly conform to the systemic preference for uniformity and predictability. Employees, constitutents, or clients will tend thus to become increasingly depersonalized in their interactions with the system.

7. *The level of alienation will tend to increase.* A 1975 Louis Harris survey reveals that in the period from 1966 to 1975, the number of people who say "I feel left-out of things going on around me" has risen from 9 percent to 41 percent. These and related data suggest that the level of public alienation may be reaching pathological proportions.

Nor is the sense of alienation limited to a particular segment of society. In a 1976 *Saturday Review* article, Leonard Silk and David Vogel examined the crisis of confidence in American business and concluded that it is a part of a larger pattern of alienation:

> The mood for business leadership is strikingly similar to that of other groups in one important respect: a feeling of impotence, a belief that its future is in the hands of outside forces. For business, as for other groups, frustration often turns to hostility. Feelings of alienation that began in the black community soon spread to the children of the middle class, moved into the white working class, and have affected the military and the police. This mood has now reached the business community.... It is a remarkable society in which so many groups, even the "Establishment," feel that "someone else" is in charge, "someone else" is to blame for whatever goes wrong.

Sociologist Melvin Seeman postulates five historical trends that may form the causal basis for the emergence of alienation. These are directly or indirectly tied to the emergence of very large social systems:

1. The expansion of scale of population and social institutions.
2. The decline of kinship and the consequential increase of anonymity and impersonality in social relations.

3. Increased physical and social mobility.
4. Social differentiation arising from specialization and division of labor.
5. Decline of traditional social forms and roles.

These observations suggest a rather direct linkage between alienation and the growth of large social systems.

8. *The appropriateness of basic value premises underlying the social system will tend to be increasingly challenged.* This proposition assumes that as a system grows, the sheer *quantitative* aggregation will ultimately result in the emergence of a *qualitatively* different system. Thus, the value premises upon which the system was initially established will become increasingly incompatible with the changing demands of a quantitatively enlarged and qualitatively altered system.

To the extent that large, complex social systems have been created by value premises that have become functionally obsolete, then either the system must change to reflect the original values, or the basic value premises themselves will have to change to reflect the character of the changed system. Social conflict will increase until either the value premises or the system itself is changed so as to reestablish congruence between them.

Contemporary challenges to the legitimacy of traditional value premises have assumed such forms as women's liberation, black power, third world ethics, the antiwar movement, the hippy counterculture, the flourishing of Eastern religions, and the conservation and ecology movement. These disparate trends do not individually signify the transformation of historic value premises. Yet, considered collectively, they suggest that major challenges to traditional values are occurring.

9. *The number and significance of unexpected consequences of policy actions will increase.* As a system grows, it may be subject to the "law of requisite variety" as stated by W. Ross Ashby in *An Introduction to Cybernetics*. This law asserts that the complexity of any policy solution must, in the long run, be equal to the complexity or variety of the problem. To the extent that diminished levels of systems comprehension (Proposition 1) force managers to apply relatively simple solutions to increasingly complex problems, then the law of requisite variety will not be satisfied and unexpected consequences of policy action may result.

Professor Jay Forrester of the Massachusetts Institute of Technology has suggested another reason why the behavior of large systems may result in outcomes that run counter to expectations. In social systems, political pressures often favor short-term policy measures, but when short-term actions, which previously produced favorable results, are redoubled without regard for their long-term consequences, changed circumstances within and without the system may produce both unexpected and even disastrous results.

With smaller and less interdependent bureaucracies, a wrong decision has only limited consequences because of the small scale and loose coupling between social systems. With very large and highly interdependent systems, however, a wrong decision can have far-reaching implications as its impact affects a pervasive and tightly interconnected web of socio-economic systems. Therefore, the number of unexpected outcomes of policy actions and the disruptive potential of these unexpected outcomes may be expected to expand as social systems grow in scale.

10. The system will tend to become more rigid since the form that it assumes inhibits the emergence of new forms. Economist Kenneth Boulding has written, "Growth creates form, but form limits growth." This principle suggests that as a system grows in size, complexity and interdependence, it will seek an enduring, predictable form that will, in turn, limit the ability of the system to generate new forms. Large bureaucracies seem to exhibit this characteristic. Richard Goodwin, writing in *The New Yorker*, describes the resistance of large social systems to fundamental structural changes:

> [T]he passion for size, reach, and growth is the soul of all bureaucracy. Within government, the fiercest battles are waged not over principles and ideas but over jurisdiction—control of old and new programs. Radically new pronouncements and policies are often digested with equanimity, but at the slightest hint of a threat to the existing structure,... the entire bureaucratic mechanism mobilizes for defense. Almost invariably, the threat is defeated or simply dissolves in fatigue, confusion, and the inevitable diversion of executive energies.

As growing bureaucracies lock themselves into relatively static and inflexible forms, creative management becomes an exercise analogous to swimming through progressively hardening concrete and the flow of social and organizational evolution is impeded.

11. The number and intensity of perturbations to the system will tend to increase disproportionately. As a social system grows, the number of elements aggregated together also grows. As Donald Michael notes in his book, *The Unprepared Society*, if the same proportion of those elements malfunction, then the increase in absolute numbers aggregated together should yield a greater number of disturbing events within the system.

Further, as the number and diversity of activities within a system increase and relationships among the activities are established, the number of interconnections within the system will tend to increase geometrically. If a significant proportion of those connections are vulnerable to disruption, then the number of perturbations could increase more rapidly than increases in scale.

Chapter IX
Economic and Political Power

12. The diversity of innovation will tend to decline. As a system grows, the span of diversity of innovation will tend to constrict, because innovation is confined within the narrowing boundaries of what the system can assimilate without itself undergoing fundamental change. Further, as the system acts to ensure its own survival, diversity of innovation may become confused with disorder.

Moreover, it seems plausible that as social forms become increasingly concretized, great reliance will be placed on technological rather than social innovation to cope with social problems. Consequently, both the breadth and the depth of innovation will tend to decline.

13. The legitimacy of leadership will tend to decline. To the extent that a system manager must draw his power to govern from the consent of the people, then, within limits, he must demonstrate to his constituency his ability to manage the system well. As the system grows in scale and complexity, relative levels of comprehension at all levels may decline, counterexpected and unexpected consequences may mount, system resilience may diminish, and, for other reasons, the performance of the system may decline. The public will hold the manager of the system responsible for the poor performance. Then, according to the rules of the game, other leaders who wish to be elected will endeavor to persuade the public that they have the "right" and "true" answers to solve the mounting problems of systems malfunction. Thus, a doubly dangerous situation is created: there is the appearance of understanding (in order to get elected or to retain power), but the reality of understanding may be diminishing. Public expectations for effective decision-making may be inordinately high at the same time that the relative capacity to make informed decisions declines. As the gap between expectation and reality grows more pronounced, the legitimacy of the decision-maker will diminish.

One of the most pervasive themes to be found in an examination of the state of health of our sociopolitical systems is the crisis of confidence in leadership and the withdrawal of legitimacy. Pollster Louis Harris described the situation this way in a 1975 talk:

> The toll on confidence in the leadership of institutions has been enormous, both in the public and private sectors.... But perhaps the most serious drops have taken place in the case of two of our most central points of power: American business and the federal government. High confidence in business has slipped from 55% in 1966 to 18% in 1975; in the White House it has fallen from 41% to 14%; Congress from 42% to 14%; the U.S. Supreme Court from 51% to 28%.... Basically, however, the startling news is that the two major institutions viewed as out of touch with the reality of what people think and want are American business, which for so long has prided itself as correctly anticipating public needs,

*Reading 29
Bureaucracies—Too Large and Complex?*

and American political leadership, which so often has claimed to head up the most responsive democratic system in the world.

Nor is this an isolated finding. The University of Michigan Survey Research Center found that the proportion of people trusting the government in Washington to do what is right "just about always" or "most of the time" dropped from 81% in 1960 to 61% in 1970, and by 1974 the proportion had dropped to 38%. A 1975 report to the Trilateral Commission stated that "Leadership is in disrepute in democratic societies."

To the extent that the capacity to govern requires the consent of those governed, then the pervasive and sustained withdrawal of legitimacy could well cripple the capacity of democracies to manage their affairs.

14. The vulnerability of the system will tend to increase. If we assume that most of the problems of large systems move in concert or on parallel paths, then with rising scale the combined effects of the problems will render the system increasingly vulnerable to disruption. Eric Sevareid forcefully describes the vulnerability of our social systems:

> We now live in and by the web of an enormously complicated, intensely interrelated technology, the whole no greater than its parts and its strongest parts at the mercy of its weakest links. This is a way of life that depends absolutely on order and continuity and predictability. But it happens that we have simultaneously reached a point of discontinuity in the political and social relations of men, where little is predictable and disorder spreads.

One hijacker can capture a multimillion dollar airplane and catapult nations into political confrontation. One defective capacitor can prevent the communication of two presidential candidates with more than 100 million constituents. The shut-down of a single brake plant can stop production at major auto assembly plants throughout the country. A localized power grid failure can plunge the entire eastern seaboard of the U.S. into darkness. The consequences of otherwise isolated and relatively insignificant events, therefore, jeopardize the continued functioning of large systems sensitive to the slightest disruption.

15. The performance of the bureaucracy will tend to decline. If we assume the previously stated propositions are valid, then as a social system grows to extremes of scale we would expect that the costs of coordination and control will escalate, the comprehensibility of the system will decline, the number and intensity of perturbations will increase, and so on. When these individual problems reach a critical threshold and thereby collectively and intensively reinforce each other, the decline of system performance will be accelerated.

There is no lack of opinion that the performance of many of our largest bureaucracies is rapidly deteriorating. This is graphically reflected in a statement by U. S. Representative James C. Cleveland:

> There is no question that the American people are coming to the conclusion that their Government couldn't run a two-car funeral without fouling up the arrangements.

16. *The full extent of declining performance of the system is not likely to be perceived.* In most large bureaucracies there are few reliable measures of systems performance. This is partially attributable to the fact that the complexity of the system obscures the operation of the system. Also, the bureaucrat, in order to acquire or retain power, may minimize the significance of malfunctions and error, and maximize the public visibility of his own achievements. Further, there may be delayed, ambiguous and conflicting feedback concerning the effectiveness of various programs. These and other forces make it difficult to monitor the performance of a massive bureaucracy and thereby make it unlikely that most persons will be able to perceive the true extent to which performance is declining....

COPING WITH INSTITUTIONAL "LIMITS TO GROWTH"

A number of different strategies could be applied in coping with the problems of large, complex bureaucracies.

- Develop alternate models of the behavior of bureaucracies as they evolve over time to ever greater levels of scale, complexity, and interdependence.
- Conduct surveys to ascertain the present status of key social bureaucracies whose continued vigor seems central to a healthy society. Such a survey could, for example, engage the politician and bureaucrat in the process of describing the behavioral properties and problems of large, complex social bureaucracies.
- Develop a spectrum of systems indicators—patterned after economic and social indicators—that may better inform us as to the state of "health" of our central social bureaucracies.
- Encourage the President to consider the state of the social bureaucracies when examining the state of the nation.
- Fund research on the least understood of the four hypothesized outcomes from a period of "systems crisis"—namely, what the nature and form of transformational change of major social bureaucracies could be.
- Explore new individual learning modes that could increase the rate and richness of our acquisition of knowledge (the internalization of information).

Reading 29
Bureaucracies—Too Large and Complex?

- Develop new group learning processes to enable more effective knowledge aggregation and patterning.
- Fund television programs (such as *Nova*) that are educational/informational at much higher levels and across a much broader range of topics and thereby attempt to inform the public of major issues of critical national importance—including the problem of the malfunctioning bureaucracies.
- Pursue governmental reorganization designed, where reasonable and possible, to reduce the scale, interdependence, and complexity of social systems.

The foregoing responses to the problems of bureaucracies are primarily restorative—they are intended to help ameliorate the severity of these problems and to help maintain the existing form of these bureaucracies. A different kind of response would be to search for innovative alternative systems whose "performance" surpasses existing bureaucracies.

Illustrative of these kinds of activities that may engender responses to surpass rather than merely maintain bureaucracies are the following:

- Fund small-scale social and technological experiments and provide "social space," relatively free of bureaucratic impingements, within which these innovations can be tested. This might take the form, for example, of a range of different types of small-scale intermediate new communities that employ different technological and social forms to cope with the new scarcity and other problems that beset our larger systems.
- Develop intermediate or appropriate technology that can increase systems resilience by increasing the self-sufficiency of local communities.
- Encourage national opinion leaders to become informed about the role that small-scale, social innovation could play in coping with larger systems problems and begin the process of building greater social legitimacy for action of this kind.

Among these various responses, perhaps the most powerful but most neglected is that of small-scale social innovation. Consequently, it seems useful to explore briefly the present status of small-scale social innovation in our society.

We are blanketed with large-scale social innovations (e.g., social security, food stamps, Medicare) and with large-scale technological innovations (e.g., mass transit, space shuttle). There are many fewer attempts at small-scale technological innovations (e.g., new agricultural technologies), and there are extremely few small-scale, diversely conceived, social innovations.

Chapter IX
Economic and Political Power

The source of creative social innovations has traditionally been the local government. However, the federal government seems to have preempted many major areas of innovation from the state and local government. Perhaps more significantly, the federal government has sapped the vitality from innovation at the local level. Richard Thompson in his book *Revenue Sharing* (Revenue Sharing Advisory Service, Washington, D.C., 1973), examined the impact of federal funding policies and observed that "the federal government has stepped in and many localities have become administrative mechanisms for implementation of national policies rather than dynamic centers of authority and creative problem solving." In a vicious circle of abdication of responsibility for local vitality, small-scale social innovation is seldom tolerated, let alone encouraged.

There seem to exist two substantial stumbling blocks to small-scale social innovation. First, our cultural "opinion leaders" (in business, government, education, and so on) perhaps do not themselves recognize the crucial role that small-scale social innovation can possibly play in responding to increasingly severe, large-scale systems problems. Consequently, small-scale social experimentation may be seen as an activity of only peripheral significance. Yet, support of the larger society appears important since truly creative innovation requires a willingness to risk the possibility of failure.

Few people at the grass roots level seem willing to engage in such risk taking without the tolerance and support of the larger community—particularly when the payoff is not windfall profits to an individual but greater resiliency of our social structures. Even if contemporary opinion leaders did no more than publicly acknowledge and affirm the importance of small-scale social experimentation, it could still result in an outpouring of creative talent.

A second barrier to innovation is that such experimentation can be viewed as a threat to existing institutions (whose participants may not perceive the larger, longer-term threat of a systems crisis). Existing institutions may act in self-defense and attempt to prevent social innovation by engulfing the process in so much "red tape" that it never gathers the momentum or the social space necessary as a precondition to success. Thus, there needs to be sufficient "institutional relaxation"—providing social space relatively free from bureaucratic impingement—to allow these small-scale, social experiments to emerge of their own accord. The advice given by Donald Michael in his book *The Unprepared Society* a decade ago seems even more relevant today in suggesting that the right place to initiate the process of social learning

> ...may very well be in a "societal interstice" where there may develop or be preserved a different standard and lifestyle. Thereby, at some later,

Reading 29
Bureaucracies—Too Large and Complex?

more propitious time, this enclave or subculture could serve as a model for many other people as our larger society struggles to find its confused and dangerous way.

Evolution is not stasis. Everything alive is impermanent. If our bureaucracies are alive, they will assuredly prove to be impermanent as well. One direct way to recognize the life and vitality of our social systems is by fostering diverse social experimentation so that, in due course, existing social forms may gradually yield to the new forms they have helped to create.

Reading 30
CITIZENSHIP

Robert N. Bellah, Richard Madsen, William M. Sullivan, Ann Swidler, Steven M. Tipton

> *Despite the erosion of confidence in government and our political leaders, most Americans remain patriotic and believe that there is some national moral consensus that should be supported. But they simultaneously believe that politics is a dirty business of competition among differing interests and regional groups. Understanding the difficulty in resolving these contradictory conceptions may help to explain the publics' political disaffection.*

THREE TYPES OF POLITICS

Like other key concepts in American moral discourse, *politics* and *citizenship* have a variety of meanings, not all of which are compatible with one another. At least three distinct conceptions of politics, with attendant notions of the meaning of citizenship, emerged from our interviews. For those who hold them, these understandings serve both to orient action and to explain it. One or more of them are conscious conceptions for some, and they seem to be implicit in the way of living of others. The three understandings are quite distinct, yet in practice they are often held simultaneously.

In the first understanding, politics is a matter of making operative the moral consensus of the community, reached through free face-to-face discussion. The process of reaching such a consensus is one of the central meanings of the word *democratic* in America. This understanding idealizes an individualism without rancor. Citizenship is virtually coextensive with "getting involved" with one's neighbors for the good of the community. Often Americans do not think of this process as "politics" at all. But where this understanding is seen as a form of politics, it is

---

From *Habits of the Heart: Individualism and Commitment in American Life*, New York: Harper & Row, 1985, pp. 200–204, 207–208. Copyright © 1985, The Regents of the University of California.

the New England township of legend, the self-governing small town singled out by Tocqueville, that remains the ideal exemplar. We call this first type "the politics of community."

In sharp contrast to the image of consensual community stands the second understanding, for which politics means the pursuit of differing interests according to agreed-upon, neutral rules. This is the realm of coalitions among groups with similar interests, of conflicts between groups with opposing interests, and of mediators and brokers of interests—the professional politicians. We call this second type the "politics of interest." It is sometimes celebrated by political scientists as "pluralism," but for ordinary Americans the connotation is often negative. The politics of interest is frequently seen as a kind of necessary evil in a large, diverse society, as a reluctantly agreed-to second best to consensual democracy.

One enters the politics of interest for reasons of utility, to get what one or one's group needs or wants, rather than because of spontaneous involvement with others to whom one feels akin. To the extent that many of those we talked to see *politics* as meaning the politics of interest, they regard it as not entirely legitimate morally. Hence the generally low opinion of the politician as a figure in American life. Politics suffers in comparison with the market. The legitimacy of the market rests in large part on the belief that it rewards individuals impartially on the basis of fair competition. By contrast, the politics of negotiation at local, state, and federal levels, though it shares the utilitarian attitudes of the market, often exposes a competition among groups in which inequalities of power, influence, and moral probity become highly visible as determinants of the outcome. At the same time, the politics of interest provides no framework for the discussion of issues other than the conflict and compromise of interests themselves. Visibly conducted by professionals, apparently rewarding all kinds of inside connections, and favoring the strong at the expense of the weak, the routine activities of interest politics thus appear as an affront to true individualism and fairness alike.

Citizenship in this second understanding of politics is more difficult and discordant for the individual than in the ideal of community consensus. It means entering the complicated, professional, yet highly personal, business of adversarial struggles, alliance building, and interest bargaining. It requires dealing with others from quite different consensual communities. For most people, it lacks the immediacy of everyday involvement unless urgent interests are at stake. Supporting candidates by voting is the typical expression of this understanding of politics for most people, keeping politics at arm's length.

Yet in the crazy quilt of conflicting and overlapping interests, Americans have traditionally, through their legislators and elected officials, been able to discover enough common interest across the discontinuities

Chapter IX
Economic and Political Power

of region, class, religion, race, and sex to order and regulate the affairs of a giant industrial society. The chief vehicle for this task has been the national political party, a party more of allied interests than, as in Europe, of ideology, led by the person who has been sufficiently adept as an interest broker to become the presidential candidate. Once elected to office, however, the party's candidate, himself a professional politician, becomes at least partly transformed in public understanding into a very different figure, the president, symbol and effective author of national unity. To some extent the members of the United States Senate and the Supreme Court also share this role as representatives not of factions but of national order and purpose. They become exemplars of the revered Constitution.

There thus emerges the third understanding we call "the politics of the nation," which exalts politics into the realm of statesmanship in which the high affairs of national life transcend particular interests. If the politics of community is seen as the realm of "natural" involvement and the politics of interest as that of semilegitimate bargaining, the politics of the nation is the sphere of impartial governance according to law and, above all, of "leadership" in the sense of uniting a disparate people for action. While in the second vision politics is the "art of the possible," the politics of the nation can on occasion be expressed in a very different language, the language of "national purpose."

Despite the erosion of public trust in governmental institutions that has been going on for two decades, Americans continue to express a degree of patriotism that is remarkable when compared to most other industrial societies (Janowitz, 1983). The increase in the number of "independent" voters not aligned with any party that has occurred in the same period, suggests that the politics of interest, with which parties are associated, has suffered more than the politics of the nation from a "legitimation crisis" (Nie, Verba, and Petrocik, 1976; Burnham, 1975 and 1980; Lipset and Schneider, 1983: chapter 12; House and Mason, 1974; Yankelovich, 1974). The citizenship that attends the third type of politics is experienced more symbolically and less in the practices of everyday life than citizenship of the first two sorts. In a variety of public rituals, in foreign relations, and above all in war, the sense of being part of a living national community colors the meaning of life.

The politics of the nation is a positive image for most citizens. It is a notion that bypasses the reality of utilitarian interest bargaining by appealing for legitimacy to the first type of politics—the vision of consensual, neighborly community. But even in the actualities of the first type of politics, the politics of community, when the local school board confronts differences with respect to curriculum content or the town council must decide about permits for developers, it is the politics of interest, as the citizens of Suffolk uncomfortably realized, that has emerged. And it is in situations such as these that even local officials can be accused of "playing politics"—that is, acting more in terms of interests than consensus. Often groups that seem exceptionally able to work their way with boards, officials, and legislatures become branded as "special interests." Perhaps this is rightly so, but it is a usage that besmirches the notion of "interests" or "interest politics" altogether. Indeed, one of the most abusive epithets an opponent can hurl at a national political figure such as the president is that he is simply playing "partisan politics," meaning that the person accused is using the prerogatives of office to advance the interests of his own party as opposed to standing virtuously "above politics" to seek the general good.

But periodically presidents have been seen as rising above politics and expressing a sense of the national community. Franklin Delano Roosevelt, a master of coalition politics, was superbly able to embody a sense of national purpose in response to the challenges of the Great Depression and World War II. It is the notion of the politics of the nation as the politics of a consensual community that helps us understand the general willingness of Americans to pay their taxes and serve in the military. But it is also this understanding of the politics of the nation that makes sense of the recurrence in the United States of social movements that insist on a new level of public morality. Major social movements from Abolition to Civil Rights to the opposition to the Vietnam War have appealed, with more than a little success, to a sense that justice and the common good can be addressed at the level of national consensus. But social movements quickly lose their moral edge if they are conceived as falling into special pleading, as when the Civil Rights movement was transformed into "Black Power." Then we are back in the only semilegitimate realm of the politics of interest.

What is paradoxical in this picture of the three types of American politics is that in an individualistic culture that highly values diversity and "pluralism," it is consensus that is appreciated and the conflict of interests that is suspect. There is something baffling and upsetting in the actual differences that divide us. We need to explore further why this is the case.

POLITICS AND THE CULTURE OF INDIVIDUALISM

...The therapeutically inclined believe that discussion between those whose "values" are different is apt to prove futile. Where moral views are seen as rooted only in subjective choice, there is no way of deciding among them except through coercion or manipulation. Even those not inclined to a therapeutic view distrust all responsibilities and agreements

Chapter IX
Economic and Political Power

that have not been explicitly negotiated for purposes of mutual advantage or arisen from the conjunction of deeply held personal values. In this cultural context, politics is not impossible so much as severely limited in scope. The fear is that where the interests involved are incommensurable and therefore almost impossible to adjudicate, interest politics must inevitably break down into coercion or fraud. This may lead to the conclusion that the only morally legitimate and worthwhile politics is our first type, the politics of consensual community. Legitimacy can also extend to certain features of the politics of the nation, our third type, when it can be understood by analogy with an idealized politics of local consensus. But politics of the second type means conflict among various groups that are quite unlike one another in their "values" and styles of life, and since there is no way to discuss or evaluate the relative merits of values and lifestyles in the culture of individualism, a generalized tolerance, dependent on strict adherence to procedural rules, is the best that can be expected. But tolerance, despite its virtues, is hardly adequate to deal with the conflict and interdependence among different groups in a complex society.

What the individualist vision of politics is least able to account for are the sources of the conflicting interests themselves. There is no generally understood account of how the divergent interests of regions, occupational groups, races, religious groups, and genders actually arise, or why they contest with very unequal power to effect their wills. The realm of interest politics seems to float disconnected from the sources of interests. Divergences make moral sense so long as they can be explained as the result of individual agency. Hence, the liberal individualist idealizing of the free market is understandable, given this cultural context, since, in theory, the economic position of each person is believed to derive from his or her own competitive effort in an open market.

The extent to which many Americans can understand the workings of our economic and social organization is limited by the capacity of their chief moral language to make sense of human interaction. The limit set by individualism is clear: events that escape the control of individual choice and will cannot coherently be encompassed in a moral calculation. But that means that much, if not most, of the workings of the interdependent American political economy, through which individuals achieve or are assigned their places and relative power in this society, cannot be understood in terms that make coherent moral sense. It further suggests why, in order to minimize "cognitive dissonance," many individuals tend not to deal with embedded inequalities of power, privilege, and esteem in a culture of self-proclaimed moral equality.

Lacking the ability to deal meaningfully with the large-scale organizational and institutional structures that characterize our society, many of those we talked to turned to the small town not only as an ideal but as a solution to our present political difficulties. Nostalgia for the small town and the use of its image in political discussion was common regardless of political views. A major reason why many who voted Republican wanted to "get government off our backs" was that if "big government" were reduced in size and less intrusive in our lives, the healthier voluntary participation of the face-to-face community might return as the most prominent mode of our political life. But those on the left who wanted "decentralization" and "citizen participation" did so for much the same reasons....

INVISIBLE COMPLEXITY

The tremendous growth of the social sciences in this century, especially economics and sociology, testifies to the widespread desire to understand the complexity of modern social relations. Whatever the achievements of social science (largely, after all, a realm of "experts"), the Americans with whom we talked had real difficulty piecing together a picture of the whole society and how they relate to it. We call this the problem of invisible complexity.

Since, as we have seen, we lack a way of making moral sense of significant cultural, social, and economic differences between groups, we also lack means for evaluating the different claims such groups make. The conflict of interests is troubling when we do not know how to evaluate those interests. In this moral vacuum, it has been tempting to translate group claims and interests into the language of individual rights, a language that makes sense in terms of our dominant individualistic ideology. But if large numbers of individuals and groups or categories of individuals begin to insist, as they have in recent years, that they are owed or are entitled to certain benefits, assistance, or preference as a matter of right, such claims are not readily accepted as matters of justice. They begin to be treated instead as simply competing wants. And since wants cannot be evaluated in terms of the ideology of individualism, the outcome of the political struggle is widely interpreted in terms of power. Wants are satisfied not in terms of their justice but in terms of the power of the wanters. Too many demands can even begin to threaten the legitimacy of the logic of individual rights, one of the few bases for making morally legitimate claims in our society. A conception of society as a whole composed of widely different, but interdependent, groups might generate a language of the common good that could adjudicate between conflicting wants and interests, thus taking the pressure off of the overstrained logic of individual rights. But such a conception would require coming to terms with the invisible complexity that Americans prefer to avoid.

As we have noted before, the image of society as a marketplace of fair

Chapter IX
Economic and Political Power

competition among roughly equal competitors is an appealing resolution to the problems of understanding the larger society, one that complements the moral balance of consensual voluntary community. But though this model continues to have wide appeal, most Americans know that it is far from descriptive of what really happens. Most are aware to some degree of things that do not fit the market model: large corporations that dominate whole sectors of the market; massive efforts to influence consumer choice through advertising; government programs that subsidize various sectors, such as agriculture; contracts for defense industries that escape reliable cost accounting; technologies that extend and intensify the centralized control of finance, production, and marketing; and so forth.

One long-standing American reaction to such facts is to suspect all groups powerful enough to avoid the operation of the free market. It is not only big government but big business and big labor that have suffered declining levels of public confidence in the past two decades (Lipset and Schneider, 1983: chapters 6-10). Such groups in one way or another "go too far" in interfering with market mechanisms for the benefit of special interests. But at the same time, many Americans are aware that large-scale organizations, however distasteful, are part of social reality in the late twentieth century and that trust-busting, union-busting, and the dismantling of government regulatory agencies are not really desirable. With that realization, the quandary deepens and leads many to believe that only effective "leadership," with the assistance of technical expertise, can meet the problems of our invisible complexity.

REFERENCES

Burnham, Walter D. 1975. "American politics in the 1970s: Beyond party?" pp. 238-277 in Louis Maisel and Paul Sacks (eds.), *The Future of Political Parties.* Beverly Hills, Calif.: Sage.

_____. 1980. "American politics in the 1980s." *Dissent* 27(Spring):149-160.

House, James, and William Mason, 1974. "Political alienation in America, 1952-1968. *American Sociological Review* 68:951-972.

Janowitz, Morris. 1983. *The Reconstruction of Patriotism.* Chicago: University of Chicago Press.

Lipset, Seymour Martin, and William Schneider. 1983. *The Confidence Gap: Business, Labor and Government in the Public Mind.* New York: Free Press.

Nie, Norman, Sidney Verba, and John Petrocik. 1976. *The Changing American Voter.* Cambridge, Mass.: Harvard University Press.

Yankelovich, Daniel. 1974. "A Crisis of Moral Legitimacy?" *Dissent* 21 (Fall):526-533.

CHAPTER X

HEALTH CARE DEFICIENCIES

Reading 31

AIDS 2000: WHERE THE FIGHT WILL BE FOUGHT

Richard Merritt, Mona J. Rowe

> *Public health is supposed to be protected by state and local governments. Today the AIDS virus presents unexpected and unprecedented challenges. How can prevention and testing insure that the infected are not stigmatized or segregated, and at the same time prevent the virus's spread? The threat of a large number of AIDS cases also forces discussion of the wider issues of the inadequacy of our private insurance and public health for the financing of any large-scale need for medical care. Various models of health care are proposed that provoke thought and raise issues about society's health care structure.*

In the United States, AIDS is the subject of unparalleled media attention and the target of millions of federal dollars in research funding and public-health efforts. But, despite the furor at the national level, it is little understood that control of the AIDS epidemic and the many social and ethical considerations associated with the disease are very much a state and local responsibility.

Constitutionally, states have been charged with the protection of public health. Moreover, state and local governments—not the federal government—have assumed primary control over public education.

States license and regulate health-care professionals and facilities. State and local governments often provide residual financial coverage or access to medical services for those who do not qualify for federal assistance or cannot obtain private health insurance. And states set the terms and conditions by which health and life insurance companies do business.

By the end of 1984, when AIDS had already claimed thousands of lives, only a handful of states regarded AIDS as a significant public-health or public-policy problem. Less than three years and many thou-

---

Reprinted, with permission, from *The Futurist,* published by the World Future Society, 4916 St. Elmo Avenue, Bethesda, MD.

Chapter X
Health Care Deficiencies

sands of deaths later, however, almost every state has come to realize some of the awesome consequences that this disease can bring.

During the 1987 legislative sessions, more than 550 AIDS-related bills were introduced and discussed in 47 of the 50 states. This represents almost a 100% increase over 1986.

Four-fifths of the states have seen the formation of an AIDS task force, commission, or advisory body whose purpose has been to review the state's current policies and recommend changes to the governor and/or legislature. Another measure of the growing involvement of the states is their increasing willingness to appropriate state general revenues for various programs and activities aimed at curbing the transmission of the virus.

Since fiscal year 1984, states have allocated more than $239 million in general revenues to AIDS activities—starting at $9.3 million in 1984, increasing to $27.5 million in 1986, and reaching $126.3 million for 1988. Generally, the level of state-only funding has increased as the number of states with expanding AIDS programs has grown.

For example, in fiscal year 1984, five states allocated their own money for AIDS programs. In 1988, 30 states will be appropriating general revenue funds to combat the disease. If Medicaid funding is added, states will spend about one-third of what total federal expenditures for AIDS programs will be in 1988.

It is widely acknowledged that, until a cure or vaccine for AIDS is discovered, the only realistic means for controlling the spread of infection and AIDS is through prevention and education. More specifically, the objective is to notify those at risk of infection of the means for reducing or eliminating their risk of exposure to the virus.

A number of public-health education strategies evolved once a test for the presence of the AIDS virus was developed. One of the most important educational strategies has been the offering of test-linked counseling.

These testing/counseling services, financed mostly by federal funds, encourage those who have practiced high-risk behavior (specifically, unsafe sex or the sharing of unclean needles) to come forward to be tested, on an anonymous basis if they wish. Those tested are then advised of the results of their tests and counseled on how to reduce their exposure risk if their tests are negative and how to reduce the risk to others if their tests are positive.

Public-health officials note that far too much attention has been devoted to the test itself as the important variable in modifying behavior, whereas, they argue, it is really the appropriate counseling that leads to the kinds of risk-reduction behavior that is desired.

*Reading 31
AIDS 2000*

AIDS TESTING

The existence of the AIDS-virus test has spawned a number of controversial issues, such as whether testing should be voluntary or mandatory and who should be tested.

The overwhelming consensus in the public-health community and, at least so far, in the political community is that prevention and educational efforts can be best achieved through voluntary means. The argument is that compulsory measures, such as mandatory testing, would tend to be counter-productive to public-health goals by keeping those most at risk of infection from coming forward to be tested and counseled.

Clearly, those who practice high-risk behavior should not feel that they will disadvantage themselves by coming forward for testing and counseling. This is why meaningful protections of confidentiality and enforceable safeguards against discrimination are essential prerequisites for a successful public-health response. Although most states have relied on existing confidentiality protections found within long-standing public health, communicable disease, sexually transmitted disease, or general medical record statutes, several states have enacted new, strengthened provisions to deal with AIDS.

One area of growing controversy involves the reporting of AIDS virus (HIV) positive test results to state health officials. While all confirmed diagnosed cases of AIDS are reported to the U.S. Centers for Disease Control and the state health departments, reporting of HIV infection is required by only 13 states at this time. The majority of these states require that some form of identification be given to receive the test result. A growing number of states, however, are considering reporting test results without personally identifying that information, to improve the quality of the data collected at the state level about the disease.

AIDS AND CONFIDENTIALITY

One growing controversy is whether physicians and other health providers have a responsibility to inform spouses or sexual partners of individuals who test HIV positive. Traditionally, the absolute confidentiality of the physician-patient relationship has been sacrosanct, but, given the possible life-and-death consequences of HIV infection, many believe that the patient's right to privacy should not serve as a pretense for inflicting harm on others.

The American Medical Association, in its recent policy recommendations on AIDS, said that "physicians who have a reason to believe that

Chapter X
Health Care Deficiencies

there is an unsuspecting sexual partner of an infected individual should be encouraged to inform public-health authorities. The duty to warn... should then reside in the public-health authorities as well as the infected person and not in the physician to the infected person."

Already, legislative proposals have been introduced in a few states and the U.S. Congress that would exempt physicians from any civil action as a result of their informing unsuspecting sexual partners of the infected status of their patients.

MANDATORY TESTING FOR AIDS

Approximately 20% of all the AIDS bills introduced over the past two years have related in one way or another to mandatory testing. And while many call for required testing of prisoners, prostitutes, and hospital patients, the overwhelming number of testing bills have focused on premarital AIDS testing. In 1987, bills requiring marriage-license applicants to be tested for AIDS were introduced in 35 states.

While this issue has garnered much publicity and legislative attention, premarital testing has thus far received little support. Only Illinois, Texas, and Louisiana have managed to enact legislation, and the Texas law may not go into effect. All other bills were either defeated or carried over until the next year's legislative session. Three states—California, Virginia, and Hawaii—amended their bills to require that, in lieu of testing, applicants for marriage licenses be provided information about AIDS and where they may be tested for AIDS if they so desire.

A few states have begun to require that individuals in certain high-risk groups be tested on a routine basis. For example, prisoners are being (or will be) routinely tested in Colorado, South Dakota, Nevada, and Idaho. In 1988, Oregon intends to start testing certain individuals convicted of drug-related or sex-related crimes. Prostitutes are routinely tested for HIV infection in Nevada, the only state that has legalized prostitution, while Florida will require under its sexually transmitted disease law that convicted prostitutes be tested. And all pregnant women with high-risk characteristics will be tested in Florida.

Policy makers who generally oppose mandatory testing are beginning to ask questions about the success of the voluntary approach. For example, one legislator in New York asks: Can we honestly say that the voluntary approach is working when we know that the number of people in New York State infected with the AIDS virus is estimated to be 300,000–500,000, but only about 40,000 people in that state have been tested?

Reading 31
AIDS 2000

THE COST OF AIDS

The cost of caring for AIDS patients can be extremely high, given that most of the costs of AIDS care are associated with hospital stays for acute care of opportunistic infections. Currently, there are no reliable estimates as to what the ultimate costs of AIDS services will be, either on an individual-patient level or in the aggregate. Estimates of inpatient hospital costs range from a low of $40,000 to a high of $140,000, based on an average survival time of 18 months between diagnosis and death.

The U.S. Public Health Service predicts that annual health-care costs for AIDS treatment will increase from a current range of between $1.2 billion and $2.4 billion to between $8 billion and $16 billion by 1991. A recent study by the Rand Corporation suggests that the total cumulative medical costs for AIDS treatment over the 1986-1991 period will range from a low of $15 billion to a high of $113 billion, with an intermediate estimate of $38 billion.

Regardless of the discrepancies in cost estimates, there is little doubt that Medicaid will play an increasingly important role in financing medical aid and other services for AIDS patients. If Rand's intermediate cost estimate is correct, spending on AIDS services could account for about 3% of Medicaid program costs by 1991, or 13% if its most pessimistic scenario occurs. It is estimated that, at any given time, 40% of all AIDS patients have some of their care covered by Medicaid.

Although for many of those with AIDS the Medicaid-eligibility process has been abbreviated, gaining eligibility is not always tantamount to obtaining access to care. Many states have reported that those with AIDS have had difficulty in finding nursing homes that would accept them.

A few states, such as Wisconsin and Florida, have tried to overcome these barriers by offering enhanced reimbursement to providers on the justification that the care provided to AIDS patients is more intense and complex and therefore more costly than the average nursing-home patient. Other states are dismantling regulatory barriers that restrict nursing-homes from accepting AIDS patients, supporting the development of specially designated nursing-home beds to care for AIDS patients, and developing intensive education programs for nursing-home staffs.

MODELS FOR AIDS CARE

Given the variability and episodic nature of the disease, AIDS patients usually require a continuum of care, from intensive acute-care services to

Chapter X
Health Care Deficiencies

various nonmedical, mostly social, services such as transportation, housing, and personal care.

Significantly, a 1986 report estimated that about half of those diagnosed with AIDS were fairly mobile, self-sufficient, and in need of outpatient care only. Data from San Francisco indicate that only 6% of those with AIDS are classified as inpatients in one of the city's hospitals.

San Francisco's provision of medical and social services to those with AIDS has been touted as a model for other cities. The San Francisco model is an integrated, community-based delivery system that provides a continuum of care to persons with AIDS. San Francisco General Hospital's AIDS-specific outpatient unit provides testing, referral, comprehensive medical treatment, mental-health and substance-abuse services, and a range of psychosocial support services. Social workers are available to assist AIDS patients with such critical problems as gaining eligibility for public assistance and securing housing and transportation. The hospital has an AIDS unit for inpatient needs and accounts for about one-third of the total number of AIDS-related patient days in the city.

This integrated, case-managed approach is largely the reason that San Francisco's inpatient costs and hospital lengths of stay are among the lowest in the nation. Supporting its success, however, is a large, unmatched corps of volunteers that helps keep costs down. Experts feel that without such volunteerism it will be difficult to equal San Francisco's success.

A different approach is exemplified by New York's initiative of designating certain hospitals to serve as centers for the care of AIDS patients. The objective is to increase the access of those with AIDS to essential health care and community resources and to address patient needs not being served by the existing health-care and social-services delivery systems.

The designated-center concept also provides for or arranges a full continuum of services that may be required by an AIDS patient. Under the plan, designated AIDS centers qualify for a higher Medicaid-reimbursement rate for providing or brokering a broad range of comprehensive services. The concept also involves the use of system-wide and regional planning.

The New York Department of Health has designated three hospitals as AIDS centers so far, expects to approve five more soon, and is considering applications from a number of other facilities.

Still another alternative involves the use of home-based and community-based waiver services by state Medicaid programs. Under this approach, Medicaid pays for a wide range of care delivered at home and in the community for patients who might otherwise be institutionalized. By law, states can target their home-based and community-based

Reading 31
AIDS 2000

services waiver at AIDS and AIDS-related complex (ARC) patients or can offer these services to all Medicaid recipients as an optional service.

In applying for the special AIDS waiver, states must provide assurances that per capita Medicaid expenditures for the specified group will not increase as a result of the waiver. Moreover, in implementing the statute, states must also implement a cost formula which ensures that total Medicaid program expenditures will not increase with the waiver.

Although there are currently over 70 general home-care and community-care waivers in effect, New Jersey is the first state to receive a waiver specifically for AIDS and ARC patients. Under the terms of the three-year waiver, the state expects to serve approximately 3,000 patients at a cost of about $68 million in Medicaid funds. Other states with such waivers include New Mexico and North Carolina; several other states are developing applications.

PAYING FOR AIDS DRUGS

One major unknown has to do with the overall impact on cost of care by introduction of antiviral drugs. Retrovir (or AZT), the only FDA-approved antiviral so far, has shown promising results in prolonging the survival times among certain AIDS patients. Preliminary data suggest that the use of AZT can mean reduced medical costs for many AIDS patients, primarily because of fewer opportunistic infections and fewer hospitalizations.

Nevertheless, the cost of the drug itself is high—$8,000 to $9,000 annually—and its use can lead to serious side effects that are costly to treat. Hence, the cost effectiveness of reimbursing expensive drug therapies such as AZT is still unclear.

Despite these ambiguities, as of June 1987, 44 states had decided to pay for the costs of AZT for AIDS patients who qualify for Medicaid coverage. Only two states with significant incidences of AIDS—Florida and Texas—have decided not to cover the drug.

HEALTH AND LIFE INSURANCE

One of the most difficult questions is to what extent, if any, states should intervene in the underwriting process for health and life insurance by regulating the conditions under which the industry can use HIV tests for underwriting purposes.

An absolute exclusion of test information runs the risk of driving insurance companies out of the market—some companies fear a large number of AIDS-related health claims, while others believe they should be able to assess claim risks for AIDS as they would for any other dis-

Chapter X
Health Care Deficiencies

ease. On the other hand, giving insurance companies complete freedom may lead to blanket exclusions from coverage for those at risk of HIV infection and even those perceived to be at risk of infection. This in turn could lead to a growing class of uninsured—for which the state may have to assume ultimate responsibility.

Currently, four states and the District of Columbia have taken specific legislative action to restrict the conditions under which insurance companies may require applicants to be tested for AIDS. Several other states are using the regulatory process to create some safeguards against discriminatory requests for and applications of AIDS tests and test results and to enhance the confidentiality of medical information. Still others are using guidelines recommended by the National Association of Insurance Commissioners.

A significant number of states, however, have taken no action at all. Thus, the prevailing practice is for companies to require blood tests from applicants for expensive or individual health and life insurance policies. Many that test positive will be denied coverage, and others will forgo coverage because they are unwilling to take a test.

One partial solution to this dilemma is the establishment of a State Health Insurance Risk Pool. A risk pool usually comprises all health insurers (except those with self-insured plans) doing business in the state. The pool offers a comprehensive health insurance plan to individuals who, because of poor health or a chronic affliction, are high risks and cannot obtain coverage through the private marketplace. Such pools work by spreading the excess financial risk of covering otherwise uninsurable individuals among all health insurers in the state.

Health Insurance Risk Pools are currently authorized in 15 states. However, to date, only two of the top 10 states most affected by AIDS and HIV infection have a state risk pool—Florida and Illinois.

The establishment of risk pools will address at least one major concern about permitting insurance companies to require applicants to take a blood test for their exposure to AIDS—i.e., what health-insurance alternatives should be available for those who test positive. However, the premiums for getting insurance under a risk pool are expensive, and only one state has decided to offer a premium-subsidy program.

Another safeguard states may use is their existing statutory or regulatory authority to prohibit insurers from canceling, not renewing, or increasing premium rates on a person's existing life or health insurance policy because of a post-issue change in the subscriber's health status. West Virginia has passed a bill specifically prohibiting insurers from canceling or failing to renew the accident and sickness insurance policy of any insured individual because of a diagnosis of AIDS.

AIDS AND THE LAW

Recently, considerable attention has been given in the media to various isolated episodes of individuals who are aware they are infected with the AIDS virus but nevertheless continue to behave in ways that endanger the public health—either by trying to donate or sell their blood or engaging in unsafe sexual practices without informing their partners of their infection.

Such episodes, while small in number, have raised public anxieties and led to demands for legislative remedies. Already, some states have responded with legislation prohibiting those with a known HIV infection from selling or donating blood, or from having sexual intercourse with another person unless they have informed the person of their status.

A different approach involves the application of targeted or limited isolation or other restrictions on an individual's freedom. Connecticut recently revised its public-health statute to allow for the detention of individuals with a communicable disease who refuse or fail to conduct themselves in a way that prevents the transmission of the disease. Several other states, upon examining their public-health statutes for their ability to protect against such situations, concluded that the statutes were outmoded and, for the most part, failed to provide appropriate civil-rights protections.

As a result, several states have amended their laws on communicable disease or sexually transmitted disease to authorize the quarantining or isolation of an individual, but only after adherence to strict due-process protections. Most states already have this ability as part of their broad authority to protect public health. The real issue for states is how broad their existing powers are and whether they can be exercised in a way that will protect individual freedom while protecting public health.

AIDS AND PUBLIC POLICY

Trying to forecast the nature of public policies related to AIDS five years into the future is a perplexing task, given the number of unknowns about the disease. However, the following observations are based on an assumption that current government projections regarding the future incidence and prevalence of HIV infection and AIDS are essentially accurate. Hence, a cumulative total of more than 270,000 AIDS cases will have occurred by the end of 1991. Also, by the end of 1991, there will have been a cumulative total of more than 179,000 deaths from AIDS in the United States, with 54,000 of those occurring in 1991 alone. Another im-

Chapter X
Health Care Deficiencies

portant assumption is that the vast majority of AIDS cases will continue to come from currently recognized high-risk groups.

Since the scientific establishment agrees that a vaccine for AIDS is at least 5–10 years away, we must rely on the only approach available—education.

One has to believe that we will learn a great deal over the next five years about which educational programs and other interventions are the most effective at modifying behavior. One also must believe that the general public will begin to take those educational messages more seriously as they come more and more into contact with friends, relatives, business associates, and colleagues who are suffering from the disease. Targeted education will be stressed, especially for minority groups hit hardest by AIDS. An increasing number of states have already heeded the U.S. Surgeon General's advice and are mandating AIDS education in schools.

Provider reluctance or refusal to care for persons with AIDS or ARC will continue to be a major problem. Reluctance will be manifest throughout the health care delivery system, from emergency personnel and private practitioners to hospital workers, nursing-home administrators, and home health aides.

States may be forced to adopt a number of practices, combining the use of both incentives and regulations, to overcome such resistance. Increased reimbursement to cover the full costs of treating an AIDS patient may be sufficient incentive for some institutions. With others, states have already begun to use their licensure or certificate-of-need authority to persuade some institutions, as well as individual health-care providers, to accept AIDS patients. Special state scholarship programs may also be needed to attract interns and residents to hospitals with a high volume of AIDS patients.

State and local policy makers—both elected and appointed—will play a significant role in defining the nature and extent of what our societal responses will be to the AIDS threat. Whether most will resist the temptation to play to the fears and anxieties of their constituents for political gain remains to be seen. One hopes that most will follow the example of one official, who said, "It is the job of the elected official not to repeat back the fears of the public but rather to lead so that the fears expressed are appropriate to the risks that exist."

PUBLIC HEALTH CARE CHALLENGES

Perhaps more than any other disease, AIDS holds the U.S. health care financing system up to the mirror, reflecting in sharp detail all its inadequacies. Even before the AIDS crisis, states were engaged in finding solutions to improving financial access to health services for a growing population of uninsured and underinsured. The growing number of ARC and AIDS cases will certainly compound the problem by adding a new subset to the uninsured population.

State Medicaid programs, most of which will continue to face considerable pressure to control costs, will have to find more creative and effective ways of organizing and delivering health-care services for AIDS patients. At the same time, the Social Security Administration will most likely expand the definition of what constitutes a diagnosis of AIDS, increasing significantly the number of individuals who may qualify for Medicaid assistance.

States will see to it that the private sector assumes some share of the increased financial responsibility for AIDS patients. The most likely response will be through the enactment of health insurance risk pools. States are likely to offer some partial subsidies of the premiums of those who fall below a certain income level.

Realistically, Medicaid expansions, risk pools, charity-care subsidies, and the like will take a state only so far. Unquestionably, many people will still find themselves uncovered.

Some argue that these cost and access pressures will lead to a more rational—and therefore national—health care financing program. A more likely scenario—at least for the next few years—has the federal government providing the states with additional financial resources, such as block grants or matching grants under Medicaid, or reducing insurance regulations, allowing states to require self-insured health plans to participate in health insurance risk pools.

The health care delivery model of the future will necessarily combine both inpatient and outpatient services with a comprehensive network of complementary, nonmedical services that enable individuals to maintain themselves outside the acute inpatient setting. Most likely, dedicated AIDS treatment centers will serve as the focal point for managing patients' medical and social needs. New antiviral drugs and improved treatment practices will mean an increased need for noninstitutional alternatives for the care and maintenance of persons with AIDS.

Case management will have increased importance, with its biggest challenge in securing alternative living arrangements for the homeless with AIDS. Nonetheless as AIDS affects an increasingly large proportion of the indigent population before it spreads to other groups, the public-health problem of trying to maintain access to quality health care will only grow.

If the scenario projections prove false and AIDS manages to spread widely beyond the current high-risk populations, no social or political institutions will remain unaffected. Despite this gloomy thought, it bears

Chapter X
Health Care Deficiencies

repeating that most state and local governments are not powerless to affect the outcome of this public-health crisis. Most states still have low numbers of citizens with AIDS and therefore have time to formulate policies and programs. These states are also in a position to benefit from the experiences of some of the high-prevalence states.

The next five years will demand extraordinary leadership from our public servants and tolerance and trust on the part of the public. As one prominent statesman said: The measure of a nation's humanity is not how it treats its least fortunate at the best of times, but how it treats them at the worst of times. The United States is just beginning to embark on one of the most difficult tests in its history.

Reading 32

THE ALL-FRILLS YUPPIE HEALTH CARE BOUTIQUE

Emily Friedman

> *Americans have always connected freedom of choice and the enjoyment of abundance as major values. When they are told that they should join HMOs (health maintenance organizations), PPOs (preferred provider organizations), or what have been called OWAs (other weird arrangements), they assume that there must necessarily be a shortage of good medical services. This leads to a competitive consumer approach to the selection and provision of health services. It also leads to "The First Corollary of Yuppie Ethics—the level of deservingness of the poor varies in direct proportion to the amount of resources available."*

The attractive, nicely groomed cowpoke rides resolutely into view on our television screens, traversing beautiful mountain country. He swings off his horse and glares accusingly into the camera. "Some people like to come up here for a couple of weeks to 'get away from it all' and 'get back to nature,' " he says with a sneer. "Well, I live here!" He produces a box of Grape-Nuts from his saddlebag and starts telling us about his with-it, back-to-nature lifestyle and his closeness to the land. While popping bits of cereal into his mouth, he tells us haughtily that Grape-Nuts fits his lifestyle perfectly. He looks down his nose at the presumably quivering television audience and issues a brutal challenge: "You see, it's obvious that Grape-Nuts is right for you. The question is, are you right for Grape-Nuts?"

This is the perfect commercial for an era in which the values associated with young upwardly mobile professionals, or Yuppies, are coming to dominate many consumer markets. Presenting a perversion of core 1960s values that have survived, such as environmental awareness and at least some questioning of the establishment, the commercial is the epit-

Reprinted by permission of Transaction Publishers, from *Society*, Vol. 23, No. 5. Copyright © 1986 by Transaction Publishers.

Chapter X
Health Care Deficiencies

ome of the Culture of Inadequacy that has grown up around the Yuppies. It is a culture that says that there is no way a young person today can be attractive enough, accomplished enough, successful enough, rich enough, or possessed of enough resources to really be secure and at the top of the heap. No matter how far you have come, we are told, there is more that you must have and more that you must do, in order to really make it.

This extreme recasting of the American dream is, in many parts of the economy, contributing to the growth (such as it is) of the gross national product. It may actually be doing some good in that if there is money to be made from environmental activism, healthier eating habits, and exercise, little harm will come of it. In health care, however, the Yuppie ethic may have a catastrophic effect on American hospitals and those they serve.

What does the Culture of Inadequacy have to do with health care, which has not traditionally been viewed as a consumer commodity and thus should not be affected by Yuppie consumerism? There is a growing connection. The seemingly unbridled inflation that characterized health care (and especially hospital) costs during the 1970s provoked several governmental attempts to stem the tide, including a stab at health planning in 1976 that today has been abandoned entirely in some states and greatly scaled down in others, and the Joseph Califano-Jimmy Carter cap on hospital expenses that was voted down by Congress. That rejection was based in part on an American Hospital Association campaign, the Voluntary Effort, that promised self-imposed cost restraint by hospitals.

The Voluntary Effort, like most crisis-inspired campaigns, dissipated. Hospitals welcomed the election of Ronald Reagan, who promised an end to regulatory cost containment. He had something else in mind. In 1983, the Reagan administration and Congress implemented with lightning speed (given the snail's pace at which health care policy is usually made), the diagnosis related group (DRG) method of prospective payment to hospitals under Medicare. Other federal budget cuts led to a domino effect in the states that in turn reduced the amount of money available for Medicaid and other health programs.

This all began just in time for the recession of 1981–82, during which unemployment contributed to the creation of more medically indigent and Medicaid patients, fewer taxpayers, and growing concern on the part of employers, who found that the negligible amounts of their budgets allocated to employee health benefits were growing faster than their profit margins. Employers' efforts to encourage employees to join health maintenance organizations (HMOs), preferred provider organizations (PPOs), and what Rob Delf of the Multnomah County, Oregon, Medical Society has dubbed OWAs, or Other Weird Arrangements, proliferated.

Reading 32
Trendy Doctor-Patient Arrangements

Greater copayments and deductibles for those same employees led to their thinking about health care expenditures more than they had during the glory days of first-dollar coverage of any health care provided by any provider the employee chose.

The effect of all this on patients and hospitals has been significant. First, cost-conscious patients who are paying $100 or $200 or even $500 out of pocket for their care are far more consumer oriented than those who are totally price-insulated. Second, cost-conscious employers, in directing employees to this or that provider, inevitably take away some of the freedom those employees once enjoyed in choosing the location and provider of their care. This is true even if the employer is mandating programs that should be welcomed, such as second opinions before elective surgery.

The appearance of a shortage of resources is inevitable under such circumstances; this is the third important effect. Americans equate denial with shortage; this derives from experience with World War II rationing for some and from the old vision of the United States as the land of unlimited plenty for others. The two American beliefs in freedom of choice (in whatever market or setting) and the availability of plenty are not organically connected; but they are connected in the minds of Americans. If we are told we can only use certain hospitals or physicians, or that we must pay a deductible expense, or that another physician must confirm the opinion of the first before a procedure can be performed, we assume that there are not enough resources for us to continue to pursue the unfettered and inexpensive (for us, if not society) freedom of choice we had enjoyed for so long.

Whether this mentality would exist in a population that had never had access to virtually unlimited choice and first-dollar coverage is questionable; the British still view their more limited health care system as a vast improvement over what they used to have. It is too late now for us to find out in America. Whether the resource shortage is real (which is not the case) or perceived (which is the case), when the postwar generation starts seeing what it thinks is a shortage of a resource that it wants, it gets very nervous—far more nervous, probably, than any other generation in the history of the United States.

Easy as it is to take potshots at Yuppies, it is important to understand that there are sound reasons for their nervousness. This generation is the most populous in history; its members have been told over and over again how many of them there are and how much of a population bulge they represent on the demographic scale. Also, they were born to a generation that had endured some of the worst hardships ever visited on Americans. Compared to the horrors that befell most of the population of the Soviet Union before and during World War II, Americans were liv-

Chapter X
Health Care Deficiencies

ing a cream-puff life even during the depression; Americans' perception of the period from 1929 to 1946 was that it was about as bad as life could get.

A rural depression was followed by an overall depression that was followed by a war. Resources of all kinds were in short supply for more than a decade. Even when the economy started to recover as a result of wartime activity and New Deal economic policy, the price of that recovery was rationing: bacon, tires, stockings, gasoline—necessities and luxuries alike were parceled out. There was grumbling, but rationing was a simple dividing up of what was available into equal portions, and although people did not like it very much, they accepted it. Unpleasant as it was, rationing was a community burden and a shared experience, and as such it affected most people on pretty much the same level.

Once the war was over and the economy started to improve, that deprived generation started to have babies, and the new parents made a solemn commitment that their children would not go through what they had. "My kid is not going to want for anything!" became the new battle cry, and it looked like an easy promise to keep in the flush 1950s as personal income rose to new highs, the infant interstate highway system began to breed the first suburbs, and the United States established dominance of the world economy.

A disproportionate number of the generation born between 1946 and 1964 were raised in an atmosphere abounding with cars at the age of sixteen, college guaranteed (and paid for without the student having to work), the promise of a professional career for the asking, and a belief that they were entitled to anything they saw or wanted. Rarely has a generation been so betrayed by its parents in terms of unwarranted and unfulfillable expectations. No wonder a futurist recently referred to the children of the late 1940s and 1950s as "the doomed generation." This population went off to college and, coming into contact with various inequities, began to call for the sharing of what seemed an endless cornucopia of resources with the less fortunate. The social movements thus spawned eventually led to enfranchisement in terms of the vote and sponsorship for health care or other benefits for black Americans, the poor, the near-poor, the elderly, and other groups. Later there would be scaled down and less successful efforts to add women and the disabled to that list.

There was even a major movement in the 1970s—the product of an unholy alliance between civil-rights-minded activists and far more cynical government officials—to enfranchise the mentally ill by freeing them from admittedly gruesome institutionalization in mental hospitals to the presumably gentler mercies of community care, which by and large did not then, and does not now, exist. The homeless mentally ill living on

Reading 32
Trendy Doctor-Patient Arrangements

our streets, who number in the hundreds of thousands, are among the most visible representations of the naiveté of the 1960s. Advocates and policymakers alike are learning that it is difficult to keep your promises when times, social values, and governmental priorities change—especially when you have made these promises to some of the most politically powerless and socially unpopular groups in the United States.

The mixed fruits of labor did not affect the Yuppies much one way or another, because they had been enfranchised from birth, and the increasing fiduciary headache their activism produced was, for the most part, unknown to them. What brought them into a head-on collision with the reality of resource constraint was the Organization of Petroleum Exporting Countries and the gas rationing bred by the Arab oil boycott. The generation that was never supposed to even hear the word *rationing* found itself subjected to it.

It is unproductive to point out that the changes in the United States and world economies in the 1970s had to do with a lot more than oil, and that there were many villains, domestic and international, that fueled the crippling inflation of that era. Oil is what got the press attention, and gasoline was what the Yuppies found themselves waiting in line to get. They began to get nervous about the future availability of gasoline, especially with widespread predictions that there would be no more oil at all by 2020 or so—when the majority of the Yuppies would still be alive. In areas such as southern California, where the car passed from being a luxury to a convenience and finally to a necessity decades ago, this was a real threat.

The security of a high-paying professional job proved more elusive than the postwar babies had supposed. In any society, the pay scale is pyramidal in nature: with many low-paying jobs at the bottom, far fewer high-paying jobs at the top. In the United States and most other countries, distribution of the positions at the top is disproportionately (although not totally) determined by education and socioeconomic class. In the United States, race plays a major negative role as well. The pyramid structure must be maintained in order to maintain the society, so although a college degree had been the determinant of higher pay in the past, if millions more young people have college degrees than the market can absorb, the rules change. Now people need a master's degree for a position that once required a baccalaureate; a Ph.D. instead of a master's. As too many postwar academics found out, if there are too many Ph.D. holders available, even that is no guarantee of a high position in academia or industry. To make matters worse, per capita income began to decline in the 1970s after spectacular increases in the 1950s and 1960s. Today, only 7 percent of those born between 1946 and 1964 earn more than $30,000 a year.

Chapter X
Health Care Deficiencies

As a result of all this, the 1960s generation, which had once marched in the streets to win a better deal for the vunerable, began to see itself in direct competition for resources with the people whose cause it had once championed. As has occurred before in the United States, the Yuppies started to reconsider just how deserving the poor and other vulnerable groups, such as the elderly, were. Thus was born the infant science of Yuppie ethics, a much-maligned discipline. Yuppie ethics is, simply put, the study of what happens to a limited resource when a powerful subgroup of the population seeking that resource wants a disproportionate share of it. When the resource is in short supply, be it cars or food or, in this case, health care, that powerful subgroup faces a problem: if it wants more than its share, some other group must receive less than its share. Because that goes against the American grain, the easiest way to justify this reallocation is to convince ourselves that the group from whom we are trying to wrest the resource is undeserving of it.

The First Corollary of Yuppie Ethics is that the level of deservingness of the poor varies in direct proportion to the amount of resources available. The Second Corollary is that if disenfranchising the poor will not free up enough resources to dissipate the fear of shortages, then some other group must also become less deserving.

In trying to define what constitutes "enough" resources in this Yuppie age, we must return to the Grape-Nuts cowpoke and his challenge that the audience prove they are worthy of the breakfast cereal he is hawking. In some cultures, when resources become scarce, quantity supersedes quality as a measure of value. In the Yuppie Culture of Inadequacy, the adequate becomes nothing less than everything. Because the Yuppies were convinced by their parents that they had a right to anything they saw, they are able to glide through the ethical gymnastics required to defend the proposition that the best way to allocate a constrained resource is to give all of it to some people while giving none to others.

The ultimate Yuppie commercial is not the one with the cowpoke. It is the beer commercial during which young professionals prove themselves able to buy and sell stocks, run farms, play softball, raise families, spend lots of time in fashionable saloons, and look perfect, all in the scope of a few hours. It is the commercial that asks the burning question of the 1980s: "Who says you can't have it all?"

...If there is anything to be learned from the erratic course of American health policymaking—what there is of it—it is that the pendulum swings broadly, but it always comes back. There is much to criticize in the Great Society health programs—chiefly the separation of the poor from the elderly in separate programs and the concentration of resources on acute, late-intervention institutional care—but they do represent a set

Reading 32
Trendy Doctor-Patient Arrangements

of values. The basis of those values is that health care is not a market commodity but a special service that should be extended as broadly as possible. Today, only the United States and South Africa among developed nations do not recognize access to health care as a right of citizenship; it is unlikely that this will always be the case. Although there will be many casualties in the meantime, health policy will return again to an understanding that frailty, pain, and suffering transcend class and income distinctions, and that ignoring the plight of those who suffer is to ignore our own humanity.

When that time comes, the Yuppie hospital—the hospital that abandoned its community—will be called to account. The fat profit margin and the free champagne with childbirth will no longer serve as a competitive edge. Hospitals will be judged on how well they honored the expectations of those they served, how well they understood the special status that society has traditionally conferred on them, and how much they fought to keep their doors open—not to the healthy but to the fragile. Those hospitals that can pass these tests will still be with us when the Yuppies become, in columnist Arthur Hoppe's lovely phrase, the Grumpies, or Grown Up Mature People. Those hospitals that chose to become slaves to a transient consumer market will be doomed along with that market. They will have proved themselves unworthy of a lot more than Grape-Nuts, and they will not be missed.

CHAPTER XI

CITIES

Reading 33

WOODLAWN: THE ZONE OF DESTRUCTION

Winston Moore, Charles P. Livermore, George F. Galland, Jr.

> *Through a case study of a Chicago neighborhood, the authors show how old urban neighborhoods fall victim to the cycle of decay, abandonment, violence, and devastation.*

America has always had slums. But for the most part they have been "good" slums, as slums go: They stayed put for a while, they had a certain stability, sometimes they endured, and if they changed, they did so slowly. Woodlawn, by contrast, was a terrible slum: *It did not last.* Large parts of it simply disappeared, and towards the end it disintegrated with extraordinary speed. In other neighborhoods in other cities across the nation, other slums are increasingly doing just what Woodlawn did—disappearing. The problem with this process is that it creates human pain and tragedy on an immense scale. That much is understood by practically everybody now, thanks to the attention paid to Woodlawn by the media. It isn't pretty to watch whole communities self-destruct in the heart of the cities of the world's richest country, nor is it good for America's self-respect to feel that it has a case of incurable cancer. But just to feel bad about it, or deplore it, is not quite enough. We also need to take a serious unsentimental look at the reasons for the collapse of neighborhoods like Woodlawn, for until we understand this process, we are not going to be able to abate the suffering and other problems it entails—and we may in fact unwittingly exacerbate them.

THE CYCLE OF ABANDONMENT

Some of the larger reasons for what happened in Woodlawn are clear enough. First, we are at the end of an historic cycle of displacement. The

---

Reprinted with permission of the authors from *The Public Interest* 30 (1973):41–59, abridged. Copyright © 1984 by National Affairs, Inc.

Chapter XI
Cities

huge European migrations of the 19th and early 20th centuries are now over, and the 20th-century migrations of blacks from the rural South to the urban North have slowed down. The succession of newly arrived population groups which caused neighborhoods to shift from older to newer immigrants is at an end, and in older neighborhoods like Woodlawn there is no new group on the horizon to succeed the blacks. These older black communities are therefore losing population and have housing surpluses. They are largely populated by a destructive residual underclass. This underclass is not something brought into the city by rural-to-urban migration or an indigenous black culture; it is instead largely the product of urban welfare policies, which institutionalize poverty, stifle upward mobility, and discourage stable family formation for large numbers of blacks. As a result, the environment of these older neighborhoods becomes so dangerous and the management of housing so risky that no new population will move into them, and no one will invest in them except as part of a large-scale development which has the capacity to *exclude* the underclass.

Second, there is the arithmetic of housing. Real estate is a business. You can make money on used housing if you can sell it or rent it for a profit. If you can't do either, there is no reason to hold it. As long as middle-class and working-class families lived in neighborhoods like Woodlawn, it was possible to charge rents sufficient to make a profit on rental housing. But along with their white counterparts, black middle-class families have been leaving Woodlawn for newer communities where they can own their own homes. Those who couldn't afford to become homeowners have had to move out as the growth of lower-class crime has made the neighborhood unsafe to live in. That has left only the very poor, who cannot move. There is money to be made by developers and builders of new subsidized housing. But there is no money to be made from used private housing for the black lower class, and neither the black or white middle class will reclaim it. So it is abandoned....

Third, much of the housing occupied by the black families who came in the big migrations during and after the World Wars was already old and worn out when they arrived. Old housing may last forever in rural New England towns and in stable communities, but it wears out rapidly when subjected to abuse or even hard use by poor people with large families.

Fourth, personal security in neighborhoods like Woodlawn has broken down so completely that few families with any choice want to live there. Traditional police techniques for maintaining order depend on assistance from ordinary community and family institutions which most neighborhoods can take for granted. When a neighborhood like Woodlawn reaches the end of its historical line of succession, these insti-

Reading 33
Woodlawn: Zone of Destruction

tutions no longer function. Being the only enforcer of neighborhood security is a new role for local government, one which it has not yet learned to perform effectively. We haven't yet found ways to deal with the problems of kids in these neighborhoods who get into trouble, or to get adequate school supervision over kids who get none at home, or to provide proper law enforcement when all fear to testify.

As conditions get worse, everybody runs who can. All that is left is a population no landlord wants, a dangerous underclass spawned by poverty, joblessness, misguided welfare policies, and ineffectual corrections and educational programs. In the final stage, the kids and young adults of this underclass cannibalize their own neighborhoods, stripping vacant apartments of anything of value, doing $30,000 worth of damage to a house to get a few pounds of brass fittings and copper wiring to sell to junk dealers for a few pennies.

These, as we said, are the general outlines of the abandonment process, which are well known. But why it happens in any particular neighborhood, and what precisely goes on there, is not so well understood. Woodlawn provides a vivid illustration of one particularly grave case of the general phenomenon. As we shall see, it does not happen altogether automatically, and both government and private institutions play a significant role.

A PORTRAIT OF AN OLD NEIGHBORHOOD

Woodlawn is a neighborhood of less than two square miles near Lake Michigan, immediately south of the University of Chicago and eight miles south of Chicago's Loop. Population began to accumulate in the Woodlawn area after 1880. Never notably fashionable, the neighborhood developed a large white transient population in boarding houses and apartment hotels built during the first decades of this century. Its major foreign groups were Irish, German, and English, but apparently it never developed the pronounced "ethnicity" characteristic of some other Chicago neighborhoods. Its racial transition covered 40 years. Blacks in Woodlawn, according to the U.S. Census, increased from 13 percent of the total population in 1930 to 39% percent in 1940. During the 1950s the transition accelerated, and by 1960 only 8,450 whites were left, most of them living on the southern fringe of the University of Chicago.

As Woodlawn went black, its total population rose—from about 66,000 in 1930 to some 81,000 in 1960. The age composition also changed: in 1930 only 4.8 percent of Woodlawn's inhabitants were under five, and only 21.7 percent were under 20, but by 1960, 13.6 percent were under five and 34.2 percent were under 20. As Woodlawn's housing grew older, it grew more crowded. The total number of dwelling units rose from

27,624 in 1950 to 29,616 in 1960, an increase due to subdivision (mostly illegal) of existing structures, since new construction came to a halt in Woodlawn during this period. Of the total number of dwelling units, only 8.8 percent were owner-occupied in 1960 (the city-wide figure was 32.7 percent). Particularly significant was the high concentration of large apartment houses: 14,359 of the 29,616 total dwelling units were in structures with 10 or more dwelling units apiece. This concentration of large, generally absentee-owned rental buildings was matched elsewhere in Chicago only by the wealthy new lakefront areas. This is a critical fact in understanding neighborhood decay, since abandonment is usually a problem of rental housing, not privately owned homes.

In 1960, at the beginning of Woodlawn's disastrous decade, the community was a crowded, largely rental-occupied black neighborhood, most of whose housing was at least 40 years old. An awesome collapse followed. During the 1960s Woodlawn's population declined from 81,000 to 52,000, a drop of 36 percent, and it is still dropping; the core of Woodlawn, between Cottage Grove Avenue and Jackson Park, lost 41 percent of its population. These losses exceeded those suffered by any other Chicago community. Between 1965 and 1971, the city demolished over 400 Woodlawn buildings. Lately the city has been demolishing at a rate of 500 dwelling units a year in Woodlawn and currently has a demolition backlog there of over 1500.

HOW THE HOUSING MARKET COLLAPSED

Numbers like these are evidence of a complete collapse in the housing market. The dismal arithmetic of Woodlawn real estate can be looked at from either the supply side or the demand side. Ironically, what originally began to deflate demand for Woodlawn's rental housing was the expansion in housing opportunities for black families in other areas of Chicago. During the 1950s and 1960s, large numbers of white families left the central city and bought homes in the suburbs. The same pattern has been taking place, on a smaller scale, within the black community. In 1940 the black population of Chicago was 282,244, three quarters of whom lived in just three neighborhoods on the Near South Side—Douglas, Grand Boulevard, and Washington Park—which were Chicago's only black-majority neighborhoods. By 1960 Chicago's black population had grown threefold, to 812,637, and 15 community areas were now predominantly black. In 1940, only about 5 percent of black-occupied dwelling units were owner-occupied; by 1960, however, the proportion had risen dramatically to almost 15 percent. The growing black population was moving into white neighborhoods where single-family houses predominated, and for the first time developers were putting up new housing to sell to blacks, especially on the far South Side.

Reading 33
Woodlawn: Zone of Destruction

The blacks are thus following the pattern set by many white immigrant groups, who first established themselves in older rental housing and then gradually moved outward toward homeownership as they moved up the economic ladder—a process described by the "trickle-down" theory of the housing market. But the difference between such previous groups and the blacks is that no one is replacing the blacks as they move out of older rental neighborhoods like Woodlawn. There is no group left for the housing to trickle down to, and middle-class blacks do not have to continue living in it. Today a middle-class black family is not forced to rent housing in older "renter" neighborhoods such as Woodlawn. It can generally buy a house in one of the changing neighborhoods, or in one of the new developments aimed at blacks.

...The result of all this is that demand for the kind of housing that predominates in Woodlawn—large, rental, walk-up apartment buildings—is increasingly concentrated at the low-income end of the spectrum. Except in a few special situations, this particular kind of housing seems to have lost favor with prevailing American tastes. Areas with large concentrations of single people or newly formed families still seem able to support large concentrations of older rental walk-up housing, but by and large this kind of housing is for people who have the least choice. The "core" of demand in the Woodlawn housing market—demand by middle-class families—has disappeared. Thus even in the absence of criminal behavior and the other disincentives of a deteriorating community, Woodlawn's housing would have held decreasing attraction for the middle class, black or white.

Woodlawn's rental housing could probably have continued to serve the many working families who had enough income to pay rents required to make the housing profitable, but who were unable to become homeowners. Such families form the nucleus of many of Chicago's white working-class communities, and rental housing in these areas still seems viable. But when the explosion of lower-class crime in Woodlawn forced out even those who could not afford to improve their housing situation, the bottom dropped out of the demand for Woodlawn's housing. In short, changing tastes and opportunities caused those to leave who could afford to move up the housing ladder; criminal terror pushed out the rest....

Perhaps the most concise description of this cycle comes from a group of predominantly black-run banks and savings and loan associations. They hold mortgages on properties in Woodlawn and similar neighborhoods. In a brief document pleading for government assistance to housing they wrote:

> The mortgage usually starts with an average mortgage of 70 per cent of the appraised value of the building, for an average term of 15 years.

Chapter XI
Cities

> When the mortgage is made the building is basically sound and in good condition.
>
> However, because these buildings are old they deteriorate at a very rapid rate. Added to this is the problem of rising expenses such as taxes, fuel, insurance and maintenance. The only expense that remains constant is the mortgage note. These expenses rise at a greater rate than the landlord can raise rents. The result is that, on the average, in five years a building that made a profit at the beginning of the mortgage term no longer makes a profit.
>
> The owner in order to make ends meet cuts back on the only expenses that he has some control over—maintenance. This reduction in maintenance is at a period in the building's economic life when more and not less maintenance is required just to retard normal deterioration—old things deteriorate at a faster rate than new things. The value of the building is, of course, diminishing during this time.
>
> The mortgage balance during this five-year period has not been reduced by a third, because a mortgage balance reduces more slowly at the beginning of the mortgage term. With the value of the building diminishing faster than the mortgage balance is reducing, what began as a 70 per cent mortgage becomes a 90–100 per cent mortgage.
>
> The regulations governing the mortgagee would not allow further advances or increases of the loan when these conditions occur, along with the fact that it would not be good business to send good money after bad. Needless to say, generally other avenues of financing repairs and rehabilitation are not available. With no repairs and rehabilitation, demolition is the ultimate result.

...Woodlawn is a perfect inner-city case study not only for the collapse of its housing market, but also for the cycle of crime that combined with the arithmetic of real estate to wipe almost the entire community off the map. Woodlawn's crime problem became nationally famous. For years its street gangs were surrounded by an aura of romanticism and ideological controversy that made it difficult for many well-meaning people to see what they really represented. But now that the drama is drawing to a close in a heap of rubble, it is possible to pick out the stages that crime in Woodlawn went through.

The cycle began with a rapid build-up of poor blacks—many of them part of large families headed by dependent mothers—in Woodlawn's dense apartment clusters. Disorganized families who cannot get into public housing have few choices. Homeowners in the black community avoid renting to them because of their destructiveness. They must seek out large, absentee-owned apartment buildings that are increasingly shunned by more prosperous families. Because of its abundance of such buildings. Woodlawn was practically guaranteed a denser concentration of disorganized families than any other black area of Chicago. While many Chicago neighborhoods were "going black" during this period, it was the older, heavily built-up neighborhoods like Woodlawn that received most of the underclass. Gangs formed, as they always have in poor neighborhoods. But until about 1963 or 1964, they were small and they seemed little different from the traditional street gangs fighting over their turf.

...The gangs fascinated people concerned with social problems. Senator Jacob Javits made a trip to Chicago and invited them to dine with him. They accepted—and kept their hats on during the meal in the hotel dining room. During this same period, Martin Luther King, launching the Southern Christian Leadership Conference's (SCLC) open housing campaign in Chicago, was encouraged to enlist the Woodlawn gangs in his cause. Already having found a sympathetic ear in some of the socially conscious newspaper reporters, [gangs such as] the Blackstone Rangers now had the mantle of racial heroes thrust upon them.

Such flattery was fuel to the gang leaders' fire. If intimidation through violence on a small scale produced a trickle of affluence, on a larger scale it could produce a flood. Their power depended on their numbers; their numbers depended on vigorous recruitment; recruitment depended on terror; and so terror became the name of the game. It was simple—join the Rangers or be shot.

THE TERROR

"Stones run it" was their claim—and as far as the streets were concerned, they did. To prevent shooting in the local high school, gang members were made hall monitors. Over one thousand students fled Hyde Park High School in a single year, many of whom apparently went to live with relatives in the South. There was hardly a doorway in any rented building in Woodlawn that was not painted with the initials of the gang. Due to the recent marketing of a spray-paint can, scores of buildings could be decorated in a very short time. The walls of schools, churches, houses, and even police stations helped carry the message. Those who couldn't read were beaten up. Murder and arson eliminated resistance.

...This expansionary phase of gang activity and underclass crime carried the death blow to a community already beset by problems and whose increasingly unprofitable rental housing was on the verge of abandonment. Even without underclass gang terror the working and middle classes had a tendency to leave Woodlawn's older rental housing for newer neighborhoods. But the terror of the gangs finally put to flight even those who couldn't afford anything better. That destroyed whatever economic viability was left in Woodlawn's rental housing. Not everybody left, of course; to this day there remain in Woodlawn many families that survived the chaos, homeowners who couldn't sell their houses or who refused to flee....

THE DEVASTATION OF WOODLAWN

A wave of arson and vandalism completed the community's criminal cycle. Vandalism is profitable to various people for various reasons. It has been speculated, although not proved, that owners sometime hire arsonists to gut their buildings. Destruction by fire is the clearest way under the income tax law to claim a tax loss. One unidentified real estate manager told a Chicago *Daily News* reporter, "It is known that if you want a fire to occur, you can arrange to have it done. And if you can't make money on a building, you sure as hell can collect insurance on it by burning it down. I know that if I wanted a fire, all I'd have to do is make a phone call—let it out—saying I wanted a fire. The word circulates and I would be contacted. The going price is $600."

But owner-sponsored arson probably accounts for only a small part of the fires. In abandoned or semi-abandoned buildings, thieves strip the fixtures, beginning with major items like water heaters and continuing down to the plumbing and wiring. Setting fires makes it easier for vandals to get at fixtures buried in the building structure and to push out the remaining tenants so that the whole building can be stripped down. And many fires probably represent arson just for the hell of it.

The theory that a real estate developers' conspiracy is responsible for the final collapse of Woodlawn has such an attraction that even experts who don't believe it sometimes espouse it, apparently just to see whether they can get away with it....

The trouble with the conspiracy theory is not that it is implausible, but that the forces dismantling Woodlawn need no help from conspirators. Conceivably a few could be found, but the Woodlawn process does not depend on them. This is becoming evident as neighborhoods in less desirable locations have begun to go through the same process. No one has thought of the west side of Chicago as a real estate developer's dream; yet when fires and abandonment began there, the Northwest Community Organization passed a resolution charging that "a conspiracy of city officials, real estate speculators, mortgage houses, and others is responsible for the fires in order to scare us so they can tear down our neighborhood to build a high-rise for people in the suburbs." Building abandonment and fires are beginning to plague other black neighborhoods far inland, which hold no self-evident charms for speculators. One such neighborhood, Lawndale, has probably suffered more heavily than Woodlawn, according to a recent federally sponsored study of abandoned buildings in Chicago and elsewhere.

SHOULD SOMETHING BE DONE?

What can be done to prevent what happened in Woodlawn from happening elsewhere? That question raises another question: *Should* anything be done? There are obvious advantages to letting the Woodlawn process go on. After all, as long as there is any housing left in the city, there will always be somewhere for the poor to live. As the more affluent classes, black and white, flee from the advancing underclass, the black poor will take over the housing they leave behind—and this, in turn, may well mean that the supply of housing for the black poor will get better. They have finally worn out much of the oldest housing; the neighborhoods they will inherit from here on will be newer.

Furthermore, while there are losses involved, they are borne largely by private investors, often other blacks, who lose their equity and by lenders who hold mortgages. This doesn't show up as a direct loss to the average taxpayer. And losses in the city may be compensated by gains elsewhere. The pressure on the white and black middle-class population to get out of reach by moving to the suburbs lays the foundation for a building boom there. There is even room in such a boom for a little suburban integration.

Moreover, the abandonment process clears land and relocates families "free." That will make it easier and cheaper to rebuild on a large scale. A few of the areas being abandoned are prime locations, such as Woodlawn, which lies between Lake Michigan, a huge park, the University of Chicago, and a large cemetery. And perhaps the problem of the underclass will wear itself out. In the next 15 or 20 years we may see declining birth rates among lower-class blacks as well as the violent death or incarceration of their more destructive underclass. In 20 years the innercity may be ready for rebuilding on a scale that will dwarf the reconstruction after the Chicago fire. And there is reason to believe that such reconstructed areas could be integrated both racially and economically.

There is another side to this, however. It is a profligate society that is willing to squander the resources generations have created. In the path of advancing decay lie not only homes but job-providing factories, schools, churches, shopping centers, universities, and other institutions. The Woodlawn process may be "accomplishing" what it took a war to "accomplish" for European cities....

People get chewed up in the Woodlawn process. Violence is already a

Chapter XI
Cities

principal cause of death among black youths under 25. Many of the victims have been good students who had the makings of community leaders, the kind of people we were expecting to depend on in the future. And the zone of destruction is a pitiful environment for people to live in, existing day and night with the threat of violence and fire, surrounded by collapse. Can a society be indifferent to such a process? Can letting such a process continue any longer be considered a defensible public policy? Can the hostilities such a process breeds ever be healed?

WHO ARE THE VICTIMS?

Look closely at who the victims of the process are. There is a tendency to focus on the poor black families who are left in the neighborhood when it finally comes crashing down. Their plight is obvious and grave. But at least in material terms they have relatively little to lose. The most threatened groups are the black and white working people, who can't afford to run away when the decay process presses against their communities: the "respectable" poor, the working poor, the elderly, the abandoned, traditional poor, the residue of hard-working ethnic communities that have yet to make it into the professional and white-collar classes. It is as if the economy has played a huge trick on them. It gave them the opportunity to become modest homeowners; then it turned around and produced a process of decay that threatens to wipe out their gains, the hard-won achievements of their lives. When applied to these people, the policy of letting-what-has-been-happening-continue not only is an affront to simple justice but also produces conflict that will increase the instability of the city and harden racial prejudice. The prospect of the poor and the near-poor fighting over a diminishing supply of cheap housing in the city is not a pretty one....

Even those members of the middle and upper classes, black and white, who can *afford* to keep running away from the problem even if it means changing cities, may not be as secure from the decay process as they think. But, more important, no family of modest means—and this applies particularly to the black middle class, struggling to establish respectable and stable communities, mostly within the limits of the central city—can feel immune from a process which could wipe out all its gains. This destroys the basic condition for a long-term resolution of America's race problem—the ability of the black middle class to develop the community, financial, commercial, and other institutions it needs so badly. Nothing is more inimical to the formation of such stable institutions than the fear that one's own neighborhood is only a few years removed from what happened in Woodlawn.

Reading 33
Woodlawn: Zone of Destruction

THE "CONTRIBUTION" OF GOVERNMENT

Ironically, what happened in Woodlawn is partly traceable to public policies that were inspired by noble national ideals. For instance, the discovery in the 1930s that a third of the nation's families were ill-housed brought to light an intolerable national condition, and on the theory that every problem would yield to a program, massive public housing projects were built to replace slums. However, these provided housing for the "worthy" poor, not the families of the underclass, who were screened out or evicted. Until very recently, the majority of families in public housing were headed by working people. The areas around the public housing projects housed many of the families who had been rejected by the housing authorities as being too disorganized. An uneasy balance developed between the two groups, confined to the ghetto as they were by the wall of segregation. In the 1950s the wall cracked. Many of the working-class and middle-class black families got out—not to integrate into white neighborhoods, but to establish black middle-class communities within a still generally segregated area.

As this process accelerated, public policy focused next on the neighborhoods to which the underclass was relegated and found them unacceptably shabby. Strict code-enforcement programs were implemented to oblige the slum owner to bring apartments up to safe and sanitary standards. Housing that could not economically be brought up to such standards was torn down. The result, for a time, was a significant shrinkage of the housing supply. In Chicago, the pressure of code enforcement seems to have played a critical role in almost one third of all demolitions in the city between 1948 and 1970, even during a period of extensive demolition as a result of expressway and public housing construction. Some of the code-enforcement programs were coupled with urban renewal projects, which focused primarily on middle-class areas threatened by the underclass.

In retrospect, it is apparent that public policy toward housing has been unwilling to make the class distinctions that have governed the behavior of families, white and black, who have had to live with the threat of the nearby underclass. As long as the neighborhoods to which that underclass was relegated lasted, it was possible to sustain the illusion that things were getting better. Urban renewal *did* transform Southwest Washington from slum to shiny new upper-class district. Code-enforcement programs *did* succeed in forcing many landlords to improve their buildings. Census statistics *did* reassure us that the total percentage of deteriorated or dilapidated dwelling units was getting smaller. It took Woodlawn and its counterparts in other cities to point out the catch: Af-

Chapter XI
Cities

ter 40 years of programs which ignored the existence of the underclass, the neighborhoods on which we implicitly depended to provide this class with housing were suddenly collapsing on a massive scale. Of course, we can continue to ignore or deny this issue—but it is no longer painless to do so.

THE CASE FOR STABILIZATION

We submit that the issue now is not how to end slums, but how to stabilize and upgrade them. This has a crass ring to it, to be sure. Years of rhetoric about making war on poverty have taken for granted the inspirational notion that, given the will and the proper means, everyone can be assured an "adequate income" and a "decent home." The idea of government policy consciously promoting the "stability" of slums goes against the grain; it lacks the sense of uncompromising high-mindedness which we have come to expect of national social policy. Yet it is precisely such "high-minded" and "inspirational" policies which have helped to create the plight of the Woodlawns of America. And in any event, what these devastated or about-to-be-devastated neighborhoods need isn't eradication, but rather assistance in stabilizing themselves. If the case of Woodlawn proves anything, it proves the urgency of finding ways to keep the communities that house black lower-class families from falling apart.

One reason for redesigning public policy so that its aim is to stabilize slums lies in the interests of the black underclass itself. The dissolution of this class, to quote Moynihan, is going to be "the work of a generation." After the early hopes of the war on poverty, the great difficulties of working with this class have become widely known. Any effort to convert the underclass into responsible, self-sufficient persons—whether through job training, school programs, welfare experiments, social work, "black capitalism," or whatnot—is undermined by their incessant drifting. Urban underclass families don't stay put very easily. This is a difficult problem even under the best of circumstances, but when neighborhoods collapse around them as Woodlawn did, they have no choice but to pack up and move on. The process of dissolving lower-class behavior depends on building up community institutions and the sense of responsibility that are the hallmark of the middle and working classes. The obvious prerequisite for this, of course, is a "community," one that lasts. Today this prerequisite does not exist.

The problem goes far beyond the suffering of people trapped in the last stages of a neighborhood like Woodlawn. The collapse of housing economics in the inner city is turning the underclass into nomads. They are the kiss of death to each successive community that they occupy. This is not to blame them in a personal sense. It is simply to state the plain fact that the economics of lower-class housing no longer work. And there is no advantage at all to the lower class in this process. If antipoverty programs must chase these people from one neighborhood to another, they will never have any meaningful impact on them.

The second part of the case for stabilizing lower-class neighborhoods stems from the interests of those who are in the path of destruction, particularly the black working and middle classes. In a city like Chicago, there are a lot of blacks who have made it. They have jobs, good incomes, homes which they own, solid neighborhoods. Some of them are becoming successful businessmen. A black investment community is beginning to form. Communities are beginning to show the capacity to respond on their own to their problems. Political power is heading their way, slowly but surely. All these gains are real, but they are recent and they are still on a very shaky basis. In general, the institutional strength of the black community is substantially less than that of otherwise comparable white communities, and this fact makes the recent gains of the blacks more vulnerable to pressure from the underclass.

The extent of this vulnerability is illustrated by the fate of a community south of Woodlawn called Chatham. Ten years ago it was the showcase of the successful Chicago black community. Today Chatham is becoming uneasy. Refugees from Woodlawn are beginning to filter into Chatham's big, solid apartment houses. Ten years ago a property owner in Chatham could sell "up"; today, it is said, he may have to sell "down." This short life of black middle-class communities should be of concern to everyone. The path to racial equality in this country depends on blacks achieving the same middle-class stability and power that the whites have. This takes time, concentration, and a modicum of security. The successive dissolving of communities under the pressure of the underclass deprives them of all three.

The third branch of the case for stabilizing our low-income neighborhoods is the question of justice for those of the poor, black and white, who take the brunt of the loss when a community falls apart. The rampage of the underclass has introduced a new factor into urban land economics. The prospect of a community's "going black," and now the prospect of its subsequent mutilation, has paralyzed the market for whole sections of inner-city land. The general tendency in the American economy over the past 30 years has been for land values to rise. Even in older sections of the inner-city land might easily be redeveloped (and in many places is redeveloped) for commercial or industrial or residential uses—were it not for a generalized fear of underclass "invasion." This

Chapter XI
Cities

hits blacks as well as whites, as the Chatham example shows. In practical terms, it freezes the urban land market and leaves the present group of owners holding the bag.

The present group of owners, of course, is usually the lower-middle class and working class. They own neighborhood after neighborhood of good, modest, cheap houses, decent if unglamorous apartment buildings, small business establishments, and the like. Without the threat of underclass violence it is hard to say what the market for this property would be. Possibly there would still be little demand for it; this is the belief of a number of authorities, such as George Sternlieb, who see an irreversible trend from urban to suburban living. But this view may be incorrect, and in any case has not been proved. Still, the paralysis of the market hurts whatever prospects present owners have both to maintain their communities and to recoup their investment when they want to sell.

To restore the economic viability of housing and to establish an acceptable level of personal security must be the two goals of any stabilization policy. We are not proposing that this be the full extent of national policy toward the central city. It is clear that most lower-class crime is the product of joblessness, bad education, and weak communal structures. But programs aimed at these fundamental problems are impossible to implement without a reasonably stable community—however shoddy from the liberal, suburban point of view—within which to develop them. Archimedes knew how to move the world, but even he acknowledged that he needed a place to stand.

The most important lesson to be drawn from the Woodlawn process, then, is that its victims are not just the inhabitants of Woodlawn. The principal victims will be the black and white working class, the lower-middle class, the traditional poor—those whom the accelerating process of decay threatens most directly. Furthermore, the Woodlawn process has become a major menace to the consolidation and growth of the black middle class itself.

The immense gains of the black population over the last 40 years—gains which the Woodlawn process menaces—were fashioned in the midst of poverty-stricken communities. The process of social advance has to start somewhere. The challenge is to assure it of a place to start. To do so will require the establishment of basic security for people and property, and more clearly focused efforts to maintain community stability in inner-city neighborhoods.

Reading 34

THE AGING CENTRAL CITY: SOME MODEST PROPOSALS

Norman Krumholz

Arguing against hopelessness or a "Marshall Plan" for cities, the author advocates "constructive shrinkage" and greater attention to residential neighborhoods than downtown investments.

Those familiar with the city planning profession are aware that its latest fad is "growth management." This year's annual conference of the American Society of Planning Officials even had "growth management" as its theme. From time to time I receive requests from Phoenix or San Diego asking what sophisticated techniques Cleveland is using to control growth and development. My response is wistful; I usually tell them I wish we had some growth to control. The absence of growth and the reality of stasis or decline call for new directions in the work of city planners and other public officials who labor in our older cities. Before considering what those new directions might be, I will first briefly outline what I see as the problems, based upon Cleveland data and generalizing where appropriate.

The population of the city of Cleveland has dropped significantly from its peak in 1950 when it was 914,000. It is now down to only... [574,000, declining 37 percent] since 1950. From 1970 to 1976, Cleveland's population loss represented one of the sharpest declines of any city in the country, a loss of 125,263 people or 16.7 percent.

Along with the decline in numbers of people has come a substantial change in the composition of the remaining population. Cleveland's white population has fallen about 50 percent since 1950 and its percentage of blacks has risen above 40 percent. Considering the fact that blacks have appreciably lower incomes than whites on the average, the relative

---

Reprinted with permission from Edward W. Hanten, Mark J. Kasoff, F. Stevens Redburn (eds.), *New Directions for the Mature Metropolis* (Cambridge, Mass.: Schenkman Publishing Co., Inc., 1980), pp. 74–85.

Chapter XI
Cities

income level of city residents has been falling when compared to the level of incomes in the metropolitan area as a whole. In the 1960s Cleveland lost 25 percent of its families with incomes over the median for our SMSA. Today, about 20 percent of all Cleveland families receive Aid to Dependent Children and one-sixth of our families earns less than $2,000 a year.

The employment base for the entire Cleveland metropolitan area has been growing more slowly than for the nation as a whole. The city lost 71,000 jobs, about 15 percent of its total employment, in the 1960s and that loss has continued in the 70s.

Population loss, relative poverty and inflation have had a destructive impact on the housing market in some Cleveland neighborhoods. Because of rising costs of operation and ownership to private landlords and the declining ability to pay among lower-income tenants, there is an economic squeeze on rental property owners. To cope with this squeeze, some owners are first resorting to tax delinquency and then to abandonment. In some neighborhoods up to one-third of all property is tax delinquent, abandonment is increasing significantly and the city spends close to $2 million a year on the demolition of abandoned property....

Let us examine more closely the structure of this decline so we can better understand the nature of the term "declining metropolitan areas." While the Cleveland SMSA lost 89,000 residents, Cleveland's suburbs still gained 24,000. This pattern appears to be characteristic of all declining metropolitan areas. In the central city, population and employment are declining, while in the suburbs they are rising. Suburbs are growing at a slower rate, but they are still growing, and central cities are losing population faster than ever. The term "metropolitan decline" tends to obscure this very important central city-suburban dichotomy. Thus, metropolitan decline is not metropolitan-wide in its impact. Central cities are absorbing the brunt of slow growth, stasis, and no growth.

These problems are not unique to Cleveland. Nearly all SMSAs east of the Mississippi and north of the Mason-Dixon Line exhibit, to some degree, the same trends. Most of these cities are oriented toward manufacturing, which is no longer a rapidly growing sector of the national economy. Northeastern cities also tend to be highly unionized and have higher wage rates and more cumbersome work rules than cities in the South and West. This encourages companies to open new plants in Dallas, Phoenix, and Houston instead of Cleveland, Buffalo and Detroit. Moreover, our increasingly hedonistic society seems to be placing an increasing value on sunshine and warm weather; and most other parts of the country have larger quantities of both. We can't do much about the weather, and it appears that labor and management are not likely to work out any agreements which will make older urban areas more com-

Reading 34
Aging Central Cities

petitive in attracting new industry. Therefore, it seems probable that, in the short run at least, the shift of economic activity and population to the South and West will continue.

Unfortunately, most of the reaction has been to the numbers involved in these trends and far too little attention has been given to their process and underlying structure. In the 1930s, Cleveland was the sixth largest city in the United States; by 1970 it ranked tenth, and [by 1980] it fell to eighteenth. This constituted a blow to the civic pride of many Clevelanders and prompted city council to pass a resolution urging the preparation of a plan calling for a central city population of one million by 1985. A population of this size may be living in the city by that year (although the probability seems slim), but it would be fair to venture that the future scale of development in Cleveland will not be determined by political desires, no matter how well meaning. In any case, the numbers mean little by themselves. Reconstruction and repopulation cannot proceed any faster than private markets can be found for cleared land, and at present the demand side appears quite weak.

The most negative aspect of metropolitan decline is rooted in declining job opportunities. The alleviation of this urban problem will require some redistribution of resources to the poor. While we have made some progress in this area, we have not done enough; and a declining local economy will make redistribution much more difficult to achieve. It is difficult to get middle and upper income groups to accept a smaller piece of a "larger pie," and I suspect it will be nearly impossible to get them to accept a smaller piece of a "smaller pie."

I perceive a very real danger of creating, perhaps perpetuating would be a better word, a permanent underclass without access to the comforts of middle class America. While there is much to criticize in the consumer life style of middle-class Americans, the sterile suburbs, the big car syndrome, ugly shopping centers, etc., few people would choose poverty over modest affluence. The problems of the urban poor are much more stark and elemental: paying the rent, feeding the kids, getting to the corner store without being mugged. Without a steady expansion of employment opportunities, many youths who are currently unemployed may never have the chance to hold a decent job. Their only alternatives will be crime and "the hustle," which will be destructive both to them and to those who live around them.

In all the discussions of our cities and their problems, we frequently overlook one very important fact—most people living in metropolitan areas, even declining ones, are not affected much by the urban crisis. The problems that constitute the heart of the urban crisis bear very heavily on some people, largely low and moderate income people living in certain neighborhoods, but never touch affluent suburbanites. If those who

Chapter XI
Cities

live outside the areas affected by the urban crisis are even dimly aware of the crisis, they generally mistake the symptoms for the real problems. They see the vacant land and abandoned buildings but ignore the social and economic realities that led to the present situation. This has led to some of the popular solutions to the urban crisis.

The first and most popular is the complete reconstruction of the central city through the massive infusion of federal funds. Nearly all the schemes presented have one thing in common; they imply that we can solve our problems by building something, a mall, a special purpose center, an arch, an automated downtown distribution system, or some other civic monument. The most recent variant of this theme is the so-called "Marshall Plan" for cities. Under this plan the federal government would initiate a massive program to rebuild the central cities in an effort to attract the fleeing middle class back into them. The keystone of this program is physical redevelopment to restore the central city in much the same manner as the "Marshall Plan" restored the countries of war-ravaged Western Europe. But, as Norton Long has pointed out, this analogy simply does not hold. An alien enemy force destoyed Western Europe in pitched battle, thus making a "Marshall Plan" necessary. The decay of our central cities was not visited upon them by some invading army, but rather was the result of social and economic forces deeply rooted in American society. They cannot be driven out like a foreign army. The much discussed "Marshall Plan" for cities differs little from the federal government's urban renewal program begun in 1949. Urban renewal did not save our cities in the 1950s, and a "Marshall Plan" won't save them in the 1970s. Such a program will not create a growing economic base, job opportunities, income, and a vigorous demand for the facilities the "Marshall Plan" would supposedly supply.

Why, then, does this idea have such staying power? There are a number of reasons. First, because massive development efforts benefit groups that have a lot of political influence; developers, builders, construction workers, landowners, etc. Building is their business and, naturally, they favor programs that stimulate building just as most of us tend to value what we produce. The second and most important reason is that this kind of proposal really does not ask us to do things any differently. It requires no changes in our values and mores, our ideology, if you will, and it ignores the really hard questions of:

- Why do children graduate from high school without learning how to read?
- Why can't our criminal justice system ensure a reasonable level of personal security?
- Why can't a sizable proportion of our work force find productive employment?

Reading 34
Aging Central Cities

Meaningful programs which would resolve the issues raised by the above questions would do far more than any "Marshall Plan" to revitalize central cities. Unfortunately, solutions would require changes in our institutional arrangements and so are probably not likely to be forthcoming in the near future.

Another reasonably popular solution for the decline of central cities is regional government. This would supposedly unite central cities and suburbs into one over-arching government and would resolve problems created by the flight of taxable resources outside the boundaries of a single municipal boundary. The metropolitan approach may be fiscally desirable from the point of view of solving many major problems cited earlier, but it is politically rejected by central city blacks who are reluctant to give up their growing influence in city government, by the city and suburban office holders who do not want to lose their jobs, and by the suburban whites who see no pay-off to assuming a share of the tax burden of the central city. So who is left to support this "logical" future? Almost no one.

It would appear that both of the solutions mentioned above have a relatively poor chance of being implemented. Pervading each is a lack of political power or a challenge to well accepted and powerful personal or institutional arrangements. Instead, it seems much more likely that most urban areas will accept a future, at least for the near term, which is an extrapolation of present trends.

1. Central cities will probably continue to lose population, although perhaps at a slower rate.
2. The population residing in the central city will probably be less affluent than the rest of the metropolitan area.
3. Development will be largely concentrated in the suburbs.
4. Today's central city problems will spread slowly to the suburbs, but they will continue to be most pronounced in the central city.

Given this probability, there are two basic public policy alternatives open. The first is "to try to recapture lost youth." Advocates of this philosophy maintain central cities can regain the preeminence they enjoyed before 1950. That middle-class white and black families can be lured back to the central city in large numbers and that this should be the focus of public policy. The urban "Marshall Plans" and regional government plans are variants on this theme.

The second alternative is "to grow old gracefully." Proponents of this philosophy argue that while returning to the 1940s might be nice, it is extraordinarily unlikely to occur. Moreover, trying to become young again will divert us from opportunities to minimize the negative consequences of present trends, thus making the aging process more painful. We

Chapter XI
Cities

should be clear about the opportunity costs of spending our increasingly limited resources in frivolous, non-productive ways. It seems much more useful to accept our situation and manage our realistic options well.

While many arguments can be put forth as to why the philosophy of "recapturing lost youth" will not work, suffice it to say that the "Marshall Plans" and energy crises will not send affluent suburbanites flocking back into central cities that have lost thirty percent of their population in the last two decades. Certain neighborhoods may experience growth, such as New York's Upper West Side, Cleveland's Ohio City area, and Lincoln Park in Chicago for examples; but they will not come close to offsetting out-migration from other parts of the central city. The middle class may return in larger numbers sometime in the future when many of the problems of central cities have manifested themselves much more intensely in the suburbs, but the prospect of this happening in the next ten years is relatively small.

What can be done to help central cities who opt for the philosophy of "growing old gracefully?" One thing central cities clearly need is some means of balancing their budgets while maintaining an adequate level of public services. Voters are increasingly reluctant to tax themselves more heavily, so cities cannot rely on increased tax rates to balance budgets. Federal transfers, except for health and job development, are likely to stabilize or decline. The alternative is clearly better management so as to realize more effective use of the resources at hand. Of course, every administration pays lip service to the goal of more and better services without more taxes. Unfortunately, few achieve it; but it need not be as elusive as it has been in the past. For example, members of the Cleveland City Planning staff worked with the city's Division of Waste Collection and Disposal for over three years in order to improve its management capacity. By reorganizing collection procedures, reassigning manpower, and spending the Division's capital resources on cost-saving equipment, the city is now realizing a savings of several million dollars a year. When this project first started, the staff of the Division possessed few planning or analytical capabilities. Now the Division head talks about picking up garbage heuristically! So approaches to improved management have some potential for success.

Perhaps the key element of any declining city's management strategy should be a program of "constructive shrinkage." As population declines, so should the need for new schools, recreation centers, and other expensive public facilities. Declining cities should be following a conscious policy of not adding to their capital stock. Most cities cannot even afford to operate and maintain the facilities they presently have. Building new ones merely increases the burden and hastens the deterioration of existing ones. The first principle of constructive shrinkage, then, should be a policy of devoting existing resources to the maintenance and improvement of present facilities rather than to the construction of new ones.

Beyond cutting back on new additions to its physical plant, cities may have to consider divesting themselves of certain responsibilities. Most cities have facilities which serve a regional population and constitute a heavy drain on the municipal treasury. Some of these can be transferred to a higher level of government with a broader financial base. In recent years the city of Cleveland has transferred its zoo, port, sewer and transit systems to regional authorities, thus relieving the city's residents of the sole responsibility for subsidizing these operations. By divesting these assets, the city has freed up millions of dollars a year that can be devoted to other purposes. There is a danger in this approach; however, for regional agencies often have little interest in central city problems. Affluent suburbanites comprise a much more potent political force than the urban working class and poor, and regional entities may choose to respond first to the suburbanites' requests regardless of the actual incidence of need. The recent history of regional transit authorities across the country is instructive in this regard. In spite of the fact that the need for increased mobility is greatest among the transit-dependent and the resources to operate transit systems are drawn from broad-based, often regressive taxes, the expenditures and programs of regional transit agencies tend to serve best the suburban commuter making a trip to work. Mass transit has become an instrument to serve the affluent at the expense of the working class and poor, many of whom don't have the option of driving since they cannot afford an automobile. As Mel Webber has written in reference to San Francisco's BART System, "the poor pay, the rich ride."

Negotiations over the transfer of the Cleveland Transit System to the Regional Transit Authority provide an excellent example. The negotiations took almost five months, but they could have been completed in a much shorter time had there not been a difference of opinion between the Cleveland City Planning staff on the one hand and the other parties to the negotiations, namely the business community, the local transit bureaucracy and the representatives of the suburbs on the other. It was the position of the Planning staff that the city should obtain firm guarantees of reduced fares and improved service—especially to the transit-dependent population—before agreeing to the transfer. The other members to the negotiation took the position that Cleveland would benefit merely by "unloading" its seventy million dollar system without prior service and fare guarantees. After prolonged conflict the city obtained its guarantees. Granted they were somewhat less than had been hoped for, but they were infinitely greater than would have been realized had the

Chapter XI
Cities

city not been prepared with a well-defined position and a willingness to fight for it.

Naturally, the transit management complained that this would reduce their flexibility which, of course, was precisely our intent. But there appeared to be no other way of ensuring an adequate level of service for the people who need mass transit the most. Cities, in the course of divesting themselves of certain functional responsibilities, must make sure that as many safeguards as possible are maintained to protect the interests of the most dependent of their residents.

At the same time older cities are learning to manage declining resources better, they must also learn to target carefully their public subsidies so as to realize maximum benefits for subsidies expended. This is vital, for central city governments are under increasing pressure to provide public subsidies and other supports for private business ventures. Since the advent of urban renewal, government officials have accepted the notion that the city stands to benefit axiomatically from private development and that the use of city money to encourage it is appropriate. While cooperation with the private sector is desirable, even necessary, cities should not invest their scarce resources in private projects unless the benefits are actually there. This means careful cost-benefit analysis on a project-by-project basis to assure these projects are consistent with city objectives. Development should never be viewed as an end in itself; it should only be viewed as a means to accomplish other goals such as reducing unemployment among city residents and increasing city tax revenues.

During the past few years the Cleveland City Planning staff has reviewed dozens of subsidy proposals. It has routinely asked one overriding question: "who gets and who pays?" In those cases where the analysis has indicated that the public costs would likely outweigh the public benefits, or where the benefits were likely to accrue to those least in need of public support, the commitment of public funds to the projects has been opposed.

It is well understood that public officials are under substantial pressure to accept promises of progress at face value. When the headlines say "$350 Million Project Proposed to Save City," public officials find skepticism an uncomfortable role. The Cleveland City Planning Commission's opposition to such projects, then, has frequently embroiled it in heated political debate. Needless to say, it has often failed to halt the expenditure of public funds on such projects; but what it has done is to gain some public acceptance for the notion that the city and its residents should expect something in return for granting subsidies—a startling concept to those who view public funds primarily as a way to take all the private risk out of what used to be called private enterprise.

Reading 34
Aging Central Cities

Cities should also begin planning for the recycling of inner city areas. Cleveland, for example, has several neighborhoods where the population is now one-third or less of its 1960 level. From 25 to 35 percent of the properties in these areas is tax delinquent and presumably on the road to abandonment. Areas like these pose special problems for local government, for prospects for redevelopment in the short run are non-existent. In the meantime, the city incurs the costs of demolishing abandoned buildings and cleaning vacant lots while receiving little or nothing from property taxes. It appears that the only sensible strategy for dealing with these areas is a program of municipal land banking.

The Cleveland City Planning Commission assisted in developing legislation in Ohio that allows municipalities to take title to all tax-delinquent property that cannot be sold at a tax sale for the sum of all public liens against it. The city will be able to land bank this property and dispose of it when development opportunities arise in the future. This strategy has several strong points. First, it will serve as a way to recoup, at least partially, back taxes and demolition costs by making it possible to hold the land until the market value increases. Second, having a large number of parcels under one ownership will facilitate redevelopment and considerably reduce the need for eminent domain. Third, ownership is a much more effective way of controlling the future reuse of this land than any kind of zoning, for if the city owns the property it can decide how it should be redeveloped.

Land banking is primarily a means of dealing with areas that cannot be saved using conventional rehabilitation methods. If such areas are to be preserved, cities will have to make some hard choices as to how a city's resources will be spent. These choices will be difficult, at best, considering the conflict between downtown interests and neighborhood interests. Property owners in the central business district are demanding more public investment in the downtown area while the neighborhood groups are demanding better municipal services and improved public facilities in their areas. This conflict grows more strident as a city's resources become more limited.

It would seem appropriate for cities to give much more attention to residential neighborhoods than to downtown investments. The rationale for this position is partly ethical and partly practical. Ethically, it seems proper to devote public resources to helping neighborhood residents because they have fewer resources of their own than do downtown investors. As a practical matter, helping central city neighborhoods is important because they represent the sole remaining source of decent, inexpensive housing still remaining in the entire metropolitan area. The price of new housing has risen to the point where only families in the top 25 percent of the income ladder can afford it. Even existing housing in

Chapter XI
Cities

the suburbs is beyond the reach of most central city residents. If we cannot preserve the housing stock in older neighborhoods, we may have to replace it at a much greater expense, or experience a significant decline in general housing standards. Moreover, a stable residential population is essential if the central city's tax base and commercial areas, downtown included, are to survive.

The foregoing concept of "growing old gracefully" may strike you as very modest in approach, not the kind of visionary proposals, the gleaming new towers in the parklike setting, that you are accustomed to hearing from city planners. In fact, the whole idea of "growing old gracefully" strikes some people as an admission of defeat. This is to be expected in a society that is as preoccupied with newness and youth as modern American society. However, it is important to remember that the aging analogy cannot be carried to its ultimate conclusion. No city is going to disappear from the map. Cleveland may be smaller in the future, it may look somewhat different; but it will still be a place where hundreds of thousands of people will work and live. The question, then, is how can Cleveland make the best of its situation?

It simply does not follow that older declining cities of the Northeast and Midwest need to be less desirable places to live than the rapidly growing cities of the South and West. If growth were an unqualified blessing there would not be so many people opposing it in other parts of the country. And, of course, if we are successful in the modest tasks previously outlined, neighborhoods will become more desirable residential locations and will be well able to compete with other locations in the region.

We must not fall into the trap of hopelessness, giving up because the city seems to be declining in so many ways, for despair is the unforgiveable sin, not only in theology, but in city planning as well, because it creates its own fulfillment. By the same token, we must not fall into the trap of pretending there are easy solutions. We cannot go back to the past. We cannot expect the federal government to bail us out. There are no grand and simple solutions, and pretending there are no serious problems is one sure way of never improving anything.

We must face the future much as a realistic person faces the whole of life itself, with all its mysterious blend of evils and potentialities. We must focus on the positive opportunities that are there with the resolution that we will persist in our efforts to take advantage of those opportunities, even though we know it will take years, even decades, to pursue them successfully. If our goal is to leave things better than we found them and we pursue this goal with verve, imagination, courage and, above all, persistence, we will succeed. After all, that is what life is all about.

CHAPTER XII

POPULATION AND ECOLOGICAL PROBLEMS

Reading 35

HIDDEN EFFECTS OF OVERPOPULATION

Paul R. Ehrlich, John P. Holdren

> *The ecosystem contains complicated balances and interrelationships that we do not yet understand. Our rapid population growth, or consumption excesses, could trigger a massive damaging interaction at any time.*

Several subtle aspects of the relationship between population growth and environmental degradation operate to make man's predicament even more perilous than superficial analyses indicate. Four to be considered here are *synergisms, threshold effects, trigger effects,* and *timelag effects.*

A *synergism* is the interaction (constructive or destructive) of two or more factors that yield a total effect greater than would occur if the factors operated independently. In colloquial terms, it is a situation in which the whole exceeds the sum of its parts. An illustrative synergism in environmental health is the interaction of sulphur dioxide (from coal-burning power plants) and asbestos particles (from automobile brake linings) in inducing lung cancer. The sulphur dioxide interferes with the process by which foreign particles are expelled from the lungs; that, in turn, increases the residence time of the carcinogenic asbestos and hence the chances of contracting the disease. Many other destructive synergisms are known, and one can speculate about even more ominous ones yet to be identified—perhaps an interaction between low-dose radiation and persistent pesticides, which could affect vital components of the ecosystem or man directly.

The connection of such effects to population growth is clear. As populations grow and the associated technologies increase in power and variety, a broadening array of biologically active wastes is distributed in ever more overlapping spheres of influence. Substances that previously rarely came in contact with each other now commonly occur together.

Reprinted with permission from *The Saturday Review,* August 1, 1970, p. 52.

Chapter XII
Population and Ecological Problems

Fertilizer residues and oil spills now pollute coastal waters once devoid of either, and pesticides, toxic lead compounds, and man-made radionuclides move simultaneously through important food chains.

A second aspect of the response of environmental systems to the wastes generated by human populations involves *threshold effects*. At levels or rates below a threshold, many sorts of impact are buffered by the environment without adverse effects. Manure is naturally processed into humus by microorganisms in the soil, and organic matter introduced into rivers is decomposed in a similar way. Increases in atmospheric carbon dioxide are partly self-correcting because they stimulate an increase in the rate of carbon dioxide-consuming photosynthesis (and part of any excess is absorbed by the oceans). Unfortunately, such systems are all too easily overloaded—the thresholds can be exceeded—with consequences ranging from nuisance odors to potential climatological disaster.

Perhaps the classic example is the plight of many of the rivers of the developed world, whose capacity to absorb sewage and industrial wastes has long since been exceeded. Although a thousand people may dump their raw sewage into a stream with impunity, ten thousand may hopelessly pollute it; activities that appear entirely innocuous when carried on by a small population may be disastrous for a larger one. We understand only a few natural systems well enough to identify their thresholds quantitatively, but we continue to play the game of growth, a procedure guaranteed to find them all by experiment. The demise of so many of our rivers does not seem to have taught us the lesson; perhaps that of the oceans will.

A related third possibility, usually overlooked by those who insist that the population/environment crisis has been exaggerated, is the *trigger effect*, in which an environmental balance is upset by a relatively small man-made input. A little-known example is the triggering of earthquakes as a result of filling the reservoirs behind large dams—dams that are built to supply the water and power needs of growing populations. The stress associated with the weight of the water impounded by the dam may lead to fault slippage, which releases far more energy than man put in. Hundreds of seismic events, with magnitudes up to 5.0 on the Richter scale, resulted from the filling of Lake Mead in the years 1935–39, and an earthquake of magnitude 6.4, caused by the filling of the Kogna Dam, killed 200 people in India in 1967. Less bizarre and perhaps much more serious trigger effects may intrude wherever the environmental status quo is maintained by opposing forces in balance: in predator-prey relationships that affect the human food supply, in the soil and water conditions that encourage or inhibit the growth of certain viruses and other agents of disease, in the chemical reactions of the upper atmo-

Reading 35
Hidden Effects of Overpopulation

sphere that maintain the Earth's protective screen against ultraviolet radiation.

The difficulties in predicting, identifying, and alleviating any of the phenomena discussed above—synergisms, threshold effects, and trigger effects—are compounded because they may operate in conjunction with a fourth factor: *time delay*. Time delay refers to situations in which causes may precede their effects by years or even decades. This can come about in a number of ways. With many persistent pesticides, the process of concentration consumes time as the substances move from level to level up the food chains. This results in a substantial lag between the original application at low concentration and the appearance of pathological effects high in the food web. For reasons not entirely understood, induction of various forms of cancer by exposure to radiation is characterized by "latency periods" ranging up to thirty years. Particulate pollution, more than 50 per cent of it dust from agricultural activities, is cooling the Earth and bringing on climatic changes. The full consequences of this trend may not be apparent for decades or longer.

Many other conditions associated with man's environmental meddling are also characterized by dormant stages preceding the appearance of identifiable symptoms (e.g., certain parasitic diseases and genetic effects associated with various chemical pollutants). Usually such a time lag means that when the symptoms finally appear, corrective action is ineffective or impossible. If *all* use of persistent pesticides were stopped tomorrow, the concentrations of these substances in many critical organisms—and the associated damage—would continue to increase for some years to come.

Consideration of the four classes of phenomena discussed here—synergisms, threshold effects, trigger effects, and time-delay effects—suggests that population growth today is committing us to a degree of environmental degradation not yet fully apparent.

Reading 36

A GUIDE TO SOME OF THE SCARIEST THINGS ON EARTH

The New York Times

> *Here is a sampling from around the world of situations environmentalists consider to be some of today's worst problems. These are not the only problems in these areas; the selection is meant to represent the variety of problems. A complete list would go on for many many more pages.*

CANADA

1. Relations between the United States and Canada came under increasing strain this year because of acid rain. Scientists say that sulfur dioxide from industries in the United States continues to kill aquatic life in hundreds of lakes in the Adirondack Mountains and in other parts of the Northeast and Canada.

UNITED STATES

2. Four decades of nuclear weapon production has polluted the air, soil and water at 16 plants and research laboratories in the United States. The contaminants include uranium, plutonium, cesium, strontium, PCB's, chromium, arsenic, mercury and solvents used in making nuclear weapons. Carcinogens leaking into an underground water reservoir from the Rocky Flats Plant north of Denver was ranked as the worst problem.

MEXICO CITY

3. Air pollution is so bad in the Mexico City area, where 20 million people live, that all schools will be closed next month so that children can stay indoors and reduce their exposure. Winter temperature inversions

---

Copyright © *The New York Times* Company. Reprinted by permission.

trap ozone, carbon monoxide, sulfur dioxide, nitrogen dioxide, lead, mercury and other pollutants, most of them generated by the city's three million cars, trucks and buses. The result is a rise in respiratory problems, fatigue, nausea and headaches.

BRAZIL

4. Fires used to clear land for agriculture and ranching in the Amazon destroyed 30,000 square miles of virgin forest last year, an area the size of Maine. The burning is so extensive that it may account for one-tenth of the global man-made production of carbon dioxide, one of the gases believed to cause the greenhouse effect. Millions of tons of methane and nitrogen oxides generated each year by the fires may help erode the earth's protective ozone shield.

ADRIATIC SEA

5. This summer the Adriatic, like many other parts of the world, suffered an outbreak of algae. Fed by phosphates and other pollutants, the algae starved the water of oxygen, killing fish in a 1,000-mile stretch along the Italian coast.

BANGLADESH

6. Tree cutting, overgrazing and agricultural erosion in the Himalayan watershed make Bangladesh's monsoons increasingly disastrous. In August mountain runoff helped swell the Ganges River, flooding the country and killing 1,200 people.

AFRICA

7. Drought and erosion from farming, grazing and wood gathering are helping the Sahara to advance as much as $3^{1}/_{2}$ miles a year into the sub-Saharan region of northwestern Africa. Erosion is also bad in the Ethiopian highlands, the headwaters of the Blue Nile, where a burgeoning population is stripping the hillsides bare. Environmentalists say that the destruction of the watershed considerably worsened a flood last summer in the Sudan that left at least 1.5 million people homeless.

ANTARCTIC OZONE HOLE

8. Last December the Antarctic ozone hole that appears each winter may have reached Australia, where scientists reported a 10 percent thinning

Chapter XII
Population and Ecological Problems

of the earth's protective shield. Problems are also believed to occur as far north as Santiago and Buenos Aires. Ozone in the upper atmosphere filters out ultraviolet light, which causes skin cancer and might depress the immune system. It can also kill phytoplankton, the microscopic organisms at the bottom of the aquatic food chain.

EASTERN EUROPE

9. Unregulated industry has turned parts of Eastern Europe into an ecological wasteland. Acid rain is killing trees in Poland, East Germany and Czechoslovakia. Pollution is blamed for cancer and mental retardation.

PHILIPPINES

10. As much as 95 percent of the coral reefs in the Philippines have been damaged by cyanide, which fishermen dump in the water to scare fish to the surface. As in other rapidly developing areas of Southeast Asia, logging and slash-and-burn agriculture consumes tens of thousands of acres of trees each year on the island of Palawan, the nation's last frontier.

CHINA

11. It is not known whether the droughts in China and the United States were related to the greenhouse effect, but environmentalists say this summer could be a preview of hotter times to come. China already suffers water shortages and pollution from farming and industry.

ARAL SEA

12. Diverting water to irrigate cotton has caused the Aral Sea to shrink 40 percent since 1960, leaving behind a vast desert waste. Twenty of the 24 native fish species are gone and dust and salt storms are killing crops.

CHERNOBYL

13. More than two and a half years after an explosion at a nuclear power plant killed 31 people and forced the evacuation of 135,000, Soviet officials and scientists are debating what to do with the ghost town of Chernobyl: demolish it or decontaminate it and allow its 10,000 inhabitants to return. Hundreds of thousands of Soviet citizens are being monitored for long-term health effects like leukemia.

Reading 37
ILL WINDS: AIR POLLUTION'S TOLL ON TREES AND CROPS

James J. Mackenzie, Mohamed T. El-Ashry

> *Air pollution has killed whole forests in Europe. It is also powerful enough to decompose statues and make lakes sterile and dead. Evidence is now available to detail the processes through which ozone and acid from fossil fuel burning weaken crops and forests and cost Americans billions of dollars yearly. Proposals for turning the tide of air pollution are presented.*

Across the United States, forest trees and crops are under attack. Many ponderosa and Jeffrey pines in southern California's San Bernardino National Forest have died over the past three decades. On well over 100,000 acres of this land, pines are aging faster, growing slower, and succumbing more easily to insects than they did 30 years ago. Likewise, at elevations about 2,500 feet in the Northeast, half the red spruce trees that appeared healthy in the early 1960s are now dead. And throughout the Farm Belt, certain major crops are growing slower than they should be or have leaves that are misshapen or discolored.

What's the assailant? In each case the evidence points to air pollution. Together or separately, ozone and acid precipitation from the burning of fossil fuels are weakening trees in U.S. forests, leaving them more vulnerable to natural stresses. And ozone is adding to the burdens of the American farmer by reducing agricultural productivity to the tune of billions of dollars a year.

Although scientists have suspected for some time that air pollution is contributing to forest declines—especially in central Europe, where the problem is more severe—evidence has until recently been scant. It is still hard to separate out the role of other factors, such as weather extremes, insects, and competititon among species. But now that numerous studies of forest declines have been completed in both the United States and

---

Reprinted with permission from *Technology Review,* copyright © 1989.

Chapter XII
Population and Ecological Problems

Europe, the evidence implicating airborne pollution is too strong to ignore. The case that air pollution, primarily ozone, is damaging crops is even more compelling. This is partly because greater resources have been devoted to crop research and partly because the ecology of agricultural systems is simpler.

As crops and trees are added to the list of entities threatened by air pollution—which already includes lakes and streams, aquatic life, materials, scenic views, and human health—the policy imperatives for the United States are now clearer than ever: the federal government must devise a more effective air-pollution control strategy and work with industry to develop clean sources of energy.

What's more, the time to act is now. In the first place, the Clean Air Act is up for renewal, and Congress will be considering ways to strengthen the legislation so that it achieves what it has thus far failed to do: protect public health and the environment from both primary pollutants and the secondary pollutants into which they are transformed. In the second place, without an effective abatement strategy for the long term, the harm caused by ozone and acid precipitation will only get worse. The use of fossil fuels is expected to increase significantly in the coming decades. Unchecked, this growth will not only hasten direct damage to the environment but also aggravate the global greenhouse problem.

OUR ENDANGERED FORESTS

Besides the declines that have hit the San Bernardino National Forest and northeastern red spruce, there are other instances of dead and dying trees that cannot be explained by natural processes:

- Surveys begun during 1983 on Mt. Mitchell in North Carolina and five other southern Appalachian peaks show that the growth of red spruce and, to a lesser extent, Fraser fir fell markedly at elevations over 6,300 feet beginning in the early 1960s. By 1987 almost half the red spruce and Fraser fir on Mt. Mitchell's west-facing slopes (the windward side) were dead.
- Tennessee, Virginia, and North Carolina contain 66,000 acres of spruce-fir forests. On a quarter of this land, more than 70 percent of the standing trees are dead.
- Throughout the Piedmont and mountain areas of the Southeast, the radial growth rates of most yellow pines under 16 inches in diameter have dropped by 30 to 50 percent over the past 30 years. The mortality rate has increased from 9 percent a year in 1975 to 15 percent in 1985.

Reading 37
Air Pollution's Toll on Trees and Crops

- White pines throughout the eastern United States have been deteriorating for several decades. They grow less in both height and diameter, and have shorter needles that die at the tips.
- In the Northeast, sugar maple, yellow birch, American beech, white ash, white spruce, and balsam fir are also showing symptoms of decline.

At some high-elevation sites, trees have been declining for almost 30 years; at others, symptoms have developed only within the past decade. What all these sites have in common, however, is that they are subject to high levels of air pollution. Most sites have much higher than average concentrations of ozone, which forms when nitrogen oxides and hydrocarbons (both produced when fossil fuels are burned in power plants, industrial boilers, and vehicles) undergo photochemical reactions in the air. The San Bernardino National Forest, for example, lies 75 miles east of the ozone-fraught Los Angeles basin. And in the high-elevation Appalachian sites where red spruce and Fraser fir are declining, ozone levels average twice those of lower neighboring elevations. This is because the ozone concentrations, for reasons not fully understood, do not fall at night as they do at lower elevations.

Acid deposition is also high at many sites, especially in eastern mountains, where forests may be covered in acidic fogs and clouds for up to 3,000 hours each year. The acids in question—nitric acid and sulfuric acid—form in the atmosphere from emissions of nitrogen oxides and another by-product of combustion, sulfur dioxide. They are carried to earth not only by clouds, fogs, and rain but also by dry deposition, in which gases and acid particles settle out of the air.

Cloud samples taken on Mt. Mitchell during 1986 showed a *p*H varying from 5.4 (slightly acidic) to as low as 2.2 (about the same as vinegar), with a mean *p*H of 3.4. The minimum, or most acidic, *p*H for two other eastern mountains was similar: Whiteface Mountain, in New York, 2.8; and Whitetop Mountain, in Virginia, 2.6. The rate of sulfate deposition on Virginia's Whitetop Mountain was about 10 times that of lower elevations from April through December of 1986. Similarly, annual hydrogen ion deposition—a direct measure of acidity—is roughly 10 times as high on Mt. Mitchell as at lower elevations.

DAMAGING EVIDENCE

Of course, it's one thing to note that ozone and acid precipitation are present where trees are dying or being injured, but quite another to prove that these pollutants are contributing to the damage. In many cases the immediate cause of the decline is a natural stress such as winter

Chapter XII
Population and Ecological Problems

cold, insects, or disease. In other cases, such as the declines in the San Bernardino mountains, the symptoms do not match those of any natural affliction. The present understanding is that these declines result from multiple stresses, with air pollution playing an important—and sometimes essential—role.

Various studies have shown that the levels of pollution at the affected sites can indeed weaken trees, causing nutrient imbalances and lowering the rate of photosynthesis. In the early 1950s, when damaged needles first appeared on San Bernardino's ponderosa pine, scientists enclosed some of the affected branches in chambers. They then fumigated the branches with the surrounding ozone-rich air, with filtered air, or with filtered air plus measured amounts of ozone. The branches in the filtered air improved, while the others continued to deteriorate. These and later fumigation experiments confirmed that ozone was causing the damage.

Subsequent research has shown that ozone enters the pores of leaves and needles. It damages the membranes of cells that contain chlorophyll, leading to reduced levels of photosynthesis and thus inhibiting growth. In addition, preliminary findings by scientists at the Boyce Thompson Institute in Ithaca, N.Y., suggest that ozone interferes with winter hardening of red spruce, making them more vulnerable to extreme cold.

Investigators have also identified a number of mechanisms by which acid deposition directly and indirectly injures trees. On Mt. Mitchell, for example, recent experiments with red spruce by Robert Bruck and his colleagues from North Carolina State University have shown that acid deposition can damage the wax plugs in the pores of needles. Since these plugs are believed to minimize water loss in the plant and help in the exchange of gases, such injury can retard growth. The same researchers have shown that acid leaches nutrients from foliage. Rainwater dripping off spruce needles on Mt. Mitchell contained a lot more magnesium, calcium, potassium, and sodium than rainwater that missed the trees. Leaching by acids is especially severe when ozone levels are also high.

More threatening than direct damage to foliage are the many indirect changes that acids can bring about by altering soils. First, acid deposition can leach important nutrients out of the soil, replacing them with hydrogen ions and acidifying the soil in the process. Trees growing on such soil may suffer nutrient imbalances that lead to decline.

Second, high levels of acid deposition can release aluminum from minerals in the soil. Aluminum ions damage the fine roots of trees and block the uptake of calcium and magnesium. George Tomlinson, a tree chemist with Domtar Research Centre in Quebec, and Walter Shortle and Kevin Smith, of the U.S. Forest Service, have observed this blocking effect in the Northeast. High levels of aluminum can also impede the flow of water within the tree, increasing its sensitivity to drought.

Finally, because of its nitric-acid component, acid precipitation can overload forest ecosystems with nitrogen. By one recent estimate, seven times as much nitrogen is deposited at a high-elevation New Hampshire site as at low elevations. Nitrogen is a vital fertilizer, but if the soil is lacking in other nutrients, the growth spurred by an overdose of nitrogen can lead to nutrient imbalances. Too much nitrogen can also make a tree more susceptible to freezing or drying out in winter.

Of course, not all these mechanisms will apply at any one site. Moreover, the actual rate at which leaching occurs—and the amount of damage it causes—depends on the condition of the soil, the amount of acid that is deposited, and other factors.

So far, the declines have hit only those forests with very high pollution levels. Nevertheless, it's possible that the damage could eventually spread to less polluted areas. If it turns out that lower levels of acid deposition lead to significant nutrient leaching, the same injuries could result over a long period as result from higher levels over a short period. Thus, it may be only a matter of time before forest declines in the United States become as serious as those in West Germany, where trees of all important species at all elevations are showing signs of damage. Indeed, a team from Oak Ridge National Laboratory that studied the soil chemistry of forests in 1986 found that 41 percent of eastern soils are susceptible to substantial nutrient leaching and thus to forest decline.

INJURED CROPS

It's hard to put a dollar value on the trees that are now declining, since most are on state or federal land. But the economic losses that air pollution causes to crops have been estimated as part of the Environmental Protection Agency's National Crop Loss Assessment Network (NCLAN), a program that ended in 1987. According to Walter Heck, of the Department of Agriculture's Air Quality Research Program, who chaired NCLAN's research committee, cutting ozone levels by 50 percent would increase yields for four major crops—soybeans, corn, wheat, and peanuts—by up to $5 billion. Overall, ozone from burning fuel is estimated to reduce crop yields by 5 to 10 percent.

Unlike forests, crops appear to suffer little or no damage from existing levels of acid deposition. Agricultural soils are well fertilized, so crops can readily replace the nutrients they may lose through leaching. But ozone is not so easily countered.

As with trees, ozone enters crops through the microscopic pores on

Chapter XII
Population and Ecological Problems

the leaves and attacks cell membranes inside the plant. If the amount of ozone in the air is small enough, plants can generally detoxify the gas or repair the damage. But the prevailing level of ozone during the growing season in most U.S. agricultural regions is double the background level. At this concentration, many plants cannot repair cell damage fast enough. The effects include yellowing, tissue death, reduced growth, decreased yield or crop quality, and greater susceptibility to stress.

In contrast to forest declines, which so far have been confined to scattered sites, the losses in crop productivity are pervasive. Various economic analysts estimate that in each of 13 states the losses exceed $100 million a year.

TURNING THE TIDE

Air pollution is already taking a heavy toll on America's forests and crops. And the toll will rise unless more is done to curb emissions. Under current regulations, nitrogen-oxide pollution from power plants is expected to double by 2030. Over the same period, nitrogen oxides from transportation, industry, residential and commercial heating, and waste incineration are likely to increase by 30 percent, and hydrocarbon emissions by 25 percent. By 2010, emissions of sulfur dioxide are expected to be no lower, and perhaps slightly higher, than they are today.

Fortunately, there is much that we as a nation can do to turn the tide. And many of the steps we take to improve the air for crops and forests will reduce ill effects on human health and global climate. In lessening the threat to one domain, we will also lessen the threat to others.

A good place to start is with more effective legislation for reducing emissions of sulfur dioxide and nitrogen oxides. In 1970 and 1977, when the last two important amendments to the Clean Air Act were passed, scientists knew much less about how pollutants form, travel, and interact, and thus did not foresee the large-scale problems of acid deposition and high rural ozone levels. Legislators also failed to anticipate how fast the number of pollutant sources would grow. The act therefore focused on limiting emissions from individual vehicles, power plants, and factories. This approach at first led to a significant drop in emissions, but it still allowed the nation's total emissions to increase.

New legislation should impose state or regional caps on the release of sulfur and nitrogen. To decrease sulfur-dioxide pollution (80 percent of which comes from power plants and industrial processes), the act should require a 50 percent reduction in such emissions—to 10 million tons a year—over a period of, say, 10 years. This goal is consistent with the National Academy of Sciences' conclusion that cutting acid deposi-

Reading 37
Air Pollution's Toll on Trees and Crops

tion in half would probably protect sensitive aquatic life. It would also go a long way toward safeguarding trees and crops.

Each state should then be permitted to choose among various options for meeting the new goal as cost-effectively as possible. A state could encourage its coal-burning power plants to convert to "clean-coal" technologies (such as fluidized-bed combustion) or to switch from one fuel to another—say, from coal to natural gas. Or a state could trade emissions, both among sources within its borders and with neighboring states. For example, if a power plant in one state could convert to clean coal more cheaply than a nearby plant in a second state, the first might offer to convert its plant in exchange for some concession from the second.

A state might also encourage the use of more efficient appliances, lighting, and other equipment, to reduce the need for electricity. According to a study of seven east-central states, such conservation measures could cut power consumption during the 1990s by 26 percent from projected levels and sulfur-dioxide emissions by 7 to 11 percent.

Nitrogen-oxide emissions (of which the main source is motor vehicles) can be reduced in much the same way. A reasonable goal would be to cut annual emissions by 5 million tons over the next decade—a 25 percent reduction from 1986 levels but a much larger reduction from projected growth. This goal can be reached through a combination of stricter emission limits for cars, buses, and trucks; strengthened inspection and maintenance; and stronger measures to prevent tampering with pollution-control equipment. The use of cleaner fuels, such as compressed natural gas, in commercial fleets and urban buses would also be beneficial.

A number of other straightforward measures could reduce pollution by cutting the total number of vehicle miles traveled. For example, cities could encourage greater use of public transit, reserve parking spaces for car pools, remove subsidies for other spaces, and designate more traffic lanes for car pools and bicycles.

To raise fuel efficiency, and thereby lower pollution levels, federal and state governments could increase fuel taxes, as well as tax new vehicles according to their gas mileage. (Annual registration fees could also vary this way.) In addition, governments might buy mostly ultra-efficient vehicles for their own fleets.

These and other measures for cutting emissions would lessen the damage to trees and crops and reduce threats to public health. Yet two serious fuel-related problems would remain: growing U.S. reliance on foreign oil and the steady increase in global warming. In principle, the nation could solve the first problem by converting to coal, which is abun-

Chapter XII
Population and Ecological Problems

dant and which could be turned into methanol (to replace gasoline) or synthetic crude oil. But this would aggravate the second problem. The burning of fossil fuels, especially coal, releases vast amounts of carbon dioxide that contribute to greenhouse warming. The only way to protect natural resources *and* contain oil imports *and* slow global climate change is to burn much less fossil fuel.

Thus, at the same time it is working to curb emissions, the United States should be preparing itself for the inevitable shift to nonfossil energy sources. The renewable-energy technologies—solar cells, wind turbines, hydropower, geothermal energy—are strong candidates to assume the burden of future power production. "Second-generation" nuclear technologies (small, inherently safe fission reactors) offer another, though less certain, option. In the long term, transporation is also due for some profound changes, perhaps a switch to electric or hydrogen-powered cars, with the electricity or hydrogen ultimately derived from nonfossil sources.

These technologies will require considerable R&D, and probably major government initiatives, before they can be applied on a grand scale. But once they are in place, nonfossil technologies will alleviate a whole range of national problems—not just tree and crop damage but urban air pollution, climate change, and dependency on foreign oil as well.

Reading 38

WHITHER WATER? THE FRAGILE FUTURE OF THE WORLD'S MOST IMPORTANT RESOURCE

Bruce K. Ferguson

> *Water appears to be an endlessly renewable resource, but it is in finite supply. Each city-dweller uses 150–200 gallons of water a day, and growing our national food supply uses 110 billion gallons per day. Eventually we may have to recycle seawater and sewage to fill our need for water.*

Although water appears to be a vast renewable resource, its future is troubled by the same problem that plagues so many other natural resources—a growing population making demands on a finite supply.

The flow of water is not increasing in proportion to population growth. Nature's rate of cycling water through the ecosystem sets a fixed limit on the amount of water that can be diverted from natural flows for human use. In many regions that limit is rapidly being approached.

Yet water is perhaps man's most important resource. It is the major agent for such necessary tasks as cooling, cleaning, cooking, firefighting, and transporting urban wastes. Heavy industries such as steel mills and power plants account for about 85 percent of the nonagricultural water consumption in the United States. Manufacturing just one ton of nitrate fertilizer requires 600 tons of water.

But even after industrial use is subtracted, the consumption of water in U.S. cities is still in the astounding range of 150 to 200 gallons per person per day. For a city of one million persons, this amounts to 625,000 tons per day—54 times the daily urban input of food and fuel combined.

The human body itself is, by weight, 70 percent water. It can be visualized as a giant plastic bag of warm water, holding about 15 gallons in addition to a few pounds of chemicals and structural materials. Every

---

Reprinted with permission from *The Futurist*, published by the World Future Society, 4916 St.Elmo Avenue, Bethesda, MD.

Chapter XII
Population and Ecological Problems

day, a person consumes another five pounds of water—more than any other substance.

Feeding the human body requires prodigious amounts of water. The irrigation systems on the 30 million irrigated acres in the United States require 110 billion gallons a day. A ton of sugar or corn, grown under irrigated conditions, requires 1,000 tons of water, and a ton of rice requires 4,000 tons of water.

But in the United States, the irrigated acreage is only a small percentage of all the land used for farming, grazing, and forestry. Growth on unirrigated lands accounts for a total of water usage many times that of the irrigated areas. For example, one acre of a typical unirrigated Pennsylvania forest uses 400 tons of water each month during the growing season. Water accounts for about 50 percent of the weight of each tree in the forest.

THE WATER CYCLE

The flow of water starts with rain and snow falling from the air to earth. Most of the water soaks into the soil, and eventually as much as half gradually goes back into the atmosphere through transpiration from the leaves of plants.

The rest of the water flows into the drainage system. Some of it becomes the flow of major rivers; some of it is stored in lakes, glaciers, and polar ice caps; and some of it soaks further down into the earth, becoming part of vast underground reservoirs in the pores and fractures of bedrock. Eventually all the water ends up in the sea, where it can evaporate into the air to start the cycle again.

When man uses water, he diverts one of these natural flows by dipping into rivers, lakes, or groundwater aquifers. Pumps and aqueducts carry this water to cities, industries, and irrigated farms. The amount of water available depends ultimately on the amount of precipitation in the watershed, which will remain fixed by nature until man achieves some sort of radical control over global weather patterns—and that control seems to be only a remote possibility.

In many areas, man's withdrawals from the watersheds now exceed nature's deposits. The problem is clearly illustrated by the depletion of the Ogallala Aquifer, which stretches from Nebraska to Texas in the U.S. High Plains. The 225,000 square miles of land overlying the aquifer comprise one of the nation's richest agricultural regions, supplying 25 percent of the nation's cotton, 38 percent of the grain sorghum, 16 percent of the wheat, and 13 percent of the corn. Forty percent of the nation's grain-fed beef is fattened there.

*Reading 38
Fragile Future of Water*

The irrigation water for all these crops comes from wells that draw water up from the aquifer, with water use increasing as farmers exploit their land more intensively. Sophisticated center-pivot irrigation devices are being installed in increasing numbers, each one spraying nearly 1.2 million gallons per day.

Although precipitation replaces some of the groundwater withdrawals, the rate of pumping exceeds the rate of replacement. Most of the water in the aquifer was deposited in a previous geologic era by the melting of receding Ice Age glaciers. Today's withdrawals therefore amount to "mining" a nonrenewable resource. So much water is being drawn from the Ogallala that the water level is falling three feet a year in some places. The farmers, who have begun to dig wells deeper into the aquifer and use more powerful pumps, are competing with each other for a limited amount of water, and are draining the water level down faster and faster in the process.

The whole region is headed for the day when the wells will run dry; researchers say that at the current rate of withdrawal the entire supply will be gone in 40 years. Before that time comes, however, many farmers may stop irrigating because of the high cost of energy to pump water from a declining water table.

Excessive withdrawals also deplete the flow of rivers, such as the Monongahela in Pittsburgh. The Monongahela is lined with the nation's greatest complex of steel mills, which use huge volumes of water. The river, crowded with barges carrying crucial supplies of coal, coke, and slag among mines and mills, conveys a greater annual tonnage than the Panama Canal. The steel companies want to divert more river water to expand their operations, but the barge navigation system requires a minimum depth of nine feet. In the early part of this century, the U.S. Army Corps of Engineers built a system of dams and locks to assure that depth. If the mills withdraw more of the water, the level will go down and the mills will lose their source of raw materials.

Meanwhile, the public is counting on a certain flow of river water to dilute industrial pollution. The steel companies are in a quandary. The economic growth of the whole region is being held back by the finite flow of river water. It may be that the capacity of the Monongahela watershed to support the development of heavy industry has already been reached.

The competition for water is aggravated in fast-growing regions such as the Sunbelt and the Rocky Mountain states, particularly in areas with low rainfall. Los Angeles, located in a desert region, has extended great aqueducts up to 444 miles, diverting water from every watershed between the Sacramento River in California and the Colorado River in Arizona. The competition for water among numerous cities and

Chapter XII
Population and Ecological Problems

irrigated-farming interests in the arid Southwest will require acts of Congress to resolve.

Even in water-rich Pennsylvania, the state legislature is considering a law to establish governmental allocation of water among competing users. New York City long ago completed a huge system of aqueducts that brings water from reservoirs in the mountains of the Delaware River Basin; because the city is fortunate in being located in a relatively humid region, its aqueducts extend to a radius of only 120 miles.

RECAPTURING THE RAIN

Ironically, while cities import water from distant reservoirs, they deliberately shunt away *all* of the rain that falls directly on them. Roofs, roads, parking lots, and sidewalks are all made of impermeable asphalt and concrete. When rain falls on them, over 90 percent is concentrated in gutters and drains and carried away quickly into lakes and streams.

If you could stand next to a river in a typical urbanizing area for several years, watching the changes as the surrounding area develops, here is what you would see: Each year the flooding of the river is higher and more frequent, because rainwater that used to soak gradually into the soil now runs directly into streams. Land and buildings near the river are damaged. The increased flooding causes shore erosion, and the resulting sediment gradually turns the water a muddy brown. Fish in the river lose their habitat and die. The groundwater table goes down because it is not replenished by natural infiltration. And since groundwater is the only source of river flow between storms, the river is actually lower during the periods of "base flow" between floods. Both groundwater and river water become less suitable as potential water supplies.

Necessity is forcing some areas to find ways to recapture their rainwater. Long Island is one such region. Separated from the Connecticut mainland by Long Island Sound, it cannot count on inland mountain reservoirs for its water, as does nearby New York City. Even if a supply pipe were laid across the Sound, Long Island would find no water to carry: all the available mainland water is already being used up by the heavily populated mainland communities. With a rapidly growing population, Long Island is stuck with just one source of fresh water—the groundwater below its surface.

Geologically, Long Island can be visualized as a bathtub full of sand, with the pores between the grains of sand filled with fresh water. The pores remain filled with water, available for pumping, only as long as the rain that falls on the island soaks down through the soil into the groundwater aquifer.

To prevent sprawling urban development from shunting the rainwater off into the sea, Long Island's county governments now require developers to build "recharge basins"—depressions in the earth where storm water from streets, driveways, and downspouts is directed. The water then soaks down into the soil, "recharging" the water in the sand aquifer.

If you were to stand next to one of Long Island's streams for several years, you would not witness the impacts suffered by a typical urbanizing area. Instead, Long Island's rainwater completes a natural cycle by perpetually replacing the water drawn out of the underlying sand. The island's water supply is assured as long as the population doesn't outgrow the replacement rate of the rainfall and as long as sewage and toxic wastes do not contaminate the groundwater.

A solution to a more acute problem of rainwater loss is found on another island, Bermuda, where the water supply is even more scarce than on Long Island. In Bermuda, every community has two completely separate water supply systems. One is a salt water system, taken directly from the ocean, which is used for flushing toilets and other purposes where the salinity is unimportant. The other system supplies fresh water, used for drinking and cooking. The fresh water is collected into cisterns from rainfall on roofs and is purified before use. Each house has its own cistern and fresh water supply. During droughts, a community water tank truck periodically refills everyone's cistern. Systems as miserly as Bermuda's are rare so far, but as populations grow and the amount of rain does not, they are likely to become more common.

Even in regions where the water supply is not such a critical issue, storm water control techniques can provide substantial benefits. Land-use planners are encouraging developers to let storm water flow into grassy roadside swales rather than channel it into gutters and drains. This method allows the water to spread out, slow down, and soak into the soil. For example, at The Woodlands, a community near Houston, developer John Mitchell and land planner Ian McHarg have created a whole 25,000-acre system of swales and ponds where water flows gradually across the land, soaking into the soil and supporting the moisture-starved oak and pine forests.

SALVAGING SEWAGE

An even greater irony than their shunting off rainfall is that cities deliberately pump *away* almost as much water, in the form of waste water and sewage, as they pump *in* each day. The major output of an American city's metabolism is water and water-borne wastes. In a city of a million persons, the daily 625,000 tons of water input becomes 500,000 tons of sewage, the residual 125,000 tons having been permanently consumed or lost. Public sewerage systems serve 150 million Americans and collect a total of 750,000 tons of waste water each day.

Chapter XII
Population and Ecological Problems

Major sewage pollution arises where, due to floods, poor maintenance, or lack of funding for adequate construction, sewage collected by one of those public systems is discharged into a lake or river without complete treatment. In the smaller towns and suburbs, the essentially untreated wastes of 70 million Americans are being piped into private backyard cesspools and septic tanks where they may contaminate groundwater supplies.

Recycling treated sewage by land application could alleviate some of this problem. At University Park, Pennsylvania, treated sewage is piped to an area of fields and woods that overlies the major limestone aquifer for the region. The liquid sewage is sprayed out over the soil. As the water seeps down, the soil filters out the potential groundwater pollutants. These same potential pollutants then act as fertilizers for feed and timber crops. The water soaks on down into the aquifer, maintaining the water level in the region's major source of water.

Fully implemented, waste-water recycling may lead to a whole new kind of American community. A community that recycles its waste water will incorporate an open area of farms and forests in addition to the conventional residential, commercial, and industrial areas. Treated waste water will be recycled on the open land.

Unlike conventional contemporary land developments, the new type of community will be a hybrid of urban and rural components. If the community is properly planned, it can preserve prime agricultural land from urban development. The water and nutrients from the community's recycled waste would then help to support the growth of crops while the excess water would seep into the soil, replacing groundwater withdrawals.

The water shortage problem can only be met by creating a linkage among water supply, sewage disposal, and storm-water control. At present, these basic components of water management are typically handled separately, as if water were an unlimited resource whose use did not require much foresight.

But man's biological need for water will never go away—and nature's rate of supply of water in each region is not likely to expand. As the population grows, the need for sophisticated water conservation and recycling systems will increase. Someday we will become used to water shortages, just as we are already used to energy shortages. Just as we have had to wait in line for gas, someday we could turn on the water faucet and wait in vain for a drop to appear.

We need to conceive of water as a complex resource, with all of its parts interconnected, so that we will build our homes and our cities with foresight for the natural resources that sustain us.

CHAPTER XIII

WORK AND TECHNOLOGY

Reading 39
LIVING DANGEROUSLY

Abigail Trafford, Andrea Gabor

> *The history of the "rocky road of progress" is made up of apparent technological wonders that turned out to be techno-threats, or outright disasters. The agencies that are supposed to assess future risks of proposed developments have not been successful, and we all better try to understand what is happening. The first step is to reduce our arrogant technological overconfidence.*

Technology was supposed to solve problems, not cause them. To free mankind, not hurt the innocent. But in the span of a few months, the dark side of technology has asserted itself.

Experts still don't know what went wrong at Chernobyl on April 26. More than two weeks later, as small amounts of radiation were settling over parts of the U.S., there was uncertainty over how much the reactor core had melted.

On the frontier of space, the worst series of rocket mishaps in U.S. history has shaken the country's confidence. Not only was the crew of Challenger lost, but in recent weeks, two other spacecraft have exploded and a research rocket misfired. Now a slew of scheduled flights have been grounded, and across America the question is being asked: Why so many disasters? What is happening to the technological fix?

According to a new *USN&WR*-Cable News Network poll, the vast majority of Americans still say that science and technology do more good than harm, but the margin has fallen from 83 percent three years ago to 72 percent today. What's more, nearly a quarter of those surveyed think that over the next 20 years, technology will cause more harm than good for the human race.

The chief source of high-tech anxiety today is nuclear power. In a kind of post-Chernobyl referendum, three Massachusetts towns voted on May 6 against opening the Seabrook, N.H., nuclear power plant, not far from the state line.

Copyright ©, May 19, 1986, *U.S. News & World Report*.

Chapter XIII
Work and Technology

At the same time, there is little chance of the nation's turning its back on new technologies. "We have chosen a life-style dependent on high technology," says management consultant John Ketteringham of the Arthur D. Little firm in Cambridge, Mass. "To revert to low-tech solutions, we have to be prepared to die young of cold, disease and hunger."

WHAT'S GONE WRONG

Often, major technological disasters occur after bureaucrats take over from scientific pioneers. Then, complacency sets in, or commercial needs are allowed to dominate.

Both these factors took hold of the National Aeronautics and Space Administration in the mid-1970s. Lulled by the exemplary safety record of the lunar flights and pared down by budget cuts, the agency tried to transform itself from a high-tech research operation into a commercial venture.

According to a recent congressional disclosure, a NASA budget squeeze over the last 15 years eliminated 70 percent of engineers who monitor the quality of equipment used for space flight. Although a 1979 memo characterized the seals on the solid-fuel rocket boosters—the main culprit in the Challenger accident—as "completely unacceptable," the space agency stuck to its design.

Critics charge that NASA treated the shuttle as a "space bus" instead of an experimental test vehicle. Teacher Christa McAuliffe was included in the crew even though an Air Force report had recently rated the chances of a fatal accident on the shuttle at 1 in 35—compared with 1 in 10,000 for a nuclear disaster or a dam failure. And more ominous for the general public is the fact that the next shuttle was to carry deadly plutonium as fuel for two space probes—a potential source of lethal radioactivity should a crash occur.

More than space flight, nuclear power is a "mature" technology that has moved from the laboratory into the commercial arena. Yet in the past 15 years, 151 "significant" incidents have been reported in nuclear plants in 14 countries.

"When things become routine, we become very sloppy," explains physicist Frank von Hipple of Princeton University. "The first team of the Nuclear Age has moved on, and now we are trying to contain a technology that we can't handle on a routine basis."

Another unique requirement of managing complex technologies, such as nuclear power and space flight, is a tricky balance of power. According to Charles Perrow, a Yale professor and author of *Normal Accidents*, both managers and technicians must retain enough control to make split-second decisions at the first sign of trouble.

Reading 39
Risks of New Technologies

At Chernobyl and Three Mile Island, the combination of "several highly improbable and therefore unforeseen failures" as the Soviet Union's Deputy Prime Minister Boris Y. Shcherbina puts it, led operators to lose control of conditions in the plants. The problems were compounded by management's failure to respond quickly. At Chernobyl, hundreds of lives may eventually be lost because authorities failed to evacuate the nearby population for 36 hours.

In contrast, Perrow argues that the airline industry "became the best example of a near-error-free technology" when it successfully balanced the central control of air-traffic controllers with the local control of pilots.

TECHNOLOGIES AT RISK

The proliferation of technologies has widened the scope of risk exponentially. With more people flying than ever before, for example, air-traffic safety—despite its former record—is a growing concern. A 33 percent drop in the number of qualified air-traffic controllers has led the independent Flight Safety Foundation to conclude that standards have slipped since 1981, when 11,400 controllers were fired after a strike. All this adds up to what retired airline captain Richard Ortman, director of airline training at Purdue University, calls a lot of "thrashing around up there."

More than 2,000 people were killed on scheduled and chartered flights worldwide last year. On large planes in the U.S. alone, the toll was 526 people, the worst since 1977, when 655 died.

In the past few years, the Federal Aviation Administration (FAA) has stepped up enforcement of airline-maintenance regulations. Last year, the agency slapped carriers with $2.8 million in fines, up from only $298,245 in 1984.

But the agency continually assures the public of aviation safety. "When you consider the numbers we deal with," says Anthony Broderick, the FAA's associate administrator for aviation standards, "the safety record is mind-boggling." Furthermore, a $12 billion modernization of the air-traffic-control system is also under way to increase the amount of traffic that controllers can safely handle.

The chemical industry is another area of worry. Only 18 months ago, a leak at a Union Carbide plant in Bhopal, India, killed more than 2,000 people and injured many thousands. Then, at Union Carbide's plant in Institute, W. Va., a leak last August of the same chemical released in the Bhopal accident—lethal methyl-isocyanate gas—sent six workers and 134 residents to hospital emergency rooms. The Occupational Safety and Health Administration charged Union Carbide with 221 safety violations at the Institute plant—a penalty the company is appealing.

Chapter XIII
Work and Technology

MILESTONES ON THE ROCKY ROAD OF PROGRESS

1945 The Atomic Age opens with the mushroom explosion of the first test bomb over the desert skies near Alamogordo, N.M.

1947 The transistor is invented at Bell Laboratories in New Jersey, paving the way for the computer revolution.

1951 The first electric power from a nuclear reactor is produced at the National Reactor Testing Station in Arco, Idaho, heralding the era of nuclear energy.

1953 The chemical structure of genes is revealed by James Watson and Francis Crick at Cambridge University, opening the way for today's biotechnology boom.

1954 The Salk vaccine against polio is tested on nearly a million children, offering the first largely effective protection against the paralyzing disease.

1957 The U.S.S.R. launches Sputnik 1, signaling the dawn of the Space Age.

1958 An accident at a plutonium weapons facility near Sverdlovsk, in the Soviet Urals, contaminates 1,500 square kilometers with radioactive debris.

1959 A patent for the first integrated circuit is filed by Jack Kilby of Texas Instruments, leading to the development of the revolutionary "computer on a chip."

1960 The laser is invented by Theodore Maiman of Hughes Research Laboratories, in California, leading to the creation of new tools for medicine, industry and the military.

1961 Soviet cosmonaut Yuri Gagarin because the first human in space, orbiting the earth in his Vostok 1 satellite for 108 minutes.

• Thalidomide is banned in West Germany and Britain after more than 2,500 deformed babies are born to European women who took the drug during pregnancy.

1967 The three-man crew of what was to have been the first Apollo flight is killed by a fire that erupts during prelaunch tests.

1969 American astronaut Neil Armstrong takes man's first step on the moon.

Continued

The dangers of a chemical accident are not confined to plants. Hundreds of mishaps occur annually in the storage and transport of hazardous chemicals. In a study made after the Bhopal disaster, the Environmental Protection Agency (EPA) found that between 1980 and 1985, 135 people died and 4,717 were injured in chemical accidents—with roughly a quarter of the accidents involving transport of lethal com-

Reading 39
Risks of New Technologies

MILESTONES ON THE ROCKY ROAD OF PROGRESS

1971 Soviet three-man crew aboard Soyuz 11 perishes when the spacecraft's cabin decompresses upon re-entry.

1973 The first genetically engineered organism is created by California researchers Stanley Cohen and Herbert Boyer, opening a new age of made-to-order microbes and plants for medicine, agriculture, energy production and the chemical industry.

1976 An explosion at a Swiss-owned chemical plant near Milan throws into the open air a cloud of the highly toxic gas dioxin. Tens of thousands of birds and animals perish, and more than 500 children develop skin rashes.

1978 First test-tube baby, Louise Brown, is delivered by Caesarean section in Oldham, England, by doctors Patrick Steptoe and Robert Edwards.

• Residents of the Love Canal section of Niagara Falls learn that their neighborhood was a dumping ground for about 21,000 tons of toxic waste in the 1940s and 1950s. Alarmed by studies pointing to high rates of cancer and other illnesses in the community, more than 2,000 residents leave their homes in the next three years. In 1980, Love Canal is declared a federal emergency area.

1979 A near-disastrous accident in the nuclear reactor at Three Mile Island, near Harrisburg, Pa., releases a cloud of low-level radioactive gas into the environment.

1981 U.S. space shuttle Columbia makes first orbital test flight, ushering in the era of the re-usable "space plane."

1984 A chemical storage tank explodes at a Union Carbide Plant in Bhopal, India, releasing a cloud of lethal methyl-isocyanate gas. More than 2,000 people are killed, and the number of injured...total tens of thousands.

1986 U.S. space shuttle Challenger blows up only moments after takeoff, killing the crew of seven, including the first teacher in space. Within weeks, three more rockets misfire, effectively grounding the U.S. space program.

• Fire burns through the core of a Soviet nuclear reactor at Chernobyl, spewing lethal radioactive debris over the Ukraine, other parts of the U.S.S.R. and Europe.

---

pounds. Barges that carry dangerous materials, including uranium, have a stunning accident rate worldwide of 1 per day.

Since the Bhopal incident, many companies have become more cautious. Monsanto, for example, has cut its inventory of hazardous chemicals by about 50 percent and increasingly uses ultrasound devices to detect ruptures in steel storage tanks.

Chapter XIII
Work and Technology

Still, the skill of those handling dangerous chemicals is a vexing issue. "I'm not terribly confident about our ability to manage these facilities," says John Henningson, a water-pollution-control expert and vice president of Malcolm-Pirnie, Inc., in New Jersey. "I've always been comfortable with the technologies but not the personnel running them."

Nowhere is the worry so deep as over the handling of the government's arsenal of nuclear weapons.

One concern is the nightmare scenario—dramatized in the 1983 movie "WarGames"—in which the U.S. receives a false warning of an attack by Soviet missiles and nearly sets off World War III with a counterattack. Occasional false alarms have gone off, but there have been no serious responses on the part of the U.S.

Recently, concern has shifted to the military's development of chemical and biological weapons. In 1968, some 6,400 sheep perished mysteriously after the Army secretly tested deadly chemical agents at the Dugway Proving Grounds in Utah. Eleven years later, 45 people near Richmond, Ky., were hospitalized after a toxic cloud formed over the Lexington-Bluegrass Army Depot when the Army tried to destroy some old canisters of nerve gas. Chemical weapons are stored in nine military facilities. The debate over safety is heating up because of Defense Department plans to develop new chemical weapons and destroy its World War II nerve-gas arsenal.

The newest technology with risks potentially as great as those of nuclear energy is genetic engineering. Late this month, the EPA is expected to allow a breakthrough experiment—the outdoor testing of bioengineered bacteria that prevent frost from forming on certain plants.

Biotechnology promises a range of miracle products from drugs for acquired-immune-deficiency syndrome to heartier plants. But critics charge that the risks associated with releasing genetically manipulated organisms into the atmosphere have not been clearly established. "These genetically engineered microbes are alive and are inherently unpredictable," charges leading biotech critic Jeremy Rifkin. "Unlike chemicals, they reproduce, migrate, grow. If something goes wrong, you can't recall them, seal them up, clean them up or do anything about them."

History shows that major accidents often lead to tighter regulations and improved safety standards. Roughly half of the safety standards for nuclear power plants were instituted after the Three Mile Island accident. In the space program, a fire in 1967 that swept through the Apollo spacecraft on a launching-pad ground test, killing three astronauts, led to a complete overhaul of NASA and redesign of the spacecraft—action that many engineers say ultimately guaranteed the lunar program's success.

To keep risks within acceptable bounds, some argue that new ways

Reading 39
Risks of New Technologies

are needed to regulate the sophisticated technologies such as biotechnology, artificial intelligence, and "smart" satellites that will dominate the next 20 years. "I think there is serious concern these days about whether we're adequately set up to handle today's technology," says Marc Vaucher, program manager of the Center for Space Policy, Inc.

Government regulators are often caught between insuring public safety and promoting new technology. The National Institutes of Health, for example, funds genetic-engineering research and helps regulate it. The FAA, too, regulates air safety and promotes the industry. The Nuclear Regulatory Commission's predecessor, the Atomic Energy Commission, was often accused of being both advocate and arbiter of nuclear power—and some make the same charge against the NRC today.

Critics say that regulators inevitably experience a conflict of interest that leads to a dimmed vigilance. Contends consultant Joseph Coates, former member of the Congress's Office of Technology Assessment: "We've always gotten ourselves into trouble because administrative bodies have conflicting duties."

Technology advocates insist that overzealous regulation has held back important advances and weakened the nation's competitive position vis-à-vis rivals such as the Japanese. Robert Gale, for example, who was called to the Soviet Union to perform lifesaving bone-marrow transplants on Chernobyl victims, was censured by the University of California at Los Angeles for conducting bone-marrow transplants in 1980 in violation of NIH guidelines.

To help bolster the spread of technology, the Reagan administration has just changed the rules governing the regulation of new technologies. On April 24, it abolished requirements that "worst case" scenarios be considered in the evaluation of potential hazards.

Warns Senator Albert Gore, Jr. (D-Tenn.): "There's a certain hubris in the Technological Age, tempting us to invest our hopes in dramatic new advances. We have to make choices along the way, instead of ducking tough decisions." Indeed, as Chernobyl, Challenger and Bhopal prove, disaster strikes when nations forget that worst-case scenarios can come true.

Reading 40
MANAGEMENT BY STRESS: BEHIND THE SCENES OF NUMMI MOTORS

Mike Parker, Jane Slaughter

> We have all heard various reasons suggested to explain the Japanese managers' secret of successful competition in mass production. Many American companies would be willing to adopt these methods to shape our industrial future. Before they do, they should look closely at the day-to-day experiences of workers in a Japanese-run plant. American managers will have to try to estimate if workers from our individualistic cultural background will adjust to this oppressive production line system.

The General Motors-Toyota assembly plant in Fremont, Calif., has probably been the site of more pilgrimages by eager managers than any other factory in the United States. These managers, from throughout the auto industry and from many other industries, are now trying to apply the lessons of this joint venture—called Nummi, for New United Motors Manufacturing Inc.—in their own factories. At conference after conference, academics, engineers, managers and union leaders extol Nummi's successes. These have become legendary:

- Consistently high quality ratings. According to a 1986 Massachusetts Institute of Technology study, Nummi rated 135 to 140 out of a possible score of 145.
- A massive increase in labor productivity—at least 50 percent higher than other General Motors Corporation plants and almost as high as at a Japanese Toyota plant.

But like other great feats, Nummi's achievements are accompanied by myths. The most important of these is that Nummi is productive because of worker involvement or even worker control. According to the

Copyright © 1988 by *The New York Times* Company. Reprinted by permission.

stories, the team concept used at Nummi encourages workers to use their brains. For the first time, workers have a say in management by planning how to carry out and share their own work. The old authoritarian foreman is replaced by a "group leader," aided by worker "team leaders."

In fact, Nummi has achieved its gains through far greater regimentation of the work force than exists in traditional American auto plants. Tight specifications and monitoring of how jobs are to be done, a bare-bones work force with no replacements for absentees and a systematic and continuing speedup are the methods used.

WORK FORCE CONTROL

We use the term "management by stress" to describe this system, which often goes by the names "team concept" or "synchronous manufacturing." It depends not only on tight control of the work force but also on extensive outside contracting and on organizing all production on a "just-in-time" basis.

Management by stress goes against traditional management notions, at least in the United States. In a traditional system—sometimes called "just in case"—management wants extra parts and extra workers on hand to cover for any glitches that may arise.

Under management by stress, the aim is to methodically locate and remove protections against glitches. Glitches are in fact welcomed because they identify the system's weak points. Breakdowns indicate where a method must be changed, perhaps a way found to perform a particular bottleneck operation more quickly. Just as important, points that never break down are assumed to waste resources. They are targeted as well—human or material resources are removed until the station can keep up, but just barely.

The "andon" board illustrates how management by stress functions. At Nummi and at other Japanese-owned car plants in the United States, a lighted board above the assembly line—called the andon board—shows the status of each work station. When a worker falls behind or needs help, he or she pulls a cord; bells chime and the board lights up. If the cord is not pulled again within a set period of time (say a minute), the line stops.

In a traditional operation, the plant manager would want to see no lights flashing. Not so under management by stress. An unlighted andon board signals inefficiency. Workers are not working as hard as they might. If the system is stressed—by speeding up the line, for example—some workers will fall behind, the lights will flash and management can focus on redesigning those jobs to make them more efficient. The ideal is for the system to run with all stations oscillating between lights on and lights off.

'TAYLORISM' REVISITED

Most glowing accounts of Nummi and other team concept plants contrast their methods to the "scientific management" principles championed by Frederick W. Taylor, the father of time-and-motion study. Former Labor Secretary Ray Marshall, speaking at a recent conference on labor-management cooperation, asserted that Nummi had "done away with Taylorism."

In fact, management by stress is an intensification of Taylorism. Engineers and group and team leaders break the required assembly tasks down into the tiniest of separate "acts" and come up with a detailed written specification of how each worker is to do each job. This chart is posted near the line so the group leader can check to see that the worker does not vary his or her methods. Workers are not allowed to work faster for a short time to create some breathing space—although the jobs are so "loaded" that this is usually not possible anyway. If they discover a method, on their own, that makes the job easier, they must ask the supervisor's permission to use it. The catch, of course, is that another task will be found to fill the time.

Thus no matter how well the workers learn their jobs, there is always room for kaizen, or continuous improvement. At Nummi recently, slow sales caused the company to slow the line speed to reduce inventories of unsold cars. Instead of letting those on the line enjoy the slightly more relaxed pace, some workers were removed from the line and the jobs rebalanced so that the pace was as killing as before. Some of the extra workers were put into kaizen groups to observe their colleagues and make suggestions as to how they could work more efficiently.

This is how management by stress differs from Taylorism. Taylor believed that management's engineers and time-study men could capture workers' knowledge of the production process all at once, after which workers would revert to being nothing but hired hands. Management-by-stress managers understand that workers continue to know more about the actual performance of their jobs than higher management does, and so make the process of appropriating that knowledge a never-ending one.

AN END TO SAFEGUARDS

Under traditional contracts, the amount of work on a job is subject to negotiation between union and management. The union has the right to file grievances over work and health and safety standards and to strike over them during the life of the contract. Management is not allowed to add extra work onto a job once the work standard has been agreed to.

In management-by-stress plants, these safeguards are replaced with a system that supposedly trusts the worker. "Why have all these bureaucratic procedures?" the argument goes. "If the worker is making an honest attempt to keep up but can't, all she has to do is pull the cord."

Of course, pulling the cord that stops the line is only a temporary help at best. It doesn't mean that a worker will be taken off the job, only that the hapless worker will receive immediate attention from the team and group leaders in the vicinity.

The stop cord works well when production has just begun and the bugs are still being worked out. Once production is up to speed, however, any problems are assumed to be the worker's fault. Workers at G.M.'s Van Nuys, Calif., assembly plant complain that management spent most of their early team meetings explaining how rare a stop-the-line situation should be.

Another myth about team concept-/management-by-stress plants is that they want workers who are highly skilled and can exercise judgment in running the highly complex factories of today. In fact, workers often find themselves feeling more like interchangeable parts than before.

Management wants flexibility to respond to the ups and downs of the market quickly. This requires that workers be able to perform many different jobs, and that contractual barriers to the group leader's right to assign workers be abolished. Thus management-by-stress plants break production jobs down into simple actions that require little special training and that can be mastered quickly. Rather than learning a marketable skill, workers become "multiskilled" by learning a series of job-specific tasks that depend mainly on manual dexterity, physical stamina and the willingness to follow instructions precisely.

WORKER ASSIGNMENTS

Related is management's other tool for flexibility—the right to assign workers to any job. Whereas in traditional plants certain workers, usually those with more seniority, could become inspectors, repairers, janitors and material handlers, in management-by-stress plants the assembly line worker is expected to handle these chores in addition to the assigned assembly tasks. One of the workers' biggest complaints about plants where such classifications have been abolished is that "there aren't any good jobs left."

The related complaint is favoritism. Flexibility means that management gets to assign its "pets" to those few "good jobs" that remain instead of using seniority or negotiated work rules. Management also gets to decide which workers get to leave the fast-paced line and serve in the kaizen groups.

All of this results in speed up, not so much by turning up the line speed itself but by giving each worker more tasks to perform. The productivity figures alone give some indication: A 1985 G.M. videotape claimed that Nummi required only 14 hours of direct labor to assemble a Nova, compared with 22 hours to produce a J car in the same plant. But the work is hard and Nummi workers often compare their jobs to eight hours of calisthenics.

SECURITY VS. THREAT

The Nummi system is supposed to provide workers with job security in exchange for management flexibility. But the system maintains a strong sense of insecurity as a primary motivation. Nummi workers and others in team-concept plants accept it mainly because they believe that without it they would have no jobs at all. Management constantly reinforces this fear by suggesting—or in many cases threatening—that if the plant is not run the way management wants, it will be closed.

Most of the auto plants in the United States that have gone as far as Nummi in implementing management-by-stress techniques are Japanese-owned or managed. It is important not to be distracted, however, by these methods' country of origin. Managers eager to reap their productivity benefits are introducing these methods the world over and, under different names, in every industry in America. They do not require the particularities of Japanese culture to work.

A March 1988 conference of rank-and-file auto workers from four continents revealed that these methods are being introduced by Ford, G.M., Mercedes and Volkswagen in plants around the world. The idea, is mistaken, that these methods will enable American industry to beat world competition. No matter how hard management by stress gets workers to work, workers elsewhere will do the same, and for less money. Management by stress may increase profits initially, but at great cost to a humane work environment.

CHAPTER XIV

CONFLICT AND WAR

Reading 41

THE SHATTERED CRYSTAL BALL: HOW MIGHT A NUCLEAR WAR BEGIN?

The Harvard Nuclear Study Group

> *This group of scenarios was created to illustrate the ways in which nuclear events could originate. Many are still quite possible, such as: regional catalytic wars, nuclear terrorism, or a faulty computer chip. Even when the scenarios seem unlikely, however, they show us new ways of thinking about possible future catastrophes. While reading, imagine other social situations in which nuclear problems could arise, and think about ways the conflicts that caused them could have been resolved.*

The question is grisly, but nonetheless it must be asked. Nuclear war cannot be avoided simply by refusing to think about it. Indeed, the task of reducing the likelihood of nuclear war should begin with an effort to understand how it might start.

When strategists in Washington or Moscow study the possible origins of nuclear war, they discuss "scenarios," imagined sequences of future events that could trigger the use of nuclear weaponry. Scenarios are, of course, speculative exercises. They often leave out the political developments that might lead to the use of force in order to focus on military dangers. That nuclear war scenarios are even more speculative than most is something for which we can be thankful, for it reflects humanity's fortunate lack of experience with atomic warfare since 1945. But imaginary as they are, nuclear scenarios can help to identify problems not understood or dangers not yet prevented because they have not been foreseen.

Many commonly held beliefs about the likely origins of nuclear war are, however, misleading. Focusing on less likely ways that nuclear war might occur creates unnecessary worries and enhances the possibility that more probable dangers will be ignored. This chapter presents sev-

---

Reprinted by permission of the publishers from *Living With Nuclear Weapons* (pp. 45–68), Harvard Nuclear Study Group, Cambridge, Mass.: Harvard Univeristy Press, Copyright © 1983 by the Harvard Nuclear Study Group.

Chapter XIV
Conflict and War

eral scenarios—some more likely than others—each a conceivable path to nuclear war. Although examining such horrible events can be frightening, creating fear is not the purpose of the exercise. Rather, constructing scenarios can underline actions already taken to reduce the likelihood of war and also point to actions that can minimize future hazards.

Nuclear war would most probably begin for reasons similar to those which began wars in the past. Governments might see opportunities for quick and easy gains and, misjudging enemy reactions, could take steps toward nuclear war without being fully aware of the risks involved. Governments might, under other circumstances, believe that beginning a war was the lesser of two evils, a plausible belief if the other evil is the enemy striking first. These and many other causes have led to war in the past.

Nuclear war is possible. It could occur through purposeful choice, through miscalculations, or through a variety of accidents. It could be started by a political leader, by a military commander, or by a group of terrorists. It could come as a sudden surprise in a time of peace or as the seemingly inevitable culmination of a prolonged conflict between nuclear armed nations. We chose the following kinds of scenarios (some of which are more plausible than others) to illustrate a gamut of possibilities as well as to explore popular and current concerns: (1) surprise attack by one superpower on all or part of the nuclear forces of the other; (2) pre-emptive attacks launched in desperation in time of crisis because one side believes (rightly or wrongly) that the other intends soon to strike first; (3) escalation of conventional wars to nuclear ones; (4) accidental uses of nuclear weapons resulting from malfunctions of machines or of minds; and (5) nuclear wars initiated by other nuclear armed nations or by terrorist organizations. These categories are not unique; additional scenarios involving elements from two or more categories could easily be constructed. Nor is the list of scenarios exhaustive; not all the possible paths to nuclear war can be foreseen. Murphy's law—which states that if something can go wrong, it will—applies here as in all other human activities: military plans go awry, controls fail, misjudgments occur, and one mistake often seems to lead to another, in peacetime and in war. This should not breed despair; it should serve as a constant reminder of the need to control events so that events do not control us.

SCENARIOS

The Bolt from the Blue

Imagine the following conversation. The date is November 1, 1991; the location, inside the Kremlin.

Reading 41
Ways a Nuclear War Might Begin

General Secretary —:"Comrade General, you have heard the debate. Some members of the Politburo favor your proposal for a surprise attack upon the United States. Others are highly opposed. We await your opinion. Can we go to war and win?"

General —, Chief of Staff, Soviet Rocket Forces: "Yes! If war is to come, it must come soon, or all is lost. The counter-revolution in Eastern Europe has put our back against the wall. The American military buildup continues to threaten our socialist nation.

"But let me explain how we can triumph if we attack quickly, with all our power. The Americans suspect nothing. We have greatly improved our hunter-killer submarine force and now can closely follow all their submarines; our ballistic missile submarines can maintain adequate attack forces off the enemy's coast. In only seven minutes our submarine missiles could destroy American bombers on their runways, the American submarines in the ports, and, as importantly, American military and civilian command centers. Without orders from these command posts, the missiles in the United States will not be immediately launched and will be destroyed when our ICBMs arrive 23 minutes after the submarine missiles land on target.

"We have, of course, supreme confidence in our military strength. But if a small number of America's nuclear missiles and bombers escape destruction from our overwhelming attack, our ballistic missile defense system and our air defense system will shoot them down. We can end the capitalist threat forever. Let us decide now to end this intolerable situation, destroy them before they gain in strength and threaten us even more."

General Secretary —: "Thank you, Comrades, the day of destiny may be upon us. How do you vote?"

Is this scenario possible? Yes. Is it likely? No. This bolt from the blue, commonly the most feared prospect, is a most unlikely scenario for the start of a nuclear war *as long as* no Russian military leader could ever report to the Politburo that a Soviet victory in nuclear war was probable or that the damage from American nuclear retaliation could be reduced to acceptable levels.

What military, political, and economic conditions would have to exist before Soviet leaders would seriously listen to the imagined general's proposal? First, nearly *all* American retaliatory forces and the entire command system would have to be highly vulnerable to a Soviet first strike. Currently, most of the Minutemen ICBMs (intercontinental ballistic missiles), U.S. bombers on airfields and submarines in port, and the American command, control, and communications network are theoretically vulnerable. But the forces that would survive a Soviet attack would still be enormously destructive. Most importantly, the American submarine force routinely at sea, which carries more nuclear warheads than does

Chapter XIV
Conflict and War

the entire Minuteman force, cannot now or in the foreseeable future be located or quickly destroyed by the Soviet navy.

Second, both Soviet ballistic missile defenses and air defenses would have to be improved greatly, perhaps beyond what is possible, before they could be expected to reduce the damage of the American retaliatory missile and bomber attacks to an acceptable level. Third, technical difficulties would plague the prospects of success in such a surprise Soviet attack: not only would it be enormously difficult to coordinate the actions of Soviet missile-bearing submarines, ICBMs, and anti-submarine warfare forces, but success would hinge on complete surprise being maintained. If Soviet strategic forces were put on full alert status, the possibility that the American intelligence network would miss the warning is exceedingly remote. Strategic Air Command bombers would be alerted and dispersed, American political leaders and military commanders could be sent to safer locations, and some submarines in port could be sent to sea. These actions would reduce still further the probability that a massive Soviet nuclear attack would be answered with only token nuclear retaliation. Finally, the United States could choose to launch its ICBMs on warning of the attack (i.e., while the attacking missiles were in flight toward their targets) or after the first attacking warheads had arrived.

The bolt from the blue is thus not likely now or any time in the foreseeable future. This scenario is, indeed, so farfetched that it is useful to consider only in one sense: it points to a set of combined circumstances which, as a matter of long-range policy, the United States must seek to avoid. There is clearly no reason that such a dangerous combination of circumstances need ever develop. The bolt from the blue could become plausible only if there was a major deterioration of Soviet-American relations and if Soviet nuclear forces, defensive preparations, and anti-submarine capabilities were greatly enhanced, while American counter-measures were unilaterally restrained.

A LIMITED ATTACK ON THE MINUTEMAN MISSILES

Some defense specialists believe that while American nuclear retaliatory capabilities might successfully deter surprise attacks on American cities, as well as bolt-from-the-blue attacks on all of the nuclear forces, limited attacks on portions of America's nuclear arsenal are substantially more likely. This is one of the concerns that has fueled the debate over the basing mode for the MX missile, a replacement for the vulnerable Minuteman system. The feared scenario often runs something like this:

The decision in Moscow: In a deep crisis over the status of Berlin, the Politburo decides not to launch an all-out pre-emptive attack against

Reading 41
Ways a Nuclear War Might Begin

American forces and command centers, but only to attack the Minuteman silos. A hot-line message is sent as soon as the warheads land: first, the Soviet Union will spare American cities if the United States refrains from retaliation and, second, the United States is urged to give in to Soviet demands in Europe.

The decision in Washington: The president asks the Joint Chiefs of Staff what military options exist, now that 90% of the Minuteman force is destroyed. They say that fifteen million Americans have just died in the Soviet attack and that an American response will likely trigger a Soviet attack on population centers. Should the president launch a retaliatory strike? Or should he give in to Soviet demands?

This Minuteman-only scenario rests upon a very questionable premise: that the Soviets would believe that the president of the United States would choose not to launch the ICBMs on warning or retaliate after 2,000 Soviet nuclear warheads have exploded here. The American submarines, moreover, could attack many Soviet military targets. A Soviet leader probably would assume that retaliation of some sort would be launched after 15 million Americans were killed. In such circumstances, it would be likely that the Soviets would try to reduce the American retaliation to whatever extent they could.

Thus, if the Soviets were to attack the United States on a large-scale basis, they would have great incentives to attack not only the land-based missiles, but also other American strategic forces and the American command, control, and communications network. There is little Soviet advantage to be gained by attacking the U.S. ICBMs alone, for they contain less than one-fourth of America's strategic nuclear warheads. It is not surprising that Soviet military doctrine, as far as American intelligence sources can determine, stresses that if nuclear war occurs, their nuclear forces would be used on a massive scale.

This Minuteman-only scenario, like the full-blown bolt from the blue, is far less likely than many other possible paths to nuclear war. These surprise attack scenarios preoccupy all too many defense analysts whose talents would be far better applied to preventing more likely dangers. And the attention of the public would be better directed to more realistic scenarios and more probable perils.

A Pre-Emptive War

Not all wars begin with coolly calculated decisions. Indeed, under certain circumstances, a nuclear war could originate from a series of hasty decisions made in the midst of uncertainty. In fact, a nuclear exchange could be precipitated by a mistaken action, originally intended to deter

Chapter XIV
Conflict and War

war, which could produce a counter-decision to launch a pre-emptive strike.

Consider the following scenario. It is the opening page of an imaginary historian's future best-seller, *The Missiles of August: The Origins of World War Three.*

What was the cause of the war? The Greek historian Thucydides, in his history of the conflict between Athens and Sparta, differentiated between the immediate causes and the underlying causes of war. The latter can be compared to the mass of combustible material; the former is the match that sets the material ablaze.

On August 2, 19—, none of the American leaders in Washington knew that they were lighting a match. A number of years earlier, Soviet Premier Brezhnev had warned the United States that if NATO deployed Pershing II and cruise missiles in Western Europe, the Soviet Union would "take retaliatory steps that would put the other side, including the United States itself, its own territory, in an analogous position." On the last day of July, American intelligence satellites spotted cruise missiles being unloaded onto Cuban soil from Soviet ships and on August 1 Premier Andropov announced that he would remove the missiles only if the United States withdrew the NATO deployments.

The sole surviving member of the National Security Council later reported that the president's decision to attack the Cuban dockyard and the Soviet ships was taken overnight. "We had no choice. In a few days, those missiles—we didn't know how many—would have been scattered all over Cuba. This was the only way to get rid of the missiles. We told the Soviets that there would be no attack on Russia itself. Our nuclear alert was only meant to signal our strength."

This was not the view from Moscow. Two Soviet staff officers who survived reported that the Politburo was informed that the Americans must be about to launch a nuclear attack. The head of the KGB told the Politburo that if the Americans launched first, the vast majority of Soviet ICBMs would be destroyed and eventually up to 100 million Soviet citizens might die. But if the Soviet arsenal was used immediately to destroy American nuclear forces and command centers, the casualties after retaliation would probably be "only" between 10 and 20 million. He even told the group that there was a small chance that a pre-emptive attack would "decapitate" the American giant and that no response would come.

He was wrong. The Russians thought war was unavoidable and launched first in desperation and fear. Thirty-five million Americans were killed instantly. The retaliation was perhaps smaller than the first strike the Soviets feared, but it still left 25 million Russians dead.

Perhaps, however, it is misleading to start this history with the immediate cause of the war. The deeper causes go back to 1945. At the close

Reading 41
Ways a Nuclear War Might Begin

of the Second World War, Soviet and American relations deteriorated rapidly....

How plausible is such a pre-emptive war scenario? Although no precise probabilities can be given, of course, it is at least a possibility that in a deep and apparently irresolvable crisis the Soviets (or the United States) might launch their nuclear weapons first with full knowledge that many of its citizens might die, but fearing far worse casualties if they allowed the other side to attack first. A desperate decision indeed, but a possible one.

What conditions would increase the likelihood of such a tragic decision being made by the leaders of a superpower? First, the leaders would have to believe that the other side intended to strike first, and soon. This would require that the adversary's forces be at or moving toward (or be perceived to be at) a high state of alert—a condition likely to be met only in times of crisis. Second, the leaders would have to believe that the other side could carry out a relatively successful disarming first strike—a judgment which would depend upon the capabilities of the adversary's forces and the vulnerabilities of their own. Lastly, the leaders must be convinced that by launching a pre-emptive attack against the other side's nuclear forces, they could substantially reduce the casualties and damage that would ultimately be suffered by their own nation.

The possibility that such a scenario might happen does not, by itself, mean that the United States should never put its forces on alert in a crisis or that we should always back down in dangerous circumstances. Nor does it mean that American nuclear forces should not be aimed at Soviet weaponry. But the possibility of such an occurrence should, at a minimum, promote great caution in times of crisis, highlight the importance of clear and unambiguous military orders, and stress the need for retaliatory forces that are invulnerable and are perceived as such by both sides. Moreover, it should serve as a constant reminder that the security of both sides is diminished by either side's fear of being struck first or by either side's temptation to strike first.

ESCALATION: CONVENTIONAL STEPS TO NUCLEAR WAR

It is difficult, though clearly not impossible, to outline a credible scenario in which, during peacetime, a Soviet or an American leader would decide to launch an all-out nuclear attack. It is less difficult to imagine a war occurring between the conventional forces of the two superpowers. And once American and Soviet troops met in combat, the likelihood of the use of nuclear weapons would be increased.

The process by which a war becomes incrementally more violent, either through the plans of the combatants or unintentionally, is called escalation. Escalation from conventional fighting to nuclear war has been a continuing concern of defense planners since the Soviets developed their nuclear arsenal. This fear has, thus far, produced prudence: each superpower has been reluctant to use even conventional forces against the other. Can this prudence continue indefinitely? What would happen if Soviet and American conventional forces did clash somewhere?

We do not know. And this inability to know whether conventional war would escalate to a nuclear exchange both enhances prudence and perpetuates fear. Consider two possible scenarios for nuclear conflict developing through escalation:

War in Europe. Step 1: East German workers, organized by an underground labor union, go on strike, demanding political changes in the government of their country. Martial law is imposed and riots ensue throughout the country. Russian troops help in the "police action." East Germans flee across the border into West Germany.

Step 2: Fighting breaks out between West German military units, who are aiding the refugees, and East German security forces. Soon Soviet forces join in the fighting. Two days later Soviet divisions cross into West Germany and the Soviet premier publicly warns the United States to "refrain from self-defeating threats."

Step 3: Other NATO forces—American, British, and Dutch—become involved in the fighting as the Soviets advance further into West Germany. As the Allies are being pushed back by the superior numbers of Soviet divisions, NATO leaders gather to decide on further military action. They publicly warn the Soviets to withdraw immediately or "suffer the gravest consequences." Four airfields along the Polish-Soviet border are attacked with nuclear-tipped cruise missiles, a communique announces, "as a demonstration of NATO resolve."

Step 4: The Soviet Union immediately fires nuclear missiles to destroy nuclear weapons sites in West Germany.

Step 5: ?? Does the war escalate to a full nuclear exchange or is a settlement possible? What would the United States do? What would the Soviet Union do next?

War in the Persian Gulf. Step 1: The Iranian Communist party overthrows the increasingly unpopular government of Ayatollah Khomeini. Civil war breaks out throughout Iran and the new government requests that Soviet troops enter the country "to help restore order." Despite American warnings against such action Soviet forces cross into Iran and move toward Teheran.

Step 2: American troops are immediately sent to southwestern Iran to protect the West's oil supply sources. Advance parties of the two armies meet and engage in combat.

Reading 41
Ways a Nuclear War Might Begin

Step 3: As Soviet reinforcements begin to move into Iran, the president orders aircraft from an American aircraft carrier in the Indian Ocean to "close the mountain passes" along the Soviet supply route. Told that nuclear bombs might be needed, he refuses to give weapons release authority to the local commander. "The United States will not be the first to go nuclear," the president's message concludes.

Step 4: The American military commander orders six conventional air strikes against mountain passes in Iran. The next morning, Soviet bombers fly south and attack the American carrier task force with nuclear-tipped missiles. The aircraft carrier and many of its supporting ships are destroyed instantly.

Step 5: ? Does the president escalate further? Does the Soviet Union stop fighting? What happens next? How does the war end?

These paths to nuclear conflict (or others like them) are more likely than the previous scenarios of initial homeland-to-homeland exchanges for an obvious reason: once war begins, the balance between political and military considerations shifts decidedly toward the military side. The leader of a government is far more likely to authorize use of a small number of nuclear weapons during a conventional war than to initiate a full-scale nuclear conflict. But unless the war is somehow terminated, there will be continued incentives for further escalation.

Once a conventional war began, there would be two other factors, in addition to possible decisions to take incremental escalatory steps, that could lead to nuclear war. First, there would be increased possibilities of miscalculation leading to nuclear war. It is possible that at some stage in a conventional conflict a field commander might be given "predelegation of authority," the president's option of allowing commanders to decide themselves when to use tactical nuclear weapons. Once this is done, the likelihood of use through miscalculation or mistake in the "fog of battle" would greatly increase. Second, the pressures for pre-emptive nuclear strikes would likely be enhanced after the line between superpower peace and superpower war was crossed. Once the fighting began, one or both governments might decide that full-scale use of nuclear weapons was inevitable or very nearly so; thus, despite the terrible risks involved, a pre-emptive attack might be chosen, on the basis that striking first is better than being stricken first, though both are worse than the unavailable option of no nuclear war at all.

The maintenance of a conventional-nuclear "firebreak"—an often used metaphor borrowed from forest fire-fighting techniques—is most strategists' goal here. If a conventional conflict between the superpowers does someday occur, every effort should be made to terminate the war without the use of nuclear weapons; escalation to full thermonuclear war should be avoided. Withdrawing tactical nuclear weapons from sites

Chapter XIV
Conflict and War

near borders, where they might be used quickly in a war, and keeping strict political control over weapons release authority widen the firebreak between conventional and nuclear war. It is not clear, however, exactly how wide such a firebreak should be because of what was earlier described as the "usability paradox": if nuclear weapons are too usable, they might be used when and in a manner not controllable by government leaders; yet if it is certain that weapons will not be used, might this not encourage conventional aggression?

TRAGIC ACCIDENTS

Could nuclear war begin purely by accident? Mechanical failures do occur, after all, even with (and perhaps especially with) the most sophisticated machinery. Human frailties always exist as well. And such frailties can produce highly irrational behavior at times, even when (and perhaps especially when) the psychological pressures to behave cautiously are enormous.

It is a common assumption that nuclear weapons are likely to be used, not through decisions of rational government leaders, but through mechanical or human accidents. Jonathan Schell, for example, has written that "the machinery of destruction is complete, poised on a hair trigger, waiting for a 'button' to be 'pushed' by some misguided or deranged human being or for some faulty computer chip to send out the instruction to fire." Is this true? Are the following scenes possible?

The Faulty Computer Chip War. Deep inside the multimillion-dollar computer, used to process the military intelligence coming from American satellites, a 35-cent computer chip malfunctions. Suddenly the radar screens begin to flash. A thousand Soviet missiles appear to be coming over the horizon. "Oh, my God," the radar screen operator says. "This is it."

In the White House, the president is informed of the warning, now ten minutes old. "In twenty minutes the missiles will destroy our retaliatory forces, sir," his military aide informs him. As the president leaves the White House for his specially equipped command post airplane, he orders that all land-based missiles be launched immediately.

"I am not going to let our missiles be destroyed on the ground," he says as he climbs aboard the helicopter. "We'll fight. But the Russians started this war. Let the history books record that fact."

The Strangelove Scenario. Individuals under pressure cannot always withstand the strain. Sometimes men snap. Late one night, a Soviet submarine commander walks into the control room of his new *Typhoon*-class submarine and, before the astonished ensign can react, he pushes a button sending a single SLBM, with twelve nuclear warheads in the nose cone, on its way to the United States.

"What have you done?" the ensign cries as he tackles the commander, wrestling him to the floor.

The commander appears startled. Then he smiles, looks up, and says, "The missile is going to down a Nazi bomber. I'm teaching those fascists a lesson. Remember Stalingrad!"

Although such imaginative scenarios are often discussed, they are, fortunately, extremely unlikely if not impossible. This is not because the problem of accidental war is not a serious concern. Rather the opposite is the case: precisely because the possibility exists that nuclear weapons could be used accidentally, the United States government has devised numerous precautions to prevent such accidents. Indeed, contrary to a popular belief, the chances of an American weapon being used accidentally are probably much less today than they were in the 1950s. For along with more sophisticated and more numerous weapons, more sophisticated and more numerous precautionary policies have been developed.

Four kinds of measures intended to minimize the chances of unauthorized or accidental use are worth noting. First is the "two-man rule," which requires parallel actions by two or more individuals at several stages in the process of communicating and carrying out any order to use nuclear weapons. Second is the system of Permissive Action Links (PALs), including a highly secure coded signal which must be inserted in the weapons before they can be used. Third, devices internal to the weapon are designed to ensure that an attempt to bypass the PALs system will disarm the weapon. Finally, the nuclear warheads themselves are designed to preclude accidental detonation as a result of exposure to heat, blast, or radiation. The Soviets share our concern with unauthorized and accidental nuclear war, and there is reason to believe that they too have taken measures to prevent it.

In this light, how credible are the two scenarios outlined above? There have been, it is true, many false alarms in the American nuclear attack warning system. Some of them have been traced to such minuscule components as an inexpensive computer chip. But none of these false alerts has even come close to leading the nation into war because the government has built redundancies into the system, precisely so that no president will ever have to rely on a single computer or single radar screen to make such important decisions. For this kind of accident to lead to war, several warning systems of different kinds (e.g., infra-red sensors on satellites, and radars on land) would have to fail simultaneously. Even that by itself would be unlikely to cause the president to order an immediate launching of ICBMs. His incentives to do so might indeed be small if the missiles were relatively invulnerable and if he had other nuclear systems at sea, not under attack. It is even possible to maintain a policy of not launching missiles in a retaliatory strike until after the damage of the enemy's first strike is assessed.

Of course, it is possible that a military commander could go insane (although the stability of American officers with such responsibilities is carefully tested). An insane American officer could not, in peacetime by himself, arm and deliver the nuclear weapons under his command. In the submarine case, to give but one example, it would take the simultaneous insanity of a number of American submarine officers for an unauthorized American launch to be possible. Given the Soviets' strong propensity for tight political control of their nuclear weapons, there is no reason to believe that the chances of unauthorized Soviet use are any greater.

Thus it is a mistake to believe that a simple accident or an unstable commander could easily lead to a nuclear exchange. In reality, the probabilities of such an event are very low. This should not, however, breed complacency about the prospect of accidental war, for two reasons. First, it is only through continual concern that the likelihood of accidental use of weapons is kept to low. Second, mechanical accidents and human frailties could become increasingly dangerous in times of deep crisis or conventional war, during which time command centers could be threatened or destroyed.

There will continue to be an uneasy balance between the degree of control required to ensure that weapons are not used accidentally and the degree of "usability" required to ensure that the weapons can be used if needed. Preventing accidental use is an important goal, but it cannot be the only objective of a nuclear weapons policy. Nuclear weapons must be usable enough to provide credible deterrence, but not so usable as to invite unintended use.

REGIONAL NUCLEAR WAR

One important reason why the world has seen nuclear peace since 1945 is that there has been no conventional war between the United States and the Soviet Union. In the future, if nuclear proliferation continues, there will be an increased danger of nuclear war breaking out between two nuclear armed Third World countries. Such an event might be more likely than nuclear war between the superpowers because many of the conditions that have led to the maintenance of nuclear peace—such as invulnerable second-strike forces, strong leadership control of nuclear weapons, and stable governments in nuclear weapons states—may be absent. The following is an imaginary future newspaper report of a nuclear war which neither Washington nor Moscow would be in a position to stop.

Reading 41
Ways a Nuclear War Might Begin

India Uses the Bomb, Pakistan Sues for Peace. New Delhi, India.—The Indian government this morning announced that four nuclear bombs were dropped on Pakistan late last night. At noon, a Defense Ministry spokesman in Islamabad read a declaration over the radio accepting "unconditional surrender" on behalf of the Revolutionary Islamic Council of Pakistan. Thus it appears that the week-long war between India and Pakistan has come to a sudden end.

Sources inside the Indian Ministry of Defense have revealed that India's entire nuclear arsenal was used in this morning's pre-emptive attack against Pakistan's three major military airfields and its nuclear weapons assembly facility. When the Pakistani forces crossed the Indian border last week, Radio Islamabad announced that any Indian use of nuclear weapons would be met in kind. After last year's Pakistani nuclear test, the government in New Delhi took the threat seriously, the Ministry of Defense officials reported, and only decided to attack pre-emptively when Indian intelligence warned that Pakistan's weapons were being readied for use. "We had no choice," an official said. "The enemy was preparing for an attack. Fortunately, we knew where the bombs were kept, and destroyed them and their bomber aircraft simultaneously."

Meanwhile, in New York, the UN Security Council met throughout the night and...

Somehow this scenario appears less farfetched than most of the previously outlined scenarios for superpower nuclear war. It also appears less apocalyptic (at least from a non-Pakistani perspective). Indeed, its less-than-apocalyptic nature may be precisely the characteristic that makes it less farfetched. The dangers of this kind of nuclear war may be comparatively small today, but they will increase in the future as more countries acquire nuclear weapons....

It is tempting, but incorrect, to think that a nuclear conflict between any two countries would not affect other nations. There is the possibility that one government in war would be allied to the Soviet Union and the other government to the United States, thereby raising the specter of the superpowers becoming involved in the war. Moreover, there is a danger that a nuclear armed country could use a weapon, intentionally or not, against a superpower.

CATALYTIC WAR

There is yet another way in which the superpowers could be dragged into nuclear war by the actions of a third party. Imagine the two scenarios described below:

The French Connection. A conventional conflict between NATO and the Warsaw Pact erupts and, despite the imminent collapse of the NATO front, the United States does not use nuclear weapons. The French government, however, launches a small number of its nuclear-tipped submarine-launched ballistic missiles against military targets, hoping to bring a halt to the Soviet advance. The Soviets do not know who launched the missiles, and respond by launching a nuclear attack against NATO military targets throughout Europe. The American president orders that NATO Pershing IIs be used against military targets in the USSR....

Mistaken Identity. A war in the Persian Gulf has broken out between the United States and the Soviet Union. After a week of conventional fighting, nuclear-tipped cruise missiles are launched against the American carrier task force. The planes are Soviet models and bear Soviet markings; they are not manned by Soviet pilots nor are they otherwise under Soviet control. Some other country has intentionally and successfully disguised its aircraft, and the Americans mistakenly conclude that it is the Soviets who have initiated use of nuclear weapons. Does the American president escalate further? What might the Soviets do in the midst of this confusion? What happens next?

Clearly, such scenarios are possible. Under a number of circumstances another nuclear power might trigger a strategic nuclear exchange between the superpowers, a war that they had thus far avoided. The possibilities of such an event are greatly increased if conventional war occurs. Few strategists place the danger of catalytic war as high as nuclear war through escalation or pre-emption, but it still is a serious concern. Indeed, during the SALT I negotiations, the Soviet Union mentioned its concern that the growing Chinese nuclear arsenal might someday be used with such results.

NUCLEAR TERRORISM

What if a terrorist organization gained possession of a nuclear bomb? Could nuclear war occur as a result? Consider the following scenario, which was invented in the best-selling novel *The Fifth Horseman*:

On a snowy December evening, the President of the United States is told by his National Security Adviser that a tape recording in Arabic has just been delivered to the White House. It appears to be a message from Muammar al-Qaddafi, President of Libya, and claims that a nuclear weapon has been placed somewhere on Manhattan. Unless the United States forces Israel to withdraw to its 1967 borders, the bomb will be detonated.

"I must further inform you that, should you make this communication public or begin in any way to evacuate New York City, I shall feel obliged to instantly explode my weapon," the message concludes.

Reading 41
Ways a Nuclear War Might Begin

"A man like Qaddafi has got to know we have the capabilities to utterly destroy him and his entire nation in retaliation. He'd be mad to do something like that," the President tells his adviser.

But what should the president do? Is nuclear terrorism possible? How could it come about?

Terrorists might gain possession of an atomic bomb in one of several ways, including theft, purchase, or manufacture. If they were to steal it, and if it were of American origin, then the Permissive Action Links should frustrate any attempt to detonate it. But it is not at all clear just how confident a president might be in the ability of the PALs to resist a concerted attempt to bypass them, especially in light of the high stakes involved. And suppose the stolen bomb was not an American one. Other current and future nuclear weapons states may not have equipped their warheads with safety systems comparable to those developed by the United States.

A terrorist organization might purchase an atomic bomb from (or be given one by) a government that shares the terrorist group's goals. Indeed, this possibility is reason enough to work to inhibit the spread of nuclear weapons to additional countries.

Finally, terrorists might fashion their own nuclear explosive device. The highly enriched uranium or plutonium essential to the project might be stolen or bought, and a crude but workable bomb assembled. The task would be difficult, but not impossible. In any event, how confident could a president be that the terrorists' bomb would not work? And against whom could he threaten retaliation?

CONCLUSION: CONTINUING ISSUES

How should one think about the various paths to war outlined in this chapter? Five points need to be stressed. First, the set of scenarios presented here is not exhaustive. Surely each reader can think of other ways in which a nuclear war might begin. How probable are such scenarios? What can be done to minimize the likelihood of their occurrence? Also, the dangers of these scenarios could be compounded. Suppose, to give but two examples, mechanical failures in warning systems developed during a deep superpower crisis, or human frailty produced unstable commanders during a conventional war. Thus, when thinking of the potential dangers to be avoided in the future, one must not assume that decisions will always be deliberate, or that accidents will always develop when they can do the least harm.

Second, this chapter suggests that it is usually misleading to concentrate one's attention on the number of nuclear weapons when analyzing the likelihood of war. It is widely assumed that changes in the numbers

Chapter XIV
Conflict and War

of weapons in the superpower arsenals—either upward or downward—are the major determinants of the risks of war. Sheer numbers, however, matter far less than factors such as the vulnerability of weapons, the credibility of commitments to allies, and imbalances in conventional forces. In the short run, to give but one example, making command and control systems less vulnerable can be as important, and probably more so, in reducing certain risks of war than would changes in the numbers of weapons: improved command and control could reduce an enemy's incentives for a "decapitating" attack, and could improve our ability to follow a policy of "no retaliation until specifically ordered." And the long-run risk of nuclear war is likely to depend more on our ability to stem proliferation than on any other single factor. The common fixation on numbers of weapons in the superpower arsenals misses such important issues.

Third, there is no reason to assume that an all-out nuclear exchange, certainly the most frightening scenario, is either the only kind of nuclear war possible or even the most likely type of nuclear war. Nuclear war occurring through the escalation of conventional conflict appears more probable. Avoiding conventional war is, therefore, one of the most important ways of avoiding nuclear war. And maintaining strong and credible conventional forces may thus be an important component of preventing nuclear war. One should never forget that, despite the incentives to keep a conventional war limited, once fighting begins it would be difficult to control escalation to the nuclear abyss. But escalation should not be considered inevitable, for that could prove to be a self-fulfilling prophecy.

Fourth, it is noted that in none of these scenarios do leaders of the United States or the Soviet Union act insanely. But departures from rationality are not inconceivable; they must be taken into account in the design of measures to prevent nuclear war.

Finally, this glimpse at the shattered crystal ball should breed neither complacency nor despair. A horrible nuclear future is not inevitable, but only because great efforts have been made in the past to decrease its likelihood. The good news for the present is, then, that nuclear war is not probable. The bad news is that nuclear war, is and will continue to be, possible. To make sure that the possible does not become the probable is the continuing task of nuclear policy.

Reading 42
THE MORAL EQUIVALENT OF WAR

William James

> *This classic statement, written in 1910 before the First World War, shows that war cannot be explained away using the greed of bad leaders. The piratical lust for land or power is the product of, and is supported by, a larger configuration of attitudes that can be characterized as a moral crusade for glorification. James suggests that this push for pride, and even the martial character, can be created without war and can be redirected toward peaceful improvements.*

The war against war is going to be no holiday excursion or camping party. The military feelings are too deeply grounded to abdicate their place among our ideals until better substitutes are offered than the glory and shame that come to nations as well as to individuals from the ups and downs of politics and the vicissitudes of trade. There is something highly paradoxical in the modern man's relation to war. Ask all our millions, north and south, whether they would vote now (were such a thing possible) to have our war for the Union expunged from history, and the record of a peaceful transition to the present time substituted for that of its marches and battles, and probably hardly a handful of eccentrics would say yes. Those ancestors, those efforts, those memories and legends, are the most ideal part of what we now own together, a sacred spiritual possession worth more than all the blood poured out. Yet ask those same people whether they would be willing in cold blood to start another civil war now to gain another similar possession, and not one man or woman would vote for the proposition. In modern eyes, precious though wars may be, they must not be waged solely for the sake of the ideal harvest. Only when forced upon one, only when an enemy's injustice leaves us no alternative, is a war now thought permissible.

It was not thus in ancient times. The earlier men were hunting men, and to hunt a neighboring tribe, kill the males, loot the village and possess the females, was the most profitable, as well as the most exciting,

---

Reprinted from *McClure's Magazine*, August, 1910, pp. 463–468.

Chapter XIV
Conflict and War

way of living. Thus were the more martial tribes selected, and in chiefs and peoples a pure pugnacity and love of glory came to mingle with the more fundamental appetite for plunder.

Modern war is so expensive that we feel trade to be a better avenue to plunder; but modern man inherits all the innate pugnacity and all the love of glory of his ancestors. Showing war's irrationality and horror is of no effect upon him. The horrors make the fascination. War is the *strong* life; it is life *in extremis;* war-taxes are the only ones men never hesitate to pay, as the budgets of all nations show us.

History is a bath of blood. The Iliad is one long recital of how Diomedes and Ajax, Sarpedon and Hector *killed.* No detail of the wounds they made is spared us, and the Greek mind fed upon the story. Greek history is a panorama of jingoism and imperialism—war for war's sake, all the citizens being warriors. It is horrible reading, because of the irrationality of it all—save for the purpose of making "history"—and the history is that of the utter ruin of a civilization in intellectual respects perhaps the highest the earth has ever seen.

Those wars were purely piratical. Pride, gold, women, slaves, excitement, were their only motives. In the Peloponnesian war for example, the Athenians ask the inhabitants of Melos (the island where the "Venus of Milo" was found), hiterto neutral, to own their lordship. The envoys meet, and hold a debate which Thucydides gives in full, and which, for sweet reasonableness of form, would have satisfied Matthew Arnold. "The powerful exact what they can," said the Athenians, "and the weak grant what they must." When the Meleans say that sooner than be slaves they will appeal to the gods, the Athenians reply: "Of the gods we believe and of men we know that, by a law of their nature, wherever they can rule they will. This law was not made by us, and we are not the first to have acted upon it; we did but inherit it, and we know that you and all mankind, if you were as strong as we are, would do as we do. So much for the gods; we have told you why we expect to stand as high in their opinion as you." Well, the Meleans still refused, and their town was taken. "The Athenians," Thucydides quietly says "thereupon put to death all who were of military age and made slaves of the women and children. They then colonized the island, sending thither five hundred settlers of their own."

Alexander's career was piracy pure and simple, nothing but an orgy of power and plunder, made romantic by the character of the hero. There was no rational principle in it, and the moment he died his generals and governors attacked one another. The cruelty of those times is incredible. When Rome finally conquered Greece, Paulus Aemilius was told by the Roman Senate to reward his soldiers for their toil by "giving" them the old kingdom of Epirus. They sacked seventy cities and carried off a hun-

Reading 42
Moral Equivalent of War

dred and fifty thousand inhabitants as slaves. How many they killed I know not; but in Etolia they killed all the senators, five hundred and fifty in number. Brutus was "the noblest Roman of them all," but to reanimate his soldiers on the eve of Philippi he similarly promises to give them the cities of Sparta and Thessalonica to ravage, if they win the fight.

Such was the gory nurse that trained societies to cohesiveness. We inherit the warlike type; and for most of the capacities of heroism that the human race is full of we have to thank this cruel history. Dead men tell no tales, and if there were any tribes of other type than this they have left no survivors. Our ancestors have bred pugnacity into our bone and marrow, and thousands of years of peace won't breed it out of us. The popular imagination fairly fattens on the thought of wars. Let public opinion once reach a certain fighting pitch, and no ruler can withstand it. In the Boer war both governments began with bluff but couldn't stay there, the military tension was too much for them. In 1898 our people had read the word "war" in letters three inches high for three months in every newspaper. The pliant politician McKinley was swept away by their eagerness, and our squalid war with Spain became a necessity.

At the present day, civilized opinion is a curious mental mixture. The military instincts and ideals are as strong as ever, but are confronted by reflective criticisms which sorely curb their ancient freedom. Innumerable writers are showing up the bestial side of military service. Pure loot and mastery seem no longer morally avowable motives, and pretexts must be found for attributing them solely to the enemy. England and we, our army and navy authorities repeat without ceasing, arm solely for "peace," Germany and Japan it is who are bent on loot and glory. "Peace" in military mouths today is a synonym for "war expected." The word has become a pure provocative, and no government wishing peace sincerely should allow it ever to be printed in a newspaper. Every up-to-date dictionary should say that "peace" and "war" mean the same thing, now *in posse*, now *in actu*. It may even reasonably be said that the intensely sharp competitive *preparation* for war by the nations *is the real war*, permanent, unceasing; and that the battles are only a sort of public verification of the mastery gained during the "peace" interval.

It is plain that on this subject civilized man has developed a sort of double personality. If we take European nations, no legitimate interest of any one of them would seem to justify the tremendous destructions which a war to compass it would necessarily entail. It would seem as though common sense and reason ought to find a way to reach agreement in every conflict of honest interests. I myself think it our bounden duty to believe in such international rationality as possible. But, as things stand, I see how desperately hard it is to bring the peace-party and the war-party together, and I believe that the difficulty is due to certain defi-

Chapter XIV
Conflict and War

ciencies in the program of pacificism which set the militarist imagination strongly, and to a certain extent justifiably, against it. In the whole discussion both sides are on imaginative and sentimental ground. It is but one utopia against another, and everything one says must be abstract and hypothetical. Subject to this criticism and caution, I will try to characterize in abstract strokes the opposite imaginative forces, and point out what to my own very fallible mind seems the best utopian hypothesis, the most promising line of conciliation.

In my remarks, pacifist though I am, I will refuse to speak of the bestial side of the war-*regime* (already done justice to by many writers) and consider only the higher aspects of militaristic sentiment. Patriotism no one thinks discreditable; nor does any one deny that war is the romance of history. But inordinate ambitions are the soul of every patriotism, and the possibility of violent death the soul of all romance. The militarily patriotic and romantic-minded everywhere, and especially the professional military class, refuse to admit for a moment that war may be a transitory phenomenon in social evolution. The notion of a sheep's paradise like that revolts, they say, our higher imagination. Where then would be the steeps of life? If war had ever stopped, we should have to re-invent it, on this view, to redeem life from flat degeneration.

Reflective apologists for war at the present day all take it religiously. It is a sort of sacrament. Its profits are to the vanquished as well as to the victor; and quite apart from any question of profit, it is an absolute good, we are told, for it is human nature at its highest dynamic. Its "horrors" are a cheap price to pay for rescue from the only alternative supposed, of a world of clerks and teachers, of co-education and zo-ophily, of "consumer's leagues," and "associated charities," of industrialism unlimited, and feminism unabashed. No scorn, no hardness, no valor any more! Fie upon such a cattleyard of a planet!

So far as the central essence of this feeling goes, no healthy-minded person, it seems to me, can help to some degree partaking of it. Militarism is the great preserver of our ideals of hardihood, and human life with no use for hardihood would be contemptible. Without risks or prizes for the darer, history would be insipid indeed; and there is a type of military character which every one feels that the race should never cease to breed, for every one is sensitive to its superiority. The duty is incumbent on mankind, of keeping military characters in stock—of keeping them, if not for use, then as ends in themselves and as pure pieces of perfection—so that Roosevelt's weaklings and mollycoddles may not end by making everything else disappear from the face of nature.

This natural sort of feeling forms, I think, the innermost soul of army-writings. Without any exception known to me, militarist authors

Reading 42
Moral Equivalent of War

take a highly mystical view of their subject, and regard war as a biological or sociological necessity, uncontrolled by ordinary psychological checks and motives. When the time of development is ripe the war must come, reason or no reason, for the justifications pleaded are invariably fictitious. War is, in short, a permanent human *obligation*. General Homer Lea, in his recent book "The Valor of Ignorance," plants himself squarely on this ground. Readiness for war is for him the essence of nationality, and ability in it the supreme measure of the health of nations.

Nations, General Lea says, are never stationary—they must necessarily expand or shrink, according to their vitality or decrepitude. Japan now is culminating; and by the fatal law in question it is impossible that her statesmen should not long since have entered, with extraordinary foresight, upon a vast policy of conquest—the game in which the first moves were her wars with China and Russia and her treaty with England, and of which the final objective is the capture of the Philippines, the Hawaiian Islands, Alaska, and the whole of our Coast west of the Sierra Passes. This will give Japan what her ineluctable vocation as a state absolutely forces her to claim, the possession of the entire Pacific Ocean; and to oppose these deep designs we Americans have, according to our author, nothing but our conceit, our ignorance, our commercialism, our corruption, and our feminism. General Lea makes a minute technical comparison of the military strength which we at present could oppose to the strength of Japan, and concludes that the islands, Alaska, Oregon, and Southern California, would fall almost without resistance, that San Francisco must surrender in a fortnight to a Japanese investment, that in three or four months the war would be over, and our republic, unable to regain what it had heedlessly neglected to protect sufficiently, would then "disintegrate," until perhaps some Caesar should arise to weld us again into a nation.

A dismal forecast indeed! Yet not unplausible, if the mentality of Japan's statesmen be of the Caesarian type of which history shows so many examples, and which is all that General Lea seems able to imagine. But there is no reason to think that women can no longer be the mothers of Napoleonic or Alexandrian characters; and if these come in Japan and find their opportunity, just such surprises as "The Valor of Ignorance" paints may lurk in ambush for us. Ignorant as we still are of the innermost recesses of Japanese mentality, we may be foolhardy to disregard such possibilities.

Other militarists are more complex and more moral in their considerations. The "Philosophie des Krieges," by S. R. Steinmetz is a good example. War, according to this author, is an ordeal instituted by God, who weighs the nations in its balance. It is the essential form of the State, and

Chapter XIV
Conflict and War

the only function in which peoples can employ all their powers at once and convergently. No victory is possible save as the resultant of a totality of virtues, no defeat for which some vice or weakness is not responsible. Fidelity, cohesiveness, tenacity, heroism, conscience, education, inventiveness, economy, wealth, physical health and vigor—there isn't a moral or intellectual point of superiority that doesn't tell, when God holds his assizes and hurls the peoples upon one another. *Die Weltgeschichte ist das Weltgericht;* and Dr. Steinmetz does not believe that in the long run chance and luck play any part in apportioning the issues.

The virtues that prevail, it must be noted, are virtues anyhow, superiorities that count in peaceful as well as in military competition; but the strain on them, being infinitely intenser in the latter case, makes war infinitely more searching as a trial. No ordeal is comparable to its winnowings. Its dread hammer is the welder of men into cohesive states, and nowhere but in such states can human nature adequately develop its capacity. The only alternative is "degeneration."

Dr. Steinmetz is a conscientious thinker, and his book, short as it is, takes much into account. Its upshot can, it seems to me, be summed up in Simon Patten's word, that mankind was nursed in pain and fear, and that the transition to a "pleasure-economy" may be fatal to a being wielding no powers of defence against its disintegrative influences. If we speak of the *fear of emancipation from the fear-regime,* we put the whole situation into a single phrase; fear regarding ourselves now taking the place of the ancient fear of the enemy.

Turn the fear over as I will in my mind, it all seems to lead back to two unwillingnesses of the imagination, one aesthetic, and the other moral; unwillingnesses, first to envisage a future in which army-life, with its many elements of charm, shall be forever impossible, and in which the destinies of peoples shall nevermore be decided quickly, thrillingly, and tragically, by force, but only gradually and insipidly by "evolution"; and, secondly, unwillingness to see the supreme theatre of human strenuousness closed, and the splendid military aptitudes of men doomed to keep always in a state of latency and never show themselves in action. These insistent unwillingnesses, no less than other aesthetic and ethical insistencies, have, it seems to me, to be listened to and respected. One cannot meet them effectively by mere counter-insistency on war's expensiveness and horror. The horror makes the thrill; and when the question is of getting the extremest and supremest out of human nature, talk of expense sounds ignominious. The weakness of so much merely negative criticism is evident—pacificism makes no converts from the military party. The military party denies neither the bestiality nor the horror, nor the expense; it only says that these things tell but half the story. It only says that war is *worth* them; that, taking human nature

Reading 42
Moral Equivalent of War

as a whole, its wars are its best protection against its weaker and more cowardly self, and that mankind cannot *afford* to adopt a peace-economy.

Pacificists ought to enter more deeply into the aesthetical and ethical point of view of their opponents. Do that first in any controversy, says J. J. Chapman, *then move the point,* and your opponent will follow. So long as anti-militarists propose no substitute for war's disciplinary function, no *moral equivalent* of war, analogous, as one might say, to the mechanical equivalent of heat, so long they fail to realize the full inwardness of the situation. And as a rule they do fail. The duties, penalties, and sanctions pictured in the utopias they paint are all too weak and tame to touch the military-minded. Tolstoi's pacificism is the only exception to this rule, for it is profoundly pessimistic as regards all this world's values, and makes the fear of the Lord furnish the moral spur provided elsewhere by the fear of the enemy. But our socialistic peace-advocates all believe absolutely in this world's values; and instead of the fear of the Lord and the fear of the enemy, the only fear they reckon with is the fear of poverty if one be lazy. This weakness pervades all the socialistic literature with which I am acquainted. Even in Lowes Dickinson's exquisite dialogue, high wages and short hours are the only forces invoked for overcoming man's distaste for repulsive kinds of labor. Meanwhile men at large still live as they always have lived, under a pain-and-fear economy—for those of us who live in an ease-economy are but an island in the stormy ocean—and the whole atmosphere of present-day utopian literature tastes mawkish and dishwatery to people who still keep a sense for life's more bitter flavors. It suggests, in truth, ubiquitous inferiority.

Inferiority is always with us, and merciless scorn of it is the keynote of the military temper. "Dogs, would you live forever?" shouted Frederick the Great. "Yes," say our utopians, "let us live forever, and raise our level gradually." The best thing about our "inferiors" to-day is that they are as tough as nails, and physically and morally almost as insensitive. Utopianism would see them soft and squeamish, while militarism would keep their callousness, but transfigure it into a meritorious characteristic, needed by "the service," and redeemed by that from the suspicion of inferiority. All the qualities of a man acquire dignity when he knows that the service of the collectivity that owns him needs them. If proud of the collectivity, his own pride rises in proportion. No collectivity is like an army for nourishing such pride; but it has to be confessed that the only sentiment which the image of pacific cosmopolitan industrialism is capable of arousing in countless worthy breasts is shame at the idea of belonging to *such* a collectivity. It is obvious that the United States of America as they exist to-day impress a mind like General Lea's as so much human blubber. Where is the sharpness and precipitousness, the contempt for life, whether one's own, or another's? Where is the savage

435

Chapter XIV
Conflict and War

"yes" and "no," the unconditional duty? Where is the conscription? Where is the blood-tax? Where is anything that one feels honored by belonging to?

Having said this much in preparation, I will now confess my own utopia. I devoutly believe in the reign of peace and in the gradual advent of some sort of a socialistic equilibrium. The fatalistic view of the war-function is to me nonsense, for I know that war-making is due to definite motives and subject to prudential checks and reasonble criticisms, just like any other form of enterprise. And when whole nations are the armies, and the science of destruction vies in intellectual refinement with the sciences of production, I see that war becomes absurd and impossible from its own monstrosity. Extravagant ambitions will have to be replaced by reasonable claims, and nations must make common cause against them. I see no reason why all this should not apply to yellow as well as to white countries, and I look forward to a future when acts of war shall be formally outlawed as between civilized peoples.

All these beliefs of mine put me squarely into the anti-militarist party. But I do not believe that peace either ought to be or will be permanent on this globe, unless the states pacifically organized preserve some of the old elements of army-discipline. A permanently successful peace-economy cannot be a simple pleasure-economy. In the more or less socialistic future towards which mankind seems drifting we must still subject ourselves collectively to those severities which answer to our real position upon this only partly hospitable globe. We must make new energies and hardihoods continue the manliness to which the military mind so faithfully clings. Martial virtues must be the enduring cement; intrepidity, contempt of softness, surrender of private interest, obedience to command, must still remain the rock upon which states are built—unless, indeed, we wish for dangerous reactions against commonwealths fit only for contempt, and liable to invite attack whenever a centre of crystallization for military-minded enterprise gets formed anywhere in their neighborhood.

The war-party is assuredly right in affirming and reaffirming that the martial virtues, although originally gained by the race through war, are absolute and permanent human goods. Patriotic pride and ambition in their military form are, after all, only specifications of a more general competitive passion. They are its first form, but that is no reason for supposing them to be its last form. Men now are proud of belonging to a conquering nation, and without a murmur they lay down their persons and their wealth, if by so doing they may fend off subjection. But who can be sure that *other aspects of one's country* may not, with time and education and suggestion enough, come to be regarded with similarly effective feelings of pride and shame? Why should men not some day feel

Reading 42
Moral Equivalent of War

that it is worth a blood-tax to belong to a collectivity superior in *any* ideal respect? Why should they not blush with indignant shame if the community that owns them is vile in any way whatsoever? Individuals, daily more numerous, now feel this civic passion. It is only a question of blowing on the spark till the whole population gets incandescent, and on the ruins of the old morals of military honor, a stable system of morals of civic honor builds itself up. What the whole community comes to believe in grasps the individual as in a vise. The war-function has grasped us so far; but constructive interests may some day seem no less imperative, and impose on the individual a hardly lighter burden.

Let me illustrate my idea more concretely. There is nothing to make one indignant in the mere fact that life is hard, that men should toil and suffer pain. The planetary conditions once for all are such, and we can stand it. But that so many men, by mere accidents of birth and opportunity, should have a life of *nothing else* but toil and pain and hardness and inferiority imposed upon them, should have *no* vacation, while others natively no more deserving never get any taste of this campaigning life at all—*this* is capable of arousing indignation in reflective minds. It may end by seeming shameful to all of us that some of us have nothing but campaigning, and others nothing but unmanly ease. If now—and this is my idea—there were, instead of military conscription, a conscription of the whole youthful population to form for a certain number of years a part of the army enlisted against *Nature*, the injustice would tend to be evened out, and numerous other goods to the commonwealth would follow. The military ideals of hardihood and discipline would be wrought into the growing fibre of the people; no one would remain blind as the luxurious classes now are blind, to man's relations to the globe he lives on, and to the permanently sour and hard foundations of his higher life. To coal and iron mines, to freight trains, to fishing fleets in December, to dishwashing, clothes-washing, and window-washing, to road-building and tunnel-making, to foundries and stoke-holes, and to the frames of skyscrapers, would our gilded youths be drafted off, according to their choice, to get the childishness knocked out of them, and to come back into society with healthier sympathies and soberer ideas. They would have paid their blood-tax, done their own part in the immemorial human warfare against nature; they would tread the earth more proudly, the women would value them more highly, they would be better fathers and teachers of the following generations.

Such a conscription, with the state of public opinion that would have required it, and the many moral fruits it would bear, would preserve in the midst of a pacific civilization the manly virtues which the military party is so afraid of seeing disappear in peace. We should get toughness without callousness, authority with as little criminal cruelty as possible,

Chapter XIV
Conflict and War

and painful work done cheerily because the duty is temporary, and threatens not, as now, to degrade the whole remainder of one's life. I spoke of the "moral equivalent" of war. So far, war has been the only force that can discipline a whole community, and until an equivalent discipline is organized, I believe that war must have its way. But I have no serious doubt that the ordinary prides and shames of social man, once developed to a certain intensity, are capable of organizing such a moral equivalent as I have sketched, or some other just as effective for preserving manliness of type. It is but a question of time, of skillful propagandism, and of opinion-making men seizing historic opportunities.

The martial type of character can be bred without war. Strenuous honor and disinterestedness abound elsewhere. Priests and medical men are in a fashion educated to it, and we should all feel some degree of it imperative if we were conscious of our work as an obligatory service to the state. We should be *owned*, as soldiers are by the army, and our pride would rise accordingly. We could be poor, then, without humiliation, as army officers now are. The only thing needed henceforward is to inflame the civic temper as past history has inflamed the military temper. H. G. Wells, as usual, sees the centre of the situation. "In many ways," he says, "military organization is the most peaceful of activities. When the contemporary man steps from the street, of clamorous insincere advertisement, push, adulteration, underselling and intermittent employment into the barrack-yard, he steps on to a higher social plane, into an atmosphere of service and cooperation and of infinitely more honorable emulations. Here at least men are not flung out of employment to degenerate because there is no immediate work for them to do. They are fed and drilled and trained for better services. Here at least a man is supposed to win promotion by self-forgetfulness and not by self-seeking. And beside the feeble and irregular endowment of research of commercialism, its little short-sighted snatches at profit by innovation and scientific economy, see how remarkable is the steady and rapid development of method and appliances in naval and military affairs! Nothing is more striking than to compare the progress of civil conveniences which has been left almost entirely to the trader, to the progress in military apparatus during the last few decades. The house-appliances of today for example, are little better than they were fifty years ago. A house of today is still almost as ill-ventilated, badly heated by wasteful fires, clumsily arranged and furnished as the house of 1858. Houses a couple of hundred years old are still satisfactory places of residence, so little have our standards risen. But the rifle or battleship of fifty years ago was beyond all comparison inferior to those we possess; in power, in speed, in convenience alike. No one has a use now for such superannuated things."

Reading 42
Moral Equivalent of War

Wells adds that he thinks that the conceptions of order and discipline, the tradition of service and devotion, of physical fitness, unstinted exertion, and universal responsibility, which universal military duty is now teaching European nations, will remain a permanent acquisition, when the last ammunition has been used in the fireworks that celebrate the final peace. I believe as he does. It would be simply preposterous if the only force that could work ideals of honor and standards of efficiency into English or American natures should be the fear of being killed by the Germans or the Japanese. Great indeed is Fear; but it is not, as our military enthusiasts believe and try to make us believe, the only stimulus known for awakening the higher ranges of men's spiritual energy. The amount of alteration in public opinion which my utopia postulates is vastly less than the difference between the mentality of those black warriors who pursued Stanley's party on the Congo with their cannibal warcry of "Meat! Meat!" and that of the "general-staff" of any civilized nation. History has seen the latter interval bridged over: the former one can be bridged over much more easily.

INDEX

AIDS, 329–40
  American Medical Association policy recommendations, 331
  antiviral drug funding, 335
  confidentiality and, 331
  health care funding and needs, 329, 338
  health insurance for, 335
  life insurance and, 335
  mandatory testing for, 332
  models for care, 333, 334
  public policy and, 337
ARC. *See* AIDS
Address Unknown, 172
Affirmative action, 164
Aggression
  relation to male anger, 80
  relation to pornography, 80, 81, 82, 85
  toward women, 78–90
Aging, problems of, 185–237
Aid to Families with Dependent Children (AFDC), 142, 144, 187
Air pollution
  effect on crops, 383–90
  effect on trees, 383–90
  endangered forests, 384, 385
  prevention, 388
  remedies, 388
Al-Anon, 42
Alateen, 42
Albigensians, 123, 124
Alcohol abuse, 21–61
Alcoholics Anonymous, 42
Alcoholics, children of 37–43
Alcoholism, education about, 42
Alexander v. Yale University, 1977, 189

American Hospital Association, 342
American Humane Association, 92
American Medical Association, AIDS policy recommendation, 331
American Psychiatric Association, 10
American Society of Planning Officials, 365–74
Anabaptists, 123, 124, 127
Anarchy, 123–31
Anger, male, 79–90
  relation to aggression, 80
  relation to pornography, 80
  relation to rape, 83
  relation to sex, 84
  types, 84–86
Antipoverty programs, 142
Arendt, Hannah, 132
Association of American Colleges, Project on Status and Education of Women, 1978, 189
Automatic teller machines, 120, 122
Autonomy, female, 215

Baader-Meinhof Gang, 127
Bach, George, 244
Banfield, 16
Banks, W. Curtis, 137
Battered women
  competence questioned, 250–68
  definition, 260
  economic dependency, 253
  experts' accounts of, 252, 256, 257, 258
  feminity, 254
  self-esteem, 258

441

Index

Battered women (*continued*)
　social construction of deviance, 250–68
　social service agency response to, 253, 258
　victimization, 258, 260
　See also Wife assault
Beals, Janette, 40
Becker, Howard S., 24
Beyond the Punitive Society, 105
Bianchi, Suzanne, 149
Bhopal, India, 401
Black, Claudia, 39
Blacks
　family income, 158
　family poverty, 149, 151
　female poverty, 149, 151, 156
　higher education rates, 158
　home ownership, 158
　poverty rates, 158
　power needs, 178
　professional employment rates, 158
　truly disadvantaged, 158–70
　welfare sectors of, 151, 153
Blalock, Hubert M., Jr., 17
Blumer, Herbert, 3, 13
Brokaw, Thomas, 173
Brown, Antoinette, 215
Bureaucracy
　administration vs. administrator, 299
　American style, 300
　authority relation masking, 301
　categorical decisions by, 300
　characteristics, 299
　complexity, 304–19
　ethos, 299–303
　European style, 299
　euphemisms in, 301
　management, 304–19
　problems
　　alienation, 308, 311
　　complexity, 305
　　comprehensiveness, 306
　　coping with, 316
　　costs, 310
　　decision making in, 307, 308, 310
　　efficiency, 311
　　growth, 305, 316
　　interdependence, 305
　　leadership, 314
　of large, 305–16
　performance decline in, 314, 315, 316
　policy consequences, 312
　rigidity, 313, 314
　size, 305, 309
　value systems, 312
　vulnerability, 314, 315
Burger, Warren, 110
Burt, Martha, 172
Bush, George, 172, 173

CETA, 152
Camus, Albert, 126
Case studies
　heroin use, 50–58
　tinydoping, 26, 27, 28
Castro, Fidel, 130
Cathari, 123
Challenger Mission, 400, 405
Chayne, Charles, 114, 115
Chernobyl, 399, 401, 405
Chickenhawks, 95
Child abuse
　crime conviction for, 227
　definition, 93, 221
　myths of, 96–99
Child molestation. *See* Pedophilia
Child neglect, 93
Children
　labelling for ability, 281–88
　middle class, bias toward, 281, 286
　of alcoholics, 37–43
　poor, bias against, 281, 288
　working class, bias against, 281, 288
Children of Alcoholics Foundation, 37
Cities, 349–74
　aging central, 365–74
　　"Marshall Plan" for, 368
　　public policy for, 369
　　reconstruction, 368
　　regional government for, 369
　growth management, 365
　labor markets, 366
　management strategies, 370–74
　metropolitan decline, 365–74
　public policy for, 361, 362
　urban crises of, 367
　See also Woodlawn
Citizenship, 321–26

442

Index

Civil rights
  race equality, 160–66
  recent history, 160–66
Civil Rights Act, 1964, 158, 188, 222
Civilian Conservation Corps, 145
Clark, Leroy D., 162
Clean Air Act, 1970, 388
Clean Air Act, 1977, 388
Clément, Jacques, 125
Cole, Ed, 114
Coleman-Herrnstein hypothesis, 286
Communication
  men's, 207
  women's, 207, 209
Community consensus, 320, 321, 323
Confidentiality, and AIDS, 331
Crain, Robert, 154
Cressey, Donald R., 118
Crime
  child abuse conviction for, 227
  computer, 119, 121, 122
  conviction rates, 225
  life structure and, 48
  patterns, 48
  prevention, 110
  punishment for, 105–7
  rape, 220, 225
  relation to drug use, 44–61
  technology and, 119
  temporal sequence, 47
  victimless, 11
  violence and, 103–38
    toward females, 225
Crimes cause drugs, 45, 47
Criminal system, 105–11
Criminals
  housing of, 105–7
  rehabilitation, 105–11
Crisis intervention, 17
Cultural differences, 175, 176

Decision making, 112–16
  bureaucratic, 307, 308, 310
  definition, 320
  immoral, 112–16
Demographic transition, 16
Deviance
  public conception of, 5
  social construction, 250–68
Diddler, definition, 95

Disadvantaged
  blacks, 158–70
  levels, 158–70
  minorities, 158–70
  program needs, 169
Discrimination
  class, 139–84
  ethnic, 139–84
  racial, 154
  sex
    and poverty, 150
  See also Sexual harassment
Disillusionment, with faculty, 198
Divorce
  attitudes toward, 269, 274
  blame in, 272
  demoralization following, 275
  disapproval of, 272
  historical perspectives on, 270
  rate, 154, 155
  self-devaluation following, 276
  social life following, 275
  social rejection result, 274
  stigma of, 269–79
Dominican Order, 123, 124
Drug abuse, 21–61
  and availability, 48, 49–58
  life structures and, 48, 49–58
  patterns, 48, 49–58
  relation to crime, 44–61
  temporal sequence, 47
  See also specific drug
Drugs cause crimes, 45, 47
Drugs-crime connection, 45–47
Dukakis, Michael, 172
Durnetti, Buenaventura, 127

ESA (Greek Army Police), 133, 138
Ecology problems, 375–96
Edens, Rudolph, 41
Education
  blacks, rates, 158
  business and industry involvement, 295
  class of 2000, 289, 290, 293
  class size, 293
  computers for, 294
  for multiculturalism, 176
  funding needs, 295
  in 2000, 290, 291, 292

443

Index

Education (*continued*)
  learning styles, 294
  priorities, 295
  quality criteria, 176
  school days and times, 293
  state-of-art, 292
  tailored courses, 294
  teaching styles, 294
Education Amendments Act, 1972, 189, 223
Educational problems, 281-96
  bias, 281-88
  expectation vs. performance, 281-88
  parental guidance for, 291
  school challenges in 2000, 290
  teaching format, 289-96
Eichmann in Jerusalem, 132
Elder abuse, 235-37
Electronic fund transfer, 120
Ellis, Judy Trent, 162
Employer-employee relations, 189
Employment, black professionals, 158
Environment
  overpopulation effects, 376-79
    synergism, 377
    threshold effects, 378
    timelag effects, 379
    trigger effects, 378
  problems threatening, 380-82
Equal Employment Opportunity Commission, 188
Exhibitionism, definition, 95

FBI Uniform Crime Report, 223
Faculty
  disillusionment with, 198
  student relations, 189-95
Fairtown, Connecticut, 205-10
Family
  black vs. white poverty, 149
  disrupted, 239-79
  economic status, 149, 153
  one-parent, 150, 154
  variation, tolerance of, 269
  women as head, 149
Family Assistance Plan, 148
Fantasy, pornography as, 85, 87
Farley, Lin, 221
Farley, Reynolds, 149

Fasteau, Marc Feigen, 218
Finkelhor, David, 231
Fetal alcohol syndrome, 40
Fiction, adults only, content analysis, 79
Fishkin, James, 162, 165
Foote, Nelson, 17, 18
Fraud
  definition, 120
  growth, 120
  prevalence, 121
Frotteur, definition, 95

Gangs, Woodlawn, 357
Gender gratification, 187-203
General Motors, Inc., 112-16
George Washington University
  Center for Family Research, 40
  Health Plan Addiction Program, 41
Ghetto
  feminine poverty in, 149-57
  program needs in, 169
  See also Slums
Giarretto, Henry, 92
Gill, Howard B, 110
God Bless the Child, 173
Goffman, Erving, 66, 74, 76
Goodwin, Donald, 38
Gram-slamming, 235
Great Depression, 144, 145, 146, 167
Great Society, 167, 168
Green Berets, 135
Groth, A. Nicholas, 231
Guevara, Che, 129

HARYOU Project, 284
HIV infections. *See* AIDS
Hall, Peter M., 13, 14, 15
Haney, Craig, 137
Haritos-Fatouros, 133
Harmful conditions, criteria for, 7, 9
Harmful people, 5
Hayes, Robert, 174
Health care
  AIDS and needs for, 329, 338
  all-frills Yuppie boutique, 341-47
  competitive consumer approach, 341-47

Index

Culture of Inadequacy, 342
  deficiencies, 327–47
  models for, 329–40
  resource adequacy, 341, 343
  trendy arrangements 341–47
Herman, Judith, 99
Heroin use
  career patterns, 49–58
    free-wheeling junkie, 53
    occasional, 50
    stabilized junkie, 52
    street junkie, 56
    typology, 50
  occasional, 48, 50
  relation to crime, 44–61
Hewitt, John P., 13, 14, 15
Home ownership, by blacks, 158
Homeless
  myths about, 171–74
  survey of, 171–74
Homicide rate, 154
Housing
  inadequate, 17
  public, 147
  Woodlawn market, 354

Ideology, definition, 218
Incessant politics, 16
Incest
  definition, 94, 100, 219
  prevalence, 92, 224
  pro-incest advocate, 100
  victim as instigator, 228
Industrial Revolution, 123
Inquisition, 124
Insurance
  health
    AIDS and, 335
    risk pools, 336
  life, AIDS and, 335
Interactional skills, 178
The Intimate Enemy, 244

Jenkins, Brian, 130
Job guarantees, 179
Job security, 410
Johnson, Jeannette, 39
Jones, Edward E., 66, 74
Jones, Ronald, 135, 136, 137

Katanga, Ron, 177
Kern, Joseph, 37, 41
Killian, Lewis M., 16
Knudsen, "Bunkie," 115

Labor market
  economic sectors, 151
  gender effects, 153
Larceny, prevalence, 121
Lazerfeld, Paul F., 17
Life structure, 48, 49
Loneliness, 245, 246
Loury, Glenn, 159, 164
Love, romantic
  artistic model, 247
  as communication, 243
  as escape from loneliness, 245, 246
  as fair exchange, 242
  as work, 244
  biological metaphor, 248
  blandness, 245
  cliches, 241–49
  contract model, 247
  dynamics, 249
  euphemisms, 241
  less-than-perfection, 249
  metaphysical model, 246

MacDonald, John M., 220
McIntosh, Mary, 119
MacKinnon, Catherine, 188
The Male Machine, 218
Management
  by stress, 406–10
  Japanese-style, 407
  scientific, 408
Mao, Tse-Tung, 130
Marijuana
  evolution of use, 23
  history of use, 23
  socialization of, 24
  tinydoping. *See* Tinydoping
  treatment for abuse, 24
Marital stability
  alternate motives, 261
  external constraints, 253
  internal constraints, 254, 261
  norms, 250
  vs. marital quality, 260
  wife assault and, 250

445

Index

Mark, definition, 66
Mathys, Jan, 124
Medicaid, 168
Medicare, 142
Mehard, Rita, 154
Men Who Rape: The Psychology of the Offender, 231
Merton, Robert K., 9, 13
Mini Manual for the Urban Guerilla, 129
Minorities
 advantaged, 162
 competitive resources, 162
 disadvantaged, 158–70
 power needs, 178
 preferential treatment, 161–66
Model, theoretical, black-white contact, 179
Molestation, definition, 95
Morehouse, Ellen, 38
Moynihan, Daniel P., 148
Multiculturalism
 additive, 175–84
 education for, 176
 future trends, 181
 need to learn, 178
 research needs, 179–81
 subtractive, 175
Myths
 about child abuse, 96–99
 about homeless, 171–74

Nader, Ralph, 113
A Nation at Risk, 295
National Advisory Council on Women's Education Survey, 1980, 189, 225
National Association of Children of Alcoholics, 39, 41, 43
National Center on Child Abuse and Neglect, 94
National Commission on Excellence in Education, 295
National Institute of Alcohol Abuse and Alcoholism, 39
Nechayev, Sergei, 127
Negotiated reality theory, 13, 14
Networks, women in social, 206
New Deal, 167, 168
New Society, 299

New United Motors Manufacturing, Inc., 406
Nisbet, Robert, 16
Norms and values, 6
Nuclear energy
 accidental release, 413, 422
 fear of, 399
Nummi Motors, 406

Occupational segregation, 150, 151
Office of Economic Opportunity, 142
Okamoto, Kozo, 125
Old Man of the Mountain, 125
One Day in the Life of Ivan Denisovich, 108
Osborne, Cy, 115
Overpopulation
 environmental effects, 376–79
 synergism, 377
 threshold effects, 378
 timelag effects, 379
 trigger effects, 378

Patriarchy
 definition, 215, 218
 violence against females in, 216
Peasant's Revolt, 124
Pederasty, definition, 94
Pedophilia
 definition, 94
 relation to pornography, 82
Penal colonies, 108, 110
Penthouse, content analysis, 79
Perpetual service, 16
Perrucci, Robert, 8
Petron, Michaelis, 133, 138
Phantom problems, 3
Pettigrew, Thomas, 177
Pilisuk, Marc, 8
Planck, Max, 3
Playboy, content analysis, 79
Pluralism, 175, 182
Polhemus, Von D., 114, 115
Political activity
 drudges of, 211
 majority whip, 210
 moralistic motivation, 212
 talk, 207

446

Index

women's roles, 204–14
work, 207
Political organization inequalities, 204–14
Political Terrorism: The Threat and the Response, 218
Politics
  definition, 320, 321, 322
  image of, 322, 323
  individualism and, 323
  types, 320
Population problems, 375–96
  overpopulation. *See* Overpopulation
Pornography, 78–90
  alternates to suppression, 86
  child, definition, 95
  as fantasy, 85, 87
  consumers of, 78
  definition, 78, 219
  relation to aggression, 80, 81, 82, 85
  relation to male anger, 80
  relation to pedophilia, 82
  relation to rape, 82, 83
  research needed, 86
Pot. *See* Marijuana
Poverty
  black vs. white families and, 149
  causes, for women, 156
  elimination, 141–48
  escape from, 152
  feminization of, 149–57
  gender effects, 153
  ghetto composition, 149
  rates, 149, 158
  sex discrimination and, 150
Power
  black, 178
  economic concentrations, 297–326
  equalization, 177, 178
  minority, 178
  political concentrations, 297–326
Preferential treatment, based on race, 161–66
Prison, 108
  guard behavior, 137, 138
  simulation of, 137
Program for Prevention Research (Arizona State University), 40
Propaganda, definition, 218
Prostitution, child, definition, 95

Psychiatric impairment, 10
Public assistance
  controversy over, 141, 142, 143
  federal taxes and, 144
Public policy
  AIDS and, 337
  for cities, 361, 362, 369
  slum stabilization, 362
  Woodlawn and, 361
Public welfare
  benefit sectors, 151, 153
  job guarantee programs, 179
  length of use, 155
  political support, 166
  targeted audiences, 167
Public Works Administration, 145
Pygmalion in the Classroom, 284

Quasi-theory, 13–19
Questioning the unquestionable, 67

Race, egalitarian principles of, 160–166
Race-specific policies, 158–70
Racial assimilation, 16
Racial justice, 177
Rape
  as crime, 220, 225
  definition, 95, 219
  forcible, definition, 95
  relation to male anger, 83
  relation to pornography, 82, 83
  statutory, definition, 95, 221
  victim as instigator, 228
Rape Offenders and Their Victims, 220
Ratchet effect, 309
Reagan, Ronald, 168, 169, 171
Research
  origins, 13–19
  replacement by quasi-theory, 15
Revolutionary Catechism, 127
Risk factors, from technology, 399–405
Robert Wood Johnson Foundation, 172
Roller, Albert, 114, 115
Roosevelt, Franklin D., 167
Russell, Diana, 92

447

Index

Schorr, Alvin, 144
Schumer, Charles, 172
Science, social responsibility of, 7
Self-confidence, 197
Self-devaluation, 276
Self-fulfilling prophecy, 281–88
Self-identity, 178
Selltiz, Claire, 18
Sex
  elements of, 85
  relation to male anger, 84
Sex education
  advocates, 69
  personal risks, 67–70
  practitioners, 69
  professional risks, 70–74
  risks in, 65–77
  See also Sex research
Sex research
  advocates, 69
  personal risks, 67–70
  practitioners, 69
  professional risks, 70–74
  risks, 65–77
Sexism, 185–237
Sexual abuse
  child, 91–102
    definition, 91, 93
    prevalence, 91
  definition, 100
  needs in area, 101
  prevalence, 101
  prevention, 100
  publicity about, 100
  reporting, 100
  symptoms, 100
  treatment, 100
  trends in area, 100
  women, 92
Sexual discrimination, sexual harassment as, 220
Sexual expressions, 63–102
Sexual harassment, 189
  bribery, 193
  costs, 197
  definition, 188, 190, 219, 221
  liability guidelines, 188
  "managing the trouble," 194, 195, 196
  on university campus, 187–203
  prevalence, 189, 190, 191, 224
  questionnaire, 189

  recognition of, 187, 190
  selective avoidance, 196
  self reports of, 191
  student status and, 195
  types, 191
  victim as instigator, 229
Sexual intercourse, definition, 95
Sexual interest
  on university campus, 187–203
  unwanted, 192
Sexual sadism, definition, 95
Sexual Shakedown: The Sexual Harassment of Women on the Job, 221
Sexual terrorism, 215–34
  characteristics, 222
  components, 217, 218, 219
  definition, 216
  men's reaction to, 217
  types, 219
  women's reaction to, 216
Sexual violence. *See* Violence, sexual
Sexually Victimized Children, 231
Sexuality, American culture and, 65
Significant numbers, 12
Slums
  stabilization of, 362
  See also Ghetto
Snyder, Mitch, 171, 172
Social insurance programs, 143
Social policy
  poor vs. non-poor, 141–48
  two-tiered, 141, 147
Social problems
  assessing, 3–12
  classification of, 8
  collective definition, 5
  concepts of, 3
  defining, 1–19
  definition, 4, 8, 9, 13
  expert interpretations, 5, 6
  harmfulness of, 10
  identification of, 4
  interrelationships, 7
  magnitude, 9
  perspectives of, 4–7
  primacy of, 7–9
  professional views, 5
  public conceptions, 4, 5
  quasi-theories, 13–19
  research origins, 13–19

Index

severity, 10
value, 5, 6, 11
Social responsibility, American business and, 112–16
Social Security, 142, 143, 145, 148, 167
Social Security Act, 1935, 145
Social welfare
  federal outlay categories, 142
  policy change, 144, 145
  programs
    history of, 144–46
    rhetoric of, 141
  recipients, 142
Society
  fair competition in, 321, 322, 325
  invisible complexity of, 325
Society for the Scientific Study of Sex, 66
Society of Jesus, 124
Sociological
  knowledge, 6
  literature, content of, 5
Sodomy, definition, 95
"Something About Amelia," 92
Stigma
  definition, 66
  occupational, 66, 74, 75
  of divorce, 269–79
  theory of, 66
  types, 66
Stone, Lucy, 215
Stress, management by, 406–10
Student Assistance Program (White Plains, NY), 38
Suicide rates, 154

Tailhade, Laurent, 127
Tappan, Paul, 45
Taxes
  federal for public assistance, 144
  rate of increase, 143, 144
Taylor, Frederick W., 408
Taylor, William L., 164
Teacher-student expectations, 281–88
Technology
  history of, 402, 403
  risks from, 399–405
  work and, 397–410
Terrorism
  failure of, 128

nuclear, 426
political, 123–31
  components, 217, 218, 219
  history of, 123–31
sexual. *See* Sexual terrorism
Terrorist, description of, 127, 128
Theft, 117–22
  definition, 117
  nature of, 118
  technology and, 119
Third Wave, 135, 136, 138
Thomas, W.I., 13
Three Mile Island, 401, 404, 405
Thurow, Lester, 168
Timerman, Jacopo, 132
Tinydoping, 23–36
Torture
  language of, 133, 134
  training in, 132–38
Transportation, public, 147

Unemployment compensation, 143
U.S. Department of Housing and Urban Development, 171
U.S. Marine Corps, 135

Value-neutrality, 5, 6
Violence
  authority of, 132
  crime and, 103–38
  effect on people, 359
  in pornography, 87
  men's fear of, 217
  sexual
    against females, 216, 222, 223, 225
    in patriarchy, 216
    not about sex, 231
    not taken seriously, 230
    victim as instigator, 228
    women's fear of, 216
  TV, 87
  toward women, 78–90
  victims of, 360

WIN, 152
Wagner Act, 146
Walzer, Michael, 127
War, 411
  double personality of, 431

449

Index

War (*continued*)
  explanations for, 429–39
  history of, 429
  moral equivalents, 429–39
  nuclear, 413–28
  prevention, 429–39
Water
  consumption, 391
  cycle of, 392
  from rain, 394
  from sewage recycling, 395
  resources, 391–96
Watson, Francis, 218
Weapons
  biological, 404
  chemical, 404
Weber, Max, 299
Werner, Cal, 115
Werner, Emily, 39
Wheeler, Harvey, 105
Wife assault
  definition, 220
  external constraints, 253
  internal constraints, 254, 261
  marital stability and, 250
  reporting, 225
  victim as instigator, 228
  See also Battered women
Wiley, George, 148
Winchell, Frank, 114, 115
Winningham, Marc, 173
Wolin, Stephen, 40
Women
  aggression toward. *See* Aggression
  as head of family, 149, 150
  as primary breadwinner, 150
  battered. *See* Battered women
  images of, 86
  political activity, 204–14
  political motivation, 212
  poverty and, 149
  roles, 208
  social networks, 206
Women Organized Against Sexual Harassment, 189, 193
Woodlawn, 351–64
  cycle of abandonment, 351
  devastation of, 358, 361
  gangs, 357
  housing market, 354
  neighborhood characteristics, 353
  population statistics, 353
  public policy and, 361
  remedies for, 359
  terror in, 357
Woodside, Migs, 43
Work, and technology, 397–410
Worker
  assignment, 409
  control, 407
  security vs. threat, 410
Working Women United Institute, 190
Works Progress Administration, 145
Wright, James (Speaker of House of Representatives), 72
Wright, James (Professor), 172
Wyden, Peter, 244

Yuppies
  ethics of, 346
  health care and, 341–47

Zimbardo, Philip, 137

THE BOOK'S MANUFACTURE

Social Problems: Contemporary Readings,
Second Edition, was typeset by
Point West, Inc., Carol Stream, Illinois.

The typeface is Palatino for text and display.

Printing and binding were done by
Braun-Brumfield, Inc., Ann Arbor, Michigan.

Cover design by Lucy Lesiak Design, Chicago, Illinois.

Internal design by John B. Goetz,
Design & Production Services, Co., Chicago, Illinois.